THE
BAPTIST
HYMN BOOK

WIPF & STOCK · Eugene, Oregon

Wipf and Stock Publishers
199 W 8th Ave, Suite 3
Eugene, OR 97401

Douds Cat Island Hymnal
By Mt. Sinai Native Baptist Church,
Copyright© Psalms and Hymns Trust
ISBN 13: 978-1-62564-731-3
Publication date 2/15/2014
Previously published by Psalms and Hymns Trust, 1980

INTRODUCTION

SINCE the eighteenth century a succession of hymn books have been prepared for use in our Baptist churches. At the end of the nineteenth century *The Baptist Hymnal* and *Psalms and Hymns* were widely used, but in 1900 these began to give way to the new *Baptist Church Hymnal*. This was prepared by a committee representing the Psalms and Hymns Trust, the trustees of *The Baptist Hymnal* and the Baptist Union. Its proprietorship was vested in the Psalms and Hymns Trust, reconstituted to include representatives of *The Baptist Hymnal* and of the Baptist Union. In its turn the *Baptist Church Hymnal* was replaced in 1933 by a Revised Edition which has rendered great service to the denomination. But every generation needs a book of its own and in 1954 the Psalms and Hymns Trust decided that the time had come to prepare not another revision but a completely new book. The work was entrusted to a representative editorial committee, which appointed a music advisory committee to assist it. Both committees held numerous and lengthy meetings. Advice was sought and obtained from many sources, including the Baptist churches of Australia, New Zealand and South Africa. A full account of the process of preparation and of the principles which guided the committee will be found in the *Baptist Hymn Book Companion*, which also contains biographical and historical information as to the hymns and tunes, their authors and composers, and many other helps to the use of the book in the churches.

While retaining those hymns in the *Baptist Church Hymnal (Revised)* which have proved their continued usefulness in public worship, the committee have omitted a number which are no longer widely used or for which better alternatives are now available. The committee are confident that both by what is omitted and by what is added a greatly enriched book has been assured and one which is more relevant to the needs of this generation. A number of old hymns have been restored and many by writers of our own times have found a place. The book draws widely upon the treasures of hymnody of the whole Church in many centuries and lands.

While the primary purpose has of course been to provide hymns for singing in congregational worship, it is hoped that like its predecessors this collection will be of service in the personal devotional life, particularly to those unable to join in public worship. One new feature is the inclusion of a section " mainly for private use ", to supplement the book as a whole in meeting such needs.

Much attention has been given to the text of the hymns. In many instances the author's original version has been restored, but it is frequently necessary to make alterations to fit a hymn for present day use. Where changes of any substance have been made this is indicated after the author's name and a detailed explanation is given in the *Companion*.

Many hymns might properly be classified under more than one heading, and a list of others on the same theme has therefore been printed at the end of each section. Hymns are arranged alphabetically within each section. A special list suggests hymns suitable for evangelistic services, a need to which the committee were very much alive. Another list provides a guide to hymns for young people and children. With the exception of those intended for little children, these are not printed in a separate section, but inserted in the appropriate sections of the book as a whole.

A notable innovation is the selection of Scripture passages. It is hoped that the choice of chants will be welcomed by those churches which use them, but the committee believe that our public worship could also be greatly enriched by the wider practice of the responsive reading of a Scripture passage by minister and congregation, not in place of the Lesson but in addition to it. The inclusion of this section in the book will facilitate this.

The committee do not favour the comparatively modern practice of singing Amen after every hymn and suggest that it should be sung only where it is printed, that is, after prayers and doxologies, or where it belongs essentially to the tune.

Any profits from the sale of this book, as of its predecessors, will be devoted by the Trust to denominational purposes, the major part being for the benefit of the widows and orphans of Baptist ministers and missionaries.

Before our work was completed we lost by death our friend and colleague, Dr. M. E. Aubrey, who had been taking an active part in all our counsels.

"The Lord is great and greatly to be praised!" The one aim of the committee in all their prolonged labours has been to provide as worthy an aid as they could fashion for His worship and for the building up of His Church.

CONTENTS

ACKNOWLEDGMENTS

FULLER and more formal acknowledgments for words and tunes will be found in the music edition, but here we express our thanks to the following for permission to include hymns:

Mrs. Alington, 45, 447; J. Arlott, Esq., 726; Association Press, New York, 187; Mrs. Bambridge & Macmillan & Co., 644; The Rev. A. F. Bayly, 84, 382, 389, 620, 751; Beacon Press, Boston, 398, 613; Messrs. A. D. & Bernard Blaxill, 470; The Rev. F. W. Boreham, D.D., 288; A. Bourne-Webb, Esq., 323; The Rt. Hon. Henry Brooke, M.P., 14, 108, 122, 133; The Rev. R. D. Browne, 396; Executors of E. M. Butler, 276, 444; Carey Kingsgate Press, 183; Messrs. Chatto & Windus and Executors of Miss E. Hull, 462; The Chautauqua Institution, 243, 689; The Rev. R. L. Child and Dr. Bernard Robinson, 717; Church Pension Fund, New York, 139, 198, 315; The Clarendon Press Oxford, 75, 137, 492, 496, 651, 699, 707; The Congregational Union, 348, 350, 380, 554, 564, 639, 729; Miss Margaret Cropper and Girls' Friendly Society, 531; J. Curwen & Sons Ltd., 520, 559, 698; Miss Mary Edgar, 472; Evans Bros. Ltd., 100; Mrs. M. D. Farrar, 345; The Fifeshire Advertiser Ltd., 92; The Rev. H. E. Fosdick, D.D., 372; E. H. Freeman Ltd., 480; The Rev. J. P. Giles, 291; Miss Mary Glover, 123; Mrs. Gould, 596; The Rev. G. O. Gregory, 327; Hope Publishing Co., Chicago, 576; The Hon. Mrs. Silvester Horne, 191, 256; The Rt. Rev. Bishop Frank Houghton, 218; The Rt. Rev. L. S. Hunter, Bishop of Sheffield, 465; Hymn Society of America, 66, 247, 655; Proprietors of *Hymns Ancient & Modern*, 156, 657; Mrs. E. R. Jackson, 131; John Lane The Bodley Head Ltd., 11; Mrs. Elvet Lewis, 193, 285, 557, 656; Longmans Green and Lady Spring Rice, 642; Headmaster, Loughborough Grammar School, 279; H. V. Lowry, Esq., 536, 652; Miss Helen MacNicol, 341, 456; The Rev. Hugh Martin, C.H., D.D., 284, 295; Mrs. J. H. B. Masterman, 660; Mrs. Basil Mathews, 366; The

Methodist Youth Dept., 135, 249, 476, 500, 670; Mrs.
T. P. Mills, 626; The Rev. L. H. Moore, 271, 691; The
Mothers' Union, 618; A. R. Mowbray & Co. Ltd., 52,
516, 647; The Rev. H. R. Moxley, 268; The National
Society, 745, 757; The National Sunday School Union,
10, 130, 233; H. E. Nichol & Son, 400; Miss E. Oxen-
ham, 490, 661; The Oxford University Press, 8, 34, 49,
102, 112, 127, 129, 146, 202, 238, 241, 312, 328, 349, 356,
390, 523, 586, 610, 619, 631, 643, 659, 666, 675, 742, 747;
Miss B. D. Page, 300; The Rev. E. A. Payne, D.D.,
362; The Rt. Rev. Bishop C. V. Pilcher, 617; Miss A. M.
Pullen, 115, 246, 529; Mrs. H. D. Rawnsley, 634; The
Community of the Resurrection, 602, 623, 765; H.
Richards, Esq., 755; The Rev. W. Robinson, D.D.,
299; S.P.C.K., 237, 503, 650; Mrs. Lesbia Scott, 259;
Mrs. E. Shillito, 181; The Rev. L. J. E. Smith, 7; Miss
D. Tarrant, 648; C. G. Thomas, Esq., 636; Miss Paula
Trump, 370, 452, 538; Mrs. W. S. Walton, 604; Joseph
Williams Ltd., 294; The World's Student Christian
Federation, 164, 408, 664; National Council of
Y.M.C.A., 716.

Thanks are also due to Thos. Nelson & Sons Ltd.,
for permission to use quotations from the Revised
Standard Version of the Bible.

HYMNS

1

ALL creatures of our God and King,
Lift up your voice and with us sing
Hallelujah, hallelujah !
Thou burning sun with golden beam,
Thou silver moon with softer gleam,
O praise Him, O praise Him,
Hallelujah, hallelujah, hallelujah !

2 Thou rushing wind that art so strong,
Ye clouds that sail in heaven along,
O praise Him, hallelujah !
Thou rising morn, in praise rejoice,
Ye lights of evening, find a voice,

3 Thou flowing water, pure and clear,
Make music for thy Lord to hear,
Hallelujah, hallelujah !
Thou fire so masterful and bright,
That givest man both warmth and light,

4 Dear mother earth, who day by day
Unfoldest blessings on our way,
O praise Him, hallelujah !
The flowers and fruits that in thee grow
Let them His glory also show,

5 And all ye men of tender heart,
Forgiving others, take your part,
O sing ye, hallelujah !
Ye who long pain and sorrow bear,
Praise God and on Him cast your care,

6 And thou, most kind and gentle death,
  Waiting to hush our latest breath,
    O praise Him, hallelujah !
  Thou leadest home the child of God,
  And Christ our Lord the way hath trod,

7 Let all things their Creator bless,
  And worship Him in humbleness,
    O praise Him, hallelujah !
  Praise, praise the Father, praise the Son,
  And praise the Spirit, Three in One,

W. H. Draper, 1855–1933.
Based on St. Francis of Assisi, 1182–1226.

2

PSALM C.

ALL people that on earth do dwell,
  Sing to the Lord with cheerful voice;
Him serve with mirth, His praise forth tell;
  Come ye before Him and rejoice.

2 The Lord, ye know, is God indeed:
  Without our aid He did us make;
We are His folk, He doth us feed;
  And for His sheep He doth us take.

3 O enter then His gates with praise,
  Approach with joy His courts unto;
Praise, laud, and bless His name always,
  For it is seemly so to do.

4 For why, the Lord our God is good;
  His mercy is for ever sure;
His truth at all times firmly stood,
  And shall from age to age endure.

William Kethe, c. 1550–1600.

3

ALL things praise Thee, Lord most high,
Heaven and earth and sea and sky,
All were for Thy glory made,
That Thy greatness, thus displayed,
Should all worship bring to Thee;
All things praise Thee: Lord, may we.

2 All things praise Thee: night to night
Sings in silent hymns of light;
All things praise Thee: day to day
Chants Thy power in burning ray;
Time and space are praising Thee;
All things praise Thee: Lord, may we.

3 All things praise Thee, high and low,
Rain and dew, and seven-hued bow,
Crimson sunset, fleecy cloud,
Rippling stream, and tempest loud,
Summer, winter,—all to Thee
Glory render: Lord, may we.

4 All things praise Thee: heaven's high shrine
Rings with melody divine;
Lowly bending at Thy feet,
Seraph and archangel meet;
This their highest bliss, to be
Ever praising: Lord, may we.

5 All things praise Thee: gracious Lord,
Great Creator, powerful Word,
Omnipresent Spirit, now
At Thy feet we humbly bow,
Lift our hearts in praise to Thee;
All things praise Thee: Lord, may we.

G. W. Conder, 1821–74.

4

ANGEL voices ever singing
 Round Thy throne of light,
Angel harps for ever ringing,
 Rest not day nor night;
Thousands only live to bless Thee
And confess Thee,
 Lord of might.

2 Thou, who art beyond the farthest
 Mortal eye can scan,
Can it be that Thou regardest
 Songs of sinful man?
Can we know that Thou art near us
And wilt hear us?
 Yea, we can.

3 Yea, we know that Thou rejoicest
 O'er each work of Thine;
Thou didst ears and hands and voices
 For Thy praise design;
Craftsman's art and music's measure
For Thy pleasure
 All combine.

4 In Thy house, great God, we offer
 Of thine own to Thee;
And for Thine acceptance proffer,
 All unworthily,
Hearts and minds and hands and voices
In our choicest
 Psalmody.

5 Honour, glory, might, and merit,
 Thine shall ever be:
Father, Son, and Holy Spirit,
 Blessèd Trinity:
Of the best that Thou hast given,
Earth and Heaven
 Render Thee.

Francis Pott, 1832–1909.

5

ANGELS holy, high and lowly,
    Sing the praises of the Lord !
Earth and sky, all living nature,
Man, the stamp of thy Creator,
    Praise ye, praise ye, God the Lord !

2 Sun and moon bright, night and noon-light,
    Starry temples azure-floored,
Cloud and rain, and wild winds' madness,
Sons of God that shout for gladness,
    Praise ye, praise ye, God the Lord !

3 Ocean hoary, tell His glory,
    Cliffs, where tumbling seas have roared,
Pulse of waters, blithely beating,
Wave advancing, wave retreating,
    Praise ye, praise ye, God the Lord !

4 Rock and high land, wood and island,
    Crag, where eagle's pride hath soared;
Mighty mountains, purple-breasted,
Peaks cloud-cleaving, snowy-crested,
    Praise ye, praise ye, God the Lord !

5 Rolling river, praise Him ever,
    From the mountain's deep vein poured;
Silver fountains, clearly gushing,
Troubled torrent, madly rushing,
    Praise ye, praise ye, God the Lord !

6 Praise Him ever, bounteous giver !
    Praise Him, Father, friend, and Lord !
Each glad soul its free course winging,
Each glad voice its free song singing,
    Praise the great and mighty Lord !

J. S. Blackie, 1809–95.

6

BEFORE Jehovah's aweful throne,
Ye nations, bow with sacred joy;
Know that the Lord is God alone:
He can create, and He destroy.

2 His sovereign power, without our aid,
Made us of clay, and formed us men;
And when like wandering sheep we strayed,
He brought us to His fold again.

3 We are His people, we His care,
Our souls, and all our mortal frame:
What lasting honours shall we rear,
Almighty Maker, to Thy name?

4 We'll crowd Thy gates with thankful songs,
High as the heavens our voices raise;
And earth, with her ten thousand tongues,
Shall fill Thy courts with sounding praise.

5 Wide as the world is Thy command;
Vast as eternity Thy love;
Firm as a rock Thy truth must stand,
When rolling years shall cease to move.

Isaac Watts, 1674–1748, *altd.*

7

FOR all the love that from our earliest days
Has gladdened life and guarded all our ways,
We bring Thee, Lord, our song of grateful praise,
Hallelujah! Hallelujah!

2 For all the truth from wisdom's lighted page,
Undimmed and pure, that shines from age to age,
God's holy Word, our priceless heritage,

3 For all the joy that childhood's days have brought,
For healthful lives and purity of thought,
For life's deep meaning to our spirits taught,

4 For all the hope that sheds its glorious ray
Along the dark and unknown future way,
And lights the path to God's eternal day,

5 For all the strength that has been gained through
     prayer,
To face life's tasks, its eager quests to share,
Till ampler powers fulfil its promise fair,

6 For Christ the Lord, our Saviour and our friend,
Upon whose love and truth our souls depend,
Our hope, our strength, our joy that knows no end.
    Hallelujah! Hallelujah!
               L. J. E. Smith, 1879–1958.

8

FOR the beauty of the earth,
    For the beauty of the skies,
For the love which from our birth
    Over and around us lies;
Christ, our Lord, to Thee we raise
This our hymn of grateful praise.

2 For the beauty of each hour
    Of the day and of the night,
Hill and vale, and tree and flower,
    Sun and moon, and stars of light;

3 For the joy of human love,
    Brother, sister, parent, child,
Friends on earth, and friends above;
    For all gentle thoughts and mild;

4 For each perfect gift of Thine
    To our race so freely given,
Graces, human and divine,
    Flowers of earth, and buds of heaven;

5 For Thy Church that evermore
   Lifteth holy hands above,
Offering up on every shore
   Its pure sacrifice of love;

F. S. Pierpoint, 1835–1917, altd.

9

GIVE to our God immortal praise;
Mercy and truth are all His ways:
Wonders of grace to God belong,
Repeat His mercies in your song.

2 Give to the Lord of lords renown;
   The King of kings with glory crown:
His mercies ever shall endure,
When lords and kings are known no more.

3 He built the earth, He spread the sky,
   And fixed the starry lights on high:
Wonders of grace to God belong,
Repeat His mercies in your song.

4 He fills the sun with morning light,
   He bids the moon direct the night:
His mercies ever shall endure,
When suns and moons shall shine no more.

5 He sent His Son with power to save
   From guilt and darkness and the grave:
Wonders of grace to God belong,
Repeat His mercies in your song.

Isaac Watts, 1674–1748, altd.

10

GOD is good;
   We come before Him
So that we may sing His praise;
Giving thanks for all His goodness,
   As we learn His wondrous ways.

2   God is great;
       We come before Him
   So that we may bow in prayer,
Seeking strength to fight our battles,
  Knowing He is everywhere.

3   God is wise;
       We come before Him
   So that we may know His law,
Learning from the men of old time
  How to serve Him more and more.

E. Mildred Nevill, 1889–

11

GOD who created me
    Nimble and light of limb,
In three elements free,
   To run, to ride, to swim:
Not when the sense is dim,
   But now from the heart of joy,
I would remember Him:
   Take the thanks of a boy.

2 Jesus, King and Lord,
   Whose are my foes to fight,
Gird me with Thy sword,
   Swift and sharp and bright.
Thee would I serve if I might,
   And conquer if I can,
From day-dawn till night:
   Take the strength of a man.

3 Spirit of love and truth,
   Breathing in grosser clay,
The light and flame of youth,
   Delight of men in the fray,

Wisdom in strength's decay,
From pain, strife, wrong to be free,
This best gift I pray,
Take my spirit to Thee.

H. C. Beeching, 1859–1919.

12

KING of glory, King of peace,
I will love Thee;
And, that love may never cease,
I will move Thee.
Thou hast granted my request,
Thou hast heard me;
Thou didst note my working breast,
Thou hast spared me.

2 Wherefore with my utmost art
I will sing Thee,
And the cream of all my heart
I will bring Thee.
Though my sins against me cried,
Thou didst clear me;
And alone, when they replied,
Thou didst hear me.

3 Seven whole days, not one in seven,
I will praise Thee;
In my heart, though not in heaven,
I can raise Thee.
Small it is, in this poor sort
To enrol Thee:
E'en eternity's too short
To extol Thee.

George Herbert, 1593–1633

13

LET all the world in every corner sing
  " My God and King ! "
The heavens are not too high;
His praise may thither fly:
The earth is not too low;
His praises there may grow.
Let all the world in every corner sing
  " My God and King ! "

2 Let all the world in every corner sing
  " My God and King ! "
The Church with psalms must shout,
No door can keep them out:
But, above all, the heart
Must bear the longest part.
Let all the world in every corner sing
  " My God and King ! "

George Herbert, 1593-1633.

14

LET the whole creation cry,
  " Glory to the Lord on high ! "
Heaven and earth, awake and sing,
" God is good and therefore King."
Praise Him, all ye hosts above,
Ever bright and fair in love;
Sun and moon, uplift your voice,
Nights and stars, in God rejoice !

2 Warriors fighting for the Lord,
Prophets burning with His word,
Those to whom the arts belong,
Add their voices to the song.
Kings of knowledge and of law,
To the glorious circle draw;
All who work and all who wait,
Sing, " The Lord is good and great ! "

3 Men and women, young and old,
Raise the anthem manifold,
And let children's happy hearts
In this worship bear their parts;
From the north to southern pole
Let the mighty chorus roll:
Holy, holy, holy One,
Glory be to God alone!

Stopford Brooke, 1832–1916.

15

PSALM CXXXVI.

LET us with a gladsome mind
Praise the Lord for He is kind:
For His mercies aye endure,
Ever faithful, ever sure.

2 He, with all-commanding might,
Filled the new-made world with light:

3 All things living He doth feed;
His full hand supplies their need:

4 He His chosen race did bless
In the wasteful wilderness:

5 He hath, with a piteous eye,
Looked upon our misery:

6 Let us then with gladsome mind,
Praise the Lord for He is kind:

John Milton, 1608–74, altd

16

LO! God is here! let us adore,
And own how holy is this place!
Let all within us feel His power,
And silent bow before His face;
Who know His power, His grace who prove,
Serve Him with awe, with reverence, love.

2 Lo ! God is here ! Him day and night
    The united choirs of angels sing:
To Him, enthroned above all height,
    Heaven's hosts their noblest praises bring:
Disdain not, Lord, our meaner song,
Who praise Thee with a stammering tongue !

3 Being of beings, may our praise
    Thy courts with grateful fragrance fill;
Still may we stand before Thy face,
    Still hear and do Thy sovereign will:
To Thee may all our thoughts arise,
Ceaseless, accepted sacrifice.

Gerhard Tersteegen, 1697–1769,
tr. *John Wesley, 1703–91,* **altd.**

17

LORD, we thank Thee for the pleasure
    That our happy lifetime gives,
For the boundless worth and treasure
    Of a soul that ever lives;
Mind that looks before and after,
    Lifting eyes to things above;
Human tears, and human laughter,
    And the depths of human love.

2 For the thrill, the leap, the gladness
    Of our pulses flowing free;
E'en for every touch of sadness
    That may bring us nearer Thee;
But, above all other kindness,
    Thine unutterable love,
Which, to heal our sin and blindness,
    Sent Thy dear Son from above.

3 Teach us so our days to number
    That we may be early wise;
Dreamy mist, or cloud, or slumber,
    Never dull our heavenward eyes.

Hearty be our work and willing,
  As to Thee, and not to men;
For we know our souls' fulfilling
  Is in heaven, and not till then.

T. W. Jex-Blake, 1832–1915, *altd.*

18

NOW thank we all our God,
  With hearts and hands and voices,
Who wondrous things hath done,
  In whom His world rejoices;
Who, from our mothers' arms,
  Hath blessed us on our way
With countless gifts of love,
  And still is ours to-day.

2 O may this bounteous God
  Through all our life be near us,
With ever-joyful hearts
  And blessèd peace to cheer us;
And keep us in His grace,
  And guide us when perplexed,
And free us from all ills
  In this world and the next.

3 All praise and thanks to God
  The Father now be given,
The Son, and Him who reigns
  With Them in highest heaven;
The one eternal God,
  Whom earth and heaven adore;
For thus it was, is now,
  And shall be evermore.

Martin Rinckart, 1586–1649,
tr. Catherine Winkworth, 1827–78.

19

O GIVE thanks to Him who made
Morning light and evening shade:
Source and giver of all good,
Nightly sleep and daily food:
Quickener of our wearied powers;
Guard of our unconscious hours.

2 O give thanks to nature's King.
Who made every breathing thing:
His, our warm and sentient frame,
His, the mind's immortal flame:
O how close the ties that bind
Spirits to the eternal Mind !

3 O give thanks with heart and lip,
For we are His workmanship,
And all creatures are His care:
Not a bird that cleaves the air
Falls unnoticed; but who can
Speak the Father's love to man ?

4 O give thanks to Him who came
In a mortal suffering frame—
Temple of the Deity,—
Came for rebel man to die;
In the path Himself hath trod,
Leading back His saints to God.

Josiah Conder, 1789-1855

20

O LOVE that wilt not let me go,
I rest my weary soul in Thee;
I give Thee back the life I owe,
That in Thine ocean depths its flow
May richer, fuller be.

2 O Light that followest all my way,
   I yield my flickering torch to Thee;
My heart restores its borrowed ray,
That in Thy sunshine's blaze its day
   May brighter, fairer be.

3 O Joy that seekest me through pain,
   I cannot close my heart to Thee;
I trace the rainbow through the rain,
And feel the promise is not vain
   That morn shall tearless be.

4 O Cross that liftest up my head,
   I dare not ask to fly from Thee;
I lay in dust life's glory dead,
And from the ground there blossoms red
   Life that shall endless be.

George Matheson, 1842–1906.

21

O SPLENDOUR of God's glory bright,
 Who bringest forth the light from light;
O Light of light, light's fountain-spring;
O Day, our days enlightening;

2 Come, very Sun of truth and love,
Come in Thy radiance from above,
And shed the Holy Spirit's ray
On all we think or do to-day.

3 Likewise to Thee our prayers ascend,
Father of glory without end,
Father of sovereign grace, for power
To conquer in temptation's hour.

4 Teach us to work with all our might;
Beat back the devil's threatening spite;
Turn all to good that seems most ill;
Help us our calling to fulfil.

5 All praise to God the Father be,
All praise, eternal Son, to Thee,
Whom with the Spirit we adore,
For ever and for evermore. Amen.

St. Ambrose (? 340–97),
tr. compilers of Hymns A. & M.

22

O WORSHIP the King,
All-glorious above;
O gratefully sing
His power and His love;
Our shield and defender,
The ancient of days,
Pavilioned in splendour,
And girded with praise.

2 O tell of His might,
O sing of His grace,
Whose robe is the light,
Whose canopy, space;
His chariots of wrath
The deep thunder-clouds form,
And dark is His path
On the wings of the storm.

3 The earth, with its store
Of wonders untold,
Almighty, Thy power
Hath founded of old:
Hath stablished it fast
By a changeless decree,
And round it hath cast,
Like a mantle, the sea.

4 Thy bountiful care
What tongue can recite?
It breathes in the air,
It shines in the light,

It streams from the hills,
  It descends to the plain,
And sweetly distils
  In the dew and the rain.

5 Frail children of dust,
  And feeble as frail,
In Thee do we trust,
  Nor find Thee to fail:
Thy mercies, how tender,
  How firm to the end,
Our maker, defender,
  Redeemer, and friend !

6 O Lord of all might,
  How boundless Thy love !
While angels delight
  To hymn Thee above,
The humbler creation,
  Though feeble their lays,
With true adoration
  Shall sing to Thy praise.

Robert Grant, 1779–1838.

23

PRAISE, my soul, the King of heaven;
  To His feet thy tribute bring;
Ransomed, healed, restored, forgiven,
  Who like thee His praise should sing ?
    Praise Him, praise Him,
  Praise the everlasting King.

2 Praise Him for His grace and favour
  To our fathers in distress;
Praise Him, still the same for ever,
  Slow to chide, and swift to bless;
    Praise Him, praise Him,
  Glorious in His faithfulness.

3 Father-like He tends and spares us;
   Well our feeble frame He knows;
In His hands He gently bears us,
   Rescues us from all our foes;
     Praise Him, praise Him,
   Widely as His mercy flows.

4 Frail as summer's flower we flourish;
   Blows the wind—and it is gone.
But while mortals rise and perish,
   God endures unchanging on.
     Praise Him, praise Him,
   Praise the high eternal One.

5 Angels, help us to adore Him,
   Ye behold Him face to face;
Sun and moon, bow down before Him,
   Dwellers all in time and space,
     Praise Him, praise Him,
   Praise with us the God of grace.

H. F. Lyte, 1793–1847.

24

PRAISE the Lord, ye heavens adore Him;
   Praise Him, angels, in the height;
Sun and moon, rejoice before Him;
   Praise Him, all ye stars and light.
Praise the Lord, for He hath spoken:
   Worlds His mighty voice obeyed;
Laws which never shall be broken,
   For their guidance He hath made.

2 Praise the Lord, for He is glorious:
   Never shall His promise fail;
God hath made His saints victorious;
   Sin and death shall not prevail.

Praise the God of our salvation;
   Hosts on high, His power proclaim;
Heaven, and earth, and all creation,
   Laud and magnify His name.

Foundling Hospital Collection, 1796.

25

Praise to the Lord, the Almighty, the King of
   creation;
O my soul, praise Him, for He is thy health and
   salvation:
   All ye who hear,
   Brothers and sisters, draw near,
Praise Him in glad adoration.

2 Praise to the Lord, who o'er all things so
   wondrously reigneth,
Shelters thee under His wings, yea, so gently
   sustaineth:
   Hast thou not seen?
   All that is needful hath been
Granted in what He ordaineth.

3 Praise to the Lord, who doth prosper thy work,
   and defend thee!
Surely His goodness and mercy here daily attend
   thee:
   Ponder anew
   What the Almighty can do,
Who with His love doth befriend thee.

4 Praise to the Lord! O let all that is in me adore
   Him!
All that hath life and breath come now with
   praises before Him!
   Let the amen
   Sound from His people again:
Gladly for aye we adore Him.

Joachim Neander, 1650–80,
tr. Catherine Winkworth, 1827–78, *and others*.

26

ISAIAH vi. 1–3.

ROUND the Lord in glory seated
    Cherubim and seraphim
Filled His temple and repeated
    Each to each the alternate hymn:
" Lord, Thy glory fills the heaven ;
    Earth is with its fulness stored ;
Unto Thee be glory given,
    Holy, holy, holy Lord ! "

2 Heaven is still with glory ringing,
    Earth takes up the angels' cry,
" Holy, holy, holy," singing,
    " Lord of hosts, Thou Lord most high ":

3 With His seraph-train before Him,
    With His holy Church below,
Thus unite we to adore Him,
    Bid we thus our anthem flow:

Richard Mant, 1776–1848, *altd.*

27

SING hallelujah forth in duteous praise,
O citizens of heaven, and sweetly raise
    An endless hallelujah.

2 Ye next, who stand before the eternal Light,
In hymning choirs re-echo to the height
    An endless hallelujah.

3 The holy city shall take up your strain,
And, with glad songs resounding, wake again
    An endless hallelujah.

4 In blissful answering strains ye thus rejoice
To render to the Lord with thankful voice
    An endless hallelujah.

5 Ye who have gained at length your palms in bliss,
Victorious ones, your chant shall still be this,
    An endless hallelujah.

6 There, in one glad acclaim, for ever ring
The strains which tell the honour of your King,
    An endless hallelujah.

7 While Thee, by whom all things were made, we
  praise
For ever, and tell out in sweetest lays
    An endless hallelujah.

8 Almighty Christ, to Thee our voices sing
Glory for evermore; to Thee we bring
    An endless hallelujah.

Latin hymn, 5th–8th cents.,
tr. John Ellerton, 1826–93

28

SING praise to God who reigns above,
  The God of all creation,
The God of power, the God of love,
  The God of our salvation:
With healing balm my soul He fills,
And every faithless murmur stills;
  To God all praise and glory!

2 What God's almighty power hath made
  His gracious mercy keepeth;
By morning glow or evening shade
  His watchful eye ne'er sleepeth;
Within the kingdom of His might,
Lo! all is just, and all is right;
  To God all praise and glory!

3 The Lord is never far away,
  But, through all grief distressing,
An ever-present help and stay,
  Our peace, and joy, and blessing;

As with a mother's tender hand,
He leads His own, His chosen band;
　　To God all praise and glory !

4 Thus all my toilsome way along
　　I sing aloud Thy praises,
That men may hear the grateful song
　　My voice unwearied raises:
Be joyful in the Lord, my heart,
Both soul and body, bear your part;
　　To God all praise and glory !

Johann Schutz, 1640–90,
tr. Frances E. Cox, 1812–97.

29

SING to the Lord a joyful song;
　　Lift up your hearts, your voices raise;
To us His gracious gifts belong,
　　To Him our songs of love and praise.

2 For life and love, for rest and food,
　　For daily help and nightly care,
Sing to the Lord, for He is good,
　　And praise His name, for it is fair.

3 For strength to those who on Him wait,
　　His truth to prove, His will to do,
Praise ye our God, for He is great;
　　Trust in His name, for it is true.

4 For joys untold, that from above
　　Cheer those who love His sweet employ,
Sing to our God, for He is love;
　　Exalt His name, for it is joy.

5 For life below, with all its bliss,
　　And for that life, more pure and high—
That inner life, which over this
　　Shall ever shine and never die,—

6 Sing to the Lord of heaven and earth,
    Whom angels serve and saints adore,
The Father, Son, and Holy Ghost,
    To whom be praise for evermore.

J. S. B. Monsell, 1811–75

30

THE God of Abraham praise,
    Who reigns enthroned above,
Ancient of everlasting days,
    And God of love.
Jehovah, great I AM !
    By earth and heaven confessed;
We bow and bless the sacred name,
    For ever blest.

2 The God of Abraham praise,
    At whose supreme command
From earth we rise, and seek the joys
    At His right hand;
We all on earth forsake,
    Its wisdom, fame, and power;
And Him our only portion make,
    Our shield and tower.

3 The God of Abraham praise,
    Whose all-sufficient grace
Shall guide us all our happy days,
    In all our ways:
He is our faithful friend;
    He is our gracious God;
And He will save us to the end,
    Through Jesus' blood.

4 He by Himself hath sworn—
    We on His oath depend—
We shall, on eagles' wings upborne,
    To heaven ascend:

We shall behold His face,
  We shall His power adore,
And sing the wonders of His grace
  For evermore.

5 The whole triumphant host
    Give thanks to God on high:
  " Hail, Father, Son, and Holy Ghost ! "
    They ever cry.
  Hail, Abraham's God and ours !
    We join the heavenly lays;
  And celebrate with all our powers
    His endless praise.

                    Thomas Olivers, 1725–99, altd.

31

THY ceaseless, unexhausted love,
    Unmerited and free,
Delights our evil to remove,
    And help our misery.

2 Thou waitest to be gracious still;
    Thou dost with sinners bear;
  That, saved, we may Thy goodness feel,
    And all Thy grace declare.

3 Thy goodness and Thy truth to me,
    To every soul, abound;
  A vast, unfathomable sea,
    Where all our thoughts are drowned.

4 Its streams the whole creation reach,
    So plenteous is the store;
  Enough for all, enough for each,
    Enough for evermore.

5 Faithful, O Lord, Thy mercies are,
    A rock that cannot move;
  A thousand promises declare
    Thy constancy of love.

6 Throughout the universe it reigns,
  Unalterably sure;
And while the truth of God remains,
  The goodness must endure.

Charles Wesley, 1707–88.

32

TO God be the glory! great things He hath
  done!
So loved He the world that He gave us His Son;
Who yielded His life an atonement for sin,
And opened the life gate that all may go in.

*Praise the Lord! praise the Lord! Let the
  earth hear His voice!*
*Praise the Lord! praise the Lord! Let the
  people rejoice!*
O come to the Father, through Jesus the Son:
*And give Him the glory! great things He hath
  done!*

2 O perfect redemption, the purchase of blood!
To every believer the promise of God;
The vilest offender who truly believes,
That moment from Jesus a pardon receives.

3 Great things He hath taught us, great things He
  hath done,
And great our rejoicing through Jesus the Son;
But purer, and higher, and greater will be
Our wonder, our rapture, when Jesus we see.

Frances van Alstyne, 1820–1915.

33

TE DEUM LAUDAMUS

WE praise, we worship Thee, O God,
  Thy sovereign power we sound abroad:
All nations bow before Thy throne,
And Thee the eternal Father own.

2 Loud hallelujahs to Thy name
  Angels and seraphim proclaim:
  The heavens and all the powers on high
  With rapture constantly do cry,

3 " O holy, holy, holy Lord !
  Thou God of hosts, by all adored;
  Earth and the heavens are full of Thee,
  Thy light, Thy power, Thy majesty."

4 Apostles join the glorious throng
  And swell the loud immortal song;
  Prophets enraptured hear the sound
  And spread the hallelujah round.

5 Victorious martyrs join their lays
  And shout the omnipotence of grace,
  While all Thy Church through all the earth
  Acknowledge and extol Thy worth.

6 Glory to Thee, O God most high !
  Father, we praise Thy majesty,
  The Son, the Spirit, we adore:
  One Godhead, blest for evermore. Amen.

Philip Gell's *Psalms and Hymns*, 1815.

34

WE thank You, Lord of heaven,
    For all the joys that greet us,
For all that You have given
  To help us and delight us,
    In earth and sky and seas;
The sunlight on the meadows,
  The rainbow's fleeting wonder,
The clouds with cooling shadows,
  The stars that shine in splendour—
    We thank You, Lord, for these.

2 For swift and gallant horses,
  For lambs in pastures springing,
For dogs with friendly faces,
  For birds with music thronging
    Their chantries in the trees;
 For herbs to cool our fever,
  For flowers of field and garden,
For bees among the clover
  With stolen sweetness laden—
    We thank You, Lord, for these.

3 For homely dwelling-places
  Where childhood's visions linger,
For friends and kindly voices,
  For bread to stay our hunger,
    And sleep to bring us ease;
For zeal and zest of living,
  For faith and understanding,
For words to tell our loving,
  For hope of peace unending—
    We thank You, Lord, for these.

Jan Struther, 1901–53.

35

WORSHIP the Lord in the beauty of holiness.
  Bow down before Him, His glory proclaim;
Gold of obedience and incense of lowliness
  Bring and adore Him; the Lord is His name!

2 Low at His feet lay thy burden of carefulness,
  High on His heart He will bear it for thee,
Comfort thy sorrows, and answer thy prayerfulness,
  Guiding thy steps as may best for thee be.

3 Fear not to enter His courts in the slenderness
    Of the poor wealth thou wouldst reckon as
      thine;
  Truth in its beauty, and love in its tenderness,
    These are the offerings to lay on His shrine.

4 These, though we bring them in trembling and
      fearfulness,
    He will accept for the name that is dear;
  Mornings of joy give for evenings of tearfulness,
    Trust for our trembling, and hope for our fear.

5 Worship the Lord in the beauty of holiness,
    Bow down before Him, His glory proclaim;
  Gold of obedience and incense of lowliness
    Bring and adore Him; the Lord is His name!
                              J. S. B. Monsell, 1811–75.

36

YE holy angels bright,
    Who wait at God's right hand,
Or through the realms of light
    Fly at your Lord's command,
      Assist our song,
        For else the theme
        Too high doth seem
      For mortal tongue.

2 Ye blessèd souls at rest,
    Who ran this earthly race,
And now, from sin released,
    Behold the Saviour's face,
      God's praises sound,
        As in His light
        With sweet delight
      Ye do abound.

3 Ye saints, who toil below,
    Adore your heavenly King,
And onward as ye go
    Some joyful anthem sing;
    Take what He gives
        And praise Him still,
        Through good or ill,
    Who ever lives !

4 My soul, bear thou thy part,
    Triumph in God above:
And with a well-tuned heart
    Sing thou the songs of love !
    Let all thy days
        Till life shall end,
        Whate'er He send,
    Be filled with praise.

Richard Baxter, 1615–91, altd.
v. 3 by J. H. Gurney, 1802–62.

37

YE servants of God,
    Your Master proclaim,
And publish abroad
    His wonderful name;
The name all-victorious
    Of Jesus extol;
His kingdom is glorious,
    And rules over all.

2 God ruleth on high,
    Almighty to save;
And still He is nigh,
    His presence we have;
The great congregation
    His triumph shall sing,
Ascribing salvation
    To Jesus our King.

3 " Salvation to God
      Who sits on the throne ",
   Let all cry aloud,
      And honour the Son;
   The praises of Jesus
      The angels proclaim,
   Fall down on their faces,
      And worship the Lamb.

4 Then let us adore,
      And give Him His right,—
   All glory and power,
      All wisdom and might;
   All honour and blessing,
      With angels above;
   And thanks never-ceasing,
      And infinite love.

Charles Wesley, 1707–88, altd.

See also—

Awake my soul, 672.
Come let us join, 200.
From all that dwell, 760.
God of mercy, 373.
Jesus, stand among us, 336.

Lord God almighty, 62.
O thou my soul, 70.
Stand up and bless the Lord
   363.

II. THE HOLY TRINITY

38

FATHER, in whom we live,
In whom we are, and move,
The glory, power, and praise receive
Of Thy creating love.

2   Incarnate Deity,
Let all the ransomed race
Render in thanks their lives to Thee,
For Thy redeeming grace.

3   Spirit of holiness,
Let all Thy saints adore
Thy sacred energy, and bless
Thine heart-renewing power.

4   Eternal, Triune Lord,
Let all the hosts above,
Let all the sons of men, record
And dwell upon Thy love.

Charles Wesley, 1707–88, *altd.*

39

FATHER of heaven, whose love profound
A ransom for our souls hath found,
Before Thy throne we sinners bend:
To us Thy pardoning love extend.

2 Almighty Son, incarnate Word,
Our prophet, priest, redeemer, Lord !
Before Thy throne we sinners bend:
To us Thy saving grace extend.

3 Eternal Spirit, by whose breath
  The soul is raised from sin and death,
  Before Thy throne we sinners bend:
  To us Thy quickening power extend.

4 Thrice holy ! Father, Spirit, Son !
  Mysterious Godhead ! Three in One !
  Before Thy throne we sinners bend:
  Grace, pardon, life to us extend.   Amen.

Edward Cooper, 1770–1833

40

GOD almighty, in Thy temple,
  Low before Thy throne we bow,
From Thy dwelling-place in glory,
  Hear our supplications now,
    While we offer
  Earnest prayer and solemn vow.

2 Christ our Saviour, Thou who carest
  For the youngest of Thy fold,
Give us now Thy heavenly blessing,
  As Thou didst in days of old—
    Priceless treasure,
  Richer far than gems or gold.

3 God the Holy Ghost, be near us,
  Ever dwell our hearts within;
Keep them pure, and brave, and earnest,
  Give us grace to conquer sin,
    And, through Jesus,
  Heaven's eternal crown to win.

4 Holy Trinity, defend us
  In a world with evil rife,
Let Thine angel-guards surround us,
  In each sore and bitter strife;
    O preserve us
  Unto everlasting life !   Amen.

R. H. Baynes, 1831–95.

41

GOD is in His temple,
The almighty Father,
Round His footstool let us gather:
  Him with adoration
Serve, the Lord most holy,
Who hath mercy on the lowly;
    Let us raise
    Hymns of praise,
  For His great salvation:
    God is in His temple!

2　　　Christ comes to His temple:
We, His word receiving,
Are made happy in believing.
  Lo! from sin delivered,
He hath turned our sadness,
Our deep gloom, to light and gladness!
    Let us raise
    Hymns of praise,
  For our bonds are severed:
    Christ comes to His temple!

3　　　Come and claim Thy temple,
Gracious Holy Spirit!
In our hearts Thy home inherit:
  Make in us Thy dwelling,
Thy high work fulfilling,
Into ours Thy will instilling,
    Till we raise
    Hymns of praise,
  Beyond mortal telling,
    In the eternal temple.

W. T. Matson, 1833–99

42

HOLY, holy, holy, Lord God almighty!
Early in the morning our song shall rise to
Thee;
Holy, holy, holy, merciful and mighty,
God in three Persons, blessèd Trinity!

2 Holy, holy, holy! all the saints adore Thee,
Casting down their golden crowns around the
glassy sea;
Cherubim and seraphim falling down before Thee,
Who wast, and art, and evermore shalt be.

3 Holy, holy, holy! though the darkness hide Thee,
Though the eye of sinful man Thy glory may not
see,
Only Thou art holy; there is none beside Thee,
Perfect in power, in love, and purity.

4 Holy, holy, holy, Lord God almighty!
All Thy works shall praise Thy name, in earth, and
sky, and sea:
Holy, holy, holy, merciful and mighty,
God in three Persons, blessèd Trinity!

Reginald Heber, 1783–1826.

43

LEAD us, heavenly Father, lead us
O'er the world's tempestuous sea;
Guard us, guide us, keep us, feed us,
For we have no help but Thee,
Yet possessing every blessing,
If our God our Father be.

2 Saviour, breathe forgiveness o'er us;
All our weakness Thou dost know;
Thou didst tread this earth before us,
Thou didst feel its keenest woe;
Son of Mary, lone and weary,
Victor through this world didst go.

3 Spirit of our God, descending,
   Fill our hearts with heavenly joy,
Love with every passion blending,
   Pleasure that can never cloy.
Thus provided, pardoned, guided,
   Nothing can our peace destroy.

James Edmeston, 1791–1867, altd.

44

O GOD of life, whose power benign
  Doth o'er the world in mercy shine,
Accept our praise, for we are Thine.

2 O Father, uncreated Lord,
  Be Thou in every land adored;
  On every soul Thy love be poured.

3 O Son of God, for sinners slain,
  We bless Thee, Lord, whose dying pain
  For us did endless life regain.

4 O Holy Ghost, whose guardian care
  Doth us for heavenly joys prepare,
  May we in Thy communion share.

5 Father, protect us here below;
  Jesus, Thy mercy may we know;
  O Holy Ghost, Thy power bestow.

6 O holy, blessèd Trinity,
  With faith we sinners bow to Thee.
  In us, O God, exalted be !

A. T. Russell, 1806–74.

45

PRAISE we God the Father's name
    For our world's creation,
And His saving health proclaim
    Unto every nation;
Till, His name by all confessed,
    Every heart enthrone Him,
And from furthest east and west
    All His children own Him.

2 Praise we God the only Son,
    Who in mercy sought us;
Born to save a world undone,
    Out of death He brought us;
Here awhile He showed His love,
    Suffered uncomplaining,
Now He pleads for us above,
    Risen, ascended, reigning !

3 Grant us, Holy Ghost, we pray,
    More and more to know Him,
More and more and every day
    In our lives to show Him;
That with hearts by Thee made brave,
    Strong and wise and tender,
We, with all the powers we have,
    Service meet may render.

4 Father, Son, and Holy Ghost,
    Help us to adore Thee,
Till, with all the angel host,
    Low we fall before Thee;
Till, throughout our earthly days
    Guided, loved, forgiven,
We can blend our songs of praise
    With the song of heaven !

C. A. Alington, 1872–1955.

46

THOU whose almighty word
Chaos and darkness heard
 And took their flight,
Hear us, we humbly pray,
And where the gospel day
Sheds not its glorious ray,
 Let there be light.

2 Thou who didst come to bring
On Thy redeeming wing
 Healing and sight,
Health to the sick in mind,
Sight to the inly blind,
O now to all mankind
 Let there be light.

3 Spirit of truth and love,
Life-giving, holy Dove,
 Speed forth Thy flight;
Move on the waters' face,
Bearing the lamp of grace,
And in earth's darkest place
 Let there be light.

4 Blessèd and holy Three,
Most glorious Trinity,
 Wisdom, love, might,
Boundless as ocean's tide
Rolling in fullest pride,
Through the world far and wide
 Let there be light.

John Marriott, 1780–1825, altd.

47

THREE in One, and One in Three.
Ruler of the earth and sea,
 Hear us, while we lift to Thee
 Holy chant and psalm.

2 Light of lights ! with morning shine;
   Lift on us Thy light divine;
   And let charity benign
      Breathe on us her balm.

3 Light of lights ! when falls the even,
   Let it close on sin forgiven;
   Fold us in the peace of heaven;
      Shed a holy calm.

4 Three in One and One in Three,
   Dimly here we worship Thee;
   Hear us while we lift to Thee
      Holy chant and psalm.

Gilbert Rorison, 1821–69, *altd.*

See also—
God hath spoken, 247.   I bind unto myself, 433.
God who created me, **11.**

III. GOD THE FATHER.

48

ALL that's good and great and true,
   All that is, and is to be,
Be it old, or be it new,
   Comes, O Father, comes from Thee.
                Hallelujah !

2 Mercies dawn with every day,
   Newer, brighter than before,
And the sun's declining ray
   Layeth others up in store.

3 Not a bird that doth not sing
   Sweetest praises to Thy name;
Nor an insect on the wing
   But Thy wonders doth proclaim.

4 Every blade and every tree,
   All in happy concert ring,
And in wondrous harmony
   Join in praises to their King.

5 Fill us then with love divine,
   Grant that we, though toiling here,
May, in spirit being Thine,
   See and hear Thee everywhere.

6 May we all with songs of praise,
   Whilst on earth Thy name adore,
Till with angel-choirs we raise
   Songs of praise for evermore.

Godfrey Thring, 1823–1903.

49

ALL things which live below the sky,
　Or move within the sea,
Are creatures of the Lord most high,
　And brothers unto me.

2 I love to hear the robin sing,
　Perched on the highest bough;
To see the rook with purple wing
　Follow the shining plough.

3 I love to watch the swallow skim
　The river in his flight;
To mark, when day is growing dim,
　The glow-worm's silvery light;

4 The sea-gull whiter than the foam,
　The fish that dart beneath;
The lowing cattle coming home;
　The goats upon the heath.

5 Beneath His heaven there's room for all;
　He gives to all their meat;
He sees the meanest sparrow fall
　Unnoticed in the street.

6 Almighty Father, King of kings,
　The lover of the meek,
Make me a friend of helpless things,
　Defender of the weak.

E. J. Brailsford, 1841–1921.

50

DEAR Lord and Father of mankind,
　Forgive our foolish ways;
Reclothe us in our rightful mind;
In purer lives Thy service find,
　In deeper reverence, praise.

2 In simple trust like theirs who heard,
   Beside the Syrian sea,
The gracious calling of the Lord,
Let us, like them, without a word
   Rise up and follow Thee.

3 O Sabbath rest by Galilee !
   O calm of hills above,
Where Jesus knelt to share with Thee
The silence of eternity,
   Interpreted by love !

4 With that deep hush subduing all
   Our words and works that drown
The tender whisper of Thy call,
As noiseless let Thy blessing fall,
   As fell Thy manna down.

5 Drop Thy still dews of quietness,
   Till all our strivings cease ;
Take from our souls the strain and stress,
And let our ordered lives confess
   The beauty of Thy peace.

6 Breathe through the heats of our desire
   Thy coolness and Thy balm ;
Let sense be dumb, let flesh retire ;
Speak through the earthquake, wind, and fire,
   O still small voice of calm !

J. G. Whittier, 1807–92.

51

1 JOHN i. 5.

ETERNAL Light ! Eternal Light !
   How pure the soul must be,
When, placed within Thy searching sight,
It shrinks not, but with calm delight
   Can live, and look on Thee.

2 The spirits that surround Thy throne
    May bear the burning bliss,
But that is surely theirs alone,
Since they have never, never known
    A fallen world like this.

3 O how shall I, whose native sphere
    Is dark, whose mind is dim,
Before the Ineffable appear,
And on my naked spirit bear
    The uncreated beam ?

4 There is a way for man to rise
    To that sublime abode ;—
An offering and a sacrifice,
A Holy Spirit's energies,
    An advocate with God.

5 These, these prepare us for the sight
    Of Holiness above;
The sons of ignorance and night
Can dwell in the eternal light,
    Through the eternal love.

Thomas Binney, 1798–1874.

52

1 JOHN iv. 8.

GOD is love: let heaven adore Him;
    God is love: let earth rejoice;
Let creation sing before Him,
    And exalt Him with one voice.
He who laid the earth's foundation,
    He who spread the heavens above,
He who breathes through all creation,
    He is love, eternal love.

2 God is love: and He enfoldeth
    All the world in one embrace;
With unfailing grasp He holdeth
    Every child of every race.

And when human hearts are breaking
  Under sorrow's iron rod,
All the sorrow, all the aching,
  Wrings with pain the heart of God.

3 God is love: and though with blindness
  Sin afflicts the souls of men,
God's eternal loving-kindness
  Holds and guides them even then.
Sin and death and hell shall never
  O'er us final triumph gain;
God is love, so love for ever
  O'er the universe must reign.

Timothy Rees, 1874–1939, *altd.*

53

GOD moves in a mysterious way,
  His wonders to perform;
He plants His footsteps in the sea,
  And rides upon the storm.

2 Deep in unfathomable mines
  Of never-failing skill
He treasures up His bright designs,
  And works His sovereign will.

3 Ye fearful saints, fresh courage take;
  The clouds ye so much dread
Are big with mercy, and shall break
  In blessings on your head.

4 Judge not the Lord by feeble sense,
  But trust Him for His grace;
Behind a frowning providence
  He hides a smiling face.

5 His purposes will ripen fast,
  Unfolding every hour;
The bud may have a bitter taste,
  But sweet will be the flower.

6 Blind unbelief is sure to err,
    And scan His work in vain;
God is His own interpreter,
    And He will make it plain.

William Cowper, 1731–1800.

54

GRACE, 'tis a charming sound,
    Harmonious to my ear;
Heaven with the echo shall resound,
    And all the earth shall hear.

2   Grace first contrived a way
        To save rebellious man;
    And all the steps that grace display
        Which drew the wondrous plan.

3   Grace taught my wandering feet
        To tread the heavenly road:
    And new supplies each hour I meet,
        While pressing on to God.

4   Grace all the work shall crown
        Through everlasting days;
    It lays in heaven the topmost stone,
        And well deserves the praise.

Philip Doddridge, 1702–51.

55

MICAH vii. 18.

GREAT God of wonders, all Thy ways
    Are matchless, godlike, and divine;
But the fair glories of Thy grace
    More godlike and unrivalled shine:
Who is a pardoning God like Thee?
Or who has grace so rich and free?

2 Such dire offences to forgive,
   Such guilty daring souls to spare;
This is Thy grand prerogative,
   And none shall in the honour share:

3 In wonder lost, with trembling joy,
   We take the pardon of our God,
Pardon for sins of deepest dye,
   A pardon sealed with Jesus' blood:

4 O may this glorious matchless love,
   This God-like miracle of grace,
Teach mortal tongues, like those above,
   To raise this song of lofty praise:

Samuel Davies, 1723–61, altd.

56

PSALM xxxvi.

HIGH in the heavens, eternal God,
   Thy goodness in full glory shines;
Thy truth shall break through every cloud
That veils and darkens Thy designs.

2 For ever firm Thy justice stands,
   As mountains their foundations keep;
Wise are the wonders of Thy hands;
   Thy judgments are a mighty deep.

3 Thy providence is kind and large,
   Both man and beast Thy bounty share;
The whole creation is Thy charge,
   But saints are Thy peculiar care.

4 My God, how excellent Thy grace,
   Whence all our hope and comfort spring !
The sons of Adam in distress
   Fly to the shadow of Thy wing.

5 From the provisions of Thy house
   We shall be fed with sweet repast;
   There mercy like a river flows,
   And brings salvation to our taste.

6 Life, like a fountain rich and free,
   Springs from the presence of the Lord;
   And in Thy light our souls shall see
   The glories promised in Thy word.

Isaac Watts, 1674–1748

57

HOW dearly God must love us
   And this poor world of ours,
To spread blue skies above us,
   And deck the earth with flowers !
There's not a weed so lowly,
   Nor bird that cleaves the air,
But tells, in accents holy,
   His kindness and His care.

2 He bids the sun to warm us,
   And light the path we tread;
At night, lest aught should harm us,
   He guards our welcome bed;
He gives our needful clothing,
   And sends our daily food;
His love denies us nothing
   His wisdom deemeth good.

3 The Bible, too, He sends us,
   That tells how Jesus came,
Whose word can save and cleanse us
   From guilt and sin and shame:
O may God's mercies move us
   To serve Him with our powers,
For O how He must love us
   And this poor world of ours !

S. W. Partridge, 1810–1903

58

I SING the almighty power of God,
　That made the mountains rise,
That spread the flowing seas abroad,
　And built the lofty skies.

2 I sing the wisdom that ordained
　The sun to rule the day;
The moon shines full at His command,
　And all the stars obey.

3 I sing the goodness of the Lord,
　That filled the earth with food;
He formed the creatures with His word,
　And then pronounced them good.

4 There's not a plant or flower below
　But makes Thy glories known;
And clouds arise and tempests blow
　By order from Thy throne.

5 Creatures, as numerous as they be,
　Are subject to Thy care;
There's not a place where we can flee
　But God is present there.

6 His hand is my perpetual guard,
　He guides me with His eye;
Why should I, then, forget the Lord,
　Whose love is ever nigh ?
　　　　　　　　　Isaac Watts, 1674–1748.

59

PSALM cxxi.

I TO the hills will lift mine eyes:
　From whence doth come mine aid ?
My safety cometh from the Lord,
　Who heaven and earth hath made.

2 Thy foot He'll not let slide, nor will
   He slumber that thee keeps.
Behold, He that keeps Israel,
   He slumbers not, nor sleeps.

3 The Lord thee keeps; the Lord thy shade
   On thy right hand doth stay;
The moon by night thee shall not smite,
   Nor yet the sun by day.

4 The Lord shall keep thy soul; He shall
   Preserve thee from all ill;
Henceforth thy going out and in
   God keep for ever will.

Francis Rous, 1579–1659.
William Barton, 1598–1678.

60

PSALM cxlvi.

I'LL praise my Maker while I've breath,
And when my voice is lost in death,
   Praise shall employ my nobler powers:
My days of praise shall ne'er be past,
While life and thought and being last,
   Or immortality endures.

2 Happy the man whose hopes rely
On Israel's God ! He made the sky
   And earth and seas, with all their train:
His truth for ever stands secure;
He saves the oppressed, He feeds the poor,
   And none shall find His promise vain.

3 The Lord hath eyes to give the blind;
The Lord supports the fainting mind;
   He sends the labouring conscience peace:
He helps the stranger in distress,
The widow and the fatherless,
   And grants the prisoner sweet release.

4 I'll praise Him while He lends me breath;
  And when my voice is lost in death,
    Praise shall employ my nobler powers:
  My days of praise shall ne'er be past,
  While life and thought and being last,
    Or immortality endures.

Isaac Watts, 1674–1748, altd.

61

1 Tim. i. 17.

IMMORTAL, invisible, God only wise,
In light inaccessible hid from our eyes,
Most blessed, most glorious, the ancient of days,
Almighty, victorious, Thy great name we praise.

2 Unresting, unhasting, and silent as light,
  Nor wanting, nor wasting, Thou rulest in might;
  Thy justice like mountains high soaring above
  Thy clouds, which are fountains of goodness and
    love.

3 To all, life Thou givest, to both great and small;
  In all life Thou livest, the true life of all;
  We blossom and flourish as leaves on the tree,
  And wither and perish: but nought changeth
    Thee.

4 Great Father of glory, pure Father of light,
  Thine angels adore Thee, all veiling their sight;
  But of all Thy rich graces this grace, Lord, impart—
  Take the veil from our faces, the veil from our
    heart.

5 All laud we would render; O help us to see,
  'Tis only the splendour of light hideth Thee;
  And so let Thy glory, Almighty, impart
  Through Christ in the story, Thy Christ to the
    heart.

W. C. Smith, 1824–1908.

62

LORD God almighty, in Thy hand
　　Rolls every world, blooms every flower;
O Maker of the sea, the land,
　　We praise Thy power.

2 For day and night that never cease;
　　For garnered wealth of harvest days;
For the pure mountains breathing peace,
　　Thy power we praise.

3 For the protected gift of life;
　　For reason; for home's sheltering bower;
For the strong love of child and wife,
　　We praise Thy power.

4 For freedom; for the sage's thought;
　　For martyrs brave; for poet's lays;
For the great word by prophets brought,
　　Thy power we praise.

5 For Him, Thy Son divine, who came
　　From Thee—Thine all-transcendent dower!
To raise us from our sin and shame,
　　We praise Thy power.

6 For all He did our souls to save,
　　And guide us in Thy heavenly ways;
For His dear life, His cross, His grave,
　　Thy power we praise.

7 Illimitable is Thy love,
　　Thy mercy endless as Thy days;
Nor shall we cease in realms above
　　Thy power to praise.

G. T. Coster, 1835–1912.

63

LORD of all being, throned afar,
Thy glory flames from sun and star;
Centre and soul of every sphere,
Yet to each loving heart how near!

2 Sun of our life, Thy quickening ray
Sheds on our path the glow of day;
Star of our hope, Thy softened light
Cheers the long watches of the night.

3 Our midnight is Thy smile withdrawn;
Our noontide is Thy gracious dawn;
Our rainbow arch, Thy mercy's sign;
All, save the clouds of sin, are Thine.

4 Lord of all life, below, above,
Whose light is truth, whose warmth is love
Before Thy ever-blazing throne
We ask no lustre of our own.

5 Grant us Thy truth to make us free,
And kindling hearts that burn for Thee,
Till all Thy living altars claim
One holy light, one heavenly flame.

Oliver Wendell Holmes, 1809-94

64

MY God, how wonderful Thou art!
Thy majesty how bright!
How beautiful Thy mercy-seat,
In depths of burning light!

2 How wonderful, how beautiful,
The sight of Thee must be,
Thine endless wisdom, boundless power,
And aweful purity!

3 Thy justice is the gladdest thing
    Creation can behold;
Thy tenderness so meek, it wins
    The guilty to be bold.

4 Yet more than all, and evermore,
    Should we, Thy creatures, bless,
Most worshipful of attributes,
    Thine aweful holiness.

5 Yet I may love Thee too, O Lord,
    Almighty as Thou art,
For thou hast stooped to ask of me
    The love of my poor heart.

6 No earthly father loves like Thee,
    No mother, half so mild,
Bears and forbears as Thou hast done
    With me, Thy sinful child.

7 O little heart of mine ! shall pain
    Or sorrow make thee moan,
When all this God is all for thee,
    A Father all thine own ?

F. W. Faber, 1814–63, *altd.*

65

1 TIM. iv. 10.

NOT, Lord, Thine ancient works alone,
    Thy wonders to past ages shown,
    Make our glad spirits glow;
Our eyes behold Thy works of might;
On us full beam Thy wonders bright:
    The living God we know.

2 We joy not only to be told
  How with Thy saints and seers of old
    Thou madest sweet abode:
  We of Thy presence bright can tell;
  Thou in Thy living saints dost dwell:
    We trust the living God.

3 Thou settest us each task divine;
  We bless that helping hand of Thine,
    This strength by Thee bestowed:
  Thou minglest in the glorious fight,
  Thine own the cause, Thine own the might;
    We serve the living God.

4 Ah! soon we droop; ah! soon we tire;
  Our fainting hearts new strength require,
    Again would quickened be:
  We ask no priest; we seek no shrine;
  To Thee we come for life divine,
    Thou living God, to Thee!

5 O more than satisfy our need;
  Our most divine desires exceed;
    Our daily quickener be:
  Thou living God, possess us still;
  Thy wondrous life in us fulfil,
    Our blessèd life in Thee!

T. H. Gill, 1819–1906, *altd*

66

O GOD of love, whose spirit wakes
    In every human breast,
Whom love, and love alone, can know,
    In whom all hearts find rest,
Help us to spread Thy gracious reign,
    Till greed and hate shall cease,
And kindness dwell in human hearts,
    And all the earth find peace.

2 O God of truth, whom science seeks
　And reverent souls adore,
Who lightest every earnest mind
　Of every clime and shore,
Dispel the gloom of error's night,
　Of ignorance and fear,
Until true wisdom from above
　Shall make life's pathway clear.

3 O God of beauty, oft revealed
　In dreams of human art,
In speech that flows to melody,
　In holiness of heart;
Teach us to ban all ugliness
　That blinds our eyes to Thee,
Till all shall know the loveliness
　Of lives made fair and free.

4 O God of righteousness and grace,
　Seen in the Christ, thy Son,
Whose life and death reveal Thy face,
　By whom Thy will was done,
Inspire Thy heralds of good news
　To live Thy life divine,
Till Christ is formed in all mankind,
　And every land is Thine.

H. H. Tweedy, 1868–1953.

67

O GOD, the rock of ages,
　Who evermore hast been,
What time the tempest rages,
　Our dwelling place serene:
Before Thy first creations,
　O Lord, the same as now;
To endless generations
　The everlasting Thou !

2 Our years are like the shadows
   On sunny hills that lie,
Or grasses in the meadows
   That blossom but to die:
A sleep, a dream, a story
   By strangers quickly told,
An unremaining glory
   Of things that soon are old.

3 O Thou, who canst not slumber,
   Whose light grows never pale,
Teach us aright to number
   Our years before they fail;
On us Thy mercy lighten,
   On us Thy goodness rest,
And let Thy Spirit brighten
   The hearts Thyself hast blest.

4 Lord, crown our faith's endeavour
   With beauty and with grace,
Till, clothed in light for ever,
   We see Thee face to face;
A joy no language measures;
   A fountain brimming o'er;
An endless flow of pleasures;
   An ocean without shore.

                E. H. Bickersteth, 1825–1906.

68

O LORD of heaven and earth and sea
   To Thee all praise and glory be!
How shall we show our love to Thee,
   Who givest all?

2 The golden sunshine, vernal air,
Sweet flowers and fruits, Thy love declare;
Where harvests ripen, Thou art there,
   Who givest all.

3 For peaceful homes and healthful days,
  For all the blessings earth displays,
  We owe Thee thankfulness and praise,
      Who givest all.

4 Thou didst not spare Thine only Son,
  But gav'st Him for a world undone;
  And freely with that blessèd One
      Thou givest all.

5 Thou giv'st the Spirit's blessèd dower,
  Spirit of life and love and power,
  And dost His sevenfold graces shower
      Upon us all.

6 For souls redeemed, for sins forgiven,
  For means of grace, and hopes of heaven,
  Father, what can to Thee be given,
      Who givest all?

7 To Thee, from whom we all derive
  Our life, our gifts, our power to give!
  O may we ever with Thee live,
      Who givest all!

Christopher Wordsworth, 1807–85, altd

69

O LOVE of God, how strong and true!
  Eternal and yet ever new;
Uncomprehended and unbought,
Beyond all knowledge and all thought.

2 O heavenly love, how precious still,
  In days of weariness and ill,
  In nights of pain and helplessness,
  To heal, to comfort, and to bless!

3 O wide-embracing, wondrous love,
  We read thee in the sky above;
  We read thee in the earth below,
  In seas that swell and streams that flow.

4 We read thee best in Him who came
   To bear for us the cross of shame,
   Sent by the Father from on high,
   Our life to live, our death to die.

5 We read thy power to bless and save
   E'en in the darkness of the grave;
   Still more in resurrection-light,
   We read the fulness of thy might.

6 O love of God, our shield and stay
   Through all the perils of our way;
   Eternal love, in thee we rest,
   For ever safe, for ever blest !

Horatius Bonar, 1808–89.

70

PSALM ciii. 1–4.

O THOU my soul, bless God the Lord;
   And all that in me is
Be stirrèd up His holy name
   To magnify and bless.

2 Bless, O my soul, the Lord thy God,
   And not forgetful be
Of all His gracious benefits
   He hath bestowed on thee:

3 All thine iniquities who doth
   Most graciously forgive;
Who thy diseases all and pains
   Doth heal, and thee relieve;

4 Who doth redeem thy life, that thou
   To death may'st not go down;
Who thee with loving kindness doth
   And tender mercies crown.

Francis Rous, 1579–1659.
William Barton, 1597–1678.

71

OUR God, our help in ages past,
 Our hope for years to come,
Our shelter from the stormy blast,
 And our eternal home;

2 Under the shadow of Thy throne
  Thy saints have dwelt secure;
 Sufficient is Thine arm alone,
  And our defence is sure.

3 Before the hills in order stood,
  Or earth received her frame,
 From everlasting Thou art God,
  To endless years the same.

4 A thousand ages in Thy sight
  Are like an evening gone;
 Short as the watch that ends the night
  Before the rising sun.

5 Time, like an ever-rolling stream,
  Bears all its sons away;
 They fly forgotten, as a dream
  Dies at the opening day.

6 Our God, our help in ages past,
  Our hope for years to come,
 Be Thou our guard while troubles last,
  And our eternal home.

Isaac Watts, 1674–1748, *altd.*

72

THE king of love my shepherd is,
  Whose goodness faileth never;
I nothing lack if I am His
  And He is mine for ever.

2 Where streams of living water flow
  My ransomed soul He leadeth,
And, where the verdant pastures grow,
  With food celestial feedeth.

3 Perverse and foolish oft I strayed;
  But yet in love He sought me,
And on His shoulder gently laid,
  And home, rejoicing, brought me.

4 In death's dark vale I fear no ill
  With Thee, dear Lord, beside me;
Thy rod and staff my comfort still,
  Thy cross before to guide me.

5 Thou spread'st a table in my sight;
  Thy unction grace l estoweth;
And O what transport of delight
  From Thy pure chalice floweth !

6 And so through all the length of days
  Thy goodness faileth never;
Good shepherd, may I sing Thy praise
  Within Thy house for ever.

H. W. Baker, 1821–77.

73

THE Lord's my shepherd, I'll not want;
 He makes me down to lie
In pastures green; He leadeth me
 The quiet waters by.

2 My soul He doth restore again,
 And me to walk doth make
Within the paths of righteousness,
 E'en for His own name's sake.

3 Yea, though I walk through death's dark vale,
 Yet will I fear none ill;
For Thou art with me, and Thy rod
 And staff me comfort still.

4 My table Thou hast furnishèd
 In presence of my foes;
My head Thou dost with oil anoint,
 And my cup overflows.

5 Goodness and mercy all my life
 Shall surely follow me;
And in God's house for evermore
 My dwelling-place shall be.

Francis Rous, 1579–1659,
revised for Scottish Psalter, 1650.

74

THE spacious firmament on high,
 With all the blue ethereal sky,
And spangled heavens, a shining frame,
Their great Original proclaim.
The unwearied sun, from day to day
Does his Creator's power display;
And publishes to every land
The work of an almighty hand.

2 Soon as the evening shades prevail,
The moon takes up the wondrous tale,
And nightly to the listening earth
Repeats the story of her birth;
While all the stars that round her burn,
And all the planets in their turn,
Confirm the tidings as they roll,
And spread the truth from pole to pole.

3 What though in solemn silence all
Move round this dark terrestrial ball ?
What though no real voice nor sound
Amidst their radiant orbs be found ?
In reason's ear they all rejoice,
And utter forth a glorious voice,
For ever singing, as they shine,
" The hand that made us is divine."

Joseph Addison, 1672–1719.

75

THEE will I love, my God and King,
Thee will I sing,
My strength and tower,
For evermore Thee will I trust,
O God most just
Of truth and power;
Who all things hast
In order placed,
Yea, for Thy pleasure hast created;
And on Thy throne
Unseen, unknown,
Reignest alone
In glory seated.

2 Set in my heart Thy love I find;
My wandering mind
To Thee Thou leadest:
My trembling hope, my strong desire
With heavenly fire
Thou kindly feedest.

Lo, all things fair
Thy path prepare,
Thy beauty to my spirit calleth,
Thine to remain
In joy or pain,
And count it gain
Whate'er befalleth.

3 O more and more Thy love extend,
My life befriend
With heavenly pleasure;
That I may win Thy paradise,
Thy pearl of price,
Thy countless treasure;
Since but in Thee
I can go free
From earthly care and vain oppression,
This prayer I make
For Jesus' sake
That Thou me take
In Thy possession.

Robert Bridges, 1844–1930

76

ROMANS i. 20.

THERE is a book, who runs may read,
Which heavenly truth imparts;
And all the lore its scholars need,
Pure eyes and Christian hearts.

2 The works of God above, below,
Within us and around,
Are pages in that book, to show
How God Himself is found.

3 The glorious sky, embracing all,
  Is like the Maker's love,
Wherewith encompassed, great and small
  In peace and order move.

4 One name, above all glorious names,
  With its ten thousand tongues,
The everlasting sea proclaims,
  Echoing angelic songs.

5 The raging fire, the roaring wind,
  Thy boundless power display:
But in the gentle breeze we find
  Thy Spirit's viewless way.

6 Two worlds are ours: 'tis only sin
  Forbids us to descry
The mystic heaven and earth within,
  Plain as the sea and sky.

7 Thou who hast given me eyes to see,
  And love this sight so fair,
Give me a heart to find out Thee,
  And read Thee everywhere.

John Keble, 1792–1866, *altd.*

77

WHEN all Thy mercies, O my God,
    My rising soul surveys,
Transported with the view, I'm lost
  In wonder, love, and praise.

2 Unnumbered comforts on my soul
  Thy tender care bestowed,
Before my infant heart conceived
  From whom those comforts flowed.

3 When in the slippery paths of youth
    With heedless steps I ran,
  Thine arm unseen conveyed me safe,
    And brought me up to man.

4 When worn with sickness, oft hast Thou
    With health renewed my face;
  And, when in sins and sorrows sunk,
    Revived my soul with grace.

5 Ten thousand thousand precious gifts
    My daily thanks employ;
  Nor is the least a cheerful heart
    That tastes those gifts with joy.

6 Through every period of my life
    Thy goodness I'll pursue;
  And after death, in distant worlds,
    The glorious theme renew.

7 Through all eternity to Thee
    A joyful song I'll raise:
  For O eternity's too short
    To utter all Thy praise.

Joseph Addison, 1672–1719.

See also—
How vast the treasure, 497.   The Lord is rich, 422.
Souls of men, 419.

IV. GOD THE SON

78

COME, Thou long-expected Jesus,
　　Born to set Thy people free;
From our fears and sins release us;
　　Let us find our rest in Thee.

2 Israel's strength and consolation,
　　Hope of all the earth Thou art;
Dear desire of every nation,
　　Joy of every longing heart.

3 Born Thy people to deliver;
　　Born a child, and yet a King;
Born to reign in us for ever;
　　Now Thy gracious kingdom bring.

4 By Thine own eternal Spirit
　　Rule in all our hearts alone:
By Thine all-sufficient merit
　　Raise us to Thy glorious throne.

Charles Wesley, 1707–88.

79

EARTH was waiting, spent and restless,
　　With a mingled hope and fear;
And the faithful few were sighing,
" Surely, Lord, the day is near;
The Desire of all the nations,
　　It is time He should appear."

2 Still the gods were in their temples,
    But the ancient faith had fled;
And the priests stood by their altars
    Only for a piece of bread;
And the oracles were silent,
    And the prophets all were dead.

3 In the sacred courts of Zion,
    Where the Lord had His abode,
There the money-changers trafficked,
    And the sheep and oxen trod;
And the world, because of wisdom,
    Knew not either Lord or God.

4 Then the Spirit of the Highest
    On a virgin meek came down,
And He burdened her with blessing,
    And He pained her with renown;
For she bare the Lord's anointed,
    For His cross and for His crown.

5 Earth for Him had groaned and travailed
    Since the ages first began;
For in Him was hid the secret
    That through all the ages ran—
Son of Mary, Son of David,
    Son of God, and Son of man.

W. C. Smith, 1824–1908.

80

PSALM lxxii.

HAIL to the Lord's anointed,
    Great David's greater Son!
Hail, in the time appointed,
    His reign on earth begun!
He comes to break oppression,
    To set the captive free,
To take away transgression.
    And rule in equity.

2 He comes with succour speedy
   To those who suffer wrong;
To help the poor and needy,
   And bid the weak be strong;
To give them songs for sighing,
   Their darkness turn to light,
Whose souls, condemned and dying,
   Were precious in His sight.

3 He shall come down like showers
   Upon the fruitful earth;
And love, joy, hope, like flowers.
   Spring in His path to birth:
Before Him on the mountains,
   Shall peace the herald go,
And righteousness in fountains
   From hill to valley flow.

4 Kings shall fall down before Him,
   And gold and incense bring;
All nations shall adore Him,
   His praise all people sing;
For He shall have dominion
   O'er river, sea, and shore,
Far as the eagle's pinion
   Or dove's light wing can soar.

5 O'er every foe victorious,
   He on His throne shall rest;
From age to age more glorious,
   All-blessing and all-blest;
The tide of time shall never
   His covenant remove;
His name shall stand for ever,
   His changeless name of Love.

James Montgomery, 1771–1854.

81

LUKE iv. 18–19.

HARK the glad sound ! the Saviour comes,
    The Saviour promised long;
Let every heart prepare a throne,
    And every voice a song.

2 He comes, the prisoners to release,
    In Satan's bondage held:
The gates of brass before Him burst,
    The iron fetters yield.

3 He comes, from thickest films of vice
    To clear the mental ray,
And on the eyeballs of the blind
    To pour celestial day.

4 He comes, the broken heart to bind,
    The bleeding soul to cure,
And with the treasures of His grace
    To enrich the humble poor.

5 Our glad hosannas, Prince of peace,
    Thy welcome shall proclaim;
And heaven's eternal arches ring
    With Thy belovèd name.

Philip Doddridge, 1702–51, altd.

82

LIFT up your heads, ye mighty gates;
    Behold the King of glory waits,
The King of kings is drawing near,
The Saviour of the world is here;
Life and salvation doth He bring,
Wherefore rejoice, and gladly sing.

2 The Lord is just, a helper tried;
  Mercy is ever at His side,
  His kingly crown is holiness,
  His sceptre, pity in distress;
  The end of all our woe He brings,
  Wherefore the earth is glad and sings.

3 O blest the land, the city blest,
  Where Christ the ruler is confessed !
  O happy hearts and happy homes,
  To whom this King in triumph comes !
  The cloudless sun of joy He is,
  Who bringeth pure delight and bliss.

4 Fling wide the portals of your heart,
  Make it a temple set apart
  From earthly use, for heaven's employ,
  Adorned with prayer, and love, and joy;
  So shall your sovereign enter in,
  And new and nobler life begin.

5 Redeemer, come ! I open wide
  My heart to Thee; here, Lord, abide !
  Let me Thine inner presence feel,
  Thy grace and love in me reveal;
  Thy Holy Spirit guide me on,
  Until the glorious crown be won !

Georg Weissel, 1590–1635,
***tr.** Catherine Winkworth, 1827–78.*

83

O COME, O come, Immanuel,
And ransom captive Israel,
That mourns in lonely exile here
Until the Son of God appear.

Rejoice ! rejoice ! Immanuel
Shall come to thee, O Israel.

2 O come, O come, Thou Lord of might,
  Who to Thy tribes on Sinai's height
  In ancient times didst give the law
  In cloud and majesty and awe.

3 O come, Thou rod of Jesse, free
  Thine own from Satan's tyranny;
  From depths of hell Thy people save,
  And give them victory o'er the grave.

4 O come, Thou dayspring, come and cheer
  Our spirits by Thine advent here;
  Disperse the gloomy clouds of night,
  And death's dark shadows put to flight.

5 O come, Thou key of David, come
  And open wide our heavenly home;
  Make safe the way that leads on high,
  And close the path to misery.

Latin, 12th cent.,
tr. J. M. Neale, 1818–66, altd.

84

ISAIAH xl. i.

O JOYFUL hope, in weary hearts awaking:
  O blessed voice of pardon and release:
Tidings of grace for souls oppressed and aching;
  Telling of liberation, life and peace.
   " Comfort ye, My people, saith your God:
    My people, comfort ye!"

2 Long was the night of exiled Israel's sorrow,
  Bitter the hours of suffering and fear,
Till on her darkness dawned the light of morrow,
  When prophet lips proclaimed redemption near.

3 Now for mankind a brighter dawn has broken;
    Bidding the gloom of sin and death be gone.
  God's voice of love His perfect word has spoken;
    Jesus the light of all the world is born.

4 Lift up your voice, O men, in exultation;
    Tell every land the tidings you have heard:
  Jesus proclaims His people's liberation;
    Speaks in the Cross His Father's saving word.

                              A. F. Bayly, 1901–

85

O F the Father's love begotten
      Ere the worlds began to be,
  He is alpha and omega,
    He the source, the ending He,
  Of the things that are, that have been,
    And that future years shall see:
      Evermore and evermore.

2 By His word was all created;
    He commanded and 'twas done;
  Earth and sky and boundless ocean,
    Universe of three in one,
  All that sees the moon's soft radiance,
    All that breathes beneath the sun.

3 This is He whom seers in old time
    Chanted of with one accord,
  Whom the voices of the prophets
    Promised in their faithful word;
  Now He shines, the long-expected;
    Let creation praise its Lord.

4 Now let old and young uniting
    Chant to Thee harmonious lays;
  Maid and matron hymn Thy glory,
    Infant lips their anthems raise,
  Boys and girls together singing
    With pure heart their song of praise.

5 O ye heights of heaven, adore Him;
    Angel hosts, His praises sing;
  All dominions, bow before Him,
    And extol our God and King;
  Let no tongue on earth be silent,
    Every voice in concert sing.

Aurelius Prudentius, 348–413,
tr. J. M. Neale, 1818–66, altd.

86

LUKE iii. 1–18.

ON Jordan's bank the Baptist's cry
  Announces that the Lord is nigh;
Come then and hearken, for he brings
Glad tidings from the King of kings.

2 Then cleansed be every breast from sin;
  Make straight the way for God within;
  Prepare we in our hearts a home,
  Where such a mighty guest may come.

3 For Thou art our salvation, Lord,
  Our refuge and our great reward;
  Without Thy grace we waste away,
  Like flowers that wither and decay.

4 To heal the sick stretch out Thine hand,
  And bid the fallen sinner stand;
  Shine forth, and let Thy light restore
  Earth's own true loveliness once more.

5 To Him who left the throne of heaven
  To save mankind, all praise be given;
  Like praise be to the Father done,
  And Holy Spirit, Three in One.   Amen.

Charles Coffin, 1676–1749.
tr. John Chandler, 1806–76, altd.

(2) His Birth

87

A GREAT and mighty wonder,
    A full and holy cure:
The Virgin bears the infant
    With virgin-honour pure.
        Repeat the hymn again!
          " To God on high be glory,
        And peace on earth to men."

2 The Word becomes incarnate
    And yet remains on high.
  And cherubim sing anthems
    To shepherds, from the sky.

3 While thus they sing your monarch,
    Those bright angelic bands,
  Rejoice, ye vales and mountains,
    Ye oceans, clap your hands !

4 Since all He comes to ransom,
    By all be He adored,
  The infant born in Bethlem,
    The Saviour and the Lord.

5 All idol forms shall perish,
    All error shall decay,
  And Christ shall wield His sceptre,
    Our Lord and God for aye.

St. Germanus, 634–732,
tr. J. M. Neale, 1818–66, altd.

88

ALL my heart this night rejoices,
    As I hear, far and near,
Sweetest angel voices;
" Christ is born ! " their choirs are singing
    Till the air everywhere
Now with joy is ringing.

2 Hark ! a voice from yonder manger,
    Soft and sweet, doth entreat:
" Flee from woe and danger;
Brethren, come: from all that grieves you
    You are freed: all you need
I will surely give you."

3 Come, then, let us hasten yonder;
    Here let all, great and small,
Kneel in awe and wonder;
Love Him who with love is yearning;
    Hail the star that from far
Bright with hope is burning.

4 Thee, dear Lord, with heed I'll cherish,
    Live to Thee, and with Thee
Dying, shall not perish,
But shall dwell with Thee for ever
    Far on high, in the joy
That can alter never.

Paul Gerhardt, 1607–76,
tr. Catherine Winkworth, 1827–78.

89

ANGELS, from the realms of glory,
    Wing your flight o'er all the earth;
Ye who sang creation's story,
    Now proclaim Messiah's birth:
Come and worship,
Worship Christ, the new-born King.

2 Shepherds, in the field abiding,
    Watching o'er your flocks by night,
God with man is now residing,
    Yonder shines the infant-light:

3 Sages, leave your contemplations,
    Brighter visions beam afar;
Seek the great desire of nations;
    Ye have seen His natal star:

4 Saints, before the altar bending,
    Watching long in hope and fear,
Suddenly the Lord descending
    In His temple shall appear:

James Montgomery, 1771–1854

90

MATT. ii. 1–11.

AS with gladness men of old
    Did the guiding star behold;
As with joy they hailed its light,
Leading onward, beaming bright,
So, most gracious God, may we
Evermore be led to Thee.

2 As with joyful steps they sped,
Saviour, to Thy lowly bed,
There to bend the knee before
Thee whom heaven and earth adore,
So may we with willing feet
Ever seek Thy mercy-seat.

3 As they offered gifts most rare
At Thy cradle rude and bare,
So may we with holy joy,
Pure, and free from sin's alloy,
All our costliest treasures bring,
Christ, to Thee, our heavenly King.

4 Holy Jesus, every day
Keep us in the narrow way;
And, when earthly things are past,
Bring our ransomed souls at last
Where they need no star to guide,
Where no clouds Thy glory hide.

5 In the heavenly country bright
Need they no created light;
Thou its light, its joy, its crown,
Thou its sun, which goes not down.
There for ever may we sing
Hallelujahs to our King.

W. C. Dix, 1837–98.

91

MATT. ii. 1–11.

BRIGHTEST and best of the sons of the
morning,
Dawn on our darkness, and lend us thine aid;
Star of the east, the horizon adorning,
Guide where our infant Redeemer is laid.

2 Cold on His cradle the dew-drops are shining;
Low lies His head with the beasts of the stall;
Angels adore Him, in slumber reclining,
Maker and monarch, and Saviour of all.

3 Say, shall we yield Him, in costly devotion,
Odours of Edom, and offerings divine;
Gems of the mountain, and pearls of the ocean,
Myrrh from the forest, or gold from the mine?

4 Vainly we offer each ample oblation;
Vainly with gifts would His favour secure;
Richer by far is the heart's adoration;
Dearer to God are the prayers of the poor.

5 Brightest and best of the sons of the morning,
   Dawn on our darkness, and lend us thine aid;
Star of the east, the horizon adorning,
   Guide where our infant Redeemer is laid.

Reginald Heber, 1783–1826

92

CHILD in the manger,
   Infant of Mary;
Outcast and stranger,
   Lord of all;
Child who inherits
   All our transgressions,
All our demerits
   On Him fall.

2 Once the most holy
   Child of salvation
Gently and lowly
   Lived below;
Now as our glorious
   Mighty Redeemer,
See Him victorious
   O'er each foe.

3 Prophets foretold Him,
   Infant of wonder;
Angels behold Him
   On His throne;
Worthy our Saviour
   Of all their praises;
Happy for ever
   Are His own.

Mary Macdonald, 1789–1872,
***tr.** Lachlan Macbean, 1853–1931.*

93

Luke ii. 10.

CHRISTIANS, awake ! salute the happy morn,
Whereon the Saviour of mankind was born;
Rise to adore the mystery of love
Which hosts of angels chanted from above;
With them the joyful tidings first begun
Of God incarnate, of the Virgin's Son.

2 Then to the watchful shepherds it was told,
Who heard the angelic herald's voice " Behold,
I bring good tidings of a Saviour's birth
To you and all the nations upon earth :
This day hath God fulfilled His promised word,
This day is born a Saviour, Christ the Lord."

3 He spake; and straightway the celestial choir,
In hymns of joy unknown before conspire;
High praise of God's redeeming love they sang,
And heaven's whole orb with hallelujahs rang :
God's highest glory was their anthem still,
" On earth be peace, and unto men goodwill."

4 O may we keep and ponder in our mind
God's wondrous love in saving lost mankind;
Trace we the Babe who hath retrieved our loss,
From His poor manger to His bitter cross;
Tread in His steps, assisted by His grace,
Till man's first heavenly state again takes place.

5 Then may we hope, the angelic hosts among,
To sing, redeemed, a glad triumphant song :
He that was born upon this joyful day
Around us all His glory shall display;
Saved by His love, incessant we shall sing
Eternal praise to heaven's almighty King.

John Byrom, 1692–1763, altd.

94

FROM east to west, from shore to shore,
    Let every heart awake and sing
The holy Child whom Mary bore,
    The Christ, the everlasting King.

2 Behold, the world's Creator wears
    The form and fashion of a slave;
Our very flesh our Maker shares,
    His fallen creature, man, to save.

3 For this how wondrously He wrought !
    A maiden, in her lowly place,
Became, in ways beyond all thought,
    The chosen vessel of His grace.

4 He shrank not from the oxen's stall,
    He lay within the manger bed,
And He, whose bounty feedeth all,
    At Mary's breast Himself was fed.

5 And while the angels in the sky
    Sang praise above the silent field,
To shepherds poor the Lord most high,
    The one great Shepherd, was revealed.

6 All glory for this blessèd morn
    To God the Father ever be;
All praise to Thee, O Virgin-born,
    All praise, O Holy Ghost, to Thee.   Amen.

Caelius Sedulius, died c. 450,
tr. John Ellerton, 1826–93, altd.

95

Matt. ii. 1–9.

FROM the eastern mountains
　Pressing on they come,
Wise men in their wisdom,
　To His humble home;
Stirred by deep devotion,
　Hasting from afar,
Ever journeying onward,
　Guided by a star.

2 There their Lord and Saviour
　Meek and lowly lay,
Wondrous Light that led them
　Onward on their way,
Ever now to lighten
　Nations from afar,
As they journey homeward
　By that guiding star.

3 Thou who in a manger
　Once hast lowly lain,
Who dost now in glory
　O'er all kingdoms reign,
Gather in the heathen,
　Who in lands afar
Ne'er have seen the brightness
　Of Thy guiding star.

4 Gather in the outcasts,
　All who've gone astray;
Throw Thy radiance o'er them;
　Guide them on their way.
Those who never knew Thee,
　Those who've wandered far,
Guide them by the brightness
　Of Thy guiding star.

5 Onward through the darkness
   Of the lonely night,
Shining still before them
   With Thy kindly light,
Guide them, Jew and Gentile,
   Homeward from afar,
Young and old together,
   By Thy guiding star.

Godfrey Thring, 1823–1903.

96

GOD rest you merry, gentlemen,
   Let nothing you dismay,
For Jesus Christ our Saviour
   Was born upon this day;
To save us all from Satan's power
   When we were gone astray.
   O tidings of comfort and joy!

2 In Bethlehem in Jewry
   This blessèd Babe was born,
And laid within a manger
   Upon this blessèd morn;
The which His mother Mary
   Did nothing take in scorn.

3 From God our heavenly Father
   A blessèd angel came,
And unto certain shepherds
   Brought tidings of the same,
How that in Bethlehem was born
   The Son of God by name.

4 The shepherds at those tidings
   Rejoicèd much in mind,
And left their flocks a-feeding
   In tempest, storm, and wind,
And went to Bethlehem straightway,
   This blessèd Babe to find.

5 And when to Bethlehem they came,
    Whereat this infant lay,
  They found Him in a manger
    Where oxen feed on hay;
  His mother Mary kneeling
    Unto the Lord did pray.

6 Now to the Lord sing praises,
    All you within this place,
  And with true love and brotherhood
    Each other now embrace;
  This holy tide of Christmas
    All anger should efface.

Traditional.

97

GOOD Christian men, rejoice
    With heart and soul and voice;
  Give ye heed to what we say,
  Jesus Christ is born to-day:
Ox and ass before Him bow,
And He is in the manger now.
    Christ is born to-day !

2 Good Christian men, rejoice
  With heart and soul and voice;
    Now ye hear of endless bliss,
    Jesus Christ was born for this:
  He hath oped the heavenly door,
  And man is blessèd evermore.
    Christ was born for this !

3 Good Christian men, rejoice
  With heart and soul and voice;
    Now ye need not fear the grave,
    Jesus Christ was born to save,
  Calls you one and calls you all,
  To gain His everlasting hall.
    Christ was born to save !

J. M. Neale, 1818-66, *altd.*

98

Luke ii. 1–20.

HARK ! the herald-angels sing
Glory to the new-born King,
Peace on earth, and mercy mild,
God and sinners reconciled.
Joyful, all ye nations rise,
Join the triumph of the skies;
With the angelic host proclaim,
" Christ is born in Bethlehem."

*Hark ! the herald-angels sing
Glory to the new-born King.*

2 Christ, by highest heaven adored,
Christ, the everlasting Lord,
Late in time behold Him come,
Offspring of a virgin's womb.
Veiled in flesh the Godhead see !
Hail, the incarnate Deity !
Pleased as man with men to dwell,
Jesus, our Immanuel.

3 Hail, the heaven-born Prince of peace !
Hail, the Sun of righteousness !
Light and life to all He brings,
Risen with healing in His wings,
Mild, He lays His glory by;
Born, that man no more may die;
Born, to raise the sons of earth;
Born, to give them second birth.

Charles Wesley, 1707–88, **altd.**

99

IN the bleak midwinter,
Frosty wind made moan,
Earth stood hard as iron.
Water like a stone;

Snow had fallen, snow on snow,
  Snow on snow,
In the bleak midwinter,
    Long ago.

2 Our God, heaven cannot hold Him,
  Nor earth sustain;
Heaven and earth shall flee away
  When He comes to reign:
In the bleak midwinter
  A stable-place sufficed
The Lord God almighty,
    Jesus Christ.

3 Angels and archangels
  May have gathered there,
Cherubim and seraphim
  Thronged the air—
But His mother only,
  In her maiden bliss,
Worshipped the belovèd
    With a kiss.

4 What can I give Him,
  Poor as I am!
If I were a shepherd
  I would bring a lamb;
If I were a wise man,
  I would do my part;
Yet what I can I give Him—
    Give my heart.

Christina Rossetti, 1830-94.

100

INFANT holy,
  Infant lowly,
For His bed a cattle stall;
  Oxen lowing,
  Little knowing
Christ the babe is Lord of all.

Swift are winging
Angels singing,
Nowells ringing,
Tidings bringing,
Christ the babe is Lord of all.

2 Flocks were sleeping,
Shepherds keeping
Vigil till the morning new
Saw the glory,
Heard the story,
Tidings of a gospel true.
Thus rejoicing,
Free from sorrow,
Praises voicing,
Greet the morrow,
Christ the babe was born for you !

Polish Carol,
tr. E. M. G. Reed, 1885–1933.

101

LUKE ii. 14.

IT came upon the midnight clear,
    That glorious song of old,
From angels bending near the earth
    To touch their harps of gold :
" Peace on the earth, goodwill to men,
    From heaven's all-gracious King ";
The world in solemn stillness lay
    To hear the angels sing.

2 Still through the cloven skies they come,
    With peaceful wings unfurled,
And still their heavenly music floats
    O'er all the weary world :
Above its sad and lowly plains
    They bend on hovering wing,
And ever o'er its Babel sounds
    The blessèd angels sing.

3 Yet with the woes of sin and strife
   The world has suffered long,
Beneath the angel-strain have rolled
   Two thousand years of wrong;
And man, at war with man, hears not
   The love-song which they bring:
O hush the noise, ye men of strife,
   And hear the angels sing.

4 For lo ! the days are hastening on,
   By prophet bards foretold,
When with the ever-circling years
   Comes round the age of gold;
When peace shall over all the earth
   Its ancient splendours fling,
And all the world send back the song
   Which now the angels sing.

E. H. Sears, 1810–76.

102

LET all mortal flesh keep silence, and with awe
   and welcome stand;
Harbour nothing earthly-minded; for, with blessing in His hand,
Christ our Lord with us abideth, loving homage
   to demand.

2 King is He, yet born a servant, Lord of all in
     humble guise,
Truly man, yet God revealing, God as love, to
     mortal eyes;
God with man, He leads and feeds us, He the
     power and He the prize.

3 Rank on rank the hosts immortal sweep in joy
     before Thy face,
Shining in the light exalted, friends and loved ones
     in embrace,
As the dark dissolves before Thee, Light of all the
     human race.

4 At Thy feet the seraphs cluster, veil their faces in
    that light,
Spirits of just men made perfect, now in timeless
    splendour dight,
Saints and angels, all adore Thee, serve and praise
    Thee in the height.

Liturgy of St. James,
tr. Percy Dearmer, 1867–1936.

103

LOVE came down at Christmas,
    Love all lovely, Love divine;
Love was born at Christmas,
    Star and angels gave the sign.

2 Worship we the Godhead,
    Love incarnate, Love divine;
Worship we our Jesus:
    But wherewith for sacred sign ?

3 Love shall be our token,
    Love be yours and love be mine,
Love to God and all men,
    Love for plea and gift and sign.

Christina Rossetti, 1830–94.

104

LUKE ii. 15.

O COME, all ye faithful,
    Joyful and triumphant,
O come ye, O come ye to Bethlehem;
    Come and behold Him,
    Born the King of angels:
    O come, let us adore Him, Christ the Lord.

2   True God of true God,
      Light of light eternal,
  Lo, He abhors not the virgin's womb;
    Son of the Father,
    Begotten not created:

3   See how the shepherds,
      Summoned to His cradle,
  Leaving their flocks, draw nigh to gaze;
    We too will thither
    Bend our joyful footsteps:

4   Lo, star-led chieftains,
      Wise men, Christ adoring,
  Offer Him incense, gold, and myrrh;
    We to the Christ-child
    Bring our hearts' oblations:

5   Sing, choirs of angels,
      Sing in exultation,
  Sing, all ye citizens of heaven above,
    " Glory to God,
    Glory in the highest ":

6   Yea, Lord, we greet Thee,
      Born this happy morning,
  Jesus, to Thee be glory given;
    Word of the Father,
    Now in flesh appearing:
      O come, let us adore Him, Christ the Lord.

Latin, 17th cent.,
tr. Frederick Oakeley, 1802–80, altd.

105

O LITTLE town of Bethlehem,
    How still we see thee lie !
Above thy deep and dreamless sleep
    The silent stars go by:
Yet in thy dark streets shineth
    The everlasting Light;
The hopes and fears of all the years
    Are met in thee to-night.

2 For Christ is born of Mary;
    And, gathered all above,
While mortals sleep, the angels keep
    Their watch of wondering love.
O morning stars, together
    Proclaim the holy birth,
And praises sing to God the King,
    And peace to men on earth.

3 How silently, how silently,
    The wondrous gift is given !
So God imparts to human hearts
    The blessings of His heaven.
No ear may hear His coming;
    But in this world of sin,
Where meek souls will receive Him, still
    The dear Christ enters in.

4 O holy child of Bethlehem,
    Descend to us, we pray;
Cast out our sin, and enter in;
    Be born in us to-day.
We hear the Christmas angels
    The great glad tidings tell;
O come to us, abide with us,
    Our Lord Immanuel.

Phillips Brooks, 1835–93.

106

ONCE in royal David's city
    Stood a lowly cattle-shed,
Where a mother laid her baby
    In a manger for His bed.
Mary was that mother mild,
Jesus Christ her little child.

2 He came down to earth from heaven,
    Who is God and Lord of all;
And His shelter was a stable,
    And His cradle was a stall:
With the poor and mean and lowly
Lived on earth our Saviour holy.

3 And through all His wondrous childhood
    He would honour and obey,
Love, and watch the lowly mother
    In whose gentle arms He lay:
Christian children all must be
Mild, obedient, good as He.

4 For He is our childhood's pattern:
    Day by day like us He grew;
He was little, weak, and helpless,
    Tears and smiles like us He knew;
And He feeleth for our sadness,
And He shareth in our gladness.

5 And our eyes at last shall see Him,
    Through His own redeeming love;
For that child so dear and gentle
    Is our Lord in heaven above;
And He leads His children on
To the place where He is gone.

6 Not in that poor lowly stable,
    With the oxen standing by,
We shall see Him, but in heaven,
    Set at God's right hand on high,
When, like stars, His children crowned
    All in white shall wait around.

Cecil Frances Alexander, 1818–95.

107

LUKE ii. 1–20.

SEE, amid the winter's snow,
Born for us on earth below,
See, the tender Lamb appears,
Promised from eternal years !

Hail, thou ever-blessed morn !
Hail, Redemption's happy dawn !
Sing through all Jerusalem,
Christ is born in Bethlehem !

2 Lo, within a manger lies
He who built the starry skies,
He who, throned in height sublime,
Sits amid the cherubim !

3 Say, ye holy shepherds, say,
What your joyful news to-day;
Wherefore have ye left your sheep
On the lonely mountain steep ?

4 " As we watched at dead of night,
Lo, we saw a wondrous light;
Angels singing ' Peace on earth '
Told us of the Saviour's birth."

5 Sacred infant, all divine,
What a tender love was Thine,
Thus to come from highest bliss
Down to such a world as this !

6 Teach, O teach us, holy child,
By Thy face so meek and mild,
Teach us to resemble Thee
In Thy sweet humility.

Edward Caswall, 1814–78, altd.

108

STILL the night, holy the night !
Sleeps the world; hid from sight,
Mary and Joseph in stable bare
Watch o'er the child beloved and fair,
Sleeping in heavenly rest.

2 Still the night, holy the night !
Shepherds first saw the light,
Heard resounding clear and long,
Far and near, the angel-song,
" Christ the Redeemer is here."

3 Still the night, holy the night !
Son of God, O how bright
Love is smiling from Thy face !
Strikes for us now the hour of grace,
Saviour, since Thou art born.

Joseph Mohr, 1792–1848,
tr. Stopford Brooke, 1832–1916, altd.

109

LUKE ii. 10–11; MATT. ii. 1–11.

THE first Nowell the angel did say,
Was to certain poor shepherds in fields as they
lay;
In fields where they lay keeping their sheep,
On a cold winter's night that was so deep.

Nowell, Nowell, Nowell, Nowell,
Born is the King of Israel.

2 They lookèd up and saw a star,
Shining in the east, beyond them far,
And to the earth it gave great light,
And so it continued both day and night.

3 And by the light of that same star,
   Three wise men came from country far;
   To seek for a king was their intent,
   And to follow the star wherever it went.

4 This star drew nigh to the north-west,
   O'er Bethlehem it took its rest,
   And there it did both stop and stay,
   Right over the place where Jesus lay.

5 Then entered in those wise men three
   Full reverently on bended knee,
   And offered there, in His presence,
   Their gold, and myrrh, and frankincense.

6 Then let us all with one accord
   Sing praises to our heavenly Lord,
   That hath made heaven and earth of nought,
   And with His blood mankind hath bought.

Traditional

110

ISAIAH ix. 2–7.

THE race that long in darkness pined
   Have seen a glorious light;
The people dwell in day, who dwelt
   In death's surrounding night.

2 To hail Thy rise, thou better Sun,
   The gathering nations come,
Joyous, as when the reapers bear
   The harvest-treasures home.

3 To us a child of hope is born,
   To us a son is given;
Him shall the tribes of earth obey,
   Him all the hosts of heaven.

4 His name shall be the Prince of peace,
　　For evermore adored;
　The wonderful, the counsellor,
　　The great and mighty Lord.

5 His power increasing still shall spread;
　　His reign no end shall know:
　Justice shall guard His throne above,
　　And peace abound below.

John Morison, 1750–98.

111

LUKE ii. 7.

THOU didst leave Thy throne and Thy kingly
　　crown
　When Thou camest to earth for me;
But in Bethlehem's home there was found no room
　For Thy holy nativity:
O come to my heart, Lord Jesus,
There is room in my heart for Thee.

2 Heaven's arches rang when the angels sang,
　　Proclaiming Thy royal degree;
　But of lowly birth cam'st Thou, Lord, on earth
　　And in great humility;
O come to my heart, Lord Jesus,
There is room in my heart for Thee.

3 The foxes found rest, and the birds their nest
　　In the shade of the cedar tree;
　But Thy couch was the sod, O Thou Son of God,
　　In the deserts of Galilee;
O come to my heart, Lord Jesus,
There is room in my heart for Thee.

4 Thou camest, O Lord, with the living word
  That should set Thy people free;
But with mocking scorn, and with crown of thorn,
  They bore Thee to Calvary;
O come to my heart, Lord Jesus,
Thy cross is my only plea.

5 When heaven's arches ring, and her choirs shall
    sing,
  At Thy coming to victory,
Let Thy voice call me home, saying, " Yet there
    is room,
  There is room at my side for thee ";
And my heart shall rejoice, Lord Jesus,
When Thou comest and callest for me.

Emily Elliott, 1836–97.

112

UNTO us a boy is born !
    King of all creation,
Came He to a world forlorn,
  The Lord of every nation.

2 Cradled in a stall was He
    With sleepy cows and asses;
But the very beasts could see
    That He all men surpasses.

3 Herod then with fear was filled:
    " A prince," he said, " in Jewry ! "
All the little boys he killed
    At Bethlem in his fury.

4 Now may Mary's son, who came
    So long ago to love us,
Lead us all with hearts aflame
    Unto the joys above us.

15th cent. carol,
tr. Percy Dearmer, 1867–1936.

113

Luke ii. 1–20.

WHILE shepherds watched their flocks by
night,
All seated on the ground,
The angel of the Lord came down,
And glory shone around:

2 " Fear not ! " said he (for mighty dread
Had seized their troubled mind)
" Glad tidings of great joy I bring
To you and all mankind.

3 " To you in David's town, this day
Is born, of David's line,
A Saviour, who is Christ the Lord;
And this shall be the sign:

4 " The heavenly babe you there shall find
To human view displayed.
All meanly wrapped in swaddling bands,
And in a manger laid."

5 Thus spake the seraph; and forthwith
Appeared a shining throng
Of angels, praising God, who thus
Addressed their joyful song:

6 " All glory be to God on high,
And to the earth be peace;
Goodwill henceforth from heaven to men
Begin and never cease."

Nahum Tate, 1652–1715.

See also—Away in a manger, 734.

114

MATT. xxi. 9.

ALL glory, laud, and honour
To Thee, Redeemer, King,
To whom the lips of children
Made sweet hosannas ring.
Thou art the King of Israel,
Thou David's royal Son,
Who in the Lord's name comest,
The King and blessèd one.

2 The company of angels
Are praising Thee on high,
And mortal men and all things
Created make reply.
The people of the Hebrews
With palms before Thee went;
Our praise and prayer and anthems
Before Thee we present.

3 To Thee before Thy passion
They sang their hymns of praise;
To Thee now high exalted
Our melody we raise.
Thou didst accept their praises;
Accept the prayers we bring,
Who in all good delightest,
Thou good and gracious King.

Theodulph of Orleans, c. 750–821,
tr. J. M. Neale, 1818–66.

115

AT work beside His father's bench,
At play when work was done,
In quiet Galilee He lived,
The friend of everyone.

Comrade of boys and girls like us,
　　Playmate so straight and true,
In all our work, in all our play,
　　Make us true comrades too.

2 And as He grew to be a man
　　He wandered far and wide,
To be a friend to all in need
　　Throughout the countryside.
　　　Comrade of men, so strong and true,
　　　　Help us strong friends to be,
　　　Make us true comrades one and all,
　　　　To others and to Thee.

Alice M. Pullen, 1889–

116

BEHOLD a little child,
　　Laid in a manger bed;
The wintry blasts blow wild
　　Around His infant head.
But who is this, so lowly laid ?
'Tis He by whom the worlds were made.

2　Where Joseph plies his trade,
　　　Lo, Jesus labours too;
　　The hands that all things made
　　　An earthly craft pursue,
That weary men in Him may rest,
And faithful toil through Him be blest.

3　Among the teachers see
　　　The boy so full of grace;
　　Say, wherefore taketh He
　　　The scholar's lowly place ?
That Christian boys, with reverence meet,
May sit and learn at Jesus' feet.

4　Christ, once Thyself a boy!
　　Our boyhood guard and guide:
　Be Thou its light and joy,
　　And still with us abide,
That Thy dear love, so great and free,
May draw us evermore to Thee.

W. W. How, 1823–97.

117

MARK iv. 37–41.

FIERCE raged the tempest o'er the deep,
　Watch did Thine anxious servants keep:
But Thou wast wrapped in guileless sleep,
　　　Calm and still.

2 " Save, Lord, we perish," was their cry,
　" O save us in our agony ";
Thy word above the storm rose high,
　　　" Peace, be still."

3 The wild winds hushed; the angry deep
Sank, like a little child, to sleep;
The sullen billows ceased to leap
　　　At Thy will.

4 So, when our life is clouded o'er,
And storm-winds drift us from the shore,
Say, lest we sink to rise no more,
　　　" Peace, be still."

Godfrey Thring, 1823–1903.

118

MARK i. 12–13.

FORTY days and forty nights
　Thou wast fasting in the wild;
Forty days and forty nights
Tempted still, yet unbeguiled:

2 Sunbeams scorching all the day,
  Chilly dew-drops nightly shed,
  Prowling beasts about Thy way,
  Stones Thy pillow, earth Thy bed.

3 Let us Thy endurance share
  And from earthly greed abstain,
  With Thee watching unto prayer,
  With Thee strong to suffer pain.

4 Then if evil on us press,
  Flesh or spirit to assail,
  Victor in the wilderness,
  Help us not to swerve or fail !

5 So shall peace divine be ours;
  Holier gladness ours shall be;
  Come to us angelic powers,
  Such as ministered to Thee.

G. H. Smyttan, 1822–70, *altd.*

119

I LOVE to hear the story
  Which angel voices tell,
How once the King of glory
  Came down on earth to dwell:
I am both weak and sinful,
  But this I surely know,
The Lord came down to save me,
  Because He loved me so.

2 I'm glad my blessèd Saviour
  Was once a child like me,
To show how pure and holy
  All boys and girls might be;
And if I try to follow
  His footsteps here below,
He never will forsake me,
  Because He loves me so.

3 To sing His love and mercy
    My sweetest songs I'll raise,
And though I cannot see Him,
    I know He hears my praise;
For He has kindly promised
    That even I may go
To sing among His angels,
    Because He loves me so.

Emily H. Miller, 1833–1913, *altd.*

120

MATT. xix. 13–15.

I THINK, when I read that sweet story of old,
    When Jesus was here among men,
How He called little children, as lambs to His fold,
    I should like to have been with them then.
I wish that His hands had been placed on my head,
    That His arm had been thrown around me,
And that I might have seen His kind look when
        He said,
    " Let the little ones come unto Me."

2 Yet still to His footstool in prayer I may go,
    And ask for a share in His love;
And if I now earnestly seek Him below,
    I shall see Him and hear Him above:
In that beautiful place He has gone to prepare
    For all who are washed and forgiven,
And many dear children are gathering there,
" For of such is the kingdom of heaven."

3 But thousands and thousands who wander and
       fall,
    Never heard of that heavenly home;
I should like them to know there is room for them
    all,
    And that Jesus has bid them to come.

I long for the joy of that glorious time,
  The sweetest, and brightest, and best,
When the dear little children of every clime
  Shall crowd to His arms and be blest.

Jemima Luke, 1813–1906.

121

IMMORTAL Love, for ever full,
  For ever flowing free,
For ever shared, for ever whole,
  A never-ebbing sea!

2 Our outward lips confess the name
    All other names above;
  Love only knoweth whence it came,
    And comprehendeth love.

3 In joy of inward peace, or sense
    Of sorrow over sin,
  He is His own best evidence,
    His witness is within.

4 For warm, sweet, tender, even yet
    A present help is He;
  And faith has still its Olivet,
    And love its Galilee.

5 The healing of His seamless dress
    Is by our beds of pain;
  We touch Him in life's throng and press,
    And we are whole again.

6 Through Him the first fond prayers are said
    Our lips of childhood frame,
  The last low whispers of our dead
    Are burdened with His name.

7 O Lord and Master of us all,
  Whate'er our name or sign,
We own Thy sway, we hear Thy call,
  We test our lives by Thine.

J. G. Whittier, 1807-92.

122

MATT. xix. 13-15.

IT fell upon a summer day,
  When Jesus walked in Galilee,
The mothers from a village brought
  Their children to His knee.

2 He took them in His arms, and laid
  His hands on each remembered head;
" Suffer these little ones to come
  To me," He gently said.

3 " Forbid them not; unless ye bear
  The childlike heart your hearts within,
Unto my kingdom ye may come,
  But may not enter in."

4 Master, I fain would enter there;
  O let me follow Thee, and share
Thy meek and lowly heart, and be
  Freed from all worldly care.

5 O happy thus to live and move,
  And sweet this world, where I shall find
God's beauty everywhere, His love,
  His good in all mankind.

6 Then, Father, grant this childlike heart,
  That I may come to Christ, and feel
His hands on me in blessing laid,
  Love-giving, strong to heal.

Stopford Brooke, 1832-1916.

123

JESUS and Joseph day after day
Chiselled and planed and hammered away,
  In the shop at Nazareth.

2 Mary, the mother, ground at the mill;
Eight little hungry mouths she must fill,
  In the home at Nazareth.

3 Four little boys for kindling were sent;
Pulling the grasses and flowers they went
  O'er the hills at Nazareth.

4 Grasses and flowers so pretty and gay,
Packed in the oven they smoulder away,
  In the yard at Nazareth.

5 Soon it grows hot, her loaves she can bake:
Bread, and not stones, for dinner they take,
  In the home at Nazareth.

6 " Where is the coin that fell ? " With her broom
Mary goes sweeping over the room,
  In the home at Nazareth.

7 " Look, there it is ! " She ran in her joy
Telling the news to the man and the boy,
  In the shop at Nazareth.

8 Patching their clothes by the candle's light,
Mary would sew far into the night,
  In the home at Nazareth.

9 Games in the market—what did they play ?
Weddings and funerals, that was their way,
  Boys and girls at Nazareth.

10 So He grew up, our Saviour dear,
Sharing the life of all of us here,
  In His home at Nazareth.

11 All that He did, He did for our sake,
   Seeking a home for us all to make
    In heav'n like that at Nazareth.

T. R. Glover, 1869–1943.

124

M Y dear Redeemer and my Lord,
   I read my duty in Thy word;
But in Thy life the law appears
Drawn out in living characters.

2 Such was Thy truth, and such Thy zeal,
   Such deference to Thy Father's will,
   Such love, and meekness so divine,
   I would transcribe and make them mine.

3 Cold mountains and the midnight air
   Witnessed the fervour of Thy prayer;
   The desert Thy temptations knew,
   Thy conflict, and Thy victory too.

4 Be Thou my pattern; make me bear
   More of Thy gracious image here;
   Then God the Judge shall own my name
   Amongst the followers of the Lamb.

Isaac Watts, 1674–1748.

125

O LORD and Master of us all!
   Whate'er our name or sign,
We own Thy sway, we hear Thy call,
   We test our lives by Thine.

2 Thou judgest us: Thy purity
   Doth all our lusts condemn;
The love that draws us nearer Thee
   Is hot with wrath to them.

3 Our thoughts lie open to Thy sight;
   And, naked to Thy glance,
Our secret sins are in the light
   Of Thy pure countenance.

4 Yet, weak and blinded though we be,
   Thou dost our service own;
We bring our varying gifts to Thee,
   And Thou rejectest none.

5 To Thee our full humanity,
   Its joys and pains, belong;
The wrong of man to man on Thee
   Inflicts a deeper wrong.

6 We faintly hear, we dimly see,
   In differing phrase we pray;
But, dim or clear, we own in Thee
   The Life, the Truth, the Way!

J. G. Whittier, 1802–92.

126

O LOVE, how deep, how broad, how high!
  It fills the heart with ecstasy,
That God, the Son of God, should take
Our mortal form for mortals' sake.

2 For us He was baptized, and bore
His holy fast, and hungered sore;
For us temptations sharp He knew;
For us the tempter overthrew.

3 For us He prayed, for us He taught,
  For us His daily works He wrought,
  By words and signs and actions, thus
  Still seeking not Himself but us.

4 For us to wicked men betrayed,
  Scourged, mocked, in purple robe arrayed,
  He bore the shameful cross and death;
  For us at length gave up His breath.

5 For us He rose from death again,
  For us He went on high to reign,
  For us He sent his Spirit here,
  To guide, to strengthen, and to cheer.

Anon., Latin, 15th cent.,
tr. Benjamin Webb, 1820–85.

127

O SON of Man, our hero strong and tender,
  Whose servants are the brave in all the earth,
Our living sacrifice to Thee we render
  Who sharest all our sorrows, all our mirth.

2 O feet so strong to climb the path of duty,
  O lips divine that taught the words of truth,
Kind eyes that marked the lilies in their beauty,
  And heart that kindled at the zeal of youth:

3 Lover of children, boyhood's inspiration,
  Of all mankind the servant and the King,
O Lord of joy and hope and consolation,
  To Thee our fears and joys and hopes we bring.

4 Not in our failures only and our sadness
  We seek Thy presence, comforter and friend;
O rich man's guest, be with us in our gladness,
  O poor man's mate, our lowliest tasks attend.

Frank Fletcher, 1870–1954.

128

Matt. xxi. 8–9.

RIDE on ! ride on in majesty !
In lowly pomp ride on to die !
O Christ, Thy triumphs now begin
O'er captive death and conquered sin.

2 Ride on ! ride on in majesty !
Hark ! all the tribes Hosanna cry;
Thine humble beast pursues his road
With palms and scattered garments strowed.

3 Ride on ! ride on in majesty !
Thy last and fiercest strife is nigh;
The Father on His sapphire throne
Expects His own anointed Son.

4 Ride on ! ride on in majesty !
In lowly pomp ride on to die !
Bow Thy meek head to mortal pain,
Then take, O God, Thy power, and reign !

H. H. Milman, 1791–1868.

129

SON of the Lord most high
Who gave the worlds their birth,
He came to live and die
The Son of man on earth.
In Bethlehem's stable born was He,
And humbly bred in Galilee.

2 Born in so low estate,
Schooled in a workman's trade,
Not with the high and great
His home the Highest made:
But labouring by His brethren's side,
Life's common lot He glorified.

3 Then, when His hour was come,
    He heard His Father's call;
And leaving friends and home,
    He gave Himself for all;
Glad news to bring, the lost to find,
To heal the sick, the lame, the blind.

4 Toiling by night and day,
    Himself oft burdened sore,
Where hearts in bondage lay,
    Himself their burden bore:
Till, scorned by them He died to save,
Himself in death, as life, He gave.

5 O lowly majesty,
    Lofty in lowliness !
Blest Saviour, who am I
    To share Thy blessedness ?
Yet Thou hast called me, even me,
Servant divine, to follow Thee.

G. W. Briggs, 1875–1959.

130

TELL me the stories of Jesus
    I love to hear;
Things I would ask Him to tell me
    If He were here;
Scenes by the wayside,
    Tales of the sea,
Stories of Jesus,
    Tell them to me.

2 First let me hear how the children
    Stood round His knee;
And I shall fancy His blessing
    Resting on me;
Words full of kindness,
    Deeds full of grace,
All in the lovelight
    Of Jesus' face.

3 Tell me, in accents of wonder,
       How rolled the sea,
   Tossing the boat in a tempest
       On Galilee;
   And how the Master,
       Ready and kind,
   Chided the billows,
       And hushed the wind.

4 Into the city I'd follow
       The children's band,
   Waving a branch of the palm-tree
       High in my hand;
   One of His heralds,
       Yes, I would sing
   Loudest hosannas,
       Jesus is King !

5 Show me that scene in the garden,
       Of bitter pain;
   And of the cross where my Saviour
       For me was slain;
   And, through the sadness,
       Help me to see
   How Jesus suffered
       For love of me.

6 Gladly I'd hear of His rising
       Out of the grave,
   Living and strong and triumphant,
       Mighty to save:
   And how He sends us
       All men to bring
   Stories of Jesus,
       Jesus, their King.

W. H. Parker, 1845–1929, altd.
v. 6 by Hugh Martin, 1890–

131

'TIS good, Lord, to be here !
　Thy glory fills the night;
Thy face and garments, like the sun,
　Shine with unborrowed light.

2　'Tis good, Lord, to be here,
　　Thy beauty to behold,
Where Moses and Elijah stand,
　　Thy messengers of old.

3　Fulfiller of the past !
　　Promise of things to be !
We hail Thy body glorified,
　　And our redemption see.

4　Before we taste of death,
　　We see Thy Kingdom come;
We fain would hold the vision bright,
　　And make this hill our home.

5　'Tis good, Lord, to be here !
　　Yet we may not remain;
But since Thou bidst us leave the mount
　　Come with us to the plain.

J. Armitage Robinson, 1858–1933.

132

WE saw Thee not when Thou didst come
　To this poor world of sin and death;
Nor e'er beheld Thy cottage home,
　In that despisèd Nazareth;
But we believe Thy footsteps trod
Its streets and plains, Thou Son of God.

2 We saw Thee not upon the wave,
    When Thou the stormy sea didst bind,
Nor marked the health Thy blessing gave
    To lame and sick, to deaf and blind;
But we believe the fount of light
Could give the darkened eyeball sight.

3 We were not with the faithful few
    Who stood Thy bitter cross around,
Nor heard Thy prayer for them that slew,
    Nor felt the earthquake rock the ground;
We saw no spear-wound pierce Thy side;
But we believe that Thou hast died.

4 We stood not by the empty tomb,
    Where late Thy sacred body lay;
Nor sat within that upper room,
    Nor met Thee in the open way;
But we believe that angels said,
" Why seek the living with the dead ? "

5 We did not mark the chosen few,
    When Thou didst through the clouds ascend
First lift to heaven their wondering view,
    Then to the earth all prostrate bend;
Yet we believe that mortal eyes
Beheld Thee rising to the skies.

6 And now that Thou dost reign on high,
    And thence Thy waiting people bless,
No ray of glory from the sky
    Doth shine upon our wilderness;
But we believe that Thou art there,
And seek Thee, Lord, in praise and prayer.

J. H. Gurney, 1802–62, *altd*

133

WHEN the Lord of love was here,
Happy hearts to Him were dear,
Though His heart was sad;
Worn and lonely for our sake,
Yet He turned aside to make
All the weary glad.

2 Meek and lowly were His ways;
From His loving grew His praise,
From His giving, prayer;
All the outcasts thronged to hear,
All the sorrowful drew near
To enjoy His care.

3 When He walked the fields, He drew
From the flowers and birds and dew
Parables of God;
For within His heart of love
All the soul of man did move,
God had His abode.

4 Fill us with Thy deep desire
All the sinful to inspire
With the Father's life;
Free us from the cares that press
On the heart of worldliness,
From the fret and strife.

5 Lord, be ours this power to keep
In the very heart of grief,
And in trial, love;
In our meekness to be wise,
And through sorrow to arise
To our God above.

Stopford Brooke, 1832–1916, *altd.*

134

WHO is He in yonder stall,
At whose feet the shepherds fall ?
'Tis the Lord, O wondrous story !
'Tis the Lord, the King of glory !
At His feet we humbly fall;
Crown Him, crown Him Lord of all.

2 Who is He in deep distress,
Fasting in the wilderness ?
'Tis the Lord, O wondrous story !
'Tis the Lord, the King of glory !

3 Who is He to whom they bring
All the sick and sorrowing ?
'Tis the Lord, O wondrous story !
'Tis the Lord, the King of glory !

4 Who is He the gathering throng
Greet with loud triumphant song ?
'Tis the Lord, O wondrous story !
'Tis the Lord, the King of glory !

5 Who is He on yonder tree
Dies in shame and agony ?
'Tis the Lord, O wondrous story !
'Tis the Lord, the King of glory !

6 Who is He that from the grave
Comes to heal and help and save ?
'Tis the Lord, O wondrous story !
'Tis the Lord, the King of glory !

7 Who is He that from His throne
Rules through all the world alone ?
'Tis the Lord, O wondrous story !
'Tis the Lord, the King of glory !
At His feet we humbly fall;
Crown Him, crown Him Lord of all.

B. R. Hanby, 1833–67, *altd.*

135

WISE men seeking Jesus
    Travelled from afar,
Guided on their journey
    By a beauteous star.

2 But if we desire Him,
    He is close at hand;
For our native country
    Is our Holy Land.

3 Prayerful souls may find Him
    By our quiet lakes,
Meet Him on our hillsides
    When the morning breaks.

4 In our fertile cornfields
    While the sheaves are bound,
In our busy markets,
    Jesus may be found.

5 Fishermen talk with Him
    By the great north sea,
As the first disciples
    Did in Galilee.

6 Every peaceful village
    In our land might be
Made by Jesus' presence
    Like sweet Bethany.

7 He is more than near us,
    If we love Him well;
For He seeketh ever
    In our hearts to dwell.

J. T. East, 1860–1937.

See also—

A stranger once, 633.   Seek ye first the kingdom, 554.
Heal us, Immanuel, 335.   Son of God, 652.
How shall I follow, 473.   Thou didst leave Thy throne, 111.

136

GOOD FRIDAY.

A TIME to watch, a time to pray,
A day of wonders is to-day:
The saddest, yet the gladdest too,
That ever man or angel knew.

2 The saddest—for our Saviour bore
His death, that man might die no more:
The agony, the scourge, the fear,
The crown of thorns, the cross, the spear;

3 And yet the gladdest—for to-day
Our load of sin was borne away:
And hopes of joy that never dies
Hang on our Saviour's sacrifice.

4 O Saviour, blessèd be Thy name!
Thine is the glory, ours the shame;
By all the pain Thy love endured
Let all our many sins be cured.

J. M. Neale, 1818–66 *altd.*

137

AH, holy Jesus, how hast Thou offended,
That man to judge Thee hath in hate
pretended?
By foes derided, by Thine own rejected,
O most afflicted.

2 Who was the guilty? Who brought this upon
Thee?
Alas, my treason, Jesus, hath undone Thee;
'Twas I, Lord Jesus, I it was denied Thee:
I crucified Thee.

3 Lo, the good Shepherd for the sheep is offered;
The slave hath sinned, and the Son hath suffered;
For man's atonement, while he nothing heedeth,
  God intercedeth.

4 For me, kind Jesus, was Thy incarnation,
Thy mortal sorrow, and Thy life's oblation;
Thy death of anguish and Thy bitter passion,
  For my salvation.

5 Therefore, kind Jesus, since I cannot pay Thee,
I do adore Thee, and will ever pray Thee,
Think on Thy pity and Thy love unswerving,
  Not my deserving.

Johann Heermann, 1585–1647,
tr. Robert Bridges, 1844–1930.

138

LAM. i. 12.

ALL ye that pass by,
 To Jesus draw nigh;
To you is it nothing that Jesus should die?
  Your ransom and peace,
  Your surety He is,
Come, see if there ever was sorrow like His.

2   He dies to atone
  For sins not His own.
Your debt He hath paid, and your work He hath
  done:
  Ye all may receive
  The peace He did leave,
Who made intercession, " My Father, forgive."

3   For you and for me
  He prayed on the tree:
The prayer is accepted, the sinner is free.
  The sinner am I,
  Who on Jesus rely,
And come for the pardon God cannot deny.

4   His death is my plea;
My advocate see,
And hear the blood speak that hath answered
for me:
He purchased the grace
Which now I embrace;
O Father, Thou knowest He hath died in my
place !

Charles Wesley, 1707–88 altd.

139

ALONE thou goest forth, O Lord,
    In sacrifice to die ;
Is this Thy sorrow naught to us
Who pass unheeding by ?

2 Our sins, not Thine, Thou bearest, Lord;
    Make us Thy sorrow feel,
Till through our pity and our shame
Love answers love's appeal.

3 This is earth's darkest hour, but Thou
    Canst light and life restore;
Then let all praise be given to Thee
Who livest evermore.

4 Grant us to suffer with Thee, Lord,
    That, as we share this hour,
Thy Cross may bring us to Thy joy
And resurrection power.

Peter Abelard, 1079–1142,
tr. F. Bland Tucker, 1895–

140

AND didst Thou love the race that loved not
    Thee ?
And didst Thou take to heaven a human brow ?
Dost plead with man's voice by the marvellous
sea ?
Art Thou his kinsman now ?

2 O God, O kinsman loved, but not enough !
　O Man, with eyes majestic after death,
Whose feet have toiled along our pathways rough,
　Whose lips drawn human breath !

3 By that one likeness which is ours and Thine,
　By that one nature which doth hold us kin,
By that high heaven where, sinless, Thou dost
　shine,
　　To draw us sinners in,

4 By Thy last silence in the judgment-hall,
　By long foreknowledge of the deadly tree,
By darkness, by the wormwood and the gall,
　I pray Thee, visit me.

5 Come, lest this heart should, cold and cast away,
　Die ere the Guest adored she entertain—
Lest eyes that never saw Thine earthly day
　Should miss Thy heavenly reign.　Amen.

Jean Ingelow, 1820–97, *altd.*

141

IN the cross of Christ I glory,
　Towering o'er the wrecks of time:
All the light of sacred story
　Gathers round its head sublime.

2 When the woes of life o'ertake me,
　Hopes deceive, and fears annoy,
Never shall the cross forsake me;
　Lo ! it glows with peace and joy.

3 When the sun of bliss is beaming
　Light and love upon my way,
From the cross the radiance streaming
　Adds more lustre to the day.

4 Bane and blessing, pain and pleasure,
    By the cross are sanctified;
  Peace is there that knows no measure,
    Joys that through all time abide.

5 In the cross of Christ I glory,
    Towering o'er the wrecks of time:
  All the light of sacred story
    Gathers round its head sublime.

John Bowring, 1792–1872.

142

IT is a thing most wonderful,
    Almost too wonderful to be,
That God's own Son should come from heaven
    And die to save a child like me.

2 And yet I know that it is true:
    He came to this poor world below,
  And wept, and toiled, and mourned, and died,
    Only because He loved us so.

3 I cannot tell how He could love
    A child so weak and full of sin;
  His love must be most wonderful,
    If He could die my love to win.

4 It is most wonderful to know
    His love for me so free and sure;
  But 'tis more wonderful to see
    My love for Him so faint and poor.

5 And yet I want to love Thee, Lord;
    O light the flame within my heart,
  And I will love Thee more and more,
    Until I see Thee as Thou art.

W. W. How, 1823–97.

143

MY song is love unknown,
My Saviour's love to me:
Love to the loveless shown,
That they might lovely be.
O who am I,
That for my sake
My Lord should take
Frail flesh, and die?

2 He came from His blest throne
Salvation to bestow;
But men made strange, and none
The longed-for Christ would know:
But O my friend,
My friend indeed,
Who at my need
His life did spend.

3 Sometimes they strew His way,
And His sweet praises sing;
Resounding all the day
Hosannas to their King:
Then " Crucify ! "
Is all their breath,
And for His death
They thirst and cry.

4 They rise and needs will have
My dear Lord made away;
A murderer they save,
The prince of life they slay;
Yet cheerful He
To suffering goes,
That He His foes
From thence might free.

5 In life, no house, no home
My Lord on earth might have;
In death, no friendly tomb,
But what a stranger gave.

What may I say?
  Heaven was His home;
  But mine the tomb
Wherein He lay.

6 Here might I stay and sing,
    No story so divine;
  Never was love, dear King!
    Never was grief like Thine.
      This is my friend,
        In whose sweet praise
        I all my days
      Could gladly spend.

Samuel Crossman, 1624–83.

144

O come and mourn with me awhile;
O, See, Jesus calls us to His side:
O come, together let us mourn:
  Jesus, our Lord, is crucified.

2 Seven times He spake, seven words of love;
    And all three hours His silence cried
  For mercy on the souls of men:
    Jesus, our Lord, is crucified.

3 Come, let us stand beneath the cross;
    The fountain opened in His side
  Shall purge our deepest stains away:
    Jesus, our Lord, is crucified.

4 A broken heart, a fount of tears,
    Ask, and they will not be denied;
  A broken heart love's offering is:
    Jesus, our Lord is crucified.

5 O love of God !   O sin of man !
  In this dread act your strength is tried,
And victory remains with love,
  For He, our Lord, is crucified.

F. W. Faber, 1814–63, *altd.*

145

O SACRED head ! sore wounded,
   With grief and shame bowed down
Now scornfully surrounded
   With thorns, Thy only crown !
How pale art Thou with anguish,
   With sore abuse and scorn !
How does that visage languish,
   Which once was bright as morn !

2 What Thou, my Lord, hast suffered,
   Was all for sinners' gain :
Mine, mine was the transgression,
   But Thine the deadly pain :
Lo ! here I fall, my Saviour ;
   'Tis I deserve Thy place ;
Look on me with Thy favour,
   Vouchsafe to me Thy grace.

3 What language shall I borrow
   To thank Thee, dearest friend,
For this, Thy dying sorrow,
   Thy pity without end ?
O make me Thine for ever ;
   And should I fainting be,
Lord, let me never, never
   Outlive my love to Thee !

4 Be near me when I'm dying,
   O show Thy cross to me,
And, for my succour flying,
   Come, Lord, and set me free !

These eyes, new faith receiving,
From Jesus shall not move;
For he who dies believing,
Dies safely through Thy love.

Attributed to Bernard of Clairvaux, 1091–1153,
tr. Paul Gerhardt, 1607–76,
tr. J. W. Alexander, 1804–59.

146

SING, my tongue, the glorious battle,
  Sing the ending of the fray;
Now above the cross, the trophy,
  Sound the loud triumphant lay:
Tell how Christ, the world's redeemer,
  As a victim won the day.

2 Tell how, when at length the fullness
  Of the appointed time was come,
He, the Word, was born of woman,
  Left for us His Father's home,
Showed to men the perfect manhood,
  Shone as light amidst the gloom.

3 Thus, with thirty years accomplished,
  Went He forth from Nazareth,
Destined, dedicate, and willing,
  Wrought His work, and met His death;
Like a lamb He humbly yielded
  On the cross His dying breath.

4 Faithful cross, thou sign of triumph,
  Now for man the noblest tree,
None in foliage, none in blossom,
  None in fruit thy peer may be;
Symbol of the world's redemption,
  For the weight that hung on thee !

5 Unto God be praise and glory:
   To the Father and the Son,
To the eternal Spirit, honour
   Now and evermore be done;
Praise and glory in the highest,
   While the timeless ages run.

Venantius Fortunatus, c. 530–609,
tr. Percy Dearmer, 1867–1936.

147

THE royal banners forward go;
   The cross shines forth in mystic glow,
Where He in flesh, our flesh who made,
Our sentence bore, our ransom paid.

2 There, whilst He hung, His sacred side
   By soldier's spear was opened wide,
   To cleanse us in the precious flood
   Of water mingled with His blood.

3 Fulfilled is now what David told
   In true prophetic song of old,
   How God the nations' King should be;
   For God is reigning from the tree.

4 O tree of glory, tree most fair,
   Ordained those holy limbs to bear,
   How bright in purple robe it stood,
   The purple of a Saviour's blood!

5 Upon its arms, so widely flung,
   The weight of this world's ransom hung:
   The price of humankind to pay
   And spoil the spoiler of his prey.

6 To thee, eternal Three in One,
   Let homage meet by all be done;
As by the cross thou dost restore,
   So rule and guide us evermore.

*Venantius Fortunatus, c. 530–609,
tr. J. M. Neale, 1818–66, altd.*

148

THERE is a fountain filled with blood
   Drawn from Immanuel's veins;
And sinners, plunged beneath that flood,
   Lose all their guilty stains.

2 The dying thief rejoiced to see
   That fountain in his day;
And there may I, as vile as he,
   Wash all my sins away.

3 Dear dying Lamb! Thy precious blood
   Shall never lose its power,
Till all the ransomed Church of God
   Be saved, to sin no more.

4 E'er since, by faith, I saw the stream
   Thy flowing wounds supply,
Redeeming love has been my theme,
   And shall be till I die.

5 Then, in a nobler, sweeter song,
   I'll sing Thy power to save,
When this poor lisping, stammering tongue
   Lies silent in the grave.

William Cowper, 1731–1800, altd.

149

THERE is a green hill far away,
   Outside a city wall,
Where the dear Lord was crucified,
   Who died to save us all.

2 We may not know, we cannot tell,
   What pains He had to bear,
But we believe it was for us
   He hung and suffered there.

3 He died that we might be forgiven,
   He died to make us good,
That we might go at last to heaven,
   Saved by His precious blood.

4 There was no other good enough
   To pay the price of sin;
He only could unlock the gate
   Of heaven, and let us in.

5 O dearly, dearly has He loved !
   And we must love Him too,
And trust in His redeeming blood,
   And try His works to do.

Cecil Frances Alexander, 1818-95.

150

WE sing the praise of Him who died,
   Of Him who died upon the cross;
The sinner's hope let men deride,
   For this we count the world but loss.

2 Inscribed upon the cross we see,
   In shining letters, " God is love ";
He bears our sins upon the tree,
   He brings us mercy from above.

3 The cross ! it takes our guilt away,
   It holds the fainting spirit up;
It cheers with hope the gloomy day,
   And sweetens every bitter cup.

4 It makes the coward spirit brave,
    And nerves the feeble arm for fight;
It takes the terror from the grave,
    And gilds the bed of death with light.

5 The balm of life, the cure of woe,
    The measure and the pledge of love;
The sinner's refuge here below,
    The angels' theme in heaven above.

Thomas Kelly, 1769-1855.

151

WHEN I survey the wondrous cross
    Where the young Prince of glory died,
My richest gain I count but loss,
    And pour contempt on all my pride.

2 Forbid it, Lord, that I should boast,
    Save in the death of Christ my God:
All the vain things that charm me most,
    I sacrifice them to His blood.

3 See from His head, His hands, His feet,
    Sorrow and love flow mingled down:
Did e'er such love and sorrow meet,
    Or thorns compose so rich a crown?

4 Were the whole realm of nature mine,
    That were a present far too small,
Love so amazing, so divine,
    Demands my soul, my life, my all.

Isaac Watts, 1674-1748.

See also—
And can it be, 426.
Beneath the cross, 427.
Drawn to the cross, 430.
I will sing, 502.
Man of sorrows, 186.

O dearest Lord, 516.
O my Saviour, 453.
O Thou who hast redeemed, 455.
One who is all unfit, 456.

152

CHRIST is risen ! hallelujah !
　　Risen our victorious Head.
Sing His praises; hallelujah !
　　Christ is risen from the dead.
Gratefully our hearts adore Him,
　　As His light once more appears;
Bowing down in joy before Him,
　　Rising up from griefs and tears.

Christ is risen! hallelujah!
　　Risen our victorious Head ;
Sing His praises; hallelujah!
　　Christ is risen from the dead.

2 Christ is risen ! all the sadness
　　Of His earthly life is o'er;
Through the open gates of gladness
　　He returns to life once more.
Death and hell before Him bending,
　　He doth rise the victor now,
Angels on His steps attending,
　　Glory round His wounded brow.

3 Christ is risen ! henceforth never
　　Death nor hell shall us enthral;
We are Christ's, in Him for ever
　　We have triumphed over all;
All the doubting and dejection
　　Of our trembling hearts have ceased,
'Tis His day of resurrection;
　　Let us rise and keep the feast.

J.S.B. Monsell, 1811–75.

153

CHRIST JESUS lay in death's strong bands,
　　For our offences given,
But now at God's right hand He stands,
　　And brings us life from heaven:
　　Wherefore let us joyful be,
And sing to God right thankfully
　　Loud songs of hallelujah !
　　　　　　　　　　Hallelujah!

2 It was a strange and dreadful strife
　　When life and death contended;
The victory remained with life,
　　The reign of death was ended:
　　Stript of power, no more he reigns,
An empty form alone remains;
　　His sting is lost for ever.

3 So let us keep the festival
　　Whereto the Lord invites us;
Christ is Himself the joy of all,
　　The sun that warms and lights us;
　　By His grace He doth impart
Eternal sunshine to the heart;
　　The night of sin is ended.

4 Then let us feast this Easter day
　　On the true Bread of heaven.
The word of grace hath purged away
　　The old and wicked leaven;
　　Christ alone our soul will feed,
He is our meat and drink indeed,
　　Faith lives upon no other.
　　　　　　　Martin Luther, 1483–1546,
　　　　　　　tr. Richard Massie, 1800–87.

154

" CHRIST the Lord is risen to-day ! "
　　　　　　　　　　Hallelujah !
Sons of men and angels say:
Raise your joy and triumph high;
Sing, ye heavens, and earth reply.

2 Love's redeeming work is done,
   Fought the fight, the battle won:
   Vain the stone, the watch, the seal;
   Christ hath burst the gates of hell.

3 Lives again our glorious King:
   Where, O death, is now thy sting?
   Once He died our souls to save;
   Where thy victory, O grave?

4 Soar we now where Christ hath led,
   Following our exalted Head;
   Made like Him, like Him we rise;
   Ours the cross, the grave, the skies.

5 King of glory! Soul of bliss!
   Everlasting life is this:
   Thee to know, Thy power to prove,
   Thus to sing, and thus to love.

Charles Wesley, 1707–88, *altd.*

155

COME, ye faithful, raise the strain
   Of triumphant gladness;
God hath brought His people now
   Into joy from sadness;
'Tis the spring of souls to-day;
   Christ hath burst His prison,
And from three days' sleep in death
   As a sun hath risen.

2 Now the queen of seasons, bright
   With the day of splendour,
With the royal feast of feasts,
   Comes its joy to render;
Comes to gladden Christian men,
   Who with true affection
Welcome in unwearied strains
   Jesus' resurrection.

3 Hallelùjah now to Thee,
    Christ, our King immortal,
Who triumphant burst the bars
    Of the tomb's dark portal;
Hallelujah, with the Son
    God the Father praising;
Hallelujah yet again
    To the Spirit raising.

John of Damascus, fl. 750,
tr. J. M. Neale, 1818–66.

156

GOOD Christian men rejoice and sing!
Now is the triumph of our King!
To all the world glad news we bring:
        Hallelujah!

2 The Lord of life is risen for aye;
Bring flowers of song to strew His way;
Let all mankind rejoice and say:

3 Praise we in songs of victory
That love, that life which cannot die,
And sing with hearts uplifted high:

4 Thy name we bless, O risen Lord,
And sing to-day with one accord
The life laid down, the life restored:

C. A. Alington, 1872–1955.

157

JESUS CHRIST is risen to-day,
        Hallelujah!
Our triumphant holy day,
        Hallelujah!
Who did once upon the cross,
        Hallelujah!
Suffer to redeem our loss.
        Hallelujah!

2 Hymns of praise then let us sing,
                    Hallelujah !
   Unto Christ, our heavenly King,
                    Hallelujah !
   Who endured the cross and grave,
                    Hallelujah !
   Sinners to redeem and save.
                    Hallelujah !

3 For the pains which He endured,
                    Hallelujah !
   Our salvation have secured,
                    Hallelujah !
   Now above the sky He's King,
                    Hallelujah !
   Where the angels ever sing.
                    Hallelujah !
              Lyra Davidica, 1708, *altd.*

158

JESUS lives ! thy terrors now
Can, O death, no more appal us;
Jesus lives ! by this we know,
Thou, O grave, canst not enthral us.
                    Hallelujah!

2   Jesus lives ! henceforth is death
But the gate of life immortal;
   This shall calm our trembling breath,
When we pass its gloomy portal.

3   Jesus lives ! for us He died;
Then, alone to Jesus living,
   Pure in heart may we abide,
Glory to our Saviour giving.

4   Jesus lives ! our hearts know well,
    Nought from us His love shall sever;
        Life, nor death, nor powers of hell,
    Tear us from His keeping ever.

5   Jesus lives ! to Him the throne
    Over all the world is given:
        May we go where He is gone,
    Rest and reign with Him in heaven.

Christian F. Gellert, 1715–69,
tr. Frances Elizabeth Cox, 1812–97.

159

LIGHT'S glittering morn bedecks the sky;
    Heaven thunders forth its victor-cry;
                                    Hallelujah !
The glad earth shouts her triumph high,
And groaning hell makes wild reply.
                                    Hallelujah !

2 While He, the King, the mighty King,
    Despoiling death of all its sting,
    And trampling down the powers of night,
    Brings forth His ransomed saints to light.

3 His tomb of late the threefold guard
    Of watch and stone and seal had barred;
    But now, in pomp and triumph high,
    He comes from death to victory.

4 The pains of hell are loosed at last;
    The days of mourning now are past;
    An angel robed in light hath said,
    "The Lord is risen from the dead."

5 All praise be Thine, O risen Lord,
    From death to endless life restored:
    All praise to God the Father be,
    And Holy Ghost eternally.

4th or 5th cent. tr. J. M. Neale, 1818–66, altd.

160

LOW in the grave He lay,
  Jesus, my Saviour;
Waiting the coming day,
  Jesus, my Lord.
  Up from the grave He arose,
  With a mighty triumph o'er His foes;
He arose a victor from the dark domain,
And He lives for ever with His saints to reign:
  He arose! Hallelujah! Christ arose!

2 Vainly they watch His bed,
    Jesus, my Saviour;
  Vainly they seal the dead,
    Jesus, my Lord.

3 Death cannot keep his prey,
    Jesus, my Saviour;
  He tore the bars away,
    Jesus, my Lord.

Robert Lowry, 1826–99.

161

ON wings of living light,
  At earliest dawn of day
Came down the angel bright,
  And rolled the stone away.
    Your voices raise with one accord,
    To bless and praise your risen Lord.

2 The keepers, watching near,
    At that dread sight and sound
  Fell down with sudden fear
    Like dead men to the ground:

3 Then rose from death's dark gloom,
   Unseen by mortal eye,
Triumphant o'er the tomb,
   The Lord of earth and sky !

4 Ye children of the light,
   Arise with Him, arise !
See how the Daystar bright
   Is burning in the skies !

5 Leave in the grave beneath
   The old things passed away;
Buried with Him in death,
   O live with Him to-day !

6 We sing Thee, Lord divine,
   With all our hearts and powers,
For we are ever Thine,
   And Thou art ever ours.

W. W. How, 1823–97.

162

THE day of resurrection !
   Earth, tell it out abroad:
The passover of gladness,
   The passover of God !
From death to life eternal,
   From earth unto the sky,
Our Christ hath brought us over
   With hymns of victory.

2 Our hearts be pure from evil,
   That we may see aright
The Lord in rays eternal
   Of resurrection-light;
And, listening to His accents,
   May hear so calm and plain
His own " All hail," and, hearing,
   May raise the victor strain.

3 Now let the heavens be joyful,
  And earth her song begin,
Let the round world keep triumph,
  And all that is therein;
Let all things seen and unseen
  Their notes of gladness blend,
For Christ the Lord hath risen,
  Our joy that hath no end.

John of Damascus, 8th cent.,
tr. J. M. Neale, 1818–66.

163

THE strife is o'er, the battle done;
  The victory of life is won;
Now be the song of praise begun,
        Hallelujah!

2 The powers of death have done their worst,
  But Christ their legions hath dispersed;
  Let shouts of holy joy outburst,

3 The three sad days have quickly sped;
  He rises glorious from the dead;
  All glory to our risen Head !

4 He brake the age-bound chains of hell;
  The bars from heaven's high portals fell;
  Let hymns of praise His triumph tell.

5 Lord, by the stripes which wounded Thee,
  From death's dread sting Thy servants free,
  That we may live, and sing to Thee,
        Hallelujah !
  Latin. tr. Francis Pott, 1832–1909.

164

THINE be the glory, risen, conquering Son,
Endless is the victory Thou o'er death hast won;
Angels in bright raiment rolled the stone away,
Kept the folded grave-clothes, where Thy body lay.
Thine be the glory, risen, conquering Son,
Endless is the victory Thou o'er death hast won.

2 Lo ! Jesus meets us, risen from the tomb;
Lovingly He greets us, scatters fear and gloom;
Let the Church with gladness hymns of triumph
sing,
For her Lord now liveth; death hath lost its sting.

3 No more we doubt Thee, glorious Prince of life;
Life is nought without Thee: aid us in our strife;
Make us more than conquerors, through Thy
deathless love:
Bring us safe through Jordan to Thy home above.

Edmond Budry, 1854–1932,
tr. R. Birch Hoyle, 1875–1939.

165

" WELCOME, happy morning ! " age to age
shall say;
Hell to-day is vanquished; heaven is won to-day !
Lo ! the Dead is living, God for evermore !
Him, their true Creator, all His works adore.
" Welcome, happy morning ! " age to age shall
say.

2 Earth with joy confesses, clothing her for spring,
All good gifts return with her returning King:
Bloom in every meadow, leaves on every bough,
Speak His sorrows ended, hail His triumph now.
Hell to-day is vanquished; heaven is won
to-day !

3 Maker and Redeemer, life and health of all,
Thou from heaven beholding human nature's fall,
Of the Father's Godhead true and only Son,
Manhood to deliver, manhood didst put on.
   " Welcome, happy morning ! " age to age shall
    say.

4 Thou, of life the author, death didst undergo,
Tread the path of darkness, saving strength to
   show :
Come, then, true and faithful, now fulfil Thy
   word ;
'Tis Thine own third morning ! Rise, O buried
   Lord !
   Hell to-day is vanquished ; heaven is won
    to-day !

5 Loose the souls long prisoned, bound with Satan's
   chain ;
All that now is fallen raise to life again ;
Show Thy face in brightness, bid the nations see ;
Bring again our daylight : day returns with Thee !
   " Welcome, happy morning ! " age to age shall
    say.

Venantius Fortunatus, 530–609,
tr. John Ellerton, 1826–93.

See also—
Father of peace, 593.   The little flowers, 755.
It is the joyful Easter, 745.

(6) HIS ASCENSION AND EXALTATION

166

GOLDEN harps are sounding,
   Angel voices ring,
Pearly gates are opened—
   Opened for the King ;
Christ, the King of glory,
   Jesus, King of love,
Is gone up in triumph
   To His throne above.

All His work is ended,
Joyfully we sing;
Jesus hath ascended!
Glory to our King!

2 He who came to save us,
   He who bled and died,
Now is crowned with glory
   At His Father's side.
Never more to suffer,
   Never more to die,
Jesus, King of glory,
   Is gone up on high !

3 Praying for His children
   In that blessèd place,
Calling them to glory,
   Sending them His grace;
His bright home preparing,
   Faithful ones, for you;
Jesus ever liveth,
   Ever loveth too.

Frances Ridley Havergal, 1836–79.

167

HAIL the day that sees Him rise,
To His throne above the skies;
Christ, awhile to mortals given,
Enters now the highest heaven.
                    Hallelujah!

2 There for Him high triumph waits;
Lift your heads, eternal gates !
Christ hath vanquished death and sin;
Take the King of glory in !

3 See ! the heaven its Lord receives,
   Yet He loves the earth He leaves:
   Though returning to His throne,
   Still He calls mankind His own.

4 See ! He lifts His hands above;
   See ! He shows the prints of love;
   Hark ! His gracious lips bestow
   Blessings on His Church below.

5 Still for us He intercedes;
   His prevailing death He pleads;
   Near Himself prepares our place,
   He the first fruits of our race.

6 Lord, though parted from our sight
   Far above the starry height,
   Grant our hearts may thither rise,
   Seeking Thee beyond the skies.

Charles Wesley, 1707–88.
Thomas Cotterill, 1779–1823.

168

HALLELUJAH ! sing to Jesus,
   His the sceptre, His the throne;
Hallelujah ! His the triumph,
   His the victory alone;
Hark ! the songs of peaceful Sion
   Thunder like a mighty flood;
Jesus out of every nation
   Hath redeemed us by His blood.

2 Hallelujah ! not as orphans
   Are we left in sorrow now;
Hallelujah ! He is near us,
   Faith believes, nor questions how:
Though the cloud from sight received Him
   When the forty days were o'er,
Shall our hearts forget His promise,
   " I am with you evermore " ?

3 Hallelujah ! bread of angels,
    Thou on earth our food, our stay;
Hallelujah ! here the sinful
    Flee to Thee from day to day;
Intercessor, friend of sinners,
    Earth's Redeemer, plead for me,
Where the songs of all the sinless
    Sweep across the crystal sea.

4 Hallelujah ! Hallelujah !
    Glory be to God on high;
To the Father, and the Saviour,
    Who has gained the victory;
Glory to the Holy Spirit,
    Fount of love and sanctity.
Hallelujah ! Hallelujah !
    To the triune Majesty.

W. C. Dix, 1837–98, altd.

169

LOOK, ye saints, the sight is glorious,
    See the Man of sorrows now
From the fight returned victorious !
    Every knee to Him shall bow:
      Crown Him ! crown Him !
    Crowns become the victor's brow.

2 Crown the Saviour, angels, crown Him !
    Rich the trophies Jesus brings;
In the seat of power enthrone Him,
    While the vault of heaven rings:
      Crown Him ! crown Him !
    Crown the Saviour King of kings !

3 Sinners in derision crowned Him,
    Mocking thus the Saviour's claim:
Saints and angels throng around Him,
    Own His title, praise His Name:
      Crown Him ! crown Him !
    Spread abroad the victor's fame !

4 Hark ! those bursts of acclamation !
  Hark ! those loud triumphant chords !
  Jesus takes the highest station:
  O what joy the sight affords !
  Crown Him ! crown Him !
  King of kings, and Lord of lords !

Thomas Kelly, 1769–1855.

170

REJOICE and be glad ! the Redeemer hath
  come :
Go, look on His cradle, His cross, and His tomb.
  Sound His praises, tell the story of Him who was
    slain ;
  Sound His praises, tell with gladness He liveth
    again.

2 Rejoice and be glad ! it is sunshine at last;
  The clouds have departed, the shadows are past.

3 Rejoice and be glad ! for the blood hath been shed;
  Redemption is finished, the price hath been paid.

4 Rejoice and be glad ! now the pardon is free;
  The just for the unjust hath died on the tree.

5 Rejoice and be glad ! for the Lamb that was slain,
  O'er death is triumphant, and liveth again.

6 Rejoice and be glad ! for our King is on high;
  He pleadeth for us on His throne in the sky.

7 Rejoice and be glad ! for He cometh again;
  He cometh in glory, the Lamb that was slain.

Horatius Bonar, 1808–89.

171

SEE the conqueror mounts in triumph,
   See the King in royal state
Riding on the clouds His chariot
   To His heavenly palace gate;
Hark, the choirs of angel voices
   Joyful hallelujahs sing,
And the portals high are lifted
   To receive their heavenly King.

2 Who is this that comes in glory,
   With the trump of jubilee?
Lord of battles, God of armies,
   He has gained the victory;
He who on the cross did suffer,
   He who from the grave arose,
He has vanquished sin and Satan,
   He by death has spoiled His foes.

3 He has raised our human nature
   In the clouds to God's right hand;
There we sit in heavenly places,
   There with Him in glory stand;
Jesus reigns, adored by angels;
   Man with God is on the throne;
Mighty Lord, in Thine ascension
   We by faith behold our own.

4 Glory be to God the Father;
   Glory be to God the Son,
Dying, risen, ascending for us,
   Who the heavenly realm has won;
Glory to the Holy Spirit;
   To One God in Persons Three;
Glory both in earth and heaven,
   Glory, endless glory be.

Christopher Wordsworth, 1807–85, altd.

172

PSALM xxiv. 7–10.

YE gates, lift up your heads on high;
    Ye doors that last for aye,
Be lifted up, that so the King
    Of glory enter may !
But who of glory is the King ?
    The mighty Lord is this,
E'en that same Lord that great in might
    And strong in battle is.

2 Ye gates, lift up your heads; ye doors,
    Doors that do last for aye,
Be lifted up, that so the King
    Of glory enter may !
But who is He that is the King
    Of glory ? who is this ?
The Lord of hosts, and none but He,
    The King of glory is.

Coda.
    Hallelujah ! Hallelujah !
    Hallelujah ! Hallelujah ! Hallelujah !
    Amen, Amen, Amen.

Francis Rous, 1579–1659.
William Barton, 1597–1678.

See also—

Praise we God, 45.   The Lord ascendeth, 177.

(7) HIS HIGH PRIESTHOOD

173

HAIL, Thou once despisèd Jesus,
    Hail, Thou Galilean King !
Thou didst suffer to release us;
    Thou didst free salvation bring:

Hail, Thou agonising Saviour,
    Bearer of our sin and shame;
By Thy merits we find favour;
    Life is given through Thy name.

2 Paschal Lamb, by God appointed,
    All our sins on Thee were laid:
By almighty love anointed,
    Thou hast full atonement made:
All Thy people are forgiven
    Through the virtue of Thy blood;
Opened is the gate of heaven;
    Man is reconciled to God.

3 Jesus, hail! enthroned in glory,
    There for ever to abide;
All the heavenly host adore Thee,
    Seated at Thy Father's side:
There for sinners Thou art pleading;
    There Thou dost our place prepare;
Ever for us interceding,
    Till in glory we appear.

4 Worship, honour, power, and blessing,
    Thou art worthy to receive;
Loudest praises, without ceasing,
    Meet it is for us to give:
Help, ye bright angelic spirits!
    Bring your sweetest, noblest lays;
Help to sing our Saviour's merits,
    Help to chant Immanuel's praise!
                    John Bakewell, 1721–1819, altd.

174

I KNOW that my Redeemer lives!
What joy the blest assurance gives!
He lives, He lives, who once was dead;
He lives, my everlasting Head!

2 He lives, to bless me with His love;
He lives, to plead for me above;
He lives, my hungry soul to feed;
He lives, to help in time of need.

3 He lives, and grants me daily breath;
He lives, and I shall conquer death:
He lives, my mansion to prepare;
He lives, to lead me safely there.

4 He lives, all glory to His name;
He lives, my Saviour, still the same;
What joy the blest assurance gives!
I know that my Redeemer lives!

Samuel Medley, 1738–99.

175

JOIN all the glorious names
Of wisdom, love, and power,
That ever mortals knew,
That angels ever bore;
All are too mean to speak His worth,
Too mean to set my Saviour forth.

2   Great prophet of my God,
My tongue would bless Thy name:
By Thee the joyful news
Of our salvation came;
The joyful news of sins forgiven,
Of hell subdued, and peace with heaven.

3   Jesus, my great high priest,
Offered His blood and died;
My guilty conscience seeks
No sacrifice beside:
His powerful blood did once atone,
And now it pleads before the throne.

4 My Saviour and my Lord,
    My conqueror and my King !
  Thy sceptre and Thy sword,
    Thy reign of grace I sing:
  Thine is the power; behold I sit
  In willing bonds before Thy feet.

Isaac Watts, 1674–1748, altd.

176

JOHN xiv. 21.

SAVIOUR, who exalted high
  In Thy Father's majesty,
Yet vouchsafest Thyself to show
To Thy faithful flock below;
Saviour, though Thy glory bright
Must be hid from mortal sight,
Still Thy presence let me see:
Manifest Thyself to me.

2 Son of God, to Thee I cry;
  By the holy mystery
  Of Thy dwelling here on earth,
  By Thy pure and holy birth,
  By Thy griefs, to us unknown,
  By Thy spirit's parting groan;
  Lord, Thy presence let me see:
  Manifest Thyself to me.

3 Prince of life, to Thee I cry:
  By Thy glorious majesty,
  By Thy triumph o'er the grave,
  Strong to conquer, strong to save,
  By the thralls of death unchained,
  By the prize of life regained;
  Lord, Thy presence let me see:
  Manifest Thyself to me.

4 Lord of glory, God most high
  Man exalted to the sky;
  With Thy love my bosom fill;
  Prompt me to perform Thy will;
  So may'st Thou, my Saviour, come,
  Make this wayward heart Thy home;
  Then Thy presence I shall see
  Manifest, my Lord, in me.

Richard Mant, 1776–1848, altd.

177

THE Lord ascendeth up on high,
  The Lord hath triumphed gloriously,
    In power and might excelling;
The grave and hell are captive led,
Lo ! He returns, our glorious Head,
    To His eternal dwelling.

2 The heavens with joy receive their Lord,
  By saints, by angel hosts adored;
    O day of exultation !
  O earth, adore thy glorious King !
  His rising, His ascension sing
    With grateful adoration !

3 Our great high priest hath gone before,
  Now on His Church His grace to pour,
    And still His love He giveth:
  O may our hearts to Him ascend;
  May all within us upward tend
    To Him who ever liveth !

Arthur T. Russell, 1806–74, altd.

178

HEBREWS, iv. 14–16.

WHERE high the heavenly temple stands,
  The house of God not made with hands,
A great high priest our nature wears,
The Saviour of mankind appears.

2 He who for men their surety stood,
  And poured on earth His precious blood,
  Pursues in heaven His mighty plan,
  The Saviour and the friend of man.

3 Though now ascended up on high,
  He bends on earth a brother's eye;
  Partaker of the human name,
  He knows the frailty of our frame.

4 Our fellow-sufferer yet retains
  A fellow-feeling of our pains;
  And still remembers, in the skies,
  His tears, and agonies, and cries.

5 In every pang that rends the heart
  The Man of sorrows had a part;
  He sympathises with our grief,
  And to the sufferer sends relief.

6 With boldness, therefore, at the throne,
  Let us make all our sorrows known;
  And ask the aid of heavenly power
  To help us in the evil hour.

Michael Bruce, 1746–67, altd.

179

WITH joy we meditate the grace
  Of our high priest above;
His heart is made of tenderness,
  It overflows with love.

2 Touched with a sympathy within,
  He knows our feeble frame;
He knows what sore temptations mean,
  For He has felt the same.

3 He, in the days of feeble flesh,
   Poured out His cries and tears;
And now exalted feels afresh
   What every member bears.

4 He'll never quench the smoking flax,
   But raise it to a flame;
The bruisèd reed He never breaks,
   Nor scorns the meanest name.

5 Then let our humble faith address
   His mercy and His power;
We shall obtain delivering grace
   In the distressing hour.

Isaac Watts, 1674–1748, altd.

See also—

And didst Thou love, 140.   High Priest divine, 348.
Behold the eternal King, 308.   Jesus, Thy blood, 208.
Golden harps, 166.   Rejoice and be glad, 170.
Hail the day, 167.   Saviour, Thy dying love, 485.

(8) HIS KINGSHIP AND FINAL TRIUMPH

180

ALL hail the power of Jesus' name!
   Let angels prostrate fall;
Bring forth the royal diadem,
   And crown Him Lord of all.

2 Crown Him, ye martyrs of our God,
   Who from His altar call;
Extol the stem of Jesse's rod,
   And crown Him Lord of all.

3 Ye seed of Israel's chosen race,
   A remnant weak and small,
Hail Him who saves you by His grace,
   And crown Him Lord of all.

4 Ye Gentile sinners, ne'er forget
   The wormwood and the gall;
Go, spread your trophies at His feet,
   And crown Him Lord of all.

5 Let every kindred, every tribe,
   On this terrestrial ball,
To Him all majesty ascribe,
   And crown Him Lord of all.

6 O that with yonder sacred throng
   We at His feet may fall,
Join in the everlasting song,
   And crown Him Lord of all !

Edward Perronet, 1726–92.
John Rippon, 1751–1836.

181

AWAY with gloom, away with doubt !
   With all the morning stars we sing;
With all the sons of God we shout
      The praises of a King,
         Hallelujah !
   Of our returning King.

2 Away with death, and welcome life;
      In Him we died and live again;
And welcome peace, away with strife !
      For He returns to reign.
         Hallelujah !
   The Crucified shall reign.

3 Then welcome beauty, He is fair;
      And welcome youth, for He is young;
And welcome spring; and everywhere
      Let merry songs be sung !
         Hallelujah !
   For such a King be sung !

Edward Shillito, 1872–1948.

182

CROWN Him with many crowns,
The Lamb upon His throne;
Hark ! how the heavenly anthem drowns
All music but its own:
Awake, my soul, and sing
Of Him who died for thee,
And hail Him as thy chosen King
Through all eternity.

2 Crown Him the Son of God
Before the worlds began;
And ye who tread where He hath trod,
Crown Him the Son of Man,
Who every grief hath known
That wrings the human breast,
And takes and bears them for His own,
That all in Him may rest.

3 Crown Him the Lord of life,
Who triumphed o'er the grave,
And rose victorious in the strife,
For those He came to save:
His glories now we sing,
Who died and rose on high,
Who died eternal life to bring,
And lives that death may die.

4 Crown Him the Lord of heaven,
Enthroned in worlds above;
Crown Him the King to whom is given
The wondrous name of love:
All hail, Redeemer, hail !
For Thou hast died for me;
Thy praise shall never, never fail
Throughout eternity.

Matthew Bridges, 1800–94.
Godfrey Thring, 1823–1903.

183

I CANNOT tell why He, whom angels worship,
  Should set His love upon the sons of men,
Or why, as shepherd, He should seek the
    wanderers,
    To bring them back, they know not how or
      when.
But this I know, that He was born of Mary,
  When Bethlehem's manger was His only home,
And that He lived at Nazareth and laboured,
  And so the Saviour, Saviour of the world, is
    come.

2 I cannot tell how silently He suffered,
    As with His peace He graced this place of
      tears,
Or how His heart upon the cross was broken,
  The crown of pain to three and thirty years.
But this I know, He heals the broken-hearted,
  And stays our sin, and calms our lurking fear,
And lifts the burden from the heavy laden,
    For yet the Saviour, Saviour of the world, is
      here.

3 I cannot tell how He will win the nations,
    How He will claim His earthly heritage,
How satisfy the needs and aspirations
  Of east and west, of sinner and of sage.
But this I know, all flesh shall see His glory,
  And He shall reap the harvest He has sown,
And some glad day His sun shall shine in splendour
  When He the Saviour, Saviour of the world, is
    known.

4 I cannot tell how all the lands shall worship,
    When, at His bidding, every storm is stilled,
Or who can say how great the jubilation
    When all the hearts of men with love are filled.

But this I know, the skies will thrill with rapture,
  And myriad, myriad human voices sing,
And earth to heaven, and heaven to earth, will
    answer,
  At last the Saviour, Saviour of the world, is
    King!

W. Y. Fullerton, 1857–1932.

184

JESUS shall reign where'er the sun
  Does his successive journeys run;
His kingdom stretch from shore to shore,
Till moons shall wax and wane no more.

2 For him shall endless prayer be made,
  And praises throng to crown His head;
His name, like sweet perfume, shall rise
With every morning sacrifice.

3 People and realms of every tongue
  Dwell on His love with sweetest song;
And infant voices shall proclaim
Their early blessings on His name.

4 Blessings abound where'er He reigns;
  The prisoner leaps to lose his chains,
The weary find eternal rest,
And all the sons of want are blest.

5 Where He displays His healing power,
  Death and the curse are known no more;
In Him the tribes of Adam boast
More blessings than their father lost.

6 Let every creature rise and bring
  Peculiar honours to our King;
Angels descend with songs again,
And earth repeat the loud " Amen."

Isaac Watts, 1674–1748, *altd.*

185

LO ! He comes, with clouds descending,
  Once for favoured sinners slain :
Thousand thousand saints attending
  Swell the triumph of His train :
    Hallelujah !
  Jesus now shall ever reign.

2 Every eye shall now behold Him
  Robed in dreadful majesty ;
Those who set at nought and sold Him,
  Pierced, and nailed Him to the tree,
    Deeply wailing,
  Shall the true Messiah see.

3 Every island, sea, and mountain,
  Heaven and earth, shall flee away ;
All who hate Him must, confounded,
  Hear the trump proclaim the day :
    Come to judgement !
  Come to judgement ! come away !

4 Yea, amen ! let all adore Thee,
  High on Thine eternal throne :
Saviour, take the power and glory,
  Claim the Kingdom for Thine own :
    O come quickly,
  Hallelujah ! come, Lord, come !

Charles Wesley, 1707–88.
Based on John Cennick, 1718–55.

186

" MAN of sorrows," wondrous name
  For the Son of God, who came
Ruined sinners to reclaim !
  Hallelujah ! what a Saviour !

2 Bearing shame and scoffing rude,
  In my place condemned He stood;
  Sealed my pardon with His blood:
    Hallelujah ! what a Saviour !

3 Guilty, vile, and helpless, we :
  Spotless Lamb of God was He:
  "Full atonement ! "—can it be ?
    Hallelujah ! what a Saviour !

4 " Lifted up " was He to die,
  " It is finished ! " was His cry;
  Now in heaven exalted high:
    Hallelujah ! what a Saviour !

5 When He comes, our glorious King,
  All His ransomed home to bring,
  Then anew this song we'll sing:
    Hallelujah ! what a Saviour !

                    Philip Bliss, 1838–76.

187

O DAY of God, draw nigh
  In beauty and in power,
Come with Thy timeless judgment now
  To match our present hour.

2   Bring to our troubled minds,
    Uncertain and afraid,
  The quiet of a steadfast faith,
    Calm of a call obeyed.

3   Bring justice to our land,
    That all may dwell secure,
  And finely build for days to come
    Foundations that endure.

4   Bring to our world of strife
     Thy sovereign word of peace,
That war may haunt the earth no more
     And desolation cease.

5   O day of God, draw nigh,
     As at creation's birth,
Let there be light again, and set
     Thy judgments in the earth.

R. B. Y. Scott, 1899–

188

O JESUS, King most wonderful,
     Thou conqueror renowned,
Thou sweetness most ineffable,
     In whom all joys are found !

2 When once Thou visitest the heart,
     Then truth begins to shine;
Then earthly vanities depart,
     Then kindles love divine.

3 O Jesus, light of all below,
     Thou fount of life and fire,
Surpassing all the joys we know,
     All that we can desire,

4 May every heart confess Thy name,
     And ever Thee adore;
And, seeking Thee, itself inflame
     To seek Thee more and more.

5 Thee may our tongues for ever bless;
     Thee may we love alone;
And ever in our lives express
     The image of Thine own.

6 Stay with us, Lord, and with Thy light
    Illume the soul's abyss;
  Scatter the darkness of our night,
    And fill the world with bliss.   Amen.

Latin, 12th cent.,
tr. Edward Caswall, 1814–78.

189

OUR Lord is now rejected
And by the world disowned;
By the many still neglected
And by the few enthroned.
But soon He'll come in glory!
The hour is drawing nigh,
For the crowning day is coming
    By and by.

O the crowning day is coming,
  Is coming by and by,
When our Lord shall come in power
  And glory from on high.
O the glorious sight will gladden
  Each waiting, watchful eye,
In the crowning day that's coming
  By and by.

2 The heavens shall glow with splendour;
  But brighter far than they
  The saints shall shine in glory,
  As Christ shall them array.
  The beauty of the Saviour
  Shall dazzle every eye,
  In the crowning day that's coming
    By and by.

3 Our pain shall then be over:
  We'll sin and sigh no more;
  Behind us all of sorrow
  And naught but joy before—

A joy in our Redeemer
As we to Him are nigh,
In the crowning day that's coming
By and by.

4 Let all that look for, hasten
The coming joyful day
By earnest consecration
To walk the narrow way;
By gathering in the lost ones
For whom our Lord did die,
For the crowning day that's coming
By and by.

D. W. Whittle, 1840–1901.

190

REJOICE ! the Lord is King.
Your Lord and King adore;
Mortals, give thanks and sing,
And triumph evermore:
Lift up your heart, lift up your voice:
Rejoice; again I say, rejoice.

2 Jesus the Saviour reigns,
The God of truth and love;
When He had purged our stains,
He took His seat above:
Lift up your heart, lift up your voice:
Rejoice; again I say, rejoice.

3 His kingdom cannot fail:
He rules o'er earth and heaven;
The keys of death and hell
Are to our Jesus given:
Lift up your heart, lift up your voice:
Rejoice; again I say, rejoice.

4   He sits at God's right hand
       Till all His foes submit,
    And bow to His command
       And fall beneath His feet.
Lift up your heart, lift up your voice:
Rejoice; again I say, rejoice.

5   Rejoice in glorious hope:
       Jesus the Judge shall come,
    And take His servants up
       To their eternal home:
We soon shall hear the archangel's voice;
The trump of God shall sound, Rejoice !

Charles Wesley, 1707–88.

191

SING we the King who is coming to reign,
Glory to Jesus, the Lamb that was slain.
Life and salvation His empire shall bring,
Joy to the nations when Jesus is King.
    Come let us sing : Praise to our King,
    Jesus our King, Jesus our King :
    This is our song, who to Jesus belong :
    Glory to Jesus, to Jesus our King.

2 All men shall dwell in His marvellous light,
Races long severed His love shall unite,
Justice and truth from His sceptre shall spring,
Wrong shall be ended when Jesus is King.

3 All shall be well in His kingdom of peace,
Freedom shall flourish and wisdom increase,
Foe shall be friend when His triumph we sing,
Sword shall be sickle when Jesus is King.

4 Souls shall be saved from the burden of sin,
Doubt shall not darken His witness within,
Hell hath no terrors, and death hath no sting;
Love is victorious when Jesus is King.

5 Kingdom of Christ, for Thy coming we pray,
Hasten, O Father, the dawn of the day
When this new song Thy creation shall sing,
Satan is vanquished and Jesus is King.

C. Silvester Horne, 1865–1914.

192

THE head that once was crowned with thorns
Is crowned with glory now:
A royal diadem adorns
The mighty victor's brow.

2 The highest place that heaven affords
Is His by sovereign right:
The King of kings and Lord of lords,
He reigns in perfect light.

3 The joy of all who dwell above,
The joy of all below,
To whom He manifests His love,
And grants His name to know.

4 To them the cross, with all its shame,
With all its grace, is given:
Their name an everlasting name,
Their joy the joy of heaven.

5 They suffer with their Lord below;
They reign with Him above;
Their profit and their joy, to know
The mystery of His love.

6 The cross He bore is life and health,
Though shame and death to Him;
His people's hope, His people's wealth,
Their everlasting theme.

Thomas Kelly, 1769–1855.

193

THE light of the morning is breaking,
  The shadows are passing away;
The nations of earth are awaking,
  New peoples are learning to pray.
Let wrong, O Redeemer, be righted,
  In knowing and doing Thy will;
And gather, as brothers united,
  All men to Thy cross on the hill.

2 Thy love is the bond of creation,
  Thy love is the peace of mankind:
Make safe with Thy love every nation
  In concord of heart and of mind.
Thy pity alone can deliver
  The earth from her sorrows, dear Lord:
Her pride and her hardness forgive her,
  Thy blood for her ransom was poured.

3 Thy throne, O Redeemer, be founded
  In radiance of wisdom and love;
Thy name through the wide world be sounded
  Till earth be as heaven above.
Though hills and high mountains should tremble,
  Though all that is seen melt away,
Thy voice shall in triumph assemble
  Thy loved ones at dawning of day.

H. Elvet Lewis, 1860–1953.

194

THE Lord is King! lift up thy voice,
  O earth, and all ye heavens rejoice;
From world to world the joy shall ring:
" The Lord omnipotent is King ! "

2 The Lord is King ! who then shall dare
Resist His will, distrust His care,
Or murmur at His wise decrees,
Or doubt His royal promises ?

3 The Lord is King ! child of the dust,
The judge of all the earth is just;
Holy and true are all His ways:
Let every creature speak His praise.

4 He reigns ! ye saints, exalt your strains;
Your God is King, your Father reigns:
And He is at the Father's side,
The man of love, the crucified.

5 One Lord, one empire, all secures;
He reigns,—and life and death are yours,
Through earth and heaven one song shall ring,
" The Lord omnipotent is King ! "

Josiah Conder, 1789–1855.

195

THE Lord will come and not be slow,
His footsteps cannot err;
Before Him righteousness shall go,
His royal harbinger.

2 Truth from the earth, like to a flower,
Shall bud and blossom then;
And justice, from her heavenly bower,
Look down on mortal men.

3 Rise, God, judge Thou the earth in might,
This wicked earth redress;
For Thou art He who shall by right
The nations all possess.

4 The nations all whom Thou hast made
　　Shall come, and all shall frame
To bow them low before Thee, Lord,
　　And glorify Thy name.

5 For great Thou art, and wonders great
　　By Thy strong hand are done:
Thou in thine everlasting seat
　　Remainest God alone.

John Milton, 1608-74.

196

THESE things shall be: a loftier race
　　Than e'er the world hath known shall rise,
With flame of freedom in their souls
　　And light of knowledge in their eyes.

2 They shall be gentle, brave, and strong
　　To spill no drop of blood, but dare
All that may plant man's lordship firm
　　On earth, and fire, and sea, and air.

3 Nation with nation, land with land,
　　Inarmed shall live as comrades free;
In every heart and brain shall throb
　　The pulse of one fraternity.

4 Man shall love man with heart as pure
　　And fervent as the young-eyed throng
Who chant their heavenly psalms before
　　God's face with undiscordant song.

5 New arts shall bloom of loftier mould,
　　And mightier music thrill the skies,
And every life shall be a song,
　　When all the earth is paradise.

6 There shall be no more sin, nor shame,
   Though pain and passion may not die;
For man shall be at one with God
   In bonds of firm necessity.

J. Addington Symonds, 1840–93.

197

LUKE xii. 36–38.

YE servants of the Lord,
   Each in his office wait,
Observant of His heavenly word,
   And watchful at His gate.

2   Let all your lamps be bright,
   And trim the golden flame;
Gird up your loins as in His sight,
   For aweful is His name.

3   Watch, 'tis your Lord's command,
   And, while we speak, He's near;
Mark the first signal of His hand,
   And ready all appear.

4   O happy servant he,
   In such a posture found;
He shall his Lord with rapture see,
   And be with honour crowned.

5   Christ shall the banquet spread
   With His own royal hand;
And raise that faithful servant's head
   Amidst the angelic band.

Philip Doddridge, 1702–51.

See also—

Christ is the world's true light, 659.
Hail to the Lord's anointed, 80.
Let us sing, 377.
Look, ye saints, 169.
Mighty God, 210.
Our God ! Our God ! 262.
Praise we God, 45.

Rejoice and be glad, 170.
Ten thousand times, 407.
The Lord is King, 488.
Thou perfect Hero-Knight, 529.
To God be the glory, 32.
We have a King, 531.
Ye servants of God, 37.

(9) HIS PRAISE AND GLORY

198

ALL praise to Thee, for Thou, O King divine,
Didst yield the glory that of right was Thine,
That in our darkened hearts Thy grace might shine.

Hallelujah!

2 Thou cam'st to us in lowliness of thought;
By Thee the outcast and the poor were sought;
And by Thy death was God's salvation wrought.

3 Let this mind be in us which was in Thee,
Who wast a servant that we might be free,
Humbling Thyself to death on Calvary.

4 Wherefore, by God's eternal purpose, Thou
Art high exalted o'er all creatures now,
And given the name to which all knees shall bow.

5 Let every tongue confess with one accord,
In heaven and earth, that Jesus Christ is Lord,
And God the Father be by all adored. Amen.

F. B. Tucker, 1895–

199

PHIL. ii. 5–11.

AT the name of Jesus
    Every knee shall bow,
Every tongue confess Him
    King of glory now.
'Tis the Father's pleasure
    We should call Him Lord,
Who from the beginning
    Was the mighty Word:

2 Mighty and mysterious
    In the highest height,
God from everlasting,
    Very light of light.
In the Father's bosom,
    With the Spirit blest,
Love, in love eternal,
    Rest, in perfect rest.

3 Humbled for a season,
    To receive a name
From the lips of sinners
    Unto whom He came,
Faithfully He bore it
    Spotless to the last,
Brought it back victorious,
    When from death He passed;

4 Bore it up triumphant
    With its human light,
Through all ranks of creatures,
    To the central height;
To the throne of Godhead,
    To the Father's breast,
Filled it with the glory
    Of that perfect rest.

5 In your hearts enthrone Him;
   There let Him subdue
All that is not holy,
   All that is not true:
Crown Him as your captain
   In temptation's hour,
Let His will enfold you
   In its light and power.

6 Brothers, this Lord Jesus
   Shall return again,
With His Father's glory,
   With His angel-train;
For all wreaths of empire
   Meet upon His brow,
And our hearts confess Him
   King of glory now.

Caroline Noel, 1817–77.

200

REV. v. 12.

COME, let us join our cheerful songs
      With angels round the throne;
Ten thousand thousand are their tongues,
   But all their joys are one.

2 " Worthy the Lamb that died ! " they cry,
   " To be exalted thus ";
" Worthy the Lamb ! " our lips reply,
   " For He was slain for us."

3 Jesus is worthy to receive
   Honour and power divine;
And blessings more than we can give
   Be, Lord, for ever Thine.

4 Let all that dwell above the sky,
   And air, and earth, and seas,
Conspire to lift Thy glories high,
   And speak Thine endless praise.

5 The whole creation join in one,
   To bless the sacred name
Of Him that sits upon the throne,
   And to adore the Lamb.

Isaac Watts, 1674–1748.

201

COME, ye people, raise the anthem,
   Cleave the sky with shouts of praise;
Sing to Him, the mighty Saviour,
   Who from death the world doth raise;
Shepherd, prophet, Word incarnate,
   Him the heart of man obeys.

2 Lo, for us and our salvation
   Hatred, scorn, and death He bore;
He, to bring mankind to freedom,
   Died that we might die no more;
Then, arising, showed His glory,
   Prince of life for evermore.

3 Now in that celestial country
   His the honour, His the might,
'Mid the circling hallelujahs
   Welling from the sons of light;
He the king and He the captain,
   Victor in the hard-won fight.

4 Laud and honour to the Father,
   Laud and honour to the Son,
Laud and honour to the Spirit,
   In the Godhead ever one.
God of life and resurrection,
   Honour, praise, to Thee be done.

Job Hupton, 1762–1849 altd.

202

FAIREST Lord Jesus,
Lord of all creation,
Jesus, of God and Mary the Son;
Thee will I cherish,
Thee will I honour,
O Thou my soul's delight and crown.

2   Fair are the meadows,
Fairer still the woodlands,
Robed in the verdure and bloom of spring.
Jesus is fairer,
Jesus is purer,
He makes the saddest heart to sing.

3   Fair are the flowers,
Fairer still the sons of men
In all the freshness of youth arrayed;
Yet is their beauty
Fading and fleeting;
My Jesus, Thine will never fade.

4   Fair is the moonlight,
Fairer still the sunshine,
Fair is the shimmering, starry sky:
Jesus shines brighter,
Jesus shines clearer
Than all the heavenly host on high.

5   All fairest beauty
Heavenly and earthly,
Wondrously, Jesus, is found in Thee;
None can be nearer,
Fairer or dearer,
Than Thou, my Saviour, art to me.

6   When I lie dying,
Still on Thee relying,

Suffer me not from Thine arms to fall:
    At my last hour
    Be Thou my power,
For Thou, Lord Jesus, art my all.

Anon. German, 1677,*
***tr.** Lilian Stevenson, 1871–1960.*

203

HOW sweet the name of Jesus sounds
        In a believer's ear !
It soothes his sorrows, heals his wounds,
    And drives away his fear.

2 It makes the wounded spirit whole,
    And calms the troubled breast;
'Tis manna to the hungry soul,
    And to the weary rest.

3 Dear name ! the rock on which I build,
    My shield and hiding-place,
My never-failing treasury, filled
    With boundless stores of grace.

4 Jesus ! my shepherd, brother, friend,
    My prophet, priest, and king;
My lord, my life, my way, my end,
    Accept the praise I bring.

5 Weak is the effort of my heart,
    And cold my warmest thought;
But when I see Thee as Thou art,
    I'll praise Thee as I ought.

6 Till then I would Thy love proclaim
    With every fleeting breath;
And may the music of Thy name
    Refresh my soul in death !

John Newton, 1725–1807, *altd.*

204

I AM not skilled to understand
What God hath willed, what God hath planned;
I only know at His right hand
    Stands one who is my Saviour.

2 I take God at His word and deed;
  " Christ died to save me," this I read;
  And in my heart I find a need
    Of Him to be my Saviour.

3 And was there then no other way
  For God to take ?—I cannot say;
  I only bless Him, day by day,
    Who saved me through my Saviour.

4 That He should leave His place on high
  And come for sinful man to die,
  You count it strange ?—so do not I,
    Since I have known my Saviour.

5 And O that He fulfilled may see
  The travail of His soul in me,
  And with His work contented be,
    As I with my dear Saviour !

6 Yea, living, dying, let me bring
  My strength, my solace, from this spring,
  That He who lives to be my King
    Once died to be my Saviour.

Dora Greenwell, 1821–82.

205

JESUS, the very thought of Thee
  With sweetness fills my breast;
But sweeter far Thy face to see,
  And in Thy presence rest.

2 Nor voice can sing, nor heart can frame,
   Nor can the memory find
A sweeter sound than Thy blest name,
   O Saviour of mankind.

3 O hope of every contrite heart,
   O joy of all the meek,
To those who fall, how kind Thou art !
   How good to those who seek !

4 But what to those who find ? Ah, this
   Nor tongue nor pen can show;
The love of Jesus, what it is,
   None but His loved ones know.

5 Jesus, our only joy be Thou,
   As Thou our prize wilt be;
Jesus, be Thou our glory now,
   And through eternity.

Latin, 12th cent.,
tr. Edward Caswall, 1814–78.

206

JESUS, these eyes have never seen
   That radiant form of Thine;
The veil of sense hangs dark between
   Thy blessèd face and mine.

2 I see Thee not, I hear Thee not,
   Yet art Thou oft with me;
And earth hath ne'er so dear a spot
   As where I meet with Thee.

3 Yet, though I have not seen, and still
   Must rest in faith alone,
I love Thee, dearest Lord, and will,
   Unseen, but not unknown.

4 When death these mortal eyes shall seal,
   And still this throbbing heart,
The rending veil shall Thee reveal,
   All glorious as Thou art.

Ray Palmer, 1808–87.

207

JESUS, Thou joy of loving hearts,
   Thou fount of life, Thou light of men;
From the best bliss that earth imparts,
   We turn unfilled to Thee again.

2 Thy truth unchanged hath ever stood;
   Thou savest those that on Thee call;
To them that seek Thee Thou art good,
   To them that find Thee, all in all !

3 We taste Thee, O Thou living bread,
   And long to feast upon Thee still;
We drink of Thee, the fountain-head,
   And thirst our souls from Thee to fill.

4 Our restless spirits yearn for Thee,
   Where'er our changeful lot is cast;
Glad, when Thy gracious smile we see,
   Blest, when our faith can hold Thee fast.

5 O Jesus, ever with us stay,
   Make all our moments calm and bright,
Chase the dark night of sin away,
   Shed o'er the world Thy holy light.

Latin, 12th cent.,
tr. Ray Palmer, 1808–87.

208

JESUS, Thy blood and righteousness
My beauty are, my glorious dress;
Midst flaming worlds, in these arrayed,
With joy shall I lift up my head.

2 Bold shall I stand in Thy great day;
For who aught to my charge shall lay?
Fully through Thee absolved I am,
From sin and fear, from guilt and shame.

3 When from the dust of death I rise
To claim my mansion in the skies,
Even then this shall be all my plea—
Jesus hath lived and died for me!

4 Jesus, be endless praise to Thee,
Whose boundless mercy hath for me,
For me and all Thy hands have made,
An everlasting ransom paid.

5 Lord, I believe, were sinners more
Than sands upon the ocean shore,
Thou hast for all a ransom paid,
For all a full atonement made.

6 Lord, I believe Thy precious blood,
Which at the mercy-seat of God
For ever doth for sinners plead,
For me, even for my soul, was shed.

7 Thou God of power, Thou God of love,
Let the whole world Thy mercy prove!
Now let Thy word o'er all prevail;
Now take the spoils of death and hell.

8 O let the dead now hear Thy voice,
Now bid Thy banished ones rejoice,
Their beauty this, their glorious dress,
Jesus, the Lord our righteousness!

Nicolaus von Zinzendorf, 1700-60,
tr. John Wesley, 1703-91.

209

LIGHT of the world, for ever, ever shining,
There is no change in Thee;
True light of life, all joy and health enshrining,
Thou canst not fade nor flee.

2 Thou hast arisen, but Thou declinest never;
To-day shines as the past;
All that Thou wast Thou art, and shalt be ever,
Brightness from first to last.

3 Night visits not Thy sky, nor storm, nor sadness;
Day fills up all its blue,
Unfailing beauty and unfaltering gladness,
And love for ever new.

4 Light of the world, undimming and unsetting,
O shine each mist away !
Banish the fear, the falsehood, and the fretting;
Be our unchanging day.

Horatius Bonar, 1808–89.

210

MIGHTY God, while angels bless Thee,
May a mortal sing Thy name ?
Lord of men as well as angels,
Thou art every creature's theme !

2 Lord of every land and nation,
Ancient of eternal days,
Sounded through the wide creation
Be Thy just and worthy praise.

3 For the grandeur of Thy nature,
Grand beyond a seraph's thought,
For created works of power,
Works with skill and kindness wrought:

4 For Thy providence that governs
   Through Thine empire's wide domain,
Wings an angel, guides a sparrow;
   Blessèd be Thy gentle reign.

5 But Thy rich, Thy free redemption
   Dark through brightness all along!—
Thought is poor, and poor expression—
   Who dare sing that wondrous song?

6 Brightness of the Father's glory,
   Shall Thy praise unuttered lie?
Break, my tongue, such guilty silence;
   Sing the Lord who came to die;

7 From the highest throne in glory,
   To the cross of deepest woe;
All to ransom guilty captives;—
   Flow, my praise, for ever flow.

8 Go, return, immortal Saviour,
   Leave Thy footstool, take Thy throne;
Thence return, and reign for ever:
   Be the kingdom all Thine own.

Robert Robinson, 1735–90, *altd.*

211

MY God, I love Thee, not because
   I hope for heaven thereby;
Nor because they who love Thee not
   Are lost eternally.

2 Thou, O my Jesus, Thou didst me
   Upon the cross embrace;
For me didst bear the nails and spear,
   And manifold disgrace;

3 And griefs and torments numberless,
    And sweat of agony;
E'en death itself,—and all for one
    Who was Thine enemy.

4 Then why, O blessèd Jesus Christ,
    Should I not love Thee well?
Not for the sake of winning heaven,
    Or of escaping hell;

5 Not with the hope of gaining aught,
    Nor seeking a reward;
But as Thyself hast lovèd me,
    O ever-loving Lord.

6 E'en so I love Thee, and will love,
    And in Thy praise will sing,
Because Thou art my loving God,
    And my redeeming King.

Attributed to Francis Xavier, 1506–52,
tr. Edward Caswall, 1814–78.

212

O FOR a thousand tongues to sing
    My great Redeemer's praise,
The glories of my God and King,
    The triumphs of His grace!

2 Jesus! The name that charms our fears,
    That bids our sorrows cease;
'Tis music in the sinner's ears,
    'Tis life, and health, and peace.

3 He breaks the power of cancelled sin,
    He sets the prisoner free;
His blood can make the foulest clean;
    His blood availed for me.

4 He speaks, and, listening to His voice,
    New life the dead receive,
The mournful, broken hearts rejoice,
    The humble poor believe.

5 Hear Him, ye deaf; His praise, ye dumb,
    Your loosened tongues employ;
Ye blind, behold your Saviour come;
    And leap, ye lame, for joy.

6 My gracious Master and my God,
    Assist me to proclaim,
To spread through all the earth abroad,
    The honours of Thy name.

Charles Wesley, 1707–88, altd.

213

O THOU my soul, forget no more
  The friend who all thy misery bore:
Let every idol be forgot,
But, O my soul, forget Him not.

2 Jesus for thee a body takes,
Thy guilt assumes, thy fetters breaks,
Discharging all thy dreadful debt;
And canst thou e'er such love forget ?

3 Renounce thy works and ways with grief,
And fly to this most sure relief;
Nor Him forget who left His throne,
And for thy life gave up His own.

4 Infinite truth and mercy shine
In Him, and He Himself is thine:
And canst thou, then, with sin beset,
Such charms, such matchless charms, forget ?

5 Ah! no; till life itself depart,
   His name shall cheer and warm my heart;
   And, lisping this, from earth I'll rise,
   And join the chorus of the skies.

Krishna Pal, 1764–1822,
tr. Joshua Marshman, 1768–1837

214

ONE there is, above all others,
   Well deserves the name of friend.
His is love beyond a brother's,
   Costly, free, and knows no end:
They who once His kindness prove,
Find it everlasting love.

2 Which of all our friends, to save us,
   Could, or would, have shed his blood?
But the Saviour died to have us
   Reconciled in Him to God:
This was boundless love indeed!
Jesus is a friend in need.

3 When He lived on earth abasèd,
   Friend of sinners was His name;
Now, above all glory raisèd,
   He rejoices in the same:
Still He calls them brethren, friends,
And to all their wants attends.

4 Could we bear from one another
   What He daily bears from us?
Yet this glorious friend and brother
   Loves us though we treat Him thus;
Though for good we render ill,
He accounts us brethren still.

5 O for grace our hearts to soften !
　　Teach us, Lord, at length to love.
　We, alas ! forget too often
　　What a friend we have above :
　But, when home our souls are brought,
　We shall love Thee as we ought.

John Newton, 1725–1807, altd.

215

PRAISE Him ! praise Him ! Jesus, our bles-
　　sèd Redeemer !
　Sing, O earth—His wonderful love proclaim !
　Hail Him ! hail Him ! highest archangels in
　　glory;
　Strength and honour give to His holy name !
　Like a shepherd, Jesus will guard His children,
　　In His arms He carries them all day long.
Praise Him ! praise Him ! tell of His excellent
　　greatness ;
Praise Him ! praise Him ever in joyful song!

2 Praise Him ! praise Him ! Jesus, our blessèd
　　Redeemer !
　For our sins He suffered, and bled, and died ;
　He—our rock, our hope of eternal salvation,
　　Hail Him ! hail Him ! Jesus, the Crucified !
　Sound His praises—Jesus who bore our sorrows,
　　Love unbounded, wonderful, deep, and strong.

3 Praise Him ! praise Him ! Jesus, our blessèd
　　Redeemer !
　Heavenly portals, loud with hosannas ring !
　Jesus, Saviour, reigneth for ever and ever :
　　Crown Him ! crown Him ! prophet, and
　　priest, and king !
　Christ is coming, over the world victorious,
　　Power and glory unto the Lord belong.

Frances van Alstyne, 1820–1915.

216

PRAISE to the Holiest in the height,
And in the depth be praise;
In all His words most wonderful,
Most sure in all His ways.

2 O loving wisdom of our God !
When all was sin and shame,
A second Adam to the fight,
And to the rescue came.

3 O wisest love ! that flesh and blood,
Which did in Adam fail,
Should strive afresh against the foe,
Should strive and should prevail;

4 And that a higher gift than grace
Should flesh and blood refine,—
God's presence, and His very self,
And essence all divine.

5 O generous love ! that He, who smote
In Man for man the foe,
The double agony in Man
For man should undergo;

6 And in the garden secretly,
And on the cross on high,
Should teach His brethren, and inspire
To suffer and to die !

7 Praise to the Holiest in the height,
And in the depth be praise;
In all His words most wonderful,
Most sure in all His ways.

J. H. Newman, 1801–90.

217

REST of the weary, joy of the sad;
Hope of the dreary, light of the glad;
Home of the stranger, strength to the end;
Refuge from danger, Saviour and friend.

2 Pillow where, lying, love rests its head;
Peace of the dying, life of the dead;
Path of the lowly, prize at the end;
Breath of the holy, Saviour and friend.

3 When my feet stumble, I to Thee cry,
Crown of the humble, cross of the high;
When my steps wander, over me bend,
Truer and fonder, Saviour and friend.

4 Ever confessing Thee, I will raise
Unto Thee blessing, glory, and praise:
All my endeavour, world without end,
Thine to be ever, Saviour and friend.

J. S. B. Monsell, 1811–75

218

STAR whose light shines o'er me,
    Rock on which I stand,
Guide who goes before me
    To my fatherland,
Daily bread reviving,
    Spring that cheers my heart,
Goal to which I'm striving—
    All, O Lord, Thou art!

2 But for Thine upholding
    Where would strength be found?
By Thine arms enfolding
    Thou dost gird me round.

Faith—a shining beacon—
    Hope, lest I lose heart—
Love that cannot weaken—
    All, O Lord, Thou art !

3 So from morn till even
    By Thy help I come,
Till the bells of heaven
    Ring my welcome home.
Then new songs I'll sing Thee
    From a joyful heart.
Naught have I to bring Thee—
    All, O Lord, Thou art !

Cornelius Krummacher, 1824–84,
tr. Frank Houghton, 1894–

219

THOU art the everlasting Word,
    The Father's only Son;
God manifestly seen and heard,
    And heaven's belovèd One:
Worthy, O Lamb of God, art Thou
That every knee to Thee should bow.

2 In Thee most perfectly expressed
    The Father's glories shine;
Of the full deity possessed,
    Eternally divine:

3 True image of the infinite,
    Whose essence is concealed;
Brightness of uncreated light;
    The heart of God revealed:

4 But the high mysteries of Thy name
   An angel's grasp transcend;
The Father only—glorious claim!
   The Son can comprehend:

5 Throughout the universe of bliss,
   The centre Thou, and sun;
The eternal theme of praise is this,
   To heaven's belovèd One:
Worthy, O Lamb of God, art Thou
That every knee to Thee should bow.

               Josiah Conder, 1789–1855.

220

JOHN xiv. 6.

THOU art the way: by Thee alone
   From sin and death we flee:
And he who would the Father seek,
   Must seek Him, Lord, in Thee.

2 Thou art the truth: Thy word alone
   True wisdom can impart;
Thou only canst instruct the mind
   And purify the heart.

3 Thou art the life; the rending tomb
   Proclaims Thy conquering arm;
And those who put their trust in Thee
   Nor death nor hell shall harm.

4 Thou art the way, the truth, the life;—
   Grant us to know that way,
That truth to keep, that life to win,
   Which leads to endless day.

               G. W. Doane, 1799–1859.

221

TO the name of our salvation
    Laud and honour let us pay,
Which for many a generation
    Hid in God's foreknowledge lay,
But with holy exultation
    We may sing aloud to-day.

2 Jesus is the name we treasure,
    Name beyond what words can tell;
Name of gladness, name of pleasure,
    Ear and heart delighting well;
Name of sweetness passing measure,
    Saving us from sin and hell.

3 'Tis the name that whoso preacheth
    Speaks like music to the ear;
Who in prayer this name beseecheth
    Sweetest comfort findeth near;
Who its perfect wisdom reacheth
    Heavenly joy possesseth here.

4 Jesus is the name exalted
    Over every other name;
In this name, whene'er assaulted,
    We can put our foes to shame;
Strength to them who else had halted,
    Eyes to blind, and feet to lame.

5 Therefore we, in love adoring,
    This most blessèd name revere,
Holy Jesus, Thee imploring
    So to write it in us here,
That hereafter, heavenward soaring,
    We may sing with angels there.

c. 15th cent. tr. J. M. Neale, 1818-66, altd.

See also—
Let all mortal flesh, 102.   Of the Father's love begotten,
Lord God almighty, 62.   85.

V. GOD THE HOLY SPIRIT

222

AWAKE, O Lord, as in the time of old !
Come down, O Spirit, in Thy power and
    might !
For lack of Thee our hearts are strangely cold,
    Our minds but blindly grope toward the light.

2 Doubts are abroad: make Thou these doubts to
    cease !
    Fears are within: set Thou these fears at rest !
Strife is among us: melt that strife to peace !
    Change marches onward: may all change be
    blest !

3 It is not knowledge that we chiefly need,
    Though knowledge sanctified by Thee is dear:
It is the will and power to love indeed;
    It is the constant thought that God is near.

4 Make us to be what we profess to be;
    Let prayer be prayer, and praise be heartfelt
    praise;
From unreality, O set us free,
    And let our words be echoed by our ways.

5 Turn us, good Lord, and so shall we be turned:
    Let every passion grieving Thee be stilled:
Then shall our race be won, our guerdons earned,
    Our Master looked on, and our joy fulfilled.

Henry Twells, 1823–1900, altd.

223

AWAY with our fears,
Our troubles and tears,
The Spirit is come,
The witness of Jesus returned to His home.

2   The pledge of our Lord
To His heaven restored,
Is sent from the sky,
And tells us our Head is exalted on high.

3   Our glorified Head
His Spirit hath shed,
With His people to stay,
And never again will He take Him away.

4   Our heavenly guide
With us shall abide,
His comforts impart,
And set up His kingdom of love in the heart.

5   The heart that believes
His kingdom receives,
His power and His peace,
His life, and His joy's everlasting increase.

Charles Wesley, 1707–88.

224

COME down, O Love divine,
Seek Thou this soul of mine,
And visit it with Thine own ardour glowing;
O Comforter, draw near,
Within my heart appear,
And kindle it, Thy holy flame bestowing.

2   O let it freely burn,
      Till earthly passions turn
  To dust and ashes, in its heat consuming;
      And let Thy glorious light
      Shine ever on my sight,
  And clothe me round, the while my path illuming.

3   Let holy charity
      Mine outward vesture be,
  And lowliness become mine inner clothing;
      True lowliness of heart,
      Which takes the humbler part,
  And o'er its own shortcomings weeps with loathing.

4   And so the yearning strong,
      With which the soul will long,
  Shall far outpass the power of human telling;
      For none can guess its grace,
      Till he become the place
  Wherein the Holy Spirit makes His dwelling.

Bianco da Siena, died 1434,
tr. R. F. Littledale, 1833–90.

225

COME, Holy Ghost, in love,
  Shed on us from above
    Thine own bright ray:
Divinely good Thou art;
Thy sacred gifts impart,
To gladden each sad heart:
    O come to-day.

2 Come, tenderest friend and best,
  Our most delightful guest,
    With soothing power:
Rest, which the weary know,
Shade, 'mid the noontide glow,
Peace, when deep griefs o'erflow,
    Cheer us this hour.

3 Come, light serene and still,
  Our inmost bosoms fill;
        Dwell in each breast:
  We know no dawn but Thine;
  Send forth Thy beams divine,
  On our dark souls to shine,
        And make us blest.

4 Exalt our low desires,
  Extinguish passion's fires,
        Heal every wound;
  Our stubborn spirits bend,
  Our icy coldness end,
  Our devious steps attend,
        While heavenward bound.

5 Come, all the faithful bless:
  Let all who Christ confess
        His praise employ:
  Give virtue's rich reward,
  Victorious death accord,
  And, with our glorious Lord,
        Eternal joy.

Attributed to Stephen Langton, died **1228,**
tr. Ray Palmer, 1808–87.

226

COME, Holy Ghost, our souls inspire
And lighten with celestial fire.

2 Thou the anointing Spirit art,
  Who dost Thy sevenfold gifts impart.

3 Thy blessèd unction from above
  Is comfort, life, and fire of love.

4 Enable with perpetual light
  The dullness of our blinded sight.

5 Anoint and cheer our soilèd face
  With the abundance of Thy grace.

6 Keep far our foes; give peace at home,
  Where Thou art guide no ill can come.

7 Teach us to know the Father, Son,
  And Thee of both, to be but One;

8 That through the ages all along
  This may be our endless song:

9 Praise to Thy eternal merit,
  Father, Son and Holy Spirit.   Amen.

Latin, 9th cent.,
tr. John Cosin, 1594–1672.

227

COME, Thou everlasting Spirit,
  Bring to every thankful mind
All the Saviour's dying merit,
  All His sufferings for mankind:

2 True recorder of His passion,
  Now the living faith impart,
Now reveal His great salvation,
  Preach His gospel to our heart.

3 Come, Thou witness of His dying;
  Come, remembrancer divine,
Let us feel Thy power, applying
  Christ to every soul, and mine.

Charles Wesley, 1707–88.

228

COME, thou Holy Spirit, come,
And from Thy celestial home
Send Thy light and brilliancy:
Father of the poor, draw near;
Giver of all gifts, be here;
Come, the soul's true radiancy.

2 O most blessèd light divine,
Shine within these hearts of thine,
And our inmost being fill;
Where Thou art not, man hath naught,
Nothing good in deed or thought,
Nothing free from taint of ill.

3 Heal our wounds; our strength renew;
On our dryness pour thy dew;
Wash the stains of guilt away:
Bend the stubborn heart and will;
Melt the frozen, warm the chill;
Guide the steps that go astray.

4 On the faithful, who adore
And confess thee, evermore
In Thy sevenfold gifts descend:
Give them virtue's sure reward,
Give them Thy salvation, Lord,
Give them joys that never end.

Attributed to Stephen Langton, died 1228,
tr. Edward Caswall, 1814–78.
J. M. Neale, 1818–66, altd.

229

COME to our poor nature's night,
With Thy blessèd inward light,
Holy Ghost, the infinite,
Comforter divine.

2 We are sinful—cleanse us, Lord;
 Sick and faint—Thy strength afford;
 Lost, until by Thee restored,
   Comforter divine.

3 Like the dew Thy peace distil;
 Guide, subdue our wayward will,
 Things of Christ unfolding still,
   Comforter divine.

4 Gentle, aweful, holy guest,
 Make Thy temple in each breast;
 There Thy presence be confessed,
   Comforter divine.

5 With us, for us, intercede,
 And with voiceless groanings plead
 Our unutterable need,
   Comforter divine.

6 In us " Abba, Father," cry,
 Earnest of the bliss on high,
 Seal of immortality,
   Comforter divine.

George Rawson, 1807–89.

230

CREATOR Spirit, by whose aid
The world's foundations first were laid,
Come, visit every waiting mind,
Come, pour Thy joys on human kind;
From sin and sorrow set us free,
And make Thy temples worthy Thee.

2 O Source of uncreated light,
 The Father's promised Paraclete,
 Thrice holy fount, thrice holy fire,
 Our hearts with heavenly love inspire;
 Come, and Thy sacred unction bring,
 To sanctify us while we sing.

3 Plenteous of grace, descend from high,
Rich in Thy sevenfold energy:
Thou strength of His almighty hand
Whose power doth heaven and earth command,
Give us Thyself, that we may see
The Father and the Son by Thee.

4 Immortal honour, endless fame,
Attend the almighty Father's name;
The Saviour Son be glorified,
Who for lost man's redemption died;
And equal adoration be,
Eternal Paraclete, to Thee !

Latin Hymn, **9th cent.**,
tr. *John Dryden*, **1631–1700**, *altd.*

231

GRACIOUS Spirit, dwell with me:
I myself would gracious be;
And, with words that help and heal,
Would Thy life in mine reveal;
And, with actions bold and meek,
Would for Christ my Saviour speak.

2 Truthful Spirit, dwell with me:
I myself would truthful be;
And with wisdom kind and clear
Let Thy life in mine appear;
And with actions brotherly
Speak my Lord's sincerity.

3 Mighty Spirit, dwell with me:
I myself would mighty be,
Mighty so as to prevail,
Where unaided man must fail;
Ever by a mighty hope
Pressing on and bearing up.

4 Holy Spirit, dwell with me:
I myself would holy be;
Separate from sin, I would
Choose and cherish all things good;
And whatever I can be,
Give to Him who gave me Thee.

T. T. Lynch, 1818–71.

232

GRACIOUS Spirit, Holy Ghost,
Taught by Thee we covet most
Of Thy gifts at Pentecost,
Holy, heavenly love.

2 Faith that mountains could remove,
Tongues of earth or heaven above,
Knowledge, all things, empty prove
Without heavenly love.

3 Love is kind, and suffers long;
Love is meek, and thinks no wrong;
Love, than death itself more strong:
Therefore give us love.

4 Prophecy will fade away,
Melting in the light of day;
Love will ever with us stay:
Therefore give us love.

5 Faith and hope and love we see
Joining hand in hand agree;
But the greatest of the three,
And the best, is love.

Christopher Wordsworth, 1807–85, altd.

233

HOLY Spirit, hear us;
Help us while we sing;
Breathe into the music
Of the praise we bring.

2 Holy Spirit, prompt us
When we kneel to pray;
Nearer come, and teach us
What we ought to say.

3 Holy Spirit, shine Thou
On the Book we read;
Gild its holy pages
With the light we need.

4 Holy Spirit, give us
Each a lowly mind;
Make us more like Jesus,
Gentle, pure, and kind.

5 Holy Spirit, help us
Daily by Thy might,
What is wrong to conquer,
And to choose the right.

W. H. Parker, 1845–1929.

234

HOLY Spirit, truth divine,
Dawn upon this soul of mine;
Word of God, and inward light,
Wake my spirit, clear my sight.

2 Holy Spirit, love divine,
Glow within this heart of mine;
Kindle every high desire;
Perish self in Thy pure fire.

3 Holy Spirit, power divine,
  Fill and nerve this will of mine;
By Thee may I strongly live,
  Bravely bear, and nobly strive.

4 Holy Spirit, peace divine,
  Still this restless heart of mine;
Speak to calm this tossing sea,
  Stayed in Thy tranquillity.

5 Holy Spirit, joy divine,
  Gladden Thou this heart of mine;
In the desert ways I'll sing,
  Spring, O well, for ever spring !

                    Samuel Longfellow, 1819–92

235

ACTS ii. 1–4.

LORD God, the Holy Ghost,
  In this accepted hour,
As on the day of Pentecost,
  Descend in all Thy power.

2   We meet with one accord
      In our appointed place,
  And wait the promise of our Lord,
      The Spirit of all grace.

3   Like mighty rushing wind
      Upon the waves beneath,
  Move with one impulse every mind;
      One soul, one feeling breathe.

4   The young, the old inspire
      With wisdom from above;
  And give us hearts and tongues of fire,
      To pray and praise and love.

5   Spirit of light, explore
    And chase our gloom away,
With lustre shining more and more
    Unto the perfect day.

6   Spirit of truth, be Thou,
    In life and death, our guide:
O Spirit of adoption, now
    May we be sanctified.

James Montgomery, 1771–1854.

236

OUR blest Redeemer, ere He breathed
    His tender last farewell,
A guide, a comforter bequeathed
    With us to dwell.

2 He came in semblance of a dove,
    With sheltering wings outspread,
The holy balm of peace and love
    On earth to shed.

3 He came in tongues of living flame,
    To teach, convince, subdue;
All powerful as the wind He came,
    As viewless too.

4 He came sweet influence to impart,
    A gracious, willing guest,
Where He can find one humble heart
    Wherein to rest.

5 And His that gentle voice we hear,
    Soft as the breath of even,
That checks each fault, that calms each fear,
    And speaks of heaven.

6 And every virtue we possess,
   And every victory won,
  And every thought of holiness,
     Are His alone.

7 Spirit of purity and grace,
   Our weakness pitying see;
  O make our hearts Thy dwelling-place,
     And worthier Thee.

Henriette Auber, 1773–1862.

237

OUR Lord, His passion ended,
Hath gloriously ascended,
Yet though from Him divided,
He leaves us not unguided;
   All His benefits to crown
   He hath sent His Spirit down,
   Burning like a flame of fire,
   His disciples to inspire.

2 God's Spirit is directing;
  No more they sit expecting,
  But forth to all the nation
  They go with exultation;
    That which God in them hath wrought
    Fills their life and soul and thought;
    So their witness now can do
    Work as great in others too.

3 The centuries go gliding,
  But still we have abiding
  With us that Spirit holy,
  To make us brave and lowly—
    Lowly, for we feel our need,
    God alone is strong indeed;
    Brave, for with the Spirit's aid
    We can venture unafraid.

F. C. Burkitt, 1864–1935.

238

Acts ii. 1-4.

REJOICE ! the year upon its way
Has brought again that blessèd day,
When on the chosen of the Lord
The Holy Spirit was outpoured.

2 On each the fire, descending, stood
In quivering tongues' similitude—
Tongues, that their words might ready prove,
And fire, to make them flame with love.

3 And now, O holy God, this day
Regard us as we humbly pray,
And send us, from Thy heavenly seat,
The blessings of the Paraclete.

4 To God the Father, God the Son,
And God the Spirit, praise be done;
May Christ the Lord upon us pour
The Spirit's gift for evermore.   Amen.

Attributed to Hilary of Poictiers, died 238,
tr. R. Ellis Roberts, 1879–1940.

239

SPIRIT divine, attend our prayers,
And make our hearts Thy home;
Descend with all Thy gracious powers,
O come, great Spirit, come.

2 Come as the light; to us reveal
Our emptiness and woe;
And lead us in those paths of life
Where all the righteous go.

3 Come as the fire; and purge our hearts
   Like sacrificial flame;
Let our whole soul an offering be
   To our Redeemer's name.

4 Come as the dew; and sweetly bless
   This consecrated hour;
May barrenness rejoice to own
   Thy fertilising power.

5 Come as the dove; and spread Thy wings,
   The wings of peaceful love;
And let Thy Church on earth become
   Blest as the Church above.

6 Come as the wind; with rushing sound
   And pentecostal grace;
That all of woman born may see
   The glory of Thy face.

7 Spirit divine, attend our prayers,
   Make a lost world Thy home;
Descend with all Thy gracious powers,
   O come, great Spirit, come.   Amen.

Andrew Reed, 1787-1862.

240

SPIRIT of God, descend upon my heart;
   Wean it from earth; through all its pulses
      move;
Stoop to my weakness, mighty as Thou art,
   And make me love Thee as I ought to love

2 Hast Thou not bid me love Thee, God and King—
   All, all Thine own, soul, heart, and strength. and
      mind ?
I see Thy cross—there teach my heart to cling:
   O let me seek Thee, and O let me find !

3 Teach me to feel that Thou art always nigh;
    Teach me the struggles of the soul to bear,
To check the rising doubt, the rebel sigh;
    Teach me the patience of unanswered prayer.

4 Teach me to love Thee as Thine angels love,
    One holy passion filling all my frame—
The baptism of the heaven-descended Dove,
    My heart an altar, and Thy love the flame.

George Croly, 1780–1860.

See also—
Breathe on me, Breath of God,   O Spirit of the living God,
    592.   387.
Come, Holy Ghost, 244.   Our God ! our God ! 262.

VI. THE HOLY SCRIPTURES

241

BOOK of books, our people's strength,
　　Statesman's, teacher's, hero's treasure,
Bringing freedom, spreading truth,
　　Shedding light that none can measure !
Wisdom comes to those who know Thee.
All the best we have we owe Thee.

2 Thank we those who toiled in thought,
　　Many diverse scrolls completing,
Poets, prophets, scholars, saints,
　　Each his word from God repeating;
Till they came, who told the story
Of the Word, and showed His glory.

3 Praise we God, Who hath inspired
　　Those whose wisdom still directs us,
Praise Him for the Word made flesh,
　　For the Spirit Who protects us.
Light of knowledge, ever burning,
Shed on us Thy deathless learning !

Percy Dearmer, 1867–1936.

242

BOOK of grace and book of glory,
　　Gift of God to age and youth,
Wondrous is thy sacred story,
　　Bright, bright with truth !

2 Book of love ! in accents tender
    Speaking unto such as we;
May it lead us, Lord, to render
    All, all to Thee.

3 Book of hope ! the spirit sighing,
    Sweetest comfort finds in thee,
As it hears the Saviour crying,
    " Come, come to Me."

4 Book of peace ! when nights of sorrow
    Fall upon us drearily,
Thou wilt bring a shining morrow,
    Full, full of thee.

5 Book of life ! when we, reposing,
    Bid farewell to friends we love,
Give us, for the life then closing,
    Life, life above.

Thomas MacKellar, 1812–99.

243

BREAK Thou the bread of life,
    Dear Lord, to me,
As Thou didst break the loaves
    Beside the sea:
Beyond the sacred page
    I seek Thee, Lord;
My spirit pants for Thee,
    O living Word !

2 O send Thy Spirit, Lord,
    Now unto me,
That He may touch my eyes,
    And make me see:

Show me the truth concealed
  Within Thy word,
That in Thy book revealed
  I see Thee Lord.

3 Bless Thou the truth, dear Lord,
    To me—to me—
  As Thou didst bless the bread
    In Galilee:
  Then shall all bondage cease,
    All fetters fall,
  And I shall find my peace,
    My all in all !

Mary Lathbury, 1841–1913,
v. 2 by Alex. Groves, 1843–1909.

244

COME, Holy Ghost, our hearts inspire;
    Let us Thine influence prove,
Source of the old prophetic fire,
    Fountain of light and love.

2 Come, Holy Ghost, for moved by Thee
    Thy prophets wrote and spoke;
  Unlock the truth, Thyself the key,
    Unseal the sacred book.

3 Expand Thy wings, celestial Dove,
    Brood o'er our nature's night;
  On our disordered spirits move,
    And let there now be light.

4 God, through Himself, we then shall know,
    If Thou within us shine;
  And sound, with all Thy saints below,
    The depths of love divine.

Charles Wesley, 1707–88.

245

FATHER of mercies, in Thy word
 What endless glory shines !
For ever be Thy name adored
 For these celestial lines.

2 Here may the blind and hungry come,
 And light and food receive;
Here shall the lowliest guest have room,
 And taste and see and live.

3 Here springs of consolation rise
 To cheer the fainting mind;
And thirsty souls receive supplies,
 And sweet refreshment find.

4 Here the Redeemer's welcome voice
 Spreads heavenly peace around;
And life and everlasting joys
 Attend the blissful sound.

5 O may these heavenly pages be
 My ever dear delight;
And still new beauties may I see,
 And still increasing light.

6 Divine instructor, gracious Lord,
 Be Thou for ever near;
Teach me to love Thy sacred word,
 And view my Saviour there.

Anne Steele, 1716–78.

246

FOR man's unceasing quest for God,
 For God's unceasing quest for man,
For records of His love and power
 Surrounding life since life began,
We thank Thee, Lord most high.

2 For those great laws of long ago
    Whose wisdom still the nations own,
For early records wise men wrought,
    Engraved on parchment, skin or stone,
We thank Thee, Lord most high.

3 For those old songs of tuneful verse,
    The music of the shepherd-king,
For songs the boy of Nazareth sang,
    And still succeeding ages sing,
We thank Thee, Lord most high.

4 For those most precious books of all,
    That show us Jesus Christ, our Lord,
Seen through the eyes of faithful friends,
    Who gave their lives to spread His word,
We thank Thee, Lord most high.

5 That still Thou speakest with mankind,
    O friend of man, O Word of God,
That every place is holy ground,
    Where'er on earth man's foot hath trod,
We thank Thee, Lord most high.

Alice M. Pullen, 1889–

247

GOD hath spoken by His prophets,
    Spoken His unchanging word;
Each from age to age proclaiming
God the one, the righteous Lord !
Mid the world's despair and turmoil
One firm anchor holding fast,
God is on His throne eternal,
He alone the first and last.

2 God hath spoken by Christ Jesus,
    Christ, the everlasting Son,
Brightness of the Father's glory,
    With the Father ever one;

Spoken by the Word Incarnate,
God of God ere time began,
Light of light, to earth descending,
Man, revealing God to man.

3 God yet speaketh by His Spirit
Speaking to the hearts of men,
In the age-long word declaring
God's own message, now as then.
Through the rise and fall of nations
One sure faith yet standeth fast:
God abides, His word unchanging,
God alone the first and last.

G. W. Briggs, 1875–1959.

248

LAMP of our feet, whereby we trace
    Our path when wont to stray;
Stream from the fount of heavenly grace,
    Brook by the traveller's way:

2 Bread of our souls, whereon we feed;
    True manna from on high;
Our guide and chart, wherein we read
    Of realms beyond the sky:

3 Pillar of fire through watches dark,
    And radiant cloud by day;
When waves would whelm our tossing bark,
    Our anchor and our stay:

4 Word of the ever-living God,
    Will of His glorious Son;
Without thee how could earth be trod,
    Or heaven itself be won?

5 Lord, grant that we aright may learn
   The wisdom it imparts;
And to its heavenly teaching turn
   With simple, childlike hearts.

Bernard Barton, 1784–1849.

249

LONG ago, when heathen darkness
   Kept our fathers chained in fears,
Dauntless strangers came and sought them,
   Showed a cross and woke their tears.

2 Strange the tongue in which they worshipped,
   Strange the altars where they prayed,
But our fathers learned of Jesus,
   And no longer were afraid.

3 Then the scholars, wise and holy,
   Brought to us the book so dear,
Clothed it in our nation's language,
   Made it homely, made it clear.

4 So the story of redemption
   All the heart of Britain stirred,
Touched the tongue of Britain, set it
   Singing of the glorious Word.

5 And its wonder, strength and virtue
   Passed into our nation's soul,
Touched with grace our common living,
   Turned us toward the heavenly goal.

6 Thanks to God for all the heroes
   Through whose toil we have this prize;
Give us grace Thy word to cherish,
   By its truth our souls make wise.

R. W. Callin. 1886–1951.

250

LORD, Thy word abideth,
And our footsteps guideth;
Who its truth believeth
Light and joy receiveth.

2 When our foes are near us,
Then Thy word doth cheer us,
Word of consolation,
Message of salvation.

3 When the storms are o'er us,
And dark clouds before us,
Then its light directeth,
And our way protecteth.

4 Who can tell the pleasure,
Who recount the treasure,
By Thy word imparted
To the simple hearted ?

5 Word of mercy, giving
Succour to the living;
Word of life, supplying
Comfort to the dying !

6 O that we, discerning
Its most holy learning,
Lord, may love and fear Thee,
Evermore be near Thee !

H. W. Baker, 1821–77.

251

O WORD of God incarnate,
O wisdom from on high,
O truth unchanged, unchanging,
O light of our dark sky,

We praise Thee for the radiance,
    That from the hallowed page,
A lantern to our footsteps,
    Shines on from age to age.

2 The Church from her dear Master
    Received the gift divine,
And still that light she lifteth
    O'er all the earth to shine:
It is the golden casket
    Where gems of truth are stored;
It is the heaven-drawn picture
    Of Christ, the living Word.

3 It floateth like a banner
    Before God's host unfurled;
It shineth like a beacon
    Above the darkling world:
It is the chart and compass
    That o'er life's surging sea,
Mid mists and rocks and quicksands
    Still guide, O Christ, to Thee.

4 O make Thy Church, dear Saviour,
    A lamp of burnished gold,
To bear before the nations
    Thy true light as of old;
O teach Thy wandering pilgrims
    By this their path to trace,
Till, clouds and darkness ended,
    They see Thee face to face!

W. W. How, 1823–97.

252

THE Spirit breathes upon the word,
    And brings the truth to sight;
Precepts and promises afford
    A sanctifying light.

2 A glory gilds the sacred page,
　　Majestic, like the sun:
It gives a light to every age;
　　It gives, but borrows none.

3 The hand that gave it still supplies
　　The gracious light and heat:
His truths upon the nations rise;
　　They rise, but never set.

4 Let everlasting thanks be Thine
　　For such a bright display
As makes a world of darkness shine
　　With beams of heavenly day.

5 My soul rejoices to pursue
　　The steps of Him I love,
Till glory breaks upon my view
　　In brighter worlds above.

William Cowper, 1731–1800

253

THY Word is like a garden, Lord,
　　With flowers bright and fair;
And every one who seeks may pluck
　　A lovely garland there.

2 Thy Word is like a deep, deep mine;
　　And jewels rich and rare
Are hidden in its mighty depths,
　　For every searcher there.

3 Thy Word is like a starry host;
　　A thousand rays of light
Are seen, to guide the traveller
　　And make his pathway bright.

4 Thy Word is like a glorious choir,
   And loud its anthems ring;
 Though many parts and tongues unite,
   It is one song they sing.

5 Thy Word is like an armoury,
   Where soldiers may repair,
 And find for life's long battle-day
   All needful weapons there.

6 O may I love Thy precious Word,
   May I explore the mine,
 May I its fragrant flowers glean,
   May light upon me shine !

7 O may I find my armour there,
   Thy Word my trusty sword;
 I'll learn to fight with every foe
   The battle of the Lord.

Edwin Hodder, 1837–1904

254

WE limit not the truth of God
   To our poor reach of mind,
By notions of our day and sect,
   Crude, partial, and confined;
No, let a new and better hope
   Within our hearts be stirred:
The Lord hath yet more light and truth
To break forth from His word.

2 Who dares to bind to his dull sense
   The oracles of heaven,
 For all the nations, tongues, and climes,
   And all the ages given ?
 That universe, how much unknown !
   That ocean unexplored !

3 Darkling our great forefathers went
    The first steps of the way;
'Twas but the dawning, yet to grow
    Into the perfect day.
And grow it shall; our glorious Sun
    More fervid rays afford:

4 O Father, Son and Spirit, send
    Us increase from above;
Enlarge, expand all Christian souls
    To comprehend Thy love:
And make us to go on to know,
    With nobler powers conferred,
The Lord hath yet more light and truth
To break forth from his word.

George Rawson, 1807–89.

See also—
God has given us a book, 740.   Jesus loves me, 749.

255

CITY of God, how broad and far
 Outspread thy walls sublime !
The true thy chartered freemen are,
 Of every age and clime.

2 One holy Church, one army strong,
 One steadfast high intent,
One working band, one harvest song,
 One King omnipotent.

3 How purely hath thy speech come down
 From man's primeval youth !
How grandly hath thine empire grown
 Of freedom, love, and truth !

4 How gleam thy watch-fires through the night
 With never-fainting ray !
How rise thy towers, serene and bright,
 To meet the dawning day !

5 In vain the surge's angry shock,
 In vain the drifting sands:
Unharmed upon the eternal Rock
 The eternal City stands.

Samuel Johnson, 1822–82.

256

FOR the might of Thine arm we bless Thee, our
God, our fathers' God;
Thou hast kept Thy pilgrim people by the strength
of Thy staff and rod;
Thou hast called us to the journey which faithless
feet ne'er trod;
*For the might of Thine arm we bless Thee, our God,
our fathers' God.*

2 For the love of Christ constraining that bound
their hearts as one;
For the faith in truth and freedom in which their
work was done:
For the peace of God's evangel wherewith their
feet were shod;

3 We are watchers of a beacon whose light must
never die;
We are guardians of an altar that shows Thee
ever nigh;
We are children of Thy freemen who sleep beneath
the sod;

4 May the shadow of Thy presence around our
camp be spread;
Baptize us with the courage with which Thou
blessed our dead;
O keep us in the pathway their saintly feet have
trod;

C. Silvester Horne, 1865–1914.

257

PSALM lxxxvii. 3.

GLORIOUS things of thee are spoken,
Zion, city of our God!
He whose word cannot be broken,
Formed thee for His own abode:

On the rock of ages founded,
  What can shake thy sure repose ?
With salvation's wall surrounded,
  Thou may'st smile at all thy foes.

2 See, the streams of living waters,
    Springing from eternal love,
  Well supply thy sons and daughters,
    And all fear of want remove :
  Who can faint, while such a river
    Ever flows their thirst to assuage—
  Grace which like the Lord the giver
    Never fails from age to age ?

3 Blest inhabitants of Zion,
    Washed in the Redeemer's blood,
  Jesus, whom their souls rely on,
    Makes them kings and priests to God.
  'Tis His love His people raises
    Over self to reign as kings ;
  And as priests, His solemn praises
    Each for a thank-offering brings.

4 Saviour, since of Zion's city
    I, through grace, a member am,
  Let the world deride or pity,
    I will glory in Thy name :
  Fading is the worldling's pleasure,
    All his boasted pomp and show ;
  Solid joys and lasting treasure
    None but Zion's children know.

John Newton, 1725–1807, altd.

258

HEAD of the Church and Lord of all,
  Hear from Thy throne our suppliant call :
We come the promised grace to seek,
Of which aforetime Thou didst speak.

2 " Lo, I am with you "—that sweet word,
   Lord Jesus, meekly be it heard,
   And stamped with all-inspiring power
   On our weak souls this favoured hour.

3 Without Thy presence, King of saints,
   Our purpose fails, our spirit faints;
   Thou must our wavering faith renew
   Ere we can yield Thee service true.

4 Thy consecrating might we ask,
   Or vain the toil, unblest the task,
   And impotent of fruit will be
   Love's holiest effort wrought for Thee.

5 " Lo, I am with you "; even so,
   Thy joy our strength, we fearless go;
   And praise shall crown the suppliant's call,
   Head of the Church, and Lord of all !

                              Joseph Tritton, 1819–87.

259

I SING a song of the saints of God,
   Patient and brave and true,
Who toiled and fought and lived and died
   For the Lord they loved and knew.
And one was a doctor, and one was a queen,
And one was a shepherdess on the green:
They were all of them saints of God; and I mean,
   God helping, to be one too.

2 They loved their Lord so good and dear,
   And His love made them strong;
And they followed the right, for Jesus' sake,
   The whole of their good lives long.

And one was a soldier, and one was a priest,
And one was slain by a fierce wild beast:
And there's not any reason, no, not the least,
    Why I shouldn't be one too.

They lived not only in ages past,
    There are hundreds of thousands still;
The world is bright with the joyous saints
    Who love to do Jesus' will.
You can meet them in school, or in lanes, or at sea,
In church, or in trains, or in shops, or at tea,
For the saints of God began just like me,
    And I mean to be one too.

Lesbia Scott, 1898–

260

JESUS, with Thy Church abide;
  Be her Saviour, Lord, and guide,
While on earth her faith is tried:
    We beseech Thee, hear us.

2 Keep her life and doctrine pure;
  Grant her patience to endure,
Trusting in Thy promise sure:
    We beseech Thee, hear us.

3 May her voice be ever clear,
  Warning of a judgment near,
Telling of a Saviour dear:
    We beseech Thee, hear us.

4 All her fettered powers release;
  Bid all strife and envy cease;
Grant the heavenly gift of peace:
    We beseech Thee, hear us.

5 May she one in doctrine be,
 One in truth and charity,
 Winning all to faith in Thee:
 　We beseech Thee, hear us.

6 May she guide the poor and blind,
 Seek the lost until she find,
 And the broken-hearted bind:
 　We beseech Thee, hear us.

7 May her lamp of truth be bright;
 Bid her bear aloft its light
 Through the realms of heathen night:
 　We beseech Thee, hear us.

8 May she holy triumphs win,
 Overthrow the hosts of sin,
 Gather all the nations in:
 　We beseech Thee, hear us. Amen.

T. B. Pollock, 1836–96.

261

LORD of our life, and God of our salvation,
Star of our night, and hope of every nation,
Hear and receive Thy Church's supplication,
 　Lord God almighty.

2 See round Thine ark the hungry billows curling;
 See how Thy foes their banners are unfurling;
 Lord, while their darts envenomed they are hurling,
 　Thou canst preserve us.

3 Lord, Thou canst help when earthly armour faileth,
 Lord, Thou canst save when deadly sin assaileth,
 Lord, o'er Thy Church nor death nor hell pre-
 　vaileth;
 　Grant us Thy peace, Lord.

4 Grant us Thy help till foes are backward driven,
Grant them Thy truth, that they may be forgiven,
Grant peace on earth, and, after we have striven,
    Peace in Thy heaven.

M. von Löwenstern, 1594–1648,
tr. Philip Pusey, 1799–1855.

262

OUR God ! our God ! Thou shinest here,
    Thine own this latter day:
To us Thy radiant steps appear;
    We watch Thy glorious way.

2 Not only olden ages felt
    The presence of the Lord;
Not only with the fathers dwelt
    Thy Spirit and Thy word.

3 Doth not the Spirit still descend
    And bring the heavenly fire ?
Doth not He still Thy Church extend,
    And waiting souls inspire ?

4 Come, Holy Ghost, in us arise;
    Be this Thy mighty hour,
And make Thy willing people wise
    To know Thy day of power.

5 Bear us aloft, more glad, more strong
    On Thy celestial wing;
And grant us grace to look and long
    For our returning King.

6 He draweth near, He standeth by,
    He fills our eyes, our ears;
Come, King of grace, Thy people cry,
    And bring the glorious years.

T. H. Gill, 1819–1906.

263

THE Church's one foundation
  Is Jesus Christ her Lord:
She is His new creation
  By water and the word:
From heaven He came and sought her
  To be His holy bride;
With His own blood He bought her,
  And for her life He died.

2 Elect from every nation,
    Yet one o'er all the earth,
  Her charter of salvation
    One Lord, one faith, one birth,
  One holy name she blesses,
    Partakes one holy food,
  And to one hope she presses,
    With every grace endued.

3 Mid toil and tribulation,
    And tumult of her war,
  She waits the consummation
    Of peace for evermore;
  Till with the vision glorious
    Her longing eyes are blest,
  And the great Church victorious
    Shall be the Church at rest.

4 Yet she on earth hath union
    With God the Three in One,
  And mystic sweet communion
    With those whose rest is won.
  O happy ones and holy!
    Lord, give us grace that we,
  Like them, the meek and lowly,
    On high may dwell with Thee.

                              S. J. Stone, 1839-1900.

264

THY hand, O God, has guided
  Thy flock from age to age;
The wondrous tale is written,
  Full clear, on every page;
Our fathers owned Thy goodness,
  And we their deeds record;
And both of this bear witness,
  One Church, one Faith, one Lord.

2 Thy heralds brought glad tidings
    To greatest, as to least;
  They bade men rise, and hasten
    To share the great King's feast;
  And this was all their teaching,
    In every deed and word,
  To all alike proclaiming
    One Church, one Faith, one Lord.

3 Through many a day of darkness,
    Through many a scene of strife,
  The faithful few fought bravely
    To guard the nation's life.
  Their gospel of redemption,
    Sin pardoned, man restored,
  Was all in this enfolded,
    One Church, one Faith, one Lord.

4 Thy mercy will not fail us,
    Nor leave Thy work undone;
  With Thy right hand to help us,
    The victory shall be won;
  And then, by men and angels,
    Thy name shall be adored,
  And this shall be their anthem,
    One Church, one Faith, one Lord.

E. H. Plumptre, 1821–91.

265

WE come unto our fathers' God:
Their rock is our salvation:
The eternal arms, their dear abode,
  We make our habitation:
We bring Thee, Lord, the praise they brought;
We seek Thee as Thy saints have sought
  In every generation.

2 The fire divine, their steps that led,
  Still goeth bright before us;
The heavenly shield, around them spread,
  Is still high holden o'er us;
The grace those sinners that subdued,
The strength those weaklings that renewed,
  Doth vanquish, doth restore us.

3 Their joy unto their Lord we bring;
  Their song to us descendeth:
The Spirit who in them did sing
  To us His music lendeth.
His song in them, in us, is one;
We raise it high, we send it on,—
  The song that never endeth!

4 Ye saints to come, take up the strain,
  The same sweet theme endeavour;
Unbroken be the golden chain,
  Keep on the song for ever!
Safe in the same dear dwelling-place,
Rich with the same eternal grace,
  Bless the same boundless giver!

T. H. Gill, 1819–1906, altd.

See also—
Faith of our fathers, 466.
Father, we thank Thee, 315.
God of grace, 372.
Let the whole creation, 14.
Lord from whom. 361.

Onward! Christian soldiers, 520
The day Thou gavest, 706.
The Son of God, 558.
Through the night, 559.
Ye holy angels bright, 36.

266

OPENING OF A NEW CHURCH BUILDING

BE with us, gracious Lord, to-day;
This house we dedicate to Thee:
O hear Thy servants as they pray,
And let Thine ear attentive be!

2 Within these walls let holy peace,
Let love and truth be always found;
May burdened hearts find sweet release,
And souls with richest grace be crowned.

3 May here be heard the suppliant's sigh,
The weary enter into rest;
Here may the contrite to Thee cry,
And waiting souls be richly blessed.

4 Here, when the gospel sound is heard,
And here proclaimed the saving name,
May hearts be quickened, moved, and stirred,
And souls be kindled into flame.

5 Here may the dead be made to live,
The dumb to sing, the deaf to hear;
And do Thou to the humble give
Pardon and peace instead of fear.

6 Make this, O Lord, Thine own abode;
Thy presence in these courts be given;
Be this, indeed, the house of God,
And this in truth the gate of heaven.

C. D. Bell, 1818–98.

267

CHRIST is our corner-stone,
   On Him alone we build;
With His true saints alone
   The courts of heaven are filled;
     On His great love
      Our hopes we place
      Of present grace
     And joys above.

2 O then with hymns of praise
   These hallowed courts shall ring;
Our voices we will raise
   The Three in One to sing;
     And thus proclaim
      In joyful song,
      Both loud and long,
     That glorious name.

3 Here, gracious God, do Thou
   For evermore draw nigh;
Accept each faithful vow,
   And mark each suppliant sigh;
     In copious shower
      On all who pray
      Each holy day
     Thy blessings pour.

4 Here may we gain from heaven
   The grace which we implore;
And may that grace, once given,
   Be with us evermore,
     Until that day
      When all the blest
      To endless rest
     Are called away.

Latin, 6th or 7th cent.,
tr. John Chandler, 1806–76.

268

FOR A STONE-LAYING

FATHER of Jesus, by whose grace
    Our souls are freed from sin and shame,
Behold us gathered in this place
    To build a temple to Thy name.

2 Lord, lest our toil be vainly done,
    Be master-builder at our side;
Let Christ Himself be corner stone,
    The one foundation, sure and tried.

3 Build us a holy house of prayer,
    Where men with Thee may keep their tryst,
And learn to cast their load of care
    Upon the loving heart of Christ.

4 Build us a holy house of truth,
    Wherein the blind shall come to see,
Where age shall hand the torch to youth
    And youth shall tell the world of Thee.

5 Build us a holy house of praise
    Where souls redeemed shall sing His worth
Who walked of old our troubled ways
    And brought salvation down to earth.

6 So shall these walls be girt with peace,
    A shelter be from storm and strife,
A home where all earth's discords cease,
    A gateway to eternal life.

H. R. Moxley, 1881–

269

HOSANNA to the living Lord!
    Hosanna to the incarnate Word!
To Christ—Creator, Saviour, King—
Let earth, let heaven, hosanna sing,
    Hosanna, Lord! Hosanna in the highest!

2 O Saviour, with protecting care
　Abide in this Thy house of prayer;
　Assembled in Thy sacred name,
　Here we Thy parting promise claim:
　　Hosanna, Lord! Hosanna in the highest!

3 But chiefest, in our cleansèd breast,
　Eternal, bid Thy Spirit rest,
　And make our secret soul to be
　A temple pure, and worthy Thee:
　　Hosanna, Lord! Hosanna in the highest!

4 So, in the last and dreadful day,
　When earth and heaven shall melt away,
　Thy flock, redeemed from sinful stain,
　Shall swell the sound of praise again,
　　Hosanna, Lord! Hosanna in the highest!
　　　　　　　　Reginald Heber, 1783–1826.

270

PSALM cxxii.

HOW pleased and blest was I
　To hear the people cry,
" Come, let us seek our God to-day! "
　Yes, with a cheerful zeal
　We haste to Zion's hill,
And there our vows and honours pay.

2　Zion, thrice happy place,
　　Adorned with wondrous grace,
And walls of strength embrace thee round:
　　In thee our tribes appear,
　　To pray and praise, and hear
The sacred gospel's joyful sound.

3   There David's greater Son
     Has fixed His royal throne,
He sits for grace and judgment there:
     He bids the saints be glad,
     He makes the sinner sad,
And humble souls rejoice with fear.

4   May peace attend thy gate,
     And joy within thee wait,
To bless the soul of every guest;
     The man that seeks thy peace,
     And wishes thine increase,
A thousand blessings on him rest!

5   My tongue repeats her vows,
     Peace to this sacred house!
For there my friends and kindred dwell;
     And, since my glorious God
     Makes thee His blest abode,
My soul shall ever love thee well.

Isaac Watts, 1674–1748.

271

FOR A SUNDAY SCHOOL ANNIVERSARY

JESUS, we love to meet Thee
    On this glad festal day:
Our songs of joy shall greet Thee,
    And sorrows flee away!
We come with lips confessing
    Thy name in gladsome praise,
And hearts that seek Thy blessing
    For all the coming days.

2 We thank Thee for the glory
    Of each returning spring:
O may we read Thy story
    In every lovely thing!

The woodlands in their splendour,
　　The starry skies above,
Their silent witness render
　　To Thee whose name is love.

3 We bring Thee all the gladness
　　With which our lives are blest;
We bring Thee, too, the sadness,
　　For Thou canst give us rest:
For whether joy or sorrow
　　Shall mark our pilgrim way,
They need not fear to-morrow,
　　Who walk with Thee to-day.

4 And so we bring the treasure
　　Of life's unfolding spring,
And seek, in growing measure,
　　To serve Thee as our King:
Then every day before us
　　Will be a day of praise
Worthy to swell the chorus
　　That angel voices raise !

Leslie H. Moore, 1909–

272

LIGHT up this house with glory, Lord;
　　Enter, and claim Thine own;
Receive the homage of our souls,
　　Erect Thy temple-throne.

2 We ask no bright shekinah-cloud
　　To glorify the place;
Give, Lord, the substance of that sign—
　　A plenitude of grace.

3 Thou risen Lord, who cam'st to bless
　　Gently as comes the dew,
Here entering breathe on all around,
　　" My peace be unto you."

4 No rushing mighty wind we ask,
    No tongues of flame desire;
Grant us the Spirit's quickening light,
    His purifying fire.

5 Light up this house with glory, Lord—
    The glory of that love
Which forms and saves a Church below,
    And makes a heaven above.

John Harris, 1802–56.

273

PSALM lxxxiv.

LORD of the worlds above,
    How pleasant and how fair
The dwellings of Thy love,
    Thine earthly temples, are !
      To thine abode
        My heart aspires
        With warm desires
      To see my God.

2 O happy souls that pray
    Where God appoints to hear !
O happy men that pay
    Their constant service there !
      They praise Thee still;
        And happy they
        That love the way
      To Zion's hill.

3 They go from strength to strength
    Through this dark vale of tears,
Till each arrives at length,
    Till each in heaven appears;

O glorious seat,
    When God our King
    Shall thither bring
Our willing feet !

4 To spend one sacred day
    Where God and saints abide,
Affords diviner joy
    Than thousand days beside:
    Where God resorts,
      I love it more
      To keep the door
    Than shine in courts.

5 God is our sun and shield,
    Our light and our defence;
With gifts His hands are filled,
    We draw our blessings thence:
    He shall bestow
      On Jacob's race
      Peculiar grace
    And glory too.

6 The Lord His people loves:
    His hand no good withholds
From those His heart approves,
    From pure and pious souls:
    Thrice happy he,
      O God of hosts,
      Whose spirit trusts
    Alone in Thee.

Isaac Watts, 1674–1748.

274

NOW let us see Thy beauty, Lord,
    As we have seen before;
And by Thy beauty quicken us
    To love Thee and adore.

2 'Tis easy when with simple mind
    Thy loveliness we see,
To consecrate ourselves afresh
    To duty and to Thee.

3 Our every feverish mood is cooled,
    And gone is every load,
When we can lose the love of self,
    And find the love of God.

4 'Tis by Thy loveliness we're won
    To home and Thee again,
And as we are Thy children true
    We are more truly men.

5 Lord, it is coming to ourselves
    When thus we come to Thee;
The bondage of Thy loveliness
    Is perfect liberty.

6 So now we come to ask again
    What Thou hast often given,
The vision of that loveliness
    Which is the life of heaven.

Benjamin Waugh, 1839-1908.

275

O DAY of rest and gladness,
    O day of joy and light,
O balm of care and sadness,
    Most beautiful, most bright !
On thee the high and lowly
    Through ages joined in tune,
Sing, " Holy, Holy, Holy,"
    To the great God Triune.

2 On thee, at the creation,
    The light first had its birth;
On thee, for our salvation,
    Christ rose from depths of earth;

On thee our Lord victorious
  The Spirit sent from heaven:
And thus on thee most glorious
  A triple light was given.

3 To-day on weary nations
    The heavenly manna falls;
  To holy convocations
    The silver trumpet calls,
  Where gospel-light is glowing
    With pure and radiant beams,
  And living water flowing
    With soul-refreshing streams.

4 New graces ever gaining
    From this our day of rest,
  We reach the rest remaining
    To spirits of the blest,
  To Holy Ghost be praises,
    To Father and to Son;
  The Church her voice upraises
    To Thee, blest Three in One.

Christopher Wordsworth, 1807–85, *altd.*

276

FOR ANNIVERSARY OF COLLEGE OR SCHOOL

O MERCIFUL and Holy
    Who still by steps unknown,
In simple hearts and lowly
    Dost build Thy loftiest throne;
As Thou of old wast near us,
    To bless our founders' care,
Bow down Thine ear and hear us
    In this Thy house of prayer.

2 For faith and hope and daring
    To do our Father's will,
  And patience and forbearing,
    Tried good and vanquished ill:

Sweet praise of our dear mother,
  And, sweeter far than fame,
The love that binds each brother—
  We glorify Thy name.

3 For memory's golden treasure,
  For hearts uplifted now,
Each pure and blameless pleasure,
  Each brave and holy vow;
And friends still clinging nearer
  As sorrows cross our way,
And some by death made dearer—
  We thank Thee, Lord, to-day.

4 Whate'er Thy will shall send us,
  If weal or woe betide,
Do Thou, our God, defend us
  Fast anchored at Thy side.
Here firm, though all be drifting,
  May thousands still adore,
Eye, heart and voice uplifting
  Till time shall be no more.

H. Montagu Butler, 1833–1918.

277

Psalm xliii. 3–5.

O SEND Thy light forth and Thy truth;
  Let them be guides to me,
And bring me to Thine holy hill,
  Even where Thy dwellings be.
Then will I to God's altar go,
  To God my chiefest joy:
Yea, God, my God, Thy name to praise
  My harp I will employ.

2 Why art thou then cast down, my soul?
  What should discourage thee?
And why with vexing thoughts art thou
  Disquieted in me?

Still trust in God; for Him to praise
Good cause I yet shall have:
He of my countenance is the health,
My God that doth me save.

Francis Rous, 1579–1659.
William Barton, 1597–1678.

278

FOR ANNIVERSARY, OR OPENING OF NEW BUILDING

O THOU whose hand hath brought us
   Unto this joyful day,
Accept our glad thanksgiving,
   And listen as we pray:
And may our preparation
   For this day's service be
With one accord to offer
   Ourselves, O Lord, to Thee.

2 For this our* house we praise Thee,
   Reared by Thine own command;
For every generous giver,
   And every willing hand;
And now within Thy temple
   Thy glory let us see;
For all its strength and beauty
   Are nothing without Thee.

3 And oft as here we gather,
   And hearts in worship blend,
May truth reveal its power,
   And fervent prayer ascend;
Here may the busy toiler
   Rise to the things above;
The young, the old, be strengthened,
   And all men learn Thy love.

* For opening a new building. the word " new " may be substituted

4 And as the years roll over,
 And strong affections twine,
And tender memories gather
 About this sacred shrine,
May this, its chief distinction,
 Its glory ever be,
That multitudes within it
 Have found their way to Thee.

5 Lord God, our fathers' helper,
 Our joy and hope and stay,
Grant now a gracious earnest
 Of many a coming day:
Our yearning hearts Thou knowest;
 We wait before Thy throne;
O come, and by Thy presence
 Make this our house Thine own.   Amen.

F. W. Goadby, 1845–80.

279

OUR Father, by whose servants
 Our house was built of old,
Whose hand hath crowned her children
 With blessings manifold,
For Thine unfailing mercies
 Far-strewn along our way,
With all who passed before us,
 We praise Thy name to-day.

2 The changeful years unresting
 Their silent course have sped,
New comrades ever bringing
 In comrades' steps to tread;
And some are long forgotten,
 Long spent their hopes and fears;
Safe rest they in Thy keeping,
 Who changest not with years.

3 They reap not where they laboured,
  We reap what they have sown;
Our harvest may be garnered
  By ages yet unknown.
The days of old have dowered us
  With gifts beyond all praise:
Our Father, make us faithful
  To serve the coming days.

4 Before us and beside us,
  Still holden in Thine hand,
A cloud unseen of witness,
  Our elder comrades stand:
One family unbroken,
  We join, with one acclaim,
One heart, one voice uplifting,
  To glorify Thy name.

G. W. Briggs, 1875-

280

PSALM lxxxiv.

PLEASANT are Thy courts above,
  In the land of light and love;
Pleasant are Thy courts below,
In this land of sin and woe:
O my spirit longs and faints
For the converse of Thy saints,
For the brightness of Thy face,
For Thy fulness, God of grace.

2 Happy birds that sing and fly
Round Thine altars, O Most High:
Happier souls that find a rest
In a heavenly Father's breast;
Like the wandering dove that found
No repose on earth around,
They can to their ark repair,
And enjoy it ever there.

3 Happy souls ! their praises flow
Even in this vale of woe;
Waters in the desert rise,
Manna feeds them from the skies;
On they go from strength to strength,
Till they reach Thy throne at length,
At Thy feet adoring fall,
Who hast led them safe through all.

4 Lord, be mine this prize to win:
Guide me through a world of sin;
Keep me by Thy saving grace;
Give me at Thy side a place:
Sun and shield alike Thou art,
Guide and guard my erring heart;
Grace and glory flow from Thee,
Shower, O shower them, Lord, on me.

H. F. Lyte, 1793–1847.

281

SWEET is the work, my God, my King,
To praise Thy name, give thanks and sing,
To show Thy love by morning light,
And talk of all Thy truth at night.

2 Sweet is the day of sacred rest,
No mortal care shall seize my breast;
O may my heart in tune be found,
Like David's harp of solemn sound.

3 My heart shall triumph in the Lord,
And bless His works and bless His word:
Thy works of grace, how bright they shine !
How deep Thy counsels ! how divine !

4 Then shall I share a glorious part,
When grace hath well refined my heart,
And fresh supplies of joy are shed
Like holy oil to cheer my head.

5 Sin, my worst enemy before,
Shall vex my eyes and ears no more;
My inward foes shall all be slain,
Nor Satan break my peace again.

6 Then shall I see and hear and know
All I desired or wished below;
And every power find sweet employ
In that eternal world of joy.

Isaac Watts, 1674–1748, altd.

282

THIS is the day of light:
Let there be light to-day;
O Dayspring, rise upon our night,
And chase its gloom away.

2   This is the day of rest :
Our failing strength renew;
On weary brain and troubled breast
Shed Thou Thy freshening dew.

3   This is the day of peace:
Thy peace our spirits fill;
Bid Thou the blasts of discord cease,
The waves of strife be still.

4   This is the day of prayer:
Let earth to heaven draw near;
Lift up our hearts to seek Thee there,
Come down to meet us here.

5   This is the first of days:
Send forth Thy quickening breath,
And wake dead souls to love and praise,
O vanquisher of death !

John Ellerton, 1826–93.

283

WE love the place, O God,
    Wherein Thine honour dwells;
The joy of Thine abode
    All earthly joy excels.

2 It is the house of prayer,
    Wherein Thy servants meet;
And Thou, O Lord, art there
    Thy chosen flock to greet.

3 We love the word of life,
    The word that tells of peace,
Of comfort in the strife,
    And joys that never cease.

4 We love to sing below
    For mercies freely given;
But O we long to know
    The triumph-song of heaven.

5 Lord Jesus, give us grace
    On earth to love Thee more,
In heaven to see Thy face,
    And with Thy saints adore.

William Bullock, 1797–1874 (w. 1–2).
H. W. Baker, 1821–77 (w. 3–5).

See also—

All people that on earth, 2.
Angel voices, 4.
Before Jehovah's aweful throne, 6.
Come let us join, 200.
Come we that love the Lord, 495.
Command Thy blessing, 357.
God almighty, 40.
God is in His temple, 41.
God of mercy, 373.
God of pity, 431.

Happy are they, 496.
Jesus, stand among us, 336.
Jesus, where'er, 338.
Lo ! God is here, 16.
Lord God the Holy Ghost, 235.
O worship the King, 22.
Our Father God, 362.
Stand up and bless, 363.
Three in one, 47.
What purpose burns, 532.

284

MARK ix. 36–37.

CHRIST who welcomed little children
To Thine arms in Galilee,
Lovingly we bring this baby
That *he* too be blessed by Thee.

2 Lord, accept the parents' praises.
Help them by Thy grace divine;
May their tender care and nurture
Train and lead *him* to be Thine.

3 In their home may Thine own presence
Guide and guard from day to day,
Filling life with love and gladness
Throughout all *his* childhood's way.

4 Then in strength of mind and body
May *he* own Thee Lord and King,
Tread the paths of Christian service,
All *his* heart's allegiance bring.

5 Christ who welcomes little children
Bid this baby welcome too.
May Thy mighty arms protect *him*.
All life's varied journey through.

Amen.

Hugh Martin, 1890–

285

MATT. xix. 13–15.

FRIEND of the home, as when in Galilee
The mothers brought their little ones to Thee,
So we, dear Lord, would now the children bring,
And seek for them the shelter of Thy wing.

2 Lord, may Thy Church, as with a mother's care,
For Thee the lambs within her bosom bear;
And grant, as morning fades to noon, that they
Still in her love and holy service stay.

3 Draw through the child the parents nearer Thee,
Endue their home with growing sanctity;
And gather all, by earthly homes made one,
In heaven, O Christ, when earthly days are done.
Amen.

H. Elvet Lewis, 1860–1953.

286

GRACIOUS Saviour, gentle shepherd,
Little ones are dear to Thee;
Gathered with Thine arms and carried
In Thy bosom may they be,
Sweetly, fondly, safely tended,
From all want and danger free.

2 Tender shepherd, never leave them
From Thy fold to go astray;
By Thy look of love directed
May they walk the narrow way;
Then direct them and protect them
Lest they fall to sin a prey.

3 Let Thy holy word instruct them,
Fill their minds with heavenly light,
Let Thy love and grace constrain them
To approve whate'er is right:
Let them feel Thy yoke is easy,
Let them prove Thy burden light.

4 Taught to voice the holy praises,
Which on earth Thy children sing,
Both with lips and hearts unfeignèd
Glad thanksgiving may they bring;
Then with all Thy saints in glory
Join to praise their Lord and King.

Jane Leeson, 1807–82,
adapted by John Keble, 1742–1866.

287

LOVING shepherd of Thy sheep,
  Keep Thy lamb, in safety keep;
Nothing can Thy power withstand,
None can pluck *him* from Thy hand.

2 May *he* praise Thee every day,
  Gladly all Thy will obey;
  Like Thy blessèd ones above,
  Happy in Thy precious love.

3 Loving shepherd, ever near,
  Teach Thy lamb Thy voice to hear;
  Suffer not *his* steps to stray
  From the straight and narrow way.

4 Where Thou leadest may *he* go,
  Walking in Thy steps below,
  Then, before Thy Father's throne,
  Saviour, claim *him* for Thine own.

Amen.

Jane Leeson, 1807–82, *altd.*

See also—

Father, in Thy presence kneeling,   Father of men, 359.
  617.

(4) BAPTISM

288

ETERNAL Father, whose great love
  Encircles us where'er we rove—
By peak or plain, by sea or shore,
By crowded street or lonely moor—
  Enfold within Thy sleepless care
  Those who this day their faith declare

2 Eternal Saviour, whose rich grace
  Did anguish, dark and drear, embrace;
  Whose sweet compassions never fail,
  Whose intercessions must prevail,
    Uphold, we pray Thee, gracious Lord,
    Those who this day obey Thy word.

3 Eternal Spirit, whose still voice
  Hath prompted every gracious choice;
  Who taught our souls to loathe our sin,
  And at the cross new life begin,
    Preserve and lead for Jesus' sake,
    Those who this day the world forsake.

F. W. Borcham, 1871-1959.

289

FIGHT the good fight with all thy might;
Christ is thy strength, and Christ thy right.
Lay hold on life, and it shall be
Thy joy and crown eternally.

2 Run the straight race through God's good grace,
  Lift up thine eyes, and seek His face;
  Life with its path before us lies;
  Christ is the way, and Christ the prize.

3 Cast care aside; lean on thy guide.
  His boundless mercy will provide;
  Trust, and thy trusting soul shall prove
  Christ is its life, and Christ its love.

4 Faint not, nor fear; His arm is near;
  He changeth not, and thou art dear;
  Only believe, and thou shalt see
  That Christ is all in all to thee.

J. S. B. Monsell. 1811-75.

290

GLORY to God, whose Spirit draws
Fresh soldiers to the Saviour's cause.
Who thus, baptized into His name,
His goodness and their faith proclaim.

2 For these now added to the host,
Who in their Lord and Saviour boast,
And consecrate to Him their days,
Accept, O God, our grateful praise.

3 Thus may Thy mighty Spirit draw
All here to love and keep His law;
Themselves His subjects to declare,
And place themselves beneath His care.

4 Lead them at once their Lord to own,
To glory in His cross alone;
And then, baptized, His truth to teach,
His love to share, His heaven to reach.

Baptist W. Noel, 1799–1873

291

HERE in this water I do vow to Thee
Of my free will a loyal child to be;
Here Thou dost pledge me, now of Jesus' kin,
That Thy grace covers evermore my sin.

2 Thine is the Kingdom; gladly I confess
Thou hast the right to all my faithfulness.
Thine is the power; and therefore I believe
Power that I need I shall from Thee receive.

3 Mine is the fulness of Thy Spirit's might;
Round me, unceasing, shines eternal light.
Here have I promised; here Thou hast fulfilled
That work of love Thou at my birth hast willed.

4 Here am I joined with those who, journeys done,
Through sun and storm their longed-for home
   have won,
That we, with countless pilgrims yet to be,
May share at last eternal joy in Thee.

John Philip Giles, 1905–

292

I'M not ashamed to own my Lord,
  Or to defend His cause;
Maintain the honour of His word,
  The glory of His cross.

2 Jesus, my Lord, I know His name;
  His name is all my trust;
Nor will He put my soul to shame,
  Nor let my hope be lost.

3 Firm as His throne His promise stands;
  And He can well secure
What I've committed to His hands
  Till the decisive hour.

4 Then will He own my worthless name
  Before His Father's face;
And in the new Jerusalem
  Appoint my soul a place.

Isaac Watts, 1674–1748.

293

JESUS, and shall it ever be,
  A mortal man ashamed of Thee,
Ashamed of Thee, whom angels praise,
Whose glories shine through endless days?

2 Ashamed of Jesus !—sooner far
Let evening blush to own a star:
He sheds the beams of light divine
O'er this benighted soul of mine.

3 Ashamed of Jesus !—just as soon
Let midnight be ashamed of noon;
'Tis midnight with my soul till He,
Bright morning star, bid darkness flee.

4 Ashamed of Jesus, that dear friend
On whom my hopes of heaven depend !
No ! when I blush, be this my shame,
That I no more revere His name.

5 Ashamed of Jesus !—Yes I may,
When I've no guilt to wash away,
No tear to wipe, no good to crave,
No fears to quell, no soul to save.

6 Till then—nor is my boasting vain—
Till then I boast a Saviour slain;
And O may this my glory be,
That Christ is not ashamed of me !

Joseph Grigg, 1722-68,
altd. by Benjamin Francis, 1734-99.

294

JESUS CHRIST, my heart's true captain,
Here I give myself to Thee.
All my strength is at Thy service
Who didst give Thy life for me.
Hence, whate'er of fame or fortune
Comes my way for weal or woe,
Thine alone am I for ever,
Where Thou leadest I will go.

2 Here before Thee stands a sinner,
  Bowed before Thy searching eyes,
  Humbled, shamed, all sin confessing,
  Trusting Thy command, " Arise ! "
  My poor heart is all unworthy
  That my God should here abide.
  Yet alone by Thine indwelling
  Can my soul be satisfied.

3 Peace can ne'er be bought or bartered,
  Vain for grace the world's whole wealth.
  Only in Thy glad adventure
  Shall my radiant heart find health.
  Nought is gain but what is given,
  All I have I count but loss,
  Save to spend it in Thy service
  For the glory of the cross.

4 God is rising up to judgment,
  Earth is waking to Thy light.
  All mankind shall yet be brothers,
  Wrong be conquered by the right.
  Tasks that call for tireless courage
  Lie before us in the way.
  Then together let us venture
  Till our God has won the day.

Greville Cooke, 1894

295

MATT. iii. 13–17.

LORD Jesus, in Thy footsteps
    We come to take our stand,
And pledge Thee loyal service
    In keeping Thy command.
As Thou in Jordan's river
    In faith and hope didst bow,
We would go through these waters
    To make our solemn vow.

2 We know we are unworthy;
    Our hearts are soiled within.
Lord, help us now to bury
    And wash away our sin.
Lord, help us in the newness
    Of risen life with Thee
Henceforth by Thine enabling
    True witnesses to be.

3 As then at Thy baptizing
    Thy Father blessed Thy name,
And from the opened heaven
    The Spirit's favour came,
So, gracious Lord and Master,
    Do Thou Thy gift bestow,
That cleansed, inspired and guided,
    We in Thy likeness grow.

4 Upon Thy grace relying
    To meet temptation's hour,
We'd face life's tests with courage
    And conquer in Thy power.
Thy Kingdom's sway extending,
    Thy will our vital breath,
O Lord, may we Thy servants
    Prove faithful unto death.

Hugh Martin. 1890–

296

MASTER, we Thy footsteps follow,
    We Thy word obey,
Hear us, Thy dear name confessing,
    While we pray.

2 Now into Thy death baptizèd,
    We ourselves would be
Dead to all the sin that made
    Thy Calvary.

3 Rising with Thee, make us like Thee,
    In Thy love and care,
In Thy zeal, and in Thy labour,
    And Thy prayer.

4 Let the love that knows no failing
    Cast out all our fears,
Let Thy pure and faithful spirit
    Fill our years

5 Till we hear the trumpets sounding
    On the other side,
And for ever, in Thy heaven
    We abide.

F. A. Jackson, 1867–1942.

297

O HAPPY day, that fixed my choice
    On Thee, my Saviour and my God !
Well may this glowing heart rejoice,
    And tell its raptures all abroad.

2 O happy bond, that seals my vows,
    To Him who merits all my love !
Let cheerful anthems fill His house,
    While to that sacred shrine I move.

3 'Tis done ! the great transaction's done;
    I am my Lord's, and He is mine;
He drew me, and I followed on,
    Charmed to confess the voice divine.

4 High heaven, that heard the solemn vow,
    That vow renewed shall daily hear,
Till in life's latest hour I bow,
    And bless in death a bond so dear.

Philip Doddridge, 1702–51, *altd.*

298

O JESUS, I have promised
    To serve Thee to the end;
Be Thou for ever near me,
  My master and my friend:
I shall not fear the battle
  If Thou art by my side,
Nor wander from the pathway
  If Thou wilt be my guide.

2 O let me feel Thee near me:
  The world is ever near;
I see the sights that dazzle,
  The tempting sounds I hear;
My foes are ever near me,
  Around me and within;
But, Jesus, draw Thou nearer,
  And shield my soul from sin.

3 O let me hear Thee speaking
  In accents clear and still,
Above the storms of passion,
  The murmurs of self-will;
O speak to reassure me,
  To hasten or control;
O speak, and make me listen,
  Thou guardian of my soul.

4 O Jesus, Thou hast promised,
  To all who follow Thee,
That where Thou art in glory
  There shall Thy servant be;
And, Jesus, I have promised
  To serve Thee to the end;
O give me grace to follow
  My master and my friend.

5 O let me see Thy footmarks,
  And in them plant mine own;
My hope to follow duly
  Is in Thy strength alone:

O guide me, call me, draw me,
Uphold me to the end;
And then in heaven receive me,
My Saviour and my friend !
Amen.

J. E. Bode, 1816–74.

299

PRAISE to God, almighty maker
Of all things, below, above;
For His might is in redemption
Manifest as holy love.

2 Praise the Son who thus revealed Him,
Love incarnate shown to us,
Living, suffering, dying, risen,
Love through death victorious.

3 Here, redemption's wondrous story
We set forth in mystic rite:
See Him die, the grave receive Him,
See Him rise, by God's great might.

4 Here, within the font we meet Him;
Here with Him we buried lie;
Here we plead His matchless merit;
Here with Him to sin we die.

5 Then, victorious through His passion,
From the grave with Him we rise,
Born again to do Him service
In the strength His grace supplies

6 Praise the Spirit, who is promised
Here to be the gift divine,
Making in our hearts His temple,
Love, joy, peace, His holy sign.

7 Praise to Father, Son and Spirit,
　　Sacred name of holy love;
　Here, baptized, the Church we enter,
　　Realm on earth of heaven above.

8 Praise to God, almighty Saviour,
　　Praises from the earth ascend;
　Praises join from saints in heaven,
　　Hallelujahs without end.

William Robinson, 1888–

300

SOLDIER, go! Thy vow is spoken:
　　Counting earthly gain but loss,
Thou henceforth must bear the token
　　Of the cross.

2 Strengthened with the sevenfold blessing
　　Of the Spirit here outpoured,
　Thou must dare to live confessing
　　Christ thy Lord.

3 Trust in Him: though sore temptation
　　Oft thy fainting heart assail,
　Yet the Prince of thy salvation
　　Shall prevail.

4 Faithful in His service ever
　　Fight, nor fear the battle's tide:
　Hosts of hell can harm thee never
　　At His side.

5 He, His mighty arm extending,
　　Still hath power from sin to save,
　Though thy warfare hath no ending
　　But the grave.

6 Then, when over death victorious
　　Thou shalt lay thine armour down,
　With the saints in heaven glorious
　　Take the crown.

T. E. Page, 1850–1936.

301

STAND, soldier of the cross,
Thy high allegiance claim,
And vow to hold the world but loss
For thy Redeemer's name.

2   Arise and be baptized,
And wash thy sins away:
Thy league with God be solemnized,
Thy faith avowed to-day.

3   No more thine own, but Christ's,—
With all the saints of old,
Apostles, seers, evangelists,
And martyr throngs enrolled,—

4   In God's whole armour strong,
Front hell's embattled powers:
The warfare may be sharp and long,
The victory must be ours.

5   O bright the conqueror's crown,
The song of triumph sweet,
When faith casts every trophy down
At our great captain's feet !

E. H. Bickersteth, 1825–1906.

302

TO Thee, O God, our hearts we raise
In humble supplication
For those who seek in early days
A life-long consecration.
To Thee they come with vows renewed,
The right from wrong discerning;
O send them forth with power endued,
With zeal and courage burning.

2 O Saviour Christ, to Thee we pray,
   With heavenly manna feed them;
Thyself the life, the truth, the way,
   Through all life's changes lead them.
When fails the heart in warfare long,
   When faith and love are dying,
O make them in their weakness strong,
   While on Thy might relying.

3 O Holy Spirit, fount of life,
   Through all their days protect them;
Their help in need, their shield in strife,
   With sevenfold gifts direct them.
Inspired with love and holy fear,
   And pledged to high endeavour,
O grant them grace to persevere,
   And seal them Thine for ever.

H. D. Dixon-Wright, 1870–1916.

303

TRUE-HEARTED, whole-hearted, faithful
      and loyal,
King of our lives, by Thy grace we will be:
Under Thy standard, exalted and royal,
   Strong in Thy strength, we will battle for
      Thee.
Peal out the watchword, and silence it never,
   Song of our spirits rejoicing and free:
" True-hearted, whole-hearted, now and for ever,
   King of our lives, by Thy grace we will be ! "

2 True-hearted, whole-hearted ! fullest allegiance
   Yielding henceforth to our glorious King,
Valiant endeavour and loving obedience
   Freely and joyously now would we bring.

3 True-hearted ! Saviour, Thou knowest our
    story:
Weak are the hearts that we lay at Thy feet,
Sinful and treacherous, yet, for Thy glory,
    Heal them, and cleanse them from sin and
    deceit.

4 Whole-hearted ! Saviour, belovèd and glorious,
    Take Thy great power and reign Thou alone
Over our wills and affections victorious,
    Freely surrendered, and wholly Thine own.

Frances Ridley Havergal, 1836–79.

304

WITNESS, ye men and angels, now,
    Before the Lord we speak;
To Him we make our solemn vow,
    A vow we dare not break;

2 That, long as life itself shall last,
    Ourselves to Christ we yield;
Nor from His cause will we depart,
    Or ever quit the field.

3 We trust not in our native strength,
    But on His grace rely,
That, with returning wants, the Lord
    Will all our need supply.

4 O guide our doubtful feet aright,
    And keep us in Thy ways;
And while we turn our vows to prayers,
    Turn Thou our prayers to praise.

Benjamin Beddome, 1717–95

305

BAPTISMAL SENTENCES

NUM. vi. 24–26; REV. v. 13; ii. 10.

THE Lord bless thee and keep thee; the Lord
make His face to shine upon thee, and be gracious
unto thee; the Lord lift up His countenance upon
thee, and give thee peace.

Blessing and honour and glory and power be
unto Him that sitteth upon the throne, and unto the
Lamb, for ever and ever.

Be thou faithful unto death and I will give thee a
crown of life.

See also—

I bind unto myself to-day, 433.

(5) THE LORD'S SUPPER

306

1 COR. xi. 24.

ACCORDING to Thy gracious word,
In meek humility
This will I do, my dying Lord,
I will remember Thee.

2 Thy body, broken for my sake,
My bread from heaven shall be;
The testamental cup I take,
And thus remember Thee.

3 Gethsemane can I forget?
Or there Thy conflict see,
Thine agony and bloody sweat,
And not remember Thee?

4 When to the cross I turn mine eyes,
And rest on Calvary,
O Lamb of God, my sacrifice,
I must remember Thee,—

5 Remember Thee, and all Thy pains,
　　And all Thy love to me;
　　Yes, while a breath, a pulse remains,
　　Will I remember Thee.

6 And when these failing lips grow dumb,
　　And mind and memory flee,
　　When Thou shalt in Thy kingdom come,
　　Jesus, remember me.

James Montgomery, 1771–1854.

307

AND now, O Father, mindful of the love
　　That bought us, once for all, on Calvary's
　　　tree,
And having with us Him that pleads above,
　　We here present, we here spread forth to Thee
That only offering perfect in Thine eyes,
The one true, pure, immortal sacrifice.

2 Look, Father, look on His anointed face,
　　And only look on us as found in Him;
　　Look not on our misusings of Thy grace,
　　　Our prayer so languid, and our faith so dim:
　　For lo, between our sins and their reward
　　We set the passion of Thy Son our Lord.

3 And then for those, our dearest and our best,
　　By this prevailing presence we appeal:
　　O fold them closer to Thy mercy's breast,
　　　O do Thine utmost for their souls' true weal;
　　From tainting mischief keep them white and clear,
　　And crown Thy gifts with strength to persevere.

4 And so we come: O draw us to Thy feet,
　　Most patient Saviour, who canst love us still;
　　And by this food, so aweful and so sweet,

Deliver us from every touch of ill:
In Thine own service make us glad and free,
And grant us nevermore to part with Thee.

308

BEHOLD the eternal king and priest
Brings forth for me the bread and wine;
Himself the master of the feast,
His flesh and blood the food divine !

2 Jesus, I come, for Thou dost call,
I eat and drink at Thy command;
Low at Thy feet I humbly fall,
O touch me with Thy piercèd hand.

3 Wash throughly clean this heart of mine,
That it may beat for Thee alone;
O let it lose its life in Thine,
And have no will except Thine own !

4 In weariness be Thou my rest,
In loneliness be Thou my friend,
In sorrow hold me to Thy breast,
And keep me, Jesus, to the end.

Anon., *Congregational Church Hymnal*, 1887.

309

BREAD of heaven ! on Thee we feed,
For Thy flesh is meat indeed;
Ever may our souls be fed
With this true and living bread;
Day by day, with strength supplied,
Through the life of Him who died.

2 Vine of heaven ! Thy blood supplies
This blest cup of sacrifice;
'Tis Thy wounds our healing give;
To Thy cross we look and live:
Thou, our life ! O let us be
Rooted, grafted, built in Thee.

Josiah Conder, 1789–1855, *altd.*

310

BREAD of the world, in mercy broken,
Wine of the soul, in mercy shed,
By whom the words of life were spoken,
And in whose death our sins are dead,

2 Look on the heart by sorrow broken,
Look on the tears by sinners shed;
And be Thy feast to us the token
That by Thy grace our souls are fed.

Reginald Heber, 1783–1826

311

1 COR. xi. 26.

BY Christ redeemed, in Christ restored,
We keep the memory adored,
And show the death of our dear Lord
Until He come.

2 His body broken in our stead
Is seen in this memorial bread,
And so our feeble love is fed
Until He come.

3 The drops of His dread agony,
His life-blood shed for us, we see;
The wine shall tell the mystery
Until He come.

4 And thus that dark betrayal-night
　　With the last advent we unite,
　　By one blest chain of loving rite,
　　　　Until He come.

5 O blessèd hope ! with this elate,
　　Let not our hearts be desolate,
　　But, strong in faith, in patience wait
　　　　Until He come.

George Rawson, 1807-89.

312

MATT. xxvi. 26.

COME, risen Lord, and deign to be our guest;
　　Nay, let us be Thy guests ; the feast is Thine ;
Thyself at Thine own board make manifest,
　　In Thine own sacrament of bread and wine.

2 We meet, as in that upper room they met ;
　　Thou at the table, blessing, yet dost stand ;
" This is my body " : so Thou givest yet ;
　　Faith still receives the cup as from Thy hand.

3 One body we, one body who partake,
　　One Church united in communion blest ;
One name we bear, one bread of life we break,
　　With all Thy saints on earth and saints at rest.

4 One with each other, Lord, for one in Thee,
　　Who art one Saviour and one living Head ;
Then open Thou our eyes, that we may see ;
　　Be known to us in breaking of the bread.

G. W. Briggs, 1875-1959.

313

DEAR Lord, before we part
From Thy sweet earthly feast,
Give us the earnest in our heart
Of Thine eternal rest.

2   Lift up our drooping eyes
To the great banquet there;
And ever for the crowning prize
Our waiting souls prepare.

3   So each a glorious seat
Shall in Thy kingdom claim;
And there, in heavenly triumph, eat
The supper of the Lamb.

Anon., Psalms and Hymns, 1858.

314

DECK thyself, my soul, with gladness,
Leave the gloomy haunts of sadness,
Come into the daylight's splendour,
There with joy thy praises render
Unto Him whose grace unbounded
Hath this wondrous banquet founded:
High o'er all the heavens He reigneth,
Yet to dwell with thee He deigneth.

2 Sun, who all my life dost brighten;
Light, who dost my soul enlighten;
Joy, the sweetest man e'er knoweth;
Fount, whence all my being floweth:
At Thy feet I cry, my Maker,
Let me be a fit partaker
Of this blessèd food from heaven,
For our good, Thy glory, given.

3 Jesus, bread of life, I pray Thee,
Let me gladly here obey Thee;
Never to my hurt invited,
Be Thy love with love requited:
From this banquet let me measure,
Lord, how vast and deep its treasure;
Through the gifts Thou here dost give me,
As Thy guest in heaven receive me.

Johann Franck, 1618–77,
tr. *Catherine Winkworth, 1827–78.*

315

FATHER, we thank Thee who hast planted
Thy holy name within our hearts.
Knowledge and faith and life immortal
Jesus Thy Son to us imparts.

2 Thou, Lord, didst make all for Thy pleasure,
Didst give man food for all his days,
Giving in Christ the bread eternal;
Thine is the power, be Thine the praise.

3 Watch o'er Thy Church, O Lord, in mercy,
Save it from evil, guard it still,
Perfect it in Thy love, unite it,
Cleansed and conformed unto Thy will.

4 As grain, once scattered on the hillsides,
Was in the broken bread made one,
So from all lands Thy Church be gathered
Into Thy kingdom by Thy Son.

From the Didache, 2nd cent.,
versified by F. Bland Tucker, 1895–

316

PART I

HERE, O my Lord, I see Thee face to face;
Here would I touch and handle things
unseen,
Here grasp with firmer hand the eternal grace,
And all my helplessness upon Thee lean.

2 Here would I feed upon the bread of God,
Here drink with Thee the royal wine of heaven;
Here would I lay aside each earthly load,
Here taste afresh the calm of sin forgiven.

3 This is the hour of banquet and of song;
This is the heavenly table spread for me;
Here let me feast, and, feasting, still prolong
The hallowed hour of fellowship with Thee.

PART II

4 Too soon we rise: the symbols disappear;
The feast, though not the love, is past and gone;
The bread and wine remove, but Thou art here,
Nearer than ever; still my shield and sun.

5 I have no help but Thine; nor do I need
Another arm save Thine to lean upon;
It is enough, my Lord, enough indeed;
My strength is in Thy might, Thy might alone.

6 Feast after feast thus comes and passes by,
Yet passing, points to the glad feast above,
Giving sweet foretaste of the festal joy,
The Lamb's great bridal feast of bliss and love.

Horatius Bonar, 1808–89, altd.

317

I HUNGER and I thirst;
  Jesus, my manna be;
Ye living waters, burst
  Out of the rock for me.

2 Thou bruised and broken bread,
  My life-long wants supply;
As living souls are fed,
  O feed me, or I die.

3 Thou true life-giving vine,
  Let me Thy sweetness prove;
Renew my life with Thine,
  Refresh my soul with love.

4 Rough paths my feet have trod,
  Since first their course began;
Feed me, Thou bread of God;
  Help me, Thou Son of Man.

5 For still the desert lies
  My fainting soul before;
O living waters, rise
  Within me evermore.

J. S. B. Monsell, 1811–75.

318

JESUS invites His saints
  To meet around His board;
Here pardoned rebels sit and hold
  Communion with their Lord.

2 Here we survey that love
  Which spoke in every breath,
Which crowned each action of His life,
  And triumphed in His death.

3   This holy bread and wine
      Maintain our fainting breath,
By union with our living Lord,
      And interest in His death.

4   Our heavenly Father calls
      Christ and His members one;
We the young children of His love,
      And He the first-born Son.

5   We are but several parts
      Of the same broken bread;
Our body hath its several limbs,
      But Jesus is the head.

6   Let all our powers be joined
      His glorious name to raise;
Pleasure and love fill every mind
      And every voice be praise.

Isaac Watts, 1674–1748.

319

JESUS, to Thy table led,
  Now let every heart be fed
With the true and living bread.

2 When we taste the mystic wine,
  Of Thine outpoured blood the sign,
  Fill our hearts with love divine.

3 While on Thy dear cross we gaze,
  Mourning o'er our sinful ways,
  Turn our sadness into praise.

4 Draw us to Thy wounded side,
  Whence there flowed the healing tide;
  There our sins and sorrows hide.

5 From the bonds of sin release;
Cold and wavering faith increase;
Grant us, Lamb of God, Thy peace.

6 Lead us by Thy piercèd hand,
Till around Thy throne we stand
In the bright and better land.   Amen.

Robert Hall Baynes, 1831–95, altd.

320

JESUS, we thus obey
Thy last and kindest word:
Here in Thine own appointed way
We come to meet our Lord.

2   Our hearts we open wide
To make the Saviour room;
And lo ! the Lamb, the crucified,
The sinner's friend is come.

3   Thus we remember Thee,
And take this bread and wine
As Thine own dying legacy,
And our redemption's sign.

4   Thy presence makes the feast;
Now let our spirits feel
The glory not to be expressed,
The joy unspeakable.

5   Now let our souls be fed
With manna from above,
And over us Thy banner spread
Of everlasting love.

Charles Wesley, 1707–88.

321

LORD, in this blest and hallowed hour
Reveal Thy presence and Thy power;
Show to my faith Thy hands and side,
My Lord and God, the crucified.

2 Fain would I find a calm retreat
From vain distractions near Thy feet;
And, borne above all earthly care,
Be joyful in Thy house of prayer.

3 Or let me through the opening skies
Catch one bright glimpse of paradise;
And realize, with raptured awe,
The vision dying Stephen saw.

4 But if unworthy of such joy,
Still shall Thy love my heart employ;
For of Thy favoured children's fare
'Twere bliss the very crumbs to share.

5 Yet never can my soul be fed
With less than Thee, the living bread;
Thyself unto my soul impart,
And with Thy presence fill my heart.

Josiah Conder, 1789–1855.

322

NO Gospel like this feast
Spread for Thy Church by Thee;
No prophet or evangelist
Preach the glad news so free.

2   All our redemption cost,
All our redemption won;
All it has won for us, the lost,
All it cost Thee, the Son.

3   Thine was the bitter price,
       Ours is the free gift given;
Thine was the blood of sacrifice,
       Ours is the wine of heaven.

4   For Thee the burning thirst,
       The shame, the mortal strife,
The broken heart, the piercèd side:
       To us the bread of life.

5   Here we would rest midway,
       As on a sacred height;
That darkest and that brightest day
       Meeting before our sight:

6   From that dark depth of woes
       Thy love for us hath trod,
Up to the heights of blest repose
       Thy love prepares with God;

7   Till, from self's chains released,
       One sight alone we see,
Still at the cross, as at the feast,
       Behold Thee, only Thee !

Elisabeth Charles, 1828–96.

323

O CHRIST, our Lord, who with Thine own
  hast been,
Our spirits cleave to Thee, the friend unseen.

2 Vouchsafe that all who on Thy bounty feed
May heed Thy love, and prize Thy gifts indeed.

3 Make every heart that is Thy dwelling-place
A watered garden filled with fruits of grace.

4 Each holy purpose help us to fulfil;
Increase our faith to feed upon Thee still.

5 Illuminate our minds, that we may see
In all around us holy signs of Thee;

6 And may such witness in our lives appear,
That all may know Thou hast been with us here.

7 O grant us peace, that by Thy peace possessed
Thy life within us we may manifest.

8 So shalt Thou be for ever, loving Lord,
Our shield and our exceeding great reward.

G. H. Bourne, 1840–1925.

324

O LEAD my blindness by the hand,
Lead me to Thy familiar feast,
Not here or now to understand,
Yet even here and now to taste,
How the eternal Word of heaven
On earth in broken bread is given.

2 We, who with one blest food are fed,
Into one body may we grow,
And one pure life from Thee, the head,
Informing all the members flow:
One pulse be felt in every vein,
One law of pleasure and of pain.

W. E. Gladstone, 1809–98.

325

SHEPHERD of souls, refresh and bless
Thy chosen pilgrim-flock,
With manna from the wilderness,
With water from the rock.

2 We would not live by bread alone,
    But by Thy word of grace,
In strength of which we travel on
    To our abiding place.

3 Be known to us in breaking bread,
    But do not then depart;
Saviour, abide with us, and spread
    Thy table in our heart.

4 Then sup with us in love divine:
    Thy body and Thy blood,
That living bread and heavenly wine,
    Be our immortal food.

James Montgomery, 1771–1854.

326

SING, my tongue, the Saviour's glory,
    Of His cross the mystery sing;
Lift on high the wondrous trophy,
    Tell the triumph of the King:
He, the world's redeemer, conquers
    Death, through death now vanquishing.

2 Born for us and for us given,
    Son of man, like us below,
He as man with men abiding
    Dwells, the seed of life to sow:
He, our heavy griefs partaking,
    Thus fulfils His life of woe.

3 Word made flesh ! His word life-giving,
    Gives His flesh our meat to be,
Bids us drink His blood believing,
    Through His death, we life shall see:
Blessed they who thus receiving
    Are from death and sin set free.

4 Low in adoration bending,
    Now our hearts our God revere;
Faith her aid to sight is lending,
    Though unseen the Lord is near;
Ancient types and shadows ending,
    Christ our paschal Lamb is here.

5 Praise for ever, thanks and blessing
    Thine, O gracious Father, be:
Praise be Thine, O Christ, who bringest
    Life and immortality:
Praise be Thine, Thou quickening Spirit,
    Praise through all eternity.   Amen.

Thomas Aquinas, 1227–74,
tr. Anon. in New Congregational Hymn Book, 1859.

327

SPREAD the table of the Lord,
    Break the bread and pour the wine;
Gathered at the sacred board,
    Share in faith the feast divine.

2 Saints and martyrs of the faith
    To the cross have turned their eyes,
Sharing, in their life and death,
    That eternal sacrifice.

3 Humbly now my place I claim
    In that glorious company,
Proud confessors of the name,
    Breaking bread, O Christ, with Thee.

4 By the memory of Thy love,
    To the glory of the Lord,
Here I raise Thy cross above,
    Here I gird me with Thy sword.

5 Guided by Thy mighty hand,
    All Thy mind I would fulfil,
Loyal to Thy least command,
    Serving Thee with steadfast will.

G. O. Gregory, 1881–

328

STRENGTHEN for service, Lord, the hands
    That holy things have taken;
Let ears that now have heard Thy songs
    To clamour never waken.

2 Lord, may the tongues which " Holy " sang
    Keep free from all deceiving;
The eyes which saw Thy love be bright,
    Thy blessèd hope perceiving.

3 The feet that tread Thy holy courts
    From light do Thou not banish;
The bodies by Thy body fed
    With Thy new life replenish.

Liturgy of Malabar,
tr. C. W. Humphreys, Percy Dearmer, 1867–1936.

329

SWEET feast of love divine !
    'Tis grace that makes us free
To feed upon this bread and wine,
    In memory, Lord, of Thee.

2 Here every welcome guest
    Waits, Lord, from Thee to learn
The secrets of Thy Father's breast,
    And all Thy grace discern.

3 Here conscience ends its strife,
    And faith delights to prove
The sweetness of the bread of life,
    The fulness of Thy love.

4 That blood that flowed for sin
    In symbol here we see,
And feel the blessed pledge within
    That we are loved of Thee.

5 O if this glimpse of love
    Is so divinely sweet,
What will it be, O Lord, above,
    Thy gladdening smile to meet !

6 To see Thee face to face,
    Thy perfect likeness wear,
And all Thy ways of wondrous grace
    Through endless years declare.

Edward Denny, 1796–1889.

330

THEE we adore, O hidden Saviour, Thee,
    Who in Thy sacrament dost deign to be:
Both flesh and spirit at Thy presence fail,
Yet here Thy presence we devoutly hail.

2 O blest memorial of our dying Lord !
Thou living Bread, who life dost here afford,
O may our souls for ever live by Thee,
And Thou to us for ever precious be.

3 Fountain of goodness, Jesus, Lord and God,
Cleanse us, unclean, with Thy most cleansing
        blood;
Make us in Thee devoutly to believe,
In Thee to hope, to Thee in love to cleave.

4 O Christ, whom now beneath a veil we see,
  May what we thirst for soon our portion be,
  There in the glory of Thy dwelling-place
  To gaze on Thee unveiled, and see Thy face.
  Amen.

Thomas Aquinas, 1227–74,
tr. J. R. Woodford, 1820–85.

331

MATT. xxvi. 26–29.

'TWAS on that night when doomed to know
  The eager rage of every foe,
That night in which He was betrayed,
The Saviour of the world took bread;

2 And after thanks and glory given
  To Him that rules in earth and heaven,
  That symbol of His flesh He broke,
  And thus to all His followers spoke:

3 " My broken body thus I give
  For you, for all; take, eat, and live:
  And oft the sacred rite renew
  That brings my wondrous love to view."

4 Then in His hands the cup He raised,
  And God anew He thanked and praised,
  While kindness in His bosom glowed,
  And from His lips salvation flowed.

5 " My blood I thus pour forth," He cries,
  " To cleanse the soul in sin that lies;
  In this the covenant is sealed,
  And heaven's eternal grace revealed.

6 " With love to man this cup is fraught,
   Let all partake the sacred draught;
   Through latest ages let it pour
   In memory of My dying hour."

John Morison, 1750–98.

See also—

Come, Thou everlasting Spirit,
   227.
Jesus, Thou joy, 207.

Lord, who in Thy perfect
   wisdom, 647.

(6) Corporate Prayer

332

APPROACH, my soul, the mercy-seat,
   Where Jesus answers prayer;
There humbly fall before His feet,
   For none can perish there.

2 Thy promise is my only plea;
   With this I venture nigh;
Thou callest burdened souls to Thee,
   And such, O Lord, am I.

3 Bowed down beneath a load of sin,
   By Satan sorely pressed,
By war without and fears within,
   I come to Thee for rest.

4 Be Thou my shield and hiding-place,
   That, sheltered near Thy side,
I may my fierce accuser face,
   And tell him Thou hast died.

5 O wondrous love, to bleed and die,
   To bear the cross and shame,
That guilty sinners, such as I,
   Might plead Thy gracious name !

John Newton, 1725–1807, *altd.*

333

COME, my soul, thy suit prepare;
Jesus loves to answer prayer;
He Himself has bid thee pray,
Therefore will not say thee nay.

2 Thou art coming to a King;
Large petitions with thee bring;
For His grace and power are such,
None can ever ask too much.

3 With my burden I begin:
Lord, remove this load of sin;
Let Thy blood, for sinners spilt,
Set my conscience free from guilt.

4 Lord, I come to Thee for rest;
Take possession of my breast;
There Thy blood-bought right maintain,
And without a rival reign.

5 While I am a pilgrim here,
Let Thy love my spirit cheer;
As my guide, my guard, my friend,
Lead me to my journey's end.

6 Show me what I have to do;
Every hour my strength renew;
Let me live a life of faith;
Let me die Thy people's death.

John Newton, 1725–1807, altd.

334

FROM every stormy wind that blows,
From every swelling tide of woes,
There is a calm, a sure retreat,
'Tis found beneath the mercy-seat.

2 There is a place where Jesus sheds
  The oil of gladness o'er our heads,
  A place than all besides more sweet;
  It is the blood-stained mercy-seat.

3 There is a spot where spirits blend,
  Where friend holds fellowship with friend;
  Though sundered far, by faith they meet
  Around one common mercy-seat.

4 There, there on eagle-wing we soar,
  And time and sense seem all no more:
  And heaven comes down our souls to greet,
  And glory crowns the mercy-seat.

Hugh Stowell, 1799–1865, *altd.*

335

LUKE viii. 43–48.

HEAL us, Immanuel ! Hear our prayer.
     We wait to feel Thy touch;
Deep-wounded souls to Thee repair,
  And, Saviour, we are such.

2 Our faith is feeble, we confess;
   We faintly trust Thy word;
  But wilt Thou pity us the less ?
   Be that far from Thee, Lord.

3 Remember him who once applied
   With trembling for relief:
  " Lord, I believe," with tears he cried,
   "O help my unbelief ! "

4 She, too, who touched Thee in the press,
   And healing virtue stole,
  Was answered, " Daughter, go in peace;
   Thy faith hath made thee whole."

5 Like her, with hopes and fears we come,
  To touch Thee, if we may;
O send us not despairing home,
  Send none unhealed away.

William Cowper, 1731–1800, altd.

336

JESUS, stand among us
  In Thy risen power;
Let this time of worship
  Be a hallowed hour.

2 Breathe the Holy Spirit
   Into every heart;
Bid the fears and sorrows
   From each soul depart.

3 Thus with quickened footsteps,
   We'll pursue our way,
Watching for the dawning
   Of eternal day.

William Pennefather, 1816–73.

337

MATT. xviii. 20.

JESUS, we look to Thee,
  Thy promised presence claim;
Thou in the midst of us shalt be,
  Assembled in Thy name.

2 Thy name salvation is,
   Which now we come to prove;
Thy name is life and health and peace
   And everlasting love.

3   We meet the grace to take
     Which Thou hast freely given;
  We meet on earth for Thy dear sake,
     That we may meet in heaven.

4   Present we know Thou art,
     But O Thyself reveal;
  Now, Lord, let every waiting heart
     Thy mighty comfort feel.

5   O may Thy quickening voice
     The death of sin remove,
  And bid our inmost souls rejoice
     In hope of perfect love.

Charles Wesley, 1707–88.

338

JESUS, where'er Thy people meet,
There they behold Thy mercy seat;
Where'er they seek Thee, Thou art found,
And every place is hallowed ground.

2 For Thou, within no walls confined,
  Inhabitest the humble mind;
  Such ever bring Thee where they come,
  And going, take Thee to their home.

3 Dear shepherd of Thy chosen few,
  Thy former mercies here renew;
  Here to our waiting hearts proclaim
  The sweetness of Thy saving name.

4 Here may we prove the power of prayer
  To strengthen faith and sweeten care;
  To teach our faint desires to rise,
  And bring all heaven before our eyes.

5 Lord, we are few, but Thou art near;
  Nor short Thine arm, nor deaf Thine ear:
  O rend the heavens, come quickly down,
  And make our waiting hearts Thine own.

William Cowper, 1731–1800.

339

O FOUNT of grace that runneth o'er,
    So full, so vast, so free !
Are none too worthless, none too poor,
    To come and take of Thee ?

2 We come, O Lord, with empty hand,
    Yet turn us not away;
For grace hath nothing to demand,
    And suppliants nought to pay.

3 'Tis ours to ask and to receive;
    To take and not to buy;
'Tis Thine in sovereign grace to give,
    Yea, give abundantly.

4 And thus, in simple faith, we dare
    Our empty urn to bring;
O nerve the feeble hand of prayer
    To dip it in the spring.

Jane Crewdson, 1809–63.

340

PRAYER is the soul's sincere desire,
    Uttered or unexpressed,
The motion of a hidden fire
    That trembles in the breast.

2 Prayer is the burden of a sigh,
　　The falling of a tear,
　　The upward glancing of an eye
　　When none but God is near.

3 Prayer is the simplest form of speech
　　That infant lips can try;
　　Prayer the sublimest strains that reach
　　The Majesty on high.

4 Prayer is the contrite sinner's voice,
　　Returning from his ways,
　　While angels in their songs rejoice,
　　And cry, " Behold, he prays ! "

5 Prayer is the Christian's vital breath,
　　The Christian's native air,
　　His watchword at the gates of death;
　　He enters heaven with prayer.

6 Nor prayer is made on earth alone;
　　The Holy Spirit pleads;
　　And Jesus, on the eternal throne,
　　For sinners intercedes.

7 O Thou by whom we come to God,
　　The life, the truth, the way,
　　The path of prayer Thyself hast trod:
　　Lord, teach us how to pray !

James Montgomery, 1771–1854.

341

PRAYER to a heart of lowly love
Opens the gate of heaven above.

2 Ah, prayer is God's high dwelling-place
Wherein His children see His face.

3 From earth to heaven we build a stair,
The name by which we call it, prayer.

4 Prayer is the gracious Father's knee;
On it the child climbs lovingly.

5 Love's rain, the Spirit's holy ray,
And tears of joy are theirs who pray.

6 Prayer to a heart of lowly love
Opens the gate of heaven above.

Narayan Vaman Tilak, 1862–1919,
tr. N. MacNicol, 1870–1952.

342

A PRAYER FOR YOUTH

STANDING forth on life's rough way,
    Father, guide them;
O we know not what of harm
    May betide them;
Neath the shadow of Thy wing,
    Father, hide them;
Waking, sleeping, Lord, we pray,
    Go beside them.

2 When in prayer they cry to Thee,
    Thou wilt hear them;
From the stains of sin and shame
    Thou wilt clear them;
Mid the quicksands and the rocks,
    Thou wilt steer them;
In temptation, trial, grief,
    Be Thou near them.

3 Unto Thee we give them up;
    Lord, receive them.
In the world we know must be
    Much to grieve them,

Many striving oft and strong
  To deceive them;
Trustful, in Thy hands of love
  We must leave them.   Amen.

William Bryant, 1850–1913.

343

WHAT a friend we have in Jesus,
    All our sins and griefs to bear !
What a privilege to carry
    Everything to God in prayer !
O what peace we often forfeit,
    O what needless pain we bear—
All because we do not carry
    Everything to God in prayer !

2 Have we trials and temptations ?
    Is there trouble anywhere ?
We should never be discouraged :
    Take it to the Lord in prayer !
Can we find a friend so faithful,
    Who will all our sorrows share ?
Jesus knows our every weakness—
    Take it to the Lord in prayer !

3 Are we weak and heavy-laden,
    Cumbered with a load of care ?
Jesus only is our refuge,
    Take it to the Lord in prayer !
Do thy friends despise, forsake thee ?
    Take it to the Lord in prayer !
In His arms He'll take and shield thee,
    Thou wilt find a solace there.

Joseph Scriven, 1819–86.

See also—
Behold us, Lord, 627.
Father, in Thy presence
  kneeling, 617.
God of pity, 431.

Master, speak ! 479.
Not for our sins alone, 449.
Revive Thy work, 391.
Speak to us, Lord, 486.

344

FATHER in heaven, we wait before Thy face.
Grant us, we pray, Thy presence in this place;
Send down to longing hearts who seek Thee here,
The message of Thy love, which knows no fear.

2 Grant us the tongues of fire that fell of old,
The vision clear that made Thy prophets bold,
The open mind, the high and pure intent,
The strenuous will on noble service bent.

3 Grant us amid the shadows of our years
The inner peace that conquers grief and tears;
Teach us the holy secret Jesus saw,
The soul's beatitude, the perfect law.

4 O living God, we need Thy help and power
To consecrate the purpose of this hour :
Grant us the shield of faith, the sword of light;
Then send us forth to battle for the right.

Amen.

Frank Phalen.

345

FATHER, O hear us, seeking now to praise
Thee;
Thou art our hope, our confidence, our Saviour,
Thou art the refuge of the generations,
Lord God almighty.

2 Maker of all things, loving all Thy creatures,
God of all goodness, infinite in mercy,
Changeless, eternal, holiest and wisest,
Hear Thou Thy children.

3 Childhood shall iearn to know Thee and revere
　　Thee;
　Manhood shall serve Thee, strong in power and
　　knowledge;
　Old age shall trust Thee, having felt Thy mercy,
　　　E'en mid the shadows.

4 Bless Thou our purpose, consecrate our labours,
　Keep us still faithful to the best and truest,
　Guide us, protect us, make us not unworthy
　　　Learners of Jesus.

5 Glory and honour, thanks and adoration,
　Still will we bring, O God of men and angels,
　To Thee, the holy, merciful and mighty
　　　Father, our Father.
　　　　　　　　　　　　　Amen.
　　　　　　　　Douglas Walmsley, 1848–1940.

346

FATHER of mercies, bow Thine ear,
Attentive to our earnest prayer:
We plead for those who plead for Thee;
Successful pleaders may they be.

2 How great their work, how vast their charge !
　Do Thou their anxious souls enlarge;
　Their best acquirements are our gain;
　We share the blessings they obtain.

3 Clothe, then, with energy divine
　Their words, and let those words be Thine;
　To them Thy sacred truth reveal,
　Suppress their fear, inflame their zeal:

4 Teach them to sow the precious seed,
　Teach them Thy chosen flock to feed,
　Teach them immortal souls to gain,
　Souls that will well reward their pain.

5 Let thronging multitudes around
　Hear from their lips the joyful sound,
　In humble strains Thy grace implore,
　And feel Thy new-creating power.

Benjamin Beddome, 1717–93.

347

G IVE me the faith which can remove
　　And sink the mountain to a plain;
Give me the childlike, praying love,
　Which longs to build Thy house again;
Thy love, let it my heart o'erpower,
Let it my ransomed soul devour.

2 I would the precious time redeem,
　　And longer live for this alone—
To spend and to be spent for them
　　Who have not yet my Saviour known;
Fully on these my mission prove,
And only breathe to breathe Thy love.

3 My talents, gifts, and graces, Lord,
　　Into Thy blessèd hands receive;
And let me live to preach Thy word,
　　And let me to Thy glory live;
My every sacred moment spend
In publishing the sinners' friend.

4 Enlarge, inflame, and fill my heart
　　With boundless charity divine;
So shall I all my strength exert,
　　And love them with a zeal like Thine;
And lead them to Thine open side,
The sheep for whom their shepherd died.

Charles Wesley, 1707–88.

348

HIGH Priest divine, from whom alone
  Can come the grace Thy suppliants need,
Our pledge this day, our purpose, own,
  Thy sheep to tend, Thy lambs to feed.
Thy blessing on Thy Church bestow,
Thy favour to Thy servants show.

2 Earnest in thought, direct in speech,
    Thy truth in love may we declare;
  Lowly to learn and apt to teach,
    Of Thy breathed messages aware.
  Thy hand unseen now on us lay,
  Lest we Thy solemn trust betray.

3 In any testing time of fear
    Deal gently with our spirit, Lord;
  Still make Thy counsel to us clear;
    And for fresh tasks new strength afford.
  Always may truth and grace control
  The inmost region of our soul.

4 Thy gifts of grace to us impart,
    That we may serve Thy Church below;
  One in design and one in heart,
    Grant us Thy threefold peace to know.
  So at the last on Thy right hand
  May we among Thy servants stand.   Amen.

H. Elvet Lewis, 1860–1953.

349

FOR TEACHERS

LORD, from whose hand we take our charge,
  The care of childhood and of youth,
To set their feet upon life's road
  In loyalty to right and truth:
    O hear us as of Thee we ask
    The strength and wisdom for our task.

2 That we may open doors on life,
  And share the visions that we see
Of the deep wonder of the world
  And man's heroic history,
    And wake in them the answering chord:
    Give us the skill and patience, Lord.

3 That we may use all law and rule,
  Not rudely to oppress and bind,
But as the needed discipline
  For freedom of the soul and mind,
    Equipped to face, with fearless eyes
    And steady faith, life's enterprise;

4 That we may understand their need,
  When comes their hour of strain and stress,
With sympathy to help and save
  From sordid thoughts and bitterness:
    Lord, use our struggles, conflicts, fears,
    To light for them the troubled years.

5 'Tis ours to give and spend ourselves,
  Nor grudge the labour and the pain
To sow the seed of noble worth;
  Yet without Thee our toil is vain:
    Great Lord of life, 'tis Thine to give
    The quickening breath by which they live.

                    W. Charter Piggott, 1872–1943.

350

FOR ORDINATIONS AND INDUCTIONS

LORD of true light, we gratefully adore Thee
    For all Thy gifts bestowed upon our race;
For saints of old, who made their vows before
    Thee,
  And told the world the wonders of Thy grace.

2 We praise Thee, Lord, that now the light is falling
    Here on Thy servant in this solemn hour;
Confirm in him his high and holy calling,
    Endue him with Thy wisdom, love and power.

3 Be in his mind, the truth of all his teaching;
    Give him the faith that welcomes all the light;
Till, from the shadows to Thy presence reaching,
    He sees the glory that shall end our night.

4 Be in his heart, the fount of all his loving;
    Make him a shepherd, kind to young and old,
Patient and watchful when Thy sheep are roving,
    Tending with care the lambs within the fold.

5 Be in his will, his strength for self-denial;
    Fit him to follow Thee through pain and loss,
Serving the world, until through every trial
    He learns at length the triumph of the cross.

6 For all Thy servants hear our supplication;
    Still give by them the word that brings release,
Till the glad song is heard in every nation,
    Glory to God on high, on earth be peace. Amen.

H. R. Moxley, 1881–

351

POUR out Thy Spirit from on high;
    Lord, Thine ordainèd servants bless;
Graces and gifts to each supply,
    And clothe them with Thy righteousness.

2 Within Thy temple when they stand,
    To teach the truth, as taught by Thee,
Saviour, like stars in Thy right hand
    The angels of the churches be !

3 Wisdom and zeal and faith impart,
    Firmness with meekness, from above,
To bear Thy people on their heart,
    And love the souls whom Thou dost love;

4 To watch and pray, and never faint;
    By day and night strict guard to keep;
To warn the sinner, cheer the saint,
    Nourish Thy lambs, and feed Thy sheep;

5 Then, when their work is finished here,
    In humble hope their charge resign.
When the chief shepherd shall appear,
    O God, may they and we be Thine. Amen.

James Montgomery, 1771–1854.

352

SEND Thou, O Lord, to every place
Swift messengers before Thy face,
The heralds of Thy wondrous grace,
Where Thou Thyself wilt come.

2 Send men whose eyes have seen the King,
Whose ears have heard His summons ring;
Send such Thy lost ones home to bring;
Send them where Thou wilt come.

3 To bring good news to souls in sin;
The bruised and broken hearts to win;
In every place to bring them in,
Where Thou Thyself wilt come.

4 Gird each one with the Spirit's sword,
The sword of Thine own deathless word;
And make them conquerors, conquering Lord,
Where Thou Thyself wilt come.

5 Raise up, O Lord, the Holy Ghost,
From this broad land a mighty host,
Their war-cry, " We will seek the lost,
Where Thou, O Christ, wilt come ! "

M. C. Gates (written 1888).

353

SHINE Thou upon us, Lord,
True light of men, to-day;
And through the written word
Thy very self display;
That so from hearts which burn
With gazing on Thy face,
The little ones may learn
The wonders of Thy grace.

2 Breathe Thou upon us, Lord,
Thy Spirit's living flame,
That so with one accord
Our lips may tell Thy name:
Give Thou the hearing ear,
Fix Thou the wandering thought,
That those we teach may hear
The great things Thou hast wrought.

3 Speak thou for us, O Lord,
In all we say of Thee:
According to Thy word
Let all our teaching be;
That so Thy lambs may know
Their own true shepherd's voice,
Where'er He leads them go,
And in His love rejoice.

4 Live Thou within us, Lord,
   Thy mind and will be ours;
Be Thou beloved, adored,
   And served with all our powers;
That so our lives may teach
   Thy children what Thou art,
And plead, by more than speech,
   For Thee with every heart.   Amen.

John Ellerton, 1826–93.

354

WE thank Thee, Lord, for using us
   For Thee to work and speak;
However trembling is the hand,
   The voice however weak.

2 We bless Thee for each seed of truth
   That we through Thee have sowed
Upon this waste and barren earth,—
   The living seed of God.

3 We thank Thee, gracious God, for all
   Of witness there hath been
From us, in any path of life,
   Though silent and unseen.

4 For solace ministered perchance
   In days of grief and pain;
For peace to troubled, weary souls,
   Not spoken all in vain.

5 Lord, keep us still the same as in
   Remembered days of old;
O keep us fervent still in love,
   Mid many waxing cold.

6 Help us, O Christ, to grasp each truth
    With hand as firm and true
As when we clasped it first to heart,
    A treasure fresh and new;

7 Thy name to name, Thyself to own
    With voice unfaltering,
And face as bold and unashamed
    As in our Christian spring.

8 O honour higher, truer far
    Than earthly fame could bring,
Thus to be used, in work like this,
    So long, by such a King!

Horatius Bonar, 1808–89.

See also—

Section VIII (6), Service and Witness.
Forget them not, 368.
Head of the Church, 258.
I bind unto myself, 433.
Lord of the living harvest, 381.

Lord, Thy servants, 383.
O Christ our Lord, 323.
O Master, when Thou callest, 552.
Witness, ye men and angels, 304.

(8) THE FELLOWSHIP OF BELIEVERS

355

BLEST be the tie that binds
  Our hearts in Christian love;
The fellowship of kindred minds
  Is like to that above.

2   Before our Father's throne
    We pour our ardent prayers;
Our fears, our hopes, our aims are one,
    Our comforts and our cares.

3   We share our mutual woes,
       Our mutual burdens bear,
  And often for each other flows
       The sympathizing tear.

4   When for awhile we part,
       This thought will soothe our pain,
  That we shall still be joined in heart,
       And hope to meet again.

5   This glorious hope revives
       Our courage by the way,
  While each in expectation lives,
       And longs to see the day.

6   From sorrow, toil, and pain,
       And sin we shall be free;
  And perfect love and friendship reign
       Through all eternity.

John Fawcett, 1740–1817, altd.

356

CHRIST is the King! O friends rejoice;
  Brothers and sisters, with one voice
Make all men know He is your choice.
Ring out ye bells, give tongue, give tongue;
Let your most merry peal be rung,
While our exultant song is sung.

2 O magnify the Lord, and raise
Anthems of joy and holy praise
For Christ's brave saints of ancient days,
Who with a faith for ever new
Followed the King, and round Him drew
Thousands of faithful men and true.

3 O Christian women, Christian men,
All the world over, seek again
The Way disciples followed then.
Christ through all ages is the same:
Place the same hope in His great name,
With the same faith His word proclaim.

4 Let love's unconquerable might
Your scattered companies unite
In service to the Lord of light:
So shall God's will on earth be done,
New lamps be lit, new tasks begun,
And the whole Church at last be one.

G. K. A. Bell, 1883–1958.

357

COMMAND Thy blessing from above,
    O God, on all assembled here;
Behold us with a Father's love,
    While we look up with filial fear.

2 Command Thy blessing, Jesus, Lord;
    May we Thy true disciples be;
Speak to each heart the mighty word,
    Say to the weakest, " Follow me."

3 Command Thy blessing in this hour,
    Spirit of truth, and fill this place
With humbling and exalting power,
    With quickening and confirming grace.

4 O Thou, our maker, saviour, guide,
    One true eternal God confessed,
May nought in life or death divide
    The saints in Thy communion blest.

5 With Thee and these for ever bound,
   May all who here in prayer unite,
With joyful songs Thy throne surround,
   Rest in Thy love and reign in light.

James Montgomery, 1771–1854.

358

ETERNAL Ruler of the ceaseless round
   Of circling planets singing on their way;
Guide of the nations from the night profound
   Into the glory of the perfect day;
Rule in our hearts, that we may ever be
Guided and strengthened, and upheld by Thee.

2 We are of Thee, the children of Thy love,
   The brothers of Thy well-belovèd Son;
Descend, O Holy Spirit, like a dove,
   Into our hearts, that we may be as one,—
As one with Thee, to whom we ever tend;
As one with Him, our brother and our friend.

3 We would be one in hatred of all wrong,
   One in our love of all things sweet and fair,
One with the joy that breaketh into song,
   One with the grief that trembles into prayer,
One in the power that makes Thy children free
To follow truth, and thus to follow Thee.

4 O clothe us with Thy heavenly armour, Lord,—
   Thy trusty shield, Thy sword of love divine;
Our inspiration be Thy constant word;
   We ask no victories that are not Thine:
Give or withhold, let pain or pleasure be,
Enough to know that we are serving Thee.

J. W. Chadwick, 1840–1904.

359

FATHER of men, in whom are one
All human kind beneath the sun,
Stablish our work in Thee begun.

2 Except the house be built by Thee
In vain the builders' toil must be;
O strengthen our infirmity.

3 Man lives not for himself alone,
In others' good he finds his own;
Life's worth in fellowship is known.

4 We, friends and comrades on life's way,
Gather within these walls to pray;
Bless Thou our fellowship to-day.

5 O Christ, our elder brother, who,
By serving man, God's will didst do,
Help us to serve our brethren too.

6 Guide us to seek the things above,
The base to shun, the pure approve,
To live by Thy free law of love.

7 In all our work, in all our play,
Be with us, Lord, our friend, our stay;
Lead onward to the perfect day.

8 Then may we know, earth's lesson o'er,
With comrades missed, or gone before,
Heaven's fellowship for evermore.

H. C. Shuttleworth, 1850–1900.

360

HE wants not friends that hath Thy love,
And may converse and walk with Thee,
And with Thy saints here and above,
With whom for ever we must be.

2 In the communion of Thy saints
   Is wisdom, safety, and delight;
And when my heart declines and faints,
   'Tis raisèd by their heat and light.

3 Our friends who leave us are not lost;
   The several vessels of Thy fleet,
Though parted now, by tempests tost,
   Shall safely in the haven meet.

4 Still we are centred all in Thee,
   Members, though distant, of one Head:
In the same family we be,
   By the same faith and spirit led.

5 Before Thy throne we daily meet
   As joint petitioners to Thee;
In spirit we each other greet,
   And shall again each other see.

6 The heavenly hosts, world without end,
   Shall be my company above;
And Thou, my best and surest friend,
   Who shall divide me from Thy love?

Richard Baxter, 1615-91.

361

LORD from whom all blessings flow,
Perfecting the Church below,
Steadfast may we cleave to Thee,
Love, the mystic union be:
Join our faithful spirits, join
Each to each, and all to Thine;
Lead us through the paths of peace
On to perfect holiness.

2 Move, and actuate, and guide;
Divers gifts to each divide:
Placed according to Thy will,
Let us all our work fulfil;
Never from our office move;
Needful to each other prove;
Use the grace on each bestowed,
Tempered by the art of God.

3 Sweetly may we all agree,
Touched with softest sympathy:
There is neither bond nor free,
Great nor servile, Lord, in Thee:
Love, like death, hath all destroyed,
Rendered all distinctions void;
Names, and sects, and parties fall,
Thou, O Christ, art all in all.

Charles Wesley, 1707–88.

362

OUR Father God, Thy name we praise,
    To Thee our hymns addressing,
And joyfully our voices raise
    Thy faithfulness confessing;
Assembled by Thy grace, O Lord,
We seek fresh guidance from Thy Word;
    Now grant anew Thy blessing.

2 Touch, Lord, the lips that speak for Thee;
    Set words of truth before us,
That we may grow in constancy,
    The light of wisdom o'er us.
Give us this day our daily bread;
May hungry souls again be fed;
    May heavenly food restore us.

3 As with our brethren here we meet,
  Thy grace alone can feed us.
As here we gather at Thy feet
  We pray that Thou wilt heed us.
The power is Thine, O Lord divine,
The kingdom and the rule are Thine.
  May Jesus Christ still lead us !

From the Anabaptist Ausbund, 16*th cent.*,
tr. E. A. Payne, 1902–

363

STAND up and bless the Lord,
  Ye people of His choice :
Stand up and bless the Lord your God,
  With heart, and soul, and voice.

2 Though high above all praise,
     Above all blessing high,
Who would not fear His holy name,
     And laud and magnify ?

3 O for the living flame
     From His own altar brought,
To touch our lips, our minds inspire,
     And wing to heaven our thought !

4 There, with benign regard,
     Our hymns He deigns to hear;
Though unrevealed to mortal sense,
     The spirit feels Him near.

5 God is our strength and song,
     And His salvation ours;
Then be His love in Christ proclaimed
     With all our ransomed powers.

6   Stand up and bless the Lord
    The Lord your God adore;
Stand up, and bless His glorious name
    Henceforth for evermore.

James Montgomery, 1771–1854.

See also—

Farewell, my friends, 759.
Father in heaven, 344.
From every stormy wind, 334.
Happy are they, 496.
Heal us, Immanuel! 335.
Jesus, we look to Thee, 337.

Jesus, where'er, 338.
O God our Father, 765.
Sing hallelujah, 27.
Through the night, 559.
We praise, we worship, 33.
Ye holy angels bright, 36.

(9) ITS WITNESS AND WORLD-WIDE MISSION

364

CHRIST for the world! we sing:
    The world to Christ we bring
        With loving zeal;
The poor, and them that mourn,
The faint and overborne.
Sin-sick and sorrow-worn,
    Whom Christ doth heal.

2 Christ for the world! we sing:
    The world to Christ we bring
        With fervent prayer;
The wayward and the lost,
By restless passion tossed,
Redeemed at countless cost
    From dark despair.

3 Christ for the world! we sing:
    The world to Christ we bring
        With one accord;
With us the work to share,
With us reproach to dare,
With us the cross to bear
    For Christ our Lord.

4 Christ for the world ! we sing:
The world to Christ we bring
  With joyful song;
The new-born souls, whose days,
Reclaimed from error's ways,
Inspired with hope and praise,
  To Christ belong.

Samuel Wolcott, 1813–86.

365

THE ROPEHOLDERS' HYMN

DOWN the mines for buried treasure,
    See our gallant comrades go,
Down into the lonely darkness,
  Seeking lost ones far below.
" Hold the ropes," their voice is calling,
  " Hold the ropes, the while we bring
Back from depths of sin and sorrow,
  Gems most precious for our King."

Hold the ropes, then, hold them bravely,
  Hold them firmly to the end;
O remember, O remember
  Precious lives on you depend.

2 Learn how Jesus loves the lost ones,
  Down amid the darkness there,
All the gold of all the mountains
  Cannot with their worth compare;
Freely of His grace receiving,
  Boldly His great cause maintain,
They most blest who give most nobly,
  Other souls for Christ to gain.

3 Work for those, who, in the darkness,
  Toil to set the captives free,
You may share in all their labour,
  Friend and helper you may be;

Pray for them with heart grown ten
You are near them when you pray,
O the power divine a prayer brings
To the labourers far away !

F. A. Jackson, 1867–1942.

366

FAR round the world Thy children sing their
song,
From east and west their voices sweetly blend,
Praising the Lord in whom young lives are strong,
Jesus, our guide, our hero, and our friend.

2 Guide of the pilgrim clambering to the height,
Hero on whom our fearful hearts depend,
Friend of the wanderer yearning for the light,
Jesus, our guide, our hero, and our friend.

3 Where Thy wide ocean, wave on rolling wave,
Beats through the ages on each island shore,
They praise their Lord whose hand alone can save,
Whose sea of love surrounds them evermore.

4 Thy sun-kissed children on earth's spreading plain,
Where Asia's rivers water all the land,
Sing, as they watch Thy fields of glowing grain,
Praise to the Lord who feeds them with His
hand.

5 Still there are lands where none have seen Thy face,
Children whose hearts have never shared Thy
joy,
Yet Thou would'st pour on these Thy radiant
grace;
Give Thy glad strength to every girl and boy.

6 All round the world let children sing Thy song,
　　From east and west their voices sweetly blend,
　Praising the Lord in whom young lives are strong,
　　Jesus, our guide, our hero, and our friend.

Basil Mathews, 1879–1951.

367

FATHER, let Thy kingdom come,—
　　Let it come with living power;
Speak at length the final word,
　　Usher in the triumph hour.

2 As it came in days of old,
　　In the deepest hearts of men,
When Thy martyrs died for Thee,
　　Let it come, O God, again.

3 Tyrant thrones and idol shrines,
　　Let them from their place be hurled:
Enter on Thy better reign,—
　　Wear the crown of this poor world.

4 O what long, sad years have gone,
　　Since Thy Church was taught this prayer !
O what eyes have watched and wept
　　For the dawning everywhere !

5 Break, triumphant day of God !
　　Break at last, our heart to cheer;
Throbbing souls and holy songs
　　Wait to hail Thy dawning here.

6 Empires, temples, sceptres, thrones,—
　　May they all for God be won !
And, in every human heart,
　　Father, let Thy kingdom come.

J. P. Hopps, 1834–1912.

368

FORGET them not, O Christ, who stand
Thy vanguard in the distant land.

2 In flood, in flame, in dark, in dread,
Sustain, we pray, each lifted head.

3 Exalt them over every fear,
In peril come Thyself more near.

4 Thine is the work they strive to do,
Their foes so many, they so few.

5 Be with Thine own, Thy loved, who stand,
Christ's vanguard, in the storm-swept land.
                                        Amen.
                    Margaret Sangster, 1838–1912.

369

LUKE xiii. 29.

FROM north and south and east and west,
When shall the peoples, long unblest,
All find their everlasting rest,
        O Christ, in Thee ?

2 When shall the climes of ageless snow
Be with the gospel light aglow,
And all men their redeemer know,
        O Christ, in Thee ?

3 When on each southern balmy coast
Shall ransomed men, in countless host,
Rise, heart and voice, to make sweet boast,
        O Christ, in Thee ?

4 O when in all the orient lands,
  From cities white and flaming sands
  Shall men lift dedicated hands,
        O Christ, to Thee ?

5 O when shall heathen darkness roll
  Away in light, from pole to pole,
  And endless day by every soul
        Be found in Thee ?

6 Bring, Lord, the long predicted hour,
  The ages' diadem and flower,
  When all shall find their refuge, tower,
        And home in Thee.

G. T. Coster, 1835–1912.

370

" GOD is with us, God is with us,"
    So our brave forefathers sang,
Far across the field of battle,
  Loud their holy war-cry rang;
Never once they feared nor faltered,
Never once they ceased to sing—
God is with us, God is with us,
  Christ our Lord shall reign as King!

2 Great the heritage they left us,
  Great the conquests to be won,
Armèd hosts to meet and scatter,
  Larger duties to be done,
Raise the song they nobly taught us,
  Round the wide world let it ring:

3 Speed the cross through all the nations,
  Speed the victories of love,
Preach the gospel of redemption
  Wheresoever men may move;
Onward, then, with ranks unbroken.
  Sure of triumph, shout and sing:
God is with us, God is with us,
  Christ our Lord shall reign as King!

W. J. Mathams, 1853–1931, *altd.*

371

Isaiah xi. 9.

GOD is working His purpose out as year
succeeds to year.
God is working His purpose out, and the time is
drawing near;
Nearer and nearer draws the time, the time that
shall surely be,
When the earth shall be filled with the glory of
God as the waters cover the sea.

2 From utmost east to utmost west where'er man's
foot hath trod,
By the mouth of many messengers goes forth the
voice of God:—
" Give ear to Me, ye continents, ye isles, give ear
to Me,
That the earth may be filled with the glory of God
as the waters cover the sea."

3 What can we do to work God's work, to prosper
and increase
The brotherhood of all mankind, the reign of the
Prince of peace ?
What can we do to hasten the time, the time that
shall surely be,
When the earth shall be filled with the glory of
God as the waters cover the sea ?

4 March we forth in the strength of God with the
banner of Christ unfurled,
That the light of the glorious gospel of truth may
shine throughout the world :
Fight we the fight with sorrow and sin, to set their
captives free,
That the earth may be filled with the glory of God
as the waters cover the sea.

5 All we can do is nothing worth unless God blesses
    the deed;
Vainly we hope for the harvest-tide till God gives
    life to the seed;
Yet nearer and nearer draws the time, the time
    that shall surely be,
When the earth shall be filled with the glory of
    God as the waters cover the sea.

A. C. Ainger, 1841–1919.

372

GOD of grace and God of glory,
    On Thy people pour Thy power;
Crown Thine ancient Church's story;
    Bring her bud to glorious flower.
        Grant us wisdom,
        Grant us courage,
    For the facing of this hour.

2 Lo ! the hosts of evil round us
    Scorn Thy Christ, assail His ways !
Fears and doubts too long have bound us;
    Free our hearts to work and praise.
        Grant us wisdom,
        Grant us courage,
    For the living of these days.

3 Heal Thy children's warring madness;
    Bend our pride to Thy control;
Shame our wanton, selfish gladness,
    Rich in things and poor in soul.
        Grant us wisdom,
        Grant us courage,
    Lest we miss Thy kingdom's goal.

4 Set our feet on lofty places;
　　Gird our lives that they may be
　Armoured with all Christlike graces
　　In the fight to set men free.
　　　　Grant us wisdom,
　　　　Grant us courage,
　　That we fail not man nor Thee.

5 Save us from weak resignation
　　To the evils we deplore;
　Let the search for Thy salvation
　　Be our glory evermore.
　　　　Grant us wisdom,
　　　　Grant us courage,
　　Serving Thee whom we adore.

H. E. Fosdick, 1878-

373

PSALM lxvii.

GOD of mercy, God of grace,
　Show the brightness of Thy face:
Shine upon us, Saviour, shine;
Fill Thy Church with light divine;
And Thy saving health extend
Unto earth's remotest end.

2 Let the people praise Thee, Lord;
　Be by all that live adored;
　Let the nations shout and sing
　Glory to their Saviour King;
　At Thy feet their tribute pay
　And Thy holy will obey.

3 Let the people praise Thee, Lord;
　Earth shall then her fruits afford,
　God to man His blessing give,
　Man to God devoted live;
　All below, and all above,
　One in joy and light and love.

H. F. Lyte, 1793–1847.

374

HILLS of the north, rejoice;
    River and mountain-spring,
Hark to the advent voice;
    Valley and lowland, sing !
Though absent long, your Lord is nigh;
He judgment brings and victory.

2 Isles of the southern seas,
    Deep in your coral caves
Pent be each warring breeze,
    Lulled be your restless waves:
He comes to reign with boundless sway,
And makes your wastes His great highway.

3 Lands of the east, awake !
    Soon shall your sons be free:
The sleep of ages break,
    And rise to liberty:
On your far hills, long cold and grey,
Has dawned the everlasting day.

4 Shores of the utmost west,
    Ye that have waited long,
Unvisited, unblest,
    Break forth to swelling song:
High raise the note, that Jesus died,
Yet lives and reigns, the crucified !

5 Shóut while ye journey home,
    Songs be in every mouth;
Lo, from the north we come,
    From east, and west, and south:
City of God, the bond are free:
We come to live and reign in Thee.

C. E. Oakley, 1832–65.

375

LEAD on, O King eternal,
   The day of march has come;
Henceforth in fields of conquest
   Thy tents shall be our home.
Through days of preparation
   Thy grace has made us strong,
And now, O King eternal,
   We lift our battle song.

2 Lead on, O King eternal,
   Till sin's fierce war shall cease,
And holiness shall whisper
   The sweet amen of peace:
For not with sword's loud clashing,
   Nor roll of stirring drums:
With deeds of love and mercy,
   The heavenly kingdom comes.

3 Lead on, O King eternal,
   We follow not with fears,
For gladness breaks like morning
   Where'er Thy face appears;
Thy cross is lifted o'er us;
   We journey in its light;
The crown awaits the conquest;
   Lead on, O God of might!

E. W. Shurtleff, 1862–1917.

376

LET the song go round the earth:
   Jesus Christ is Lord!
Sound His praises, tell His worth,
   Be His name adored;
Every clime and every tongue
Join the grand, the glorious song.

2 Let the song go round the earth !
  From the eastern sea,
Where the daylight has its birth,
  Glad, and bright, and free;
China's millions join the strains,
Waft them on to India's plains.

3 Let the song go round the earth !
  Lands where Islam's sway
Darkly broods o'er home and hearth,
  Cast their bonds away;
Let His praise from Afric's shore
Rise and swell her wide lands o'er.

4 Let the song go round the earth !
  Where the summer smiles,
Let the notes of holy mirth
  Break from distant isles;
Inland forests, dark and dim,
Snow-bound coasts give back the hymn.

5 Let the song go round the earth :
  Jesus Christ is King !
With the story of His worth,
  Let the whole world ring,
Him creation all adore
Evermore and evermore.

Sarah G. Stock, 1838–96.

377

PSALM xlv

LET us sing the King Messiah,
  King of righteousness and peace;
Hail Him, all His happy subjects,
  Never let His praises cease:
    Ever hail Him;
  Never let His praises cease.

2 How transcendent are Thy glories,
　　Fairer than the sons of men,
While Thy blessèd mediation
　　Brings us back to God again:
　　　　Blest redeemer,
　　How we triumph in Thy reign !

3 Gird Thy sword on, mighty hero,
　　Make the word of truth Thy car;
Prosper in Thy course majestic;
　　All success attend Thy war:
　　　　Gracious victor,
　　Let mankind before Thee bow.

4 Majesty combined with meekness,
　　Righteousness and peace unite
To ensure Thy blessèd conquests;
　　On, great prince, assert Thy right:
　　　　Ride triumphant
　　All around the conquered globe.

5 Blest are all that touch Thy sceptre;
　　Blest are all that own Thy reign,
Freed from sin, that worst of tyrants,
　　Rescued from its galling chain:
　　　　Saints and angels,
　　All who know Thee bless Thy reign.

John Ryland, 1753–1825, altd.

378

LIFT up your heads, ye gates of brass,
　　Ye bars of iron, yield,
And let the King of glory pass,
　　The cross is in the field.

2 Ye armies of the living God,
　　His dedicated host,
Where hallowed footstep never trod
　　Take your appointed post.

3 Follow the cross; the ark of peace
   Accompany your path;
To slaves and rebels bring release
   From bondage and from wrath.

4 Though few and small and weak your bands,
   Strong in your captain's strength,
Go to the conquest of all lands;
   All must be His at length.

5 Then fear not, faint not, halt not now,
   Quit you like men, be strong:
To Christ shall all the nations bow,
   And sing the triumph song:

6 Uplifted are the gates of brass,
   The bars of iron yield;
Behold the King of glory pass:
   The cross has won the field.

James Montgomery, 1771–1854.

379

LORD, her watch Thy Church is keeping;
   When shall earth Thy rule obey?
When shall end the night of weeping?
   When shall break the promised day?
See the whitening harvest languish,
   Waiting still the labourers' toil;
Was it vain—Thy Son's deep anguish?
   Shall the strong retain the spoil?

2 Tidings sent to every creature
   Millions yet have never heard;
Can they hear without a preacher?
   Lord almighty, give the word.

Give the word; in every nation
  Let the gospel trumpet sound,
Witnessing a world's salvation,
  To the earth's remotest bound.

3 Then the end,—Thy Church completed,
  All Thy chosen gathered in,
With their King in glory seated,
  Satan bound, and banished sin;
Gone for ever parting, weeping,
  Hunger, sorrow, death, and pain:
Lo ! her watch Thy Church is keeping;
  Come, Lord Jesus, come to reign.

Henry Downton, 1818–85.

380

LORD of light, whose name outshineth
  All the stars and suns of space,
Deign to make us Thy co-workers
  In the kingdom of Thy grace;
Use us to fulfil Thy purpose
  In the gift of Christ Thy Son:
  Father, as in highest heaven,
  So on earth Thy will be done.

2 By the toil of lonely workers
  In some far outlying field;
By the courage where the radiance
  Of the cross is still revealed;
By the victories of meekness,
  Through reproach and suffering won:

3 Grant that knowledge, still increasing,
  At Thy feet may lowly kneel;
With Thy grace our triumphs hallow,
  With Thy charity our zeal;
Lift the nations from the shadows
  To the gladness of the sun:

4 By the prayers of faithful watchmen,
   Never silent day or night;
By the cross of Jesus bringing
   Peace to men, and healing light;
By the love that passeth knowledge,
   Making all Thy children one:
      Father, as in highest heaven,
      So on earth Thy will be done.
                              Amen.
                    H. Elvet Lewis, 1860–1953.

381

LUKE X. 2.

L ORD of the living harvest
      That whitens o'er the plain,
Where angels soon shall gather
   Their sheaves of golden grain,
Accept these hands to labour,
   These hearts to trust and love,
And deign with them to hasten
   Thy kingdom from above.

2 As labourers in Thy vineyard,
   Send us out, Christ, to be,
Content to bear the burden
   Of weary days for Thee;
We ask no other wages,
   When Thou shalt call us home,
But to have shared the travail
   That makes Thy kingdom come.

3 Come down, Thou Holy Spirit,
   And fill our souls with light;
Clothe us in spotless raiment,
   In linen clean and white;
Within Thy sacred temple
   Be with us, where we stand,
And sanctify Thy people
   Throughout this happy land.

4 Be with us, God the Father,
  Be with us, God the Son,
Be with us, God the Spirit,
  O blessèd Three in One !
Make us a royal priesthood,
  Thee rightly to adore,
And fill us with Thy fulness,
  Now, and for evermore. Amen.

J. S. B. Monsell, 1811–75.

382

LORD, Thy kingdom bring triumphant,
  Give this world Thy liberty,
May Thy Spirit's strong compulsion
  Rule our tides of energy:

2 Where the vessel cleaves the ocean,
  Or the pilot steers his plane,
Where the miner toils in darkness,
  And the farmer sows the grain.

3 Consecrate Thy people's labour
  At the airfield, mill and port;
With the gladness of Thy presence
  Bless our homes and grace our sport.

4 Let Thy mercy and Thy wisdom
  Rule our courts and parliament,
And to soldier, sage and scholar
  May Thy light and truth be sent.

5 By the pioneer's endeavour,
  By the word of printed page,
By the martyr's dying witness,
  And Thy saints in every age:

6 By the living voice of preacher,
    By the skill of surgeon's hand,
  By the far borne broadcast tidings
    Speaking peace from land to land:

7 Lord, Thy kingdom bring triumphant,
    Visit us this living hour,
  Let Thy toiling, sinning children
    See Thy kingdom come in power.

A. F. Bayly, 1901–

383

LORD, Thy servants forth are going,
    Each has heard the Master's call,
Seeds of life eternal sowing
    In His name who died for all;
        O sustain them
    Till the shades of evening fall.

2 Then, where desert sands are glowing
    Neath the noontide's sultry heat,
  Living streams shall soon be flowing
    Mid the meadow fair and sweet;
        And a harvest
    Shall their raptured vision greet.

3 Lo ! Thy hand is now bestowing
    Gifts abundant, rich and free;
  Love, her wondrous debt still owing,
    Brings Thy gifts again to Thee
        That Thy kingdom
    May extend from sea to sea.

4 Like the south wind gently blowing
    Comes Thy Spirit's breath of balm;
  List ! the sound is louder growing !
    Look ! the Lord makes bare His arm !
        Hallelujah !
    Wakes the universal psalm.

W. E. Winks, 1842–1926.

384

O CHRIST, our true and only light,
Illumine those who sit in night,
Let those afar now hear Thy voice,
And in Thy fold with us rejoice.

2 And all who else have strayed from Thee,
O gently seek ! Thy healing be
To every wounded conscience given,
And let them also share Thy heaven.

3 O make the deaf to hear Thy word,
And teach the dumb to speak, dear Lord,
Who dare not yet the faith avow,
Though secretly they hold it now.

4 Shine on the darkened and the cold,
Recall the wanderers from Thy fold,
Those now unite who walk apart,
Confirm the weak and doubting heart.

5 So they with us may evermore
Such grace with wondering thanks adore,
And endless praise to Thee be given
By all Thy Church in earth and heaven.

Johann Heerman, 1585–1647.
tr. *Catherine Winkworth*, 1827–78.

385

O LORD our God, arise;
The cause of truth maintain,
And wide o'er all the peopled world
Extend her blessèd reign.

2   Thou Prince of life, arise;
Nor let Thy glory cease;
Far spread the conquests of Thy grace,
And bless the earth with peace.

3 Thou Holy Ghost, arise;
Expand Thy quickening wing,
And o'er a dark and ruined world
Let light and order spring.

4 All on the earth, arise;
To God the Saviour sing;
From shore to shore, from earth to heaven,
Let echoing anthems ring.

Ralph Wardlaw, 1779–1853.

386

O NORTH, with all thy vales of green !
O south, with all thy palms !
From peopled towns and fields between
Uplift the voice of psalms,
Raise, ancient east, the anthem high,
And let the youthful west reply.

2 Lo ! in the clouds of heaven appears
God's well-belovèd Son;
He brings a train of brighter years,
His kingdom is begun :
He comes a guilty world to bless
With mercy, truth and righteousness.

3 O Father, haste the promised hour
When at His feet shall lie
All rule, authority, and power
Beneath the ample sky :
When He shall reign from pole to pole,
The Lord of every human soul;

4 When all shall heed the words He said,
Amid their daily cares,
And by the loving life He led
Shall strive to pattern theirs :
And He who conquered death shall win
The mightier conquest over sin.

W. Cullen Bryant, 1794–1878.

387

O SPIRIT of the living God,
In all Thy plenitude of grace,
Where'er the foot of man has trod,
Descend on our apostate race.

2 Give tongues of fire and hearts of love
To preach the reconciling word;
Give power and unction from above,
Whene'er the joyful sound is heard.

3 Be darkness, at Thy coming, light;
Confusion, order in Thy path;
Souls without strength inspire with might;
Bid mercy triumph over wrath.

4 O Spirit of the Lord, prepare
All the round earth her God to meet;
Breathe Thou abroad like morning air
Till hearts of stone begin to beat.

5 Baptize the nations; far and nigh,
The triumphs of the cross record;
The name of Jesus glorify,
Till every kindred call Him Lord.

Amen.

James Montgomery, 1771-1854.

388

O'ER the gloomy hills of darkness
Look, my soul; be still, and gaze;
All the promises do travail
With a glorious day of grace:
Blessèd jubilee !
Let thy glorious morning dawn.

2 Kingdoms wide, that sit in darkness,
    Grant them, Lord, Thy glorious light;
And from eastern coast to western
    May the morning chase the night;
      And redemption,
    Freely purchased, win the day.

3 May the glorious day approaching,
    End their night of sin and shame;
And the everlasting gospel
    Spread abroad Thy holy name
      O'er the borders
    Of the great Immanuel's land.

4 Fly abroad, thou mighty gospel,
    Win and conquer, never cease;
May Thy lasting, wide dominion
    Multiply and still increase:
      May Thy sceptre,
    Saviour, rule the world around.

William Williams, 1717–91,
revised by John Rippon, 1751–1836, altd.

389

REJOICE, O people, in the mounting years,
  Wherein God's mighty purposes unfold:
From age to age His righteous reign appears,
  From land to land the love of Christ is told.
Rejoice, O people, in your glorious Lord;
Lift up your hearts in jubilant accord.

2 Rejoice, O people, in the years of old,
  When prophets' glowing visions lit the way;
Till saint and martyr sped the venture bold,
  And eager hearts awoke to greet the day.
Rejoice in God's glad messengers of peace,
Who bore the Saviour's gospel of release.

3 Rejoice, O people, in this living hour:
    Low lies man's pride and human wisdom dies;
But on the cross God's love reveals His power;
    And from His waiting Church new hopes arise.
Rejoice that while the sin of man divides,
One Christian fellowship of love abides.

4 Rejoice, O people, in the days to be,
    When o'er the strife of nations sounding clear,
Shall ring love's gracious song of victory,
    To east and west His kingdom bringing near.
Rejoice, rejoice, His Church on earth is one,
And binds the ransomed nations neath the sun.

5 Rejoice, O people, in that final day
    When all the travail of creation ends;
Christ now attains His universal sway,
    O'er heaven and earth His royal word extends:
That word proclaimed where saints and martyrs
    trod:
The glorious gospel of the blessèd God.

A. F. Bayly, 1901–

390

REMEMBER all the people
    Who live in far-off lands,
In strange and lovely cities,
    Or roam the desert sands,
Or farm the mountain pastures,
    Or till the endless plains,
Where children wade through rice-fields
    And watch the camel-trains.

2 Some work in sultry forests
    Where apes swing to and fro;
Some fish in mighty rivers,
    Some hunt across the snow:
Remember all God's children,
    Who yet have never heard
The truth that comes from Jesus,
    The glory of His word.

3 God bless the men and women
    Who serve Him oversea;
God raise up more to help them
    To set the nations free,
Till all the distant people
    In every foreign place,
Shall understand His kingdom,
    And come into His grace.

Percy Dearmer, 1867–1936,

391

REVIVE Thy work, O Lord,
    Thy mighty arm make bare;
Speak with the voice that wakes the dead
    And make Thy people hear.

2   Revive Thy work, O Lord,
        Disturb this sleep of death;
Quicken the smouldering embers now
        By Thine almighty breath.

3   Revive Thy work, O Lord,
        Create soul-thirst for Thee;
And hungering for the bread of life
        O may our spirits be !

4   Revive Thy work, O Lord,
        Exalt Thy precious name;
And, by the Holy Ghost, our love
        For Thee and Thine inflame.

5   Revive Thy work, O Lord,
        Give pentecostal showers;
The glory shall be all Thine own,
        The blessing, Lord, be ours.

Albert Midlane, 1825–1909.

392

SAVIOUR, quicken many nations,
  Fruitful let Thy sorrows be;
By Thy pains and consolations
  Draw the peoples unto Thee;
Of Thy cross the wondrous story
  Be to all the nations told;
Let them see Thee in Thy glory,
  And Thy mercy manifold.

2 Far and wide, though all unknowing,
    Pants for Thee each mortal breast;
  Human tears for Thee are flowing,
    Human hearts in Thee would rest:
  Thirsting, as for dews of even,
    As the new-mown grass for rain,
  Thee they seek, as God of heaven,
    Thee, as Man for sinners slain.

3 Saviour, lo ! the isles are waiting,
    Stretched the hand, and strained the sight,
  For Thy Spirit new creating,
    Love's pure flame and wisdom's light;
  Give the word, and of the preacher
    Speed the foot and touch the tongue,
  Till on earth by every creature
    Glory to the Lamb be sung.

A. C. Coxe, 1818–96.

393

SEND forth the gospel ! Let it run
  Southward and northward, east and west:
Tell all the earth Christ died and lives,
  Who giveth pardon, life, and rest.

2 Send forth Thy gospel, mighty Lord !
    Out of the chaos bring to birth
Thine own creation's promised hope;
    The better days of heaven on earth.

3 Send forth Thy gospel, gracious Lord !
    Thine was the blood for sinners shed;
Thy voice still pleads in human hearts;
    To Thee Thine other sheep be led.

4 Send forth Thy gospel, holy Lord !
    Kindle in us love's sacred flame;
Love giving all and grudging naught
    For Jesus' sake, in Jesus' name.

5 Send forth the gospel ! Tell it out !
    Go, brothers, at the Master's call;
Prepare His way, who comes to reign
    The King of kings and Lord of all.

H. E. Fox, 1841--1926.

394

SPREAD, O spread, thou mighty word,
Spread the kingdom of the Lord,
Wheresoe'er His breath has given
Life to beings meant for heaven.

2 Tell them how the Father's will
Made the world, and keeps it still,
How He sent His Son to save
All who help and comfort crave.

3 Tell of our Redeemer's love,
Who for ever doth remove
By His holy sacrifice
All the guilt that on us lies.

4 Tell them of the Spirit given
　Now to guide us up to heaven,
　Strong and holy, just and true,
　Working both to will and do.

5 Word of life, most pure and strong,
　Lo, for Thee the nations long;
　Spread, till from its dreary night
　All the world awakes to light.

Jonathan Bahnmaier, 1774–1841,
tr. Catherine Winkworth, 1827–78.

395

THE whole wide world for Jesus !
　This shall our watchword be,
Upon the highest mountains,
　Down by the widest sea :
The whole wide world for Jesus !
　To Him shall all men bow,
In city or in prairie.
　The world for Jesus now !

The whole wide world, the whole wide world !
Proclaim the gospel tidings through the whole wide
　world:
Lift up the cross for Jesus, His banner be unfurled,
Till every tongue confess Him through the whole wide
　world.

2 The whole wide world for Jesus !
　　The marching order sound;
　Go ye and preach the gospel
　　Wherever man is found.
　The whole wide world for Jesus !
　　Our banner is unfurled;
　We battle now for Jesus,
　　And faith demands the world.

3 The whole wide world for Jesus !
   In the Father's house above
Are many wondrous mansions,
   Mansions of light and love.
The whole wide world for Jesus !
   Ride forth, O conquering King,
Through all the mighty nations
   The world to glory bring.

Catherine Johnson, 1835-1907.

396

THOU, Lord, hast given Thyself for our healing
   Poured out Thy life that our souls might
      be freed.
Love, from the heart of the Father, revealing
   Light for our darkness and grace for our need.

2 Saviour of men, our humanity sharing
   Give us a passion for souls that are lost.
Help us to follow, Thy gospel declaring;
   Daily to serve Thee and count not the cost.

3 Pray we for men who to-day in their blindness
   Wander from Thee and Thy kingdom of truth :
Grant them a sight of Thy great loving-kindness,
   Lord of their manhood and guide of their youth.

4 Come, Holy Spirit, to cleanse and renew us :
   Purge us from evil and fill us with power :
Thus shall the waters of healing flow through us;
   So shall revival be born in this hour.

5 Give to Thy Church, as she tells forth the story,
   Strength for her weakness and trust for her
      fears :
Make her a channel of grace for Thy glory,
   Answer her prayers in the midst of the years.

R. D. Browne, 1905–

397

THY kingdom come, O God,
　Thy rule, O Christ, begin;
Break with Thine iron rod
　The tyrannies of sin.

2 Where is Thy reign of peace,
　And purity, and love?
When shall all hatred cease,
　As in the realms above?

3 When comes the promised time,
　That war shall be no more,
And lust, oppression, crime
　Shall flee Thy face before?

4 We pray Thee, Lord, arise,
　And come in Thy great might;
Revive our longing eyes,
　Which languish for Thy sight.

5 Men scorn Thy sacred name,
　And wolves devour Thy fold;
By many deeds of shame
　We learn that love grows cold.

6 O'er lands both near and far
　Thick darkness broodeth yet:
Arise, O morning star,
　Arise, and never set!

Lewis Hensley, 1824–1905, altd.

398

THY kingdom come! on bended knee
　The passing ages pray;
And faithful souls have yearned to see
　On earth that kingdom's day.

2 But the slow watches of the night
   Not less to God belong;
And for the everlasting right
   The silent stars are strong.

3 And lo, already on the hills
   The flags of dawn appear;
Gird up your loins, ye prophet souls,
   Proclaim the day is near;

4 The day in whose clear-shining light
   All wrong shall stand revealed,
When justice shall be throned in might,
   And every hurt be healed;

5 When knowledge, hand in hand with peace,
   Shall walk the earth abroad;—
The day of perfect righteousness,
   The promised day of God.

F. L. Hosmer, 1840–1929.

399

WE have heard a joyful sound:
         Jesus saves !
Spread the gladness all around:
         Jesus saves !
Bear the news to every land,
Climb the steeps and cross the waves;
Onward ! 'tis our Lord's command:
         Jesus saves !

2 Sing above the battle's strife:
            Jesus saves !
By His death and endless life,
         Jesus saves !
Sing it softly through the gloom,
When the heart for mercy craves;
Sing in triumph o'er the tomb:
         Jesus saves !

3 Give the winds a mighty voice:
                    Jesus saves !
Let the nations now rejoice:
                    Jesus saves !
Shout salvation full and free
To every strand that ocean laves—
This our song of victory:
                    Jesus saves !

Priscilla Owens, 1829–1907.

400

WE'VE a story to tell to the nations,
        That shall turn their hearts to the right,
A story of truth and sweetness,
        A story of peace and light:
*For the darkness shall turn to dawning,
And the dawning to noon-day bright,
And Christ's great kingdom shall come on earth,
The kingdom of love and light.*

2 We've a song to be sung to the nations,
        That shall lift their hearts to the Lord;
A song that shall conquer evil,
        And shatter the spear and sword:

3 We've a message to give to the nations,
        That the Lord who reigneth above
Hath sent us His Son to save us,
        And show us that God is love:

4 We've a Saviour to show to the nations,
        Who the path of sorrow has trod,
That all of the world's great peoples
        Might come to the truth of God:

Colin Sterne, 1862–1926.

401

WHEN mothers of Salem,
Their children brought to Jesus,
The stern disciples drove them back
And bade them depart;
But Jesus saw them ere they fled,
And sweetly smiled, and kindly said:
"Suffer the children to come unto Me."

2 How kind was our Saviour
To bid those children welcome;
But there are many thousands
Who have never heard His name;
The Bible they have never read,
They know not what the Saviour said,
"Suffer the children to come unto Me."

3 And soon may the heathen
Of every tribe and nation
Fulfil Thy blessèd word, and cast
Their idols all away;
O shine upon them from above,
And show Thyself a God of love;
Teach them, dear Saviour, to come unto Thee.

W. M. Hutchings, 1827–76.

See also—

Christ is the King, 356.
Christ is the world's true
    light, 659.
Faith of our fathers, 466.
Father, whose will is life and
    good, 634.
From the eastern mountains,
    95.
Hail to the Lord's anointed,
    80.
I cannot tell, 183.
I think when I read, 120.
In Christ there is no east or
    west, 661.
Jesus shall reign, 184.

Jesus, with Thy Church abide
    260.
Long ago when Jesus, 751.
O Christ our Lord, 323.
O Lord of life, 483.
O Master, when Thou callest,
    552.
Send Thou, O Lord, 352.
The day Thou gavest, 706.
Thine arm, O Christ, 637.
Thou whose almighty word,
    46.
Workman of God, 535.
Ye who are banded, 536.

402

COME, let us join our friends above,
    That have obtained the prize,
And on the eagle wings of love,
    To joys celestial rise.

2 Let saints below in concert sing
    With those to glory gone;
For all the servants of our King
    In earth and heaven are one.

3 One family we dwell in Him,
    One Church, above, beneath,
Though now divided by the stream,
    The narrow stream, of death.

4 One army of the living God,
    To His command we bow;
Part of His host have crossed the flood,
    And part are crossing now.

5 Our spirits too shall quickly join
    With theirs in glory crowned,
And shout to see our captain's sign,
    To hear His trumpet sound.

6 Jesus, be Thou our constant guide;
    Then, when the word is given,
Bid Jordan's narrow stream divide,
    And bring us safe to heaven.

Charles Weslev, 1707–88. *altd.*

403

FOR all the saints who from their labours rest,
    Who Thee by faith before the world confessed,
Thy name, O Jesus, be for ever blest.
        Hallelujah !

2 Thou wast their rock, their fortress, and their
     might;
Thou, Lord, their captain in the well-fought fight;
Thou, in the darkness still their one true light.
       Hallelujah !

3 O may Thy soldiers, faithful, true, and bold,
Fight as the saints who nobly fought of old,
And win, with them, the victor's crown of gold.
       Hallelujah !

4 O blest communion, fellowship divine !
We feebly struggle, they in glory shine,
Yet all are one in Thee, for all are Thine.
       Hallelujah !

5 And when the strife is fierce, the warfare long,
Steals on the ear the distant triumph-song,
And hearts are brave again, and arms are strong.
       Hallelujah !

6 The golden evening brightens in the west;
Soon, soon to faithful warriors comes their rest;
Sweet is the calm of paradise the blest.
       Hallelujah !

7 But lo ! there breaks a yet more glorious day:
The saints triumphant rise in bright array;
The King of glory passes on His way.
       Hallelujah !

8 From earth's wide bounds, from ocean's farthest
     coast,
Through gates of pearl streams in the countless
     host,
Singing to Father, Son, and Holy Ghost,
       Hallelujah !

W. W. How, 1823–97, *altd.*

404

GIVE me the wings of faith to rise
　　Within the veil, and see
The saints above, how great their joys,
　How bright their glories be.

2 Once they were mourning here below,
　　With sighing and with tears;
They wrestled hard, as we do now,
　With sins, and doubts, and fears.

3 I ask them whence their victory came:
　　They, with united breath,
Ascribe their victory to the Lamb,
　Their triumph to His death.

4 They marked the footsteps where He trod,
　　His zeal inspired their breast;
And, following their incarnate God,
　Possess the promised rest.

5 Our glorious leader claims our praise
　　For His own pattern given;
While the great cloud of witnesses
　Show the same path to heaven.

Isaac Watts, 1674–1748, *altd.*

405

REV. vii. 13–17.

HOW bright these glorious spirits shine!
　　Whence all their white array?
How came they to the blissful seats
　Of everlasting day?

2 Lo ! these are they, from sufferings great,
　　Who came to realms of light,
　And in the blood of Christ have washed
　　Those robes that shine so bright.

3 Now with triumphal palms they stand
　　Before the throne on high,
　And serve the God they love, amidst
　　The glories of the sky.

4 His presence fills each heart with joy,
　　Tunes every voice to sing;
　By day, by night, the sacred courts
　　With glad hosannas ring.

5 Hunger and thirst are felt no more,
　　Nor sun with scorching ray;
　God is their sun, whose cheering beams
　　Diffuse eternal day.

6 The Lamb who dwells amidst the throne,
　　Shall o'er them still preside,
　Feed them with nourishment divine,
　　And all their footsteps guide.

7 In pastures green He'll lead His flock
　　Where living streams appear;
　And God Himself from every eye
　　Shall wipe away the tear.

Isaac Watts, 1674–1748,
revised by W. Cameron, 1751–1811

406

JERUSALEM the golden,
　　With milk and honey blest,
Beneath thy contemplation
　Sink heart and voice oppressed !
I know not, O I know not,
　What joys await us there,
What radiancy of glory,
　What light beyond compare.

2 They stand, those halls of Zion,
   All jubilant with song,
And bright with many an angel,
   And all the martyr throng;
The Prince is ever in them,
   The daylight is serene;
The pastures of the blessèd
   Are decked in glorious sheen.

3 There is the throne of David,
   And there, from care released,
The shout of them that triumph,
   The song of them that feast;
And they who, with their Leader,
   Have conquered in the fight,
For ever and for ever
   Are clad in robes of white.

4 And now we watch and struggle
   And now we live in hope;
And Zion in her anguish
   With Babylon must cope.
But He, whom now we trust in,
   Shall then be seen and known,
And they that know and see Him
   Shall have Him for their own.

5 O sweet and blessèd country,
   The home of God's elect !
O sweet and blessèd country,
   That eager hearts expect !
Jesus, in mercy bring us
   To that dear land of rest,
Who art, with God the Father
   And Spirit, ever blest.

Bernard of Morlaix, 12th cent.,
tr. J. M. Neale, 1818–66.

407

TEN thousand times ten thousand,
  In sparkling raiment bright,
The armies of the ransomed saints
  Throng up the steeps of light:
'Tis finished, all is finished,
  Their fight with death and sin;
Fling open wide the golden gates,
  And let the victors in.

2 What rush of hallelujahs
    Fills all the earth and sky !
  What ringing of a thousand harps
    Bespeaks the triumph nigh !
  O day for which creation
    And all its tribes were made !
  O joy, for all its former woes
    A thousandfold repaid !

3 O then what raptured greetings
    On Canaan's happy shore,
  What knitting severed friendships up,
    Where partings are no more !
  Then eyes with joy shall sparkle
    That brimmed with tears of late;
  Orphans no longer fatherless,
    Nor widows desolate.

4 Bring near Thy great salvation,
    Thou Lamb for sinners slain;
  Fill up the roll of Thine elect,
    Then take Thy power and reign;
  Appear, desire of nations,
    Thine exiles long for home;
  Show in the heavens Thy promised sign:
    Thou Prince and Saviour, come.

                    Henry Alford, 1810–71.

408

WHAT joy, to think of that vast host,
Of every tribe and tongue,
Who come from every clime and coast,
Who raise in heaven their song,
Their glad triumphal song.

2 Glad thought, that all who served the Lord,—
The apostolic band,
The myriads trusting in their word,
Shall all together stand,
Redeemed at God's right hand.

3 What bliss, their loves and joys to tell,
What wondrous strains they sing,
Exultant anthems rise and swell
Till heaven's high arches ring,
As they adore their King.

4 Great God, in mercy save us all;
Raise us to dwell with Thee.
With souls redeemed, when Thou shalt call,
Grant that our place may be,
Through all eternity.

W. A. Wexels, 1796–1866,
tr. R. Birch Hoyle, 1875–1939.

See also—

He wants not friends, 360.
Holy ! Holy ! Holy ! 42.
Sing hallelujah, 27.
The Church's one foundation,
263.

The God of Abraham, 30.
Through the night, 559.
We praise, we worship Thee,
33.
Ye holy angels bright, 36.

VIII. THE CHRISTIAN LIFE

(1) THE GOSPEL CALL

409

ART thou weary, heavy laden,
    Art thou sore distressed ?
" Come to Me," saith One, " and, coming,
        Be at rest."

2 " Hath He marks to lead me to Him,
    If He be my guide ? "
In His feet and hands are wound-prints,
        And His side.

3 " Is there diadem, as monarch,
    That His brow adorns ? "
Yea, a crown in very surety;
        But of thorns.

4 " If I find Him, if I follow,
    What His guerdon here ? "
Many a sorrow, many a labour,
        Many a tear.

5 " If I still hold closely to Him,
    What hath He at last ? "
Sorrow vanquished, labour ended,
        Jordan past.

6 " If I ask Him to receive me,
    Will He say me nay ? "
Not till earth, and not till heaven
        Pass away.

7 " Finding, following, keeping, struggling,
    Is He sure to bless ? "
Saints, apostles, prophets, martyrs,
        Answer, " Yes ! "

J. M. Neale, 1818–66.
Based on Stephen the Sabaite, 725-94.

410

BEHOLD Me standing at the door,
And hear Me pleading evermore,
With gentle voice: O heart of sin,
May I come in ? May I come in ?
Behold Me standing at the door,
And hear Me pleading evermore :
Say, weary heart, oppressed with sin,
May I come in ? May I come in ?

2 I bore the cruel thorns for thee,
I waited long and patiently:
Say, weary heart, oppressed with sin,
May I come in ? May I come in ?

3 I would not plead with thee in vain;
Remember all My grief and pain !
I died to ransom thee from sin,
May I come in ? May I come in ?

4 I bring thee joy from heaven above,
I bring thee pardon, peace, and love:
Say, weary heart, oppressed with sin,
May I come in ? May I come in ?

Frances van Alstyne, 1820-1915.

411

COME let us sing of a wonderful love,
Tender and true;
Out of the heart of the Father above,
Streaming to me and to you:
Wonderful love
Dwells in the heart of the Father above.

2 Jesus, the Saviour, this gospel to tell,
    Joyfully came;
Came with the helpless and hopeless to dwell,
  Sharing their sorrow and shame;
    Seeking the lost,
Saving, redeeming at measureless cost.

3 Jesus is seeking the wanderers yet;
    Why do they roam?
Love only waits to forgive and forget;
  Home! weary wanderers, home!
    Wonderful love
Dwells in the heart of the Father above.

4 Come to my heart, O Thou wonderful love,
    Come and abide,
Lifting my life till it rises above
  Envy and falsehood and pride;
    Seeking to be
Lowly and humble, a learner of Thee.

Robert Walmsley, 1831–1905.

412

" COME unto Me, ye weary,
    And I will give you rest."
O blessèd voice of Jesus,
  Which comes to hearts oppressed!
It tells of benediction,
  Of pardon, grace, and peace,
Of joy that has no ending,
  Of love which cannot cease.

2 " Come unto Me, ye wanderers,
  And I will give you light."
O loving voice of Jesus,
  Which comes to cheer the night!
Our hearts were filled with sadness,
  And we had lost our way;
But morning brings us gladness,
  And songs at break of day.

3 " Come unto Me, ye fainting,
   And I will give you life."
O cheering voice of Jesus,
   Which comes to aid our strife !
The foe is stern and eager,
   The fight is fierce and long;
But Thou hast made us mighty,
   And stronger than the strong.

4 " And whosoever cometh,
   I will not cast him out."
O welcome voice of Jesus,
   Which drives away our doubt;
Which calls us very sinners,
   Unworthy though we be
Of love so free and boundless,
   To come, dear Lord, to Thee !

W. C. Dix, 1837–98.

413

COME, ye souls by sin afflicted,
   Bowed with fruitless sorrow down,
By the broken law convicted,
   Through the cross behold the crown;
      Look to Jesus;
   Mercy flows through Him alone.

2 Blessèd are the eyes that see Him,
   Blest the ears that hear His voice;
Blessèd are the souls that trust Him,
   And in Him alone rejoice;
      His commandments
   Then become their happy choice.

3 Sweet as home to pilgrims weary,
   Light to newly opened eyes,
Or full springs in deserts dreary,
   Is the rest the cross supplies;
      All who taste it
   Shall to bliss immortal rise.

4 Take His easy yoke and wear it;
  Love will make obedience sweet;
Christ will give you strength to bear it,
  While His wisdom guides your feet
    Safe to glory,
  Where His ransomed captives meet.

Joseph Swain, 1761–96.

414

HARK, my soul ! it is the Lord;
  'Tis thy Saviour, hear His word:
Jesus speaks, and speaks to thee:
" Say, poor sinner, lov'st thou me ?

2 " I delivered thee when bound,
  And, when bleeding, healed thy wound;
Sought thee wandering, set thee right,
Turned thy darkness into light.

3 " Can a woman's tender care
  Cease towards the child she bare ?
Yes, she may forgetful be,
Yet will I remember thee.

4 " Mine is an unchanging love,
  Higher than the heights above,
Deeper than the depths beneath,
Free and faithful, strong as death.

5 " Thou shalt see My glory soon,
  When the work of grace is done;
Partner of My throne shalt be:
Say, poor sinner, lov'st thou Me ? "

6 Lord, it is my chief complaint
  That my love is weak and faint;
Yet I love Thee, and adore;
O for grace to love Thee more !

William Cowper, 1731–1800.

415

I LOVE to tell the story
  Of unseen things above,
Of Jesus and His glory,
  Of Jesus and His love.
I love to tell the story,
  Because I know it's true;
It satisfies my longings
  As nothing else can do.
    I love to tell the story,
      'Twill be my theme in glory,
    To tell the old, old story
      Of Jesus and His love.

2 I love to tell the story:
    'Tis pleasant to repeat
  What seems, each time I tell it,
    More wonderfully sweet.
  I love to tell the story:
    For some have never heard
  The message of salvation
    From God's own holy Word.

3 I love to tell the story:
    For those who know it best
  Seem hungering and thirsting
    To hear it like the rest.
  And when, in scenes of glory,
    I sing the new, new song,
  'Twill be the old, old story,
    That I have loved so long.

                    Arabella C. Hankey, 1834–1911.

416

JESUS calls us; o'er the tumult
  Of our life's wild restless sea,
Day by day His voice is sounding,
  Saying, " Christian, follow me ";

2 As of old apostles heard it
    By the Galilean lake,
Turned from home, and toil, and kindred,
    Leaving all for His dear sake.

3 Jesus calls us from the worship
    Of the vain world's golden store,
From each idol that would keep us,
    Saying, " Christian, love Me more."

4 In our joys and in our sorrows,
    Days of toil and hours of ease,
Still He calls, in cares and pleasures,
    " Christian, love Me more than these."

5 Jesus calls us ! By Thy mercies,
    Saviour, may we hear Thy call,
Give our hearts to Thine obedience,
    Serve and love Thee best of all.

Cecil Frances Alexander, 1818–95.

417

JESUS is tenderly calling thee home—
    Calling to-day, calling to-day !
Why from the sunshine of love wilt thou roam,
    Farther and farther away ?
        Calling to-day! calling to-day!
        Jesus is calling, is tenderly calling to-day!

2 Jesus is calling the weary to rest—
    Calling to-day, calling to-day !
Bring Him thy burden, and thou shalt be blest:
    He will not turn thee away.

3 Jesus is waiting, O come to Him now—
    Waiting to-day, waiting to-day !
Come with thy sins, at His feet lowly bow;
    Come, and no longer delay !

4 Jesus is pleading; O list to His voice—
  Hear Him to-day, hear Him to-day !
They who believe on His name shall rejoice;
  Answer His call and obey.

Frances van Alstyne, 1820–1915.

418

O JESUS, Thou art standing
    Outside the fast-closed door,
In lowly patience waiting
  To pass the threshold o'er.
Shame on us, Christian brothers,
  His name and sign who bear,
O shame, thrice shame upon us,
  To keep Him standing there !

2 O Jesus, Thou art knocking;
    And lo, that hand is scarred,
And thorns Thy brow encircle,
  And tears Thy face have marred.
O love that passeth knowledge,
  So patiently to wait !
O sin that hath no equal,
  So fast to bar the gate !

3 O Jesus, Thou art pleading
    In accents meek and low,
" I died for you, My children,
  And will ye treat Me so ? "
O Lord, with shame and sorrow
  We open now the door;
Dear Saviour, enter, enter,
  And leave us nevermore.

W. W. How, 1823–97.

419

[Souls of men ! why will ye scatter
  Like a crowd of frightened sheep ?
Foolish hearts ! why will ye wander
  From a love so true and deep ?]

THERE'S a wideness in God's mercy,
  Like the wideness of the sea :
There's a kindness in His justice,
  Which is more than liberty.

2 There is no place where earth's sorrows
  Are more felt than up in heaven;
There is no place where earth's failings
  Have such kindly judgment given.

3 For the love of God is broader
  Than the measures of man's mind;
And the heart of the Eternal
  Is most wonderfully kind.

4 But we make His love too narrow
  By false limits of our own;
And we magnify His strictness
  With a zeal He will not own.

5 There is plentiful redemption
  In the blood that has been shed;
There is joy for all the members
  In the sorrows of the Head.

6 If our love were but more simple,
  We should take Him at His word;
And our lives be filled with gladness,
  From the presence of the Lord.

F. W. Faber, 1814–63, altd.

420

TELL me the old, old story
   Of unseen things above,
Of Jesus and His glory,
   Of Jesus and His love.
Tell me the story simply,
   As to a little child,
For I am weak and weary,
   And helpless and defiled.
Tell me the old, old story,
   Of Jesus and His love.

2 Tell me the story slowly,
   That I may take it in—
That wonderful redemption,
   God's remedy for sin.
Tell me the story often,
   For I forget so soon:
The early dew of morning
   Has passed away at noon.

3 Tell me the story softly,
   With earnest tones and grave;
Remember ! I'm the sinner
   Whom Jesus came to save.
Tell me the story always,
   If you would really be,
In any time of trouble,
   A comforter to me.

4 Tell me the same old story,
   When you have cause to fear
That this world's empty glory
   Is costing me too dear.
Yes, and when that world's glory
   Is dawning on my soul,
Tell me the old, old story;
   " Christ Jesus makes thee whole."

Arabella C. Hankey, 1834–1911, *altd*

421

THE gospel bells are ringing
Over land, from sea to sea;
Blessèd news of free salvation
Do they offer you and me.
For God so loved the world
That His only Son He gave;
Whoso'er believeth in Him
Everlasting life shall have.
>   *Gospel bells, how they ring*
>   *Over land, from sea to sea ;*
>   *Gospel bells freely bring*
>   *Blessèd news to you and me.*

2 The gospel bells invite us
To a feast prepared for all;
Do not slight the invitation
Nor reject the gracious call.
"I am the bread of life;
Eat of Me, thou hungry soul;
Though your sins be red as crimson,
They shall be as white as wool."

3 The gospel bells are joyful
As they echo far and wide,
Bearing news of perfect pardon
Through a Saviour crucified.
"Good tidings of great joy
To all people do I bring;
Unto you is born a Saviour
Which is Christ the Lord and King."

S. W. Martin, 1839– ?

422

THE Lord is rich and merciful,
　　The Lord is very kind;
O come to Him, come now to Him,
　　With a believing mind.
His comforts they shall strengthen thee,
　　Like flowing waters cool;
And He shall for thy spirit be
　　A fountain ever full.

2 The Lord is glorious and strong,
　　Our God is very high;
O trust in Him, trust now in Him
　　And have security.
He shall be to thee like the sea,
　　And thou shalt surely feel
His wind that bloweth healthily
　　Thy sicknesses to heal.

3 The Lord is wonderful and wise,
　　As all the ages tell;
O learn of Him, learn now of Him,
　　Then with thee it is well.
And with His light thou shalt be blest,
　　Therein to work and live;
And He shall be to thee a rest
　　When evening hours arrive.

T. T. Lynch, 1818-71.

423

THE Saviour calls; let every ear
　　Attend the heavenly sound;
Ye doubting souls, dismiss your fear,
　　Hope smiles reviving round.

2 For every thirsty, longing heart,
　　Here streams of bounty flow;
And life, and health, and bliss impart,
　　To banish mortal woe.

3 Ye sinners, come, 'tis mercy's voice,
   The gracious call obey;
Mercy invites to heavenly joys,
   And can you yet delay?

4 Dear Saviour, draw reluctant hearts,
   To Thee let sinners fly,
And take the bliss Thy love imparts
   And drink and never die.

Anne Steele, 1717–78.

424

THERE is no love like the love of Jesus,
   Never to fade or fall,
Till into the fold of the peace of God
   He has gathered us all.

   Jesus' love, precious love,
     Boundless and pure and free!
   O turn to that love, weary wandering soul,
     Jesus pleadeth with thee.

2 There is no heart like the heart of Jesus,
   Filled with a tender love,
No throb nor throe that our hearts can know
   But He feels it above.

3 O let us hark to the voice of Jesus!
   O may we never roam,
Till safe we rest on His loving breast
   In the dear heavenly home.

W. E. Littlewood, 1831–86.

425

THERE were ninety and nine that safely lay
   In the shelter of the fold;
But one was out on the hills away,
   Far off from the gates of gold;—
Away on the mountains wild and bare,
   Away from the tender Shepherd's care.

2 " Lord, Thou hast here Thy ninety and nine,
    Are they not enough for Thee ? "
  But the shepherd made answer: " This of Mine
    Has wander'd away from Me;
  And although the road be rough and steep,
    I go to the desert to find My sheep."

3 But none of the ransomed ever knew
    How deep were the waters crossed;
  Nor how dark was the night that the Lord passed
    through,
  Ere He found His sheep that was lost:
  Out in the desert He heard its cry,
    Sick and helpless and ready to die.

4 " Lord, whence are those blood-drops all the way,
    That mark out the mountain's track ? "
  " They were shed for one who had gone astray,
    Ere the Shepherd could bring him back."
  " Lord, whence are Thy hands so rent and torn ? "
    " They are piercèd to-night by many a thorn."

5 And all through the mountains, thunder-riven,
    And up from the rocky steep,
  There rose a cry to the gate of heaven,
    " Rejoice, I have found My sheep ! "
  And the angels echoed around the throne,
    " Rejoice ! for the Lord brings back His own ! "

Elizabeth Clephane, 1830–69.

See also—

I am not skilled, 204.
I am so glad, 498.
Jesus, Thy blood, 208.
Man of sorrows, 186.
O for a thousand tongues, 212.

Praise Him ! 215.
Rejoice and be glad, 170.
To God be the glory, 32.
What a friend, 343.

426

AND can it be that I should gain
      An interest in the Saviour's blood ?
Died He for me, who caused His pain ?
   For me, who Him to death pursued ?
Amazing love ! how can it be
That Thou, my God, shouldst die for me !

2 'Tis mystery all ! The Immortal dies :
   Who can explore His strange design ?
In vain the first-born seraph tries
   To sound the depths of love divine.
'Tis mercy all ! let earth adore,
Let angel minds inquire no more.

3 He left His Father's throne above—
   So free, so infinite His grace—
Emptied Himself of all but love,
   And bled for Adam's helpless race.
'Tis mercy all, immense and free ;
For, O my God, it found out me !

4 Long my imprisoned spirit lay
   Fast bound in sin and nature's night ;
Thine eye diffused a quickening ray—
   I woke, the dungeon flamed with light ;
My chains fell off, my heart was free,
I rose, went forth, and followed Thee.

5 No condemnation now I dread ;
   Jesus, and all in Him, is mine !
Alive in Him, my living Head,
   And clothed in righteousness divine,
Bold I approach the eternal throne,
And claim the crown, through Christ, my own.

Charles Wesley, 1707–88.

427

BENEATH the cross of Jesus
   I fain would take my stand—-
The shadow of a mighty rock,
   Within a weary land:
A home within the wilderness,
   A rest upon the way,
From the burning of the noontide heat,
   And the burden of the day.

2 O safe and happy shelter,
   O refuge tried and sweet,
O trysting-place where heaven's love
   And heaven's justice meet!
As to the holy patriarch
   That wondrous dream was given,
So seems my Saviour's cross to me,
   A ladder up to heaven.

3 Upon that cross of Jesus
   Mine eyes at times can see
The very dying form of One
   Who suffered there for me;
And from my smitten heart with tears
   Two wonders I confess—
The wonders of His glorious love,
   And my own worthlessness.

4 I take, O cross, thy shadow,
   For my abiding-place!
I ask no other sunshine than
   The sunshine of His face;
Content to let the world go by,
   To know no gain nor loss—
My sinful self my only shame,
   My glory all—the cross.

Elizabeth Clephane, 1830–69.

428

COME and rejoice with me !
For once my heart was poor,
And I have found a treasury
Of love, a boundless store.

2   Come and rejoice with me !
I, once so sick at heart,
Have met with One who knows my case,
And knows the healing art.

3   Come and rejoice with me !
For I was wearied sore,
And I have found a mighty arm
Which holds me evermore.

4   Come and rejoice with me !
My feet so wide did roam,
And One has sought me from afar,
And beareth me safe home.

5   Come and rejoice with me !
For I have found a Friend
Who knows my heart's most secret depths
Yet loves me without end.

6   I knew not of His love;
And He had loved so long,
With love so faithful and so deep,
So tender and so strong.

7   And now I know it all,
Have heard and known His voice,
And hear it still from day to day,—
Can I enough rejoice ?

Elisabeth R. Charles, 1828-**96**.

429

HOSEA vi, 1–3.

COME, let us to the Lord our God
　　With contrite hearts return;
Our God is gracious, nor will leave
　　The desolate to mourn.

2 His voice commands the tempest forth,
　　And stills the stormy wave;
And though His arm be strong to smite,
　　'Tis also strong to save.

3 Long hath the night of sorrow reigned;
　　The dawn shall bring us light;
God shall appear, and we shall rise
　　With gladness in His sight.

4 Our hearts, if God we seek to know,
　　Shall know Him, and rejoice;
His coming like the morn shall be,
　　Like morning songs His voice.

5 As dew upon the tender herb,
　　Diffusing fragrance round;
As showers that usher in the spring,
　　And cheer the thirsty ground;

6 So shall His presence bless our souls,
　　And shed a joyful light;
That hallowed morn shall chase away
　　The sorrows of the night.

John Morison, 1750–98.

430

DRAWN to the cross which Thou hast blessed
　　With healing gifts for souls distressed,
To find in Thee my life, my rest,
　　Christ crucified, I come!

2 Stained with the sins which I have wrought
  In word and deed and secret thought,
  For pardon which Thy blood has bought,
    Christ crucified, I come !

3 Weary of selfishness and pride,
  False pleasures gone, vain hopes denied,
  Deep in Thy wounds my shame to hide,
    Christ crucified, I come !

4 Thou knowest all my griefs and fears,
  Thy grace abused, my misspent years;
  Yet now to Thee, for cleansing tears,
    Christ crucified, I come !

5 I would not, if I could, conceal
  The ills which only Thou canst heal,
  So to the cross, where sinners kneel,
    Christ crucified, I come !

6 Wash me, and take away each stain,
  Let nothing of my sin remain:
  For cleansing, though it be through pain,
    Christ crucified, I come !

7 To be what Thou wouldst have me be,
  Accepted, sanctified in Thee,
  Through what Thy grace shall work in me,
    Christ crucified, I come !

Genevieve Irons, 1855–1928.

431

GOD of pity, God of grace,
When we humbly seek Thy face,
Bend from heaven, Thy dwelling-place:
  Hear, forgive, and save.

2 When we in Thy temple meet,
  Spread our wants before Thy feet,
  Pleading at the mercy-seat:
      Look from heaven and save.

3 When Thy love our hearts shall fill,
  And we long to do Thy will,
  Turning to Thy holy hill:
      Lord, accept and save.

4 Should we wander from Thy fold,
  And our love to Thee grow cold,
  With a pitying eye behold:
      Lord, forgive and save.

5 Should the hand of sorrow press,
  Earthly care and want distress,
  May our souls Thy peace possess:
      Jesus, hear and save.

6 And whate'er our cry may be,
  When we lift our hearts to Thee,
  From our burden set us free:
      Hear, forgive and save.   Amen.

Eliza Morris, 1821–74.

432

I AM trusting Thee, Lord Jesus,
    Trusting only Thee,
Trusting Thee for full salvation,
    Great and free.

2 I am trusting Thee for pardon:
    At Thy feet I bow,
For Thy grace and tender mercy
    Trusting now.

3 I am trusting Thee to guide me;
    Thou alone shalt lead,
Every day and hour supplying
    All my need.

4 I am trusting Thee for power:
    Thine can never fail;
Words which Thou Thyself shalt give me
    Must prevail.

5 I am trusting Thee, Lord Jesus;
    Never let me fall:
I am trusting Thee for ever,
    And for all.

Frances Ridley Havergal, 1836–79

433

I BIND unto myself to-day
    The strong Name of the Trinity,
By invocation of the same,
    The Three in One, and One in Three.

2 I bind this day to me for ever,
    By power of faith, Christ's incarnation;
His baptism in the Jordan river;
    His death on cross for my salvation;
His bursting from the spicèd tomb;
    His riding up the heavenly way;
His coming at the day of doom:
    I bind unto myself to-day.

3 I bind unto myself to-day
    The power of God to hold and lead,
His eye to watch, His might to stay,
    His ear to hearken to my need,
The wisdom of my God to teach,
    His hand to guide, His shield to ward,
The word of God to give me speech,
    His heavenly host to be my guard.

4 Christ be with me, Christ within me,
   Christ behind me, Christ before me,
Christ beside me, Christ to win me,
   Christ to comfort and restore me,
Christ beneath me, Christ above me,
   Christ in quiet, Christ in danger,
Christ in hearts of all that love me,
   Christ in mouth of friend and stranger.

5 I bind unto myself the name,
   The strong name of the Trinity;
By invocation of the same,
   The Three in One, and One in Three,
Of whom all nature hath creation,
   Eternal Father, Spirit, Word.
Praise to the Lord of my salvation:
   Salvation is of Christ the Lord.

Attributed to St. Patrick, 385–461,
tr. Cecil Frances Alexander, 1818–95.

434

I BLESS the Christ of God;
   I rest on love divine;
And with unfaltering lip and heart,
   I call the Saviour mine.

2   His cross dispels each doubt:
     I bury in His tomb
Each thought of unbelief and fear,
     Each lingering shade of gloom.

3   I praise the God of grace;
     I trust His truth and might;
He calls me His, I call Him mine,
     My God, my joy, my light.

4   In Him is only good,
     In me is only ill;
My ill but draws His goodness forth,
     And me He loveth still.

5   'Tis He who saveth me,
        And freely pardon gives:
I love because He loveth me,
        I live because He lives.

6   My life with Him is hid,
        My death has passed away,
My clouds have melted into light,
        My midnight into day.

Horatius Bonar, 1808–89.

435

I GIVE my heart to Thee,
  O Jesus most desired !
And heart for heart the gift shall be,
    For Thou my soul hast fired:
    Thou hearts alone wouldst move,
    Thou only hearts dost love:
I would love Thee as Thou lov'st me,
  O Jesus most desired!

2   What offering can I make,
      Dear Lord, to love like Thine ?
That Thou, the Word, didst stoop to take
    A human form like mine.
    " Give Me thy heart, My son ":
    Lord, Thou my heart hast won:

3   Here finds my heart its rest,
      Repose that knows no shock,
The strength of love that keeps it blest:
    In Thee, the riven rock,
    My soul, as girt around,
    Her citadel hath found:
I would love Thee as Thou lov'st me,
  O Jesus most desired !

Latin Hymn, 9th cent.,
tr. Ray Palmer, 1808–87.

436

I HEARD the voice of Jesus say,
   " Come unto Me and rest;
Lay down, thou weary one, lay down
   Thy head upon My breast ":
I came to Jesus as I was,
   Weary, and worn, and sad;
I found in Him a resting-place,
   And He has made me glad.

2 I heard the voice of Jesus say,
   " Behold, I freely give
The living water; thirsty one,
   Stoop down, and drink, and live ":
I came to Jesus and I drank
   Of that life-giving stream;
My thirst was quenched, my soul revived,
   And now I live in Him.

3 I heard the voice of Jesus say,
   " I am this dark world's light;
Look unto Me, thy morn shall rise,
   And all thy day be bright ":
I looked to Jesus, and I found
   In Him my star, my sun;
And in that light of life I'll walk
   Till travelling days are done.

Horatius Bonar, 1808–89.

437

I KNOW not why God's wondrous grace
   To me has been made known;
Nor why—unworthy as I am—
   He claimed me for His own.

*But " I know whom I have believed; and
am persuaded that He is able to keep that
which I've committed unto Him against that
day."*

2 I know not how this saving faith
   To me He did impart;
Or how believing in His word
   Wrought peace within my heart.

3 I know not how the Spirit moves,
   Convincing men of sin;
Revealing Jesus through the word,
   Creating faith in Him.

4 I know not what of good or ill
   May be reserved for me—
Of weary ways or golden days
   Before his face I see.

                    D. W. Whittle, 1840–1901.

438

I LIFT my heart to Thee,
   Saviour divine;
For Thou art all to me,
   And I am Thine.
Is there on earth a closer bond than this.
That "my belovèd's mine, and I am His "?

2 Thine am I by all ties;
   But chiefly Thine,
That through Thy sacrifice
   Thou, Lord, art mine.
By Thine own cords of love, so sweetly wound
Around me, I to Thee am closely bound.

3 To Thee, Thou dying Lamb,
   I all things owe;
All that I have and am
   And all I know.
All that I have is now no longer mine,
And I am not my own; Lord, I am Thine.

4 I pray Thee, Saviour, keep
   Me in Thy love,
Until death's holy sleep
   Shall me remove
To that fair realm where, sin and sorrow o'er,
Thou and Thine own are one for evermore.

C. E. Mudie, 1818–90

439

IN full and glad surrender,
   I give myself to Thee,
Thine utterly and only
   And evermore to be.

2 O Son of God, who lov'st me,
   I will be Thine alone;
And all I have, and am, Lord,
   Shall henceforth be Thine own.

3 Reign over me, Lord Jesus,
   O make my heart Thy throne;
It shall be Thine, dear Saviour,
   It shall be Thine alone.

4 O come and reign, Lord Jesus,
   Rule over everything;
And keep me always loyal
   And true to Thee, my King.

Frances Ridley Havergal, 1836–79.

440

I'VE found a friend; O such a friend!
   He loved me ere I knew Him;
He drew me with the cords of love,
   And thus He bound me to Him:
And round my heart still closely twine
   Those ties which nought can sever,
For I am His, and He is mine,
   For ever and for ever.

2 I've found a friend; O such a friend !
   He bled, He died to save me;
And not alone the gift of life,
   But His own self He gave me:
Nought that I have my own I call,
   I hold it for the giver;
My heart, my strength, my life, my all,
   Are His, and His for ever.

3 I've found a friend; O such a friend !
   So kind, and true, and tender !
So wise a counsellor and guide,
   So mighty a defender !
From Him who loves me now so well
   What power my soul can sever ?
Shall life, or death, or earth, or hell ?
   No ! I am His for ever.

J. G. Small, **1817–88.**

441

JESUS, lover of my soul,
   Let me to Thy bosom fly,
While the nearer waters roll,
   While the tempest still is high:
Hide me, O my Saviour, hide,
   Till the storm of life is past;
Safe into the haven guide;
   O receive my soul at last !

2 Other refuge have I none,
   Hangs my helpless soul on Thee;
Leave, ah ! leave me not alone,
   Still support and comfort me:
All my trust on Thee is stayed;
   All my help from Thee I bring;
Cover my defenceless head
   With the shadow of Thy wing.

3 Thou, O Christ, art all I want;
   More than all in Thee I find;
Raise the fallen, cheer the faint,
   Heal the sick, and lead the blind.
Just and holy is Thy name,
   I am all unrighteousness;
False, and full of sin I am,
   Thou art full of truth and grace.

4 Plenteous grace with Thee is found,
   Grace to cover all my sin;
Let the healing streams abound,
   Make and keep me pure within.
Thou of life the fountain art,
   Freely let me take of Thee:
Spring Thou up within my heart,
   Rise to all eternity.

Charles Wesley, 1707–88, *altd.*

442

JUST as I am, Thine own to be,
Friend of the young, who lovest me,
To consecrate myself to Thee,
   O Jesus Christ, I come.

2 I would live ever in the light,
I would work ever for the right,
I would serve Thee with all my might,
   Therefore to Thee I come.

3 Just as I am, young, strong, and free,
To be the best that I can be
For truth, and righteousness, and Thee,
   Lord of my life, I come.

4 With many dreams of fame and gold,
Success and joy to make me bold;
But dearer still my faith to hold;
   For my whole life, I come.

5 And for Thy sake to win renown,
  And then to take my victor's crown,
  And at Thy feet to cast it down;
    O Master, Lord, I come.

6 In the glad morning of my day,
  My life to give, my vows to pay,
  With no reserve and no delay,
    With all my heart I come.

Marianne Farningham, 1834–1909.

443

JUST as I am—without one plea,
  But that Thy blood was shed for me,
And that Thou bidd'st me come to Thee,
    O Lamb of God, I come.

2 Just as I am—and waiting not
  To rid my soul of one dark blot,
  To Thee, whose blood can cleanse each spot,
    O Lamb of God, I come.

3 Just as I am—though tossed about
  With many a conflict, many a doubt,
  Fightings and fears within, without,
    O Lamb of God, I come.

4 Just as I am—poor, wretched, blind;
  Sight, riches, healing of the mind,
  Yea, all I need, in Thee to find,
    O Lamb of God, I come.

5 Just as I am—Thou wilt receive,
  Wilt welcome, pardon, cleanse, relieve;
  Because Thy promise I believe,
    O Lamb of God, I come.

6 Just as I am—Thy love unknown
  Has broken every barrier down;
  Now to be Thine, yea, Thine alone,
      O Lamb of God, I come.

7 Just as I am—of that free love
  The breadth, length, depth, and height to prove,
  Here for a season, then above,
      O Lamb of God, I come.

Charlotte Elliott, 1789–1871.

444

LIFT up your hearts! We lift them, Lord, to
      Thee;
Here, at Thy feet, none other may we see;
"Lift up your hearts!" E'en so, with one accord,
We lift them up, we lift them to the Lord.

2 Above the level of the former years,
  The mire of sin, the slough of guilty fears,
  The mist of doubt, the blight of love's decay;
  O Lord of light, lift all our hearts to-day.

3 Above the swamps of subterfuge and shame,
  The deeds, the thoughts, that honour may not
      name,
  The halting tongue that dares not tell the whole,
  O Lord of truth, lift every Christian soul.

4 Lift every gift that Thou Thyself hast given;
  Low lies the best till lifted up to heaven:
  Low lie the bounding heart, the teeming brain,
  Till, sent from God, they mount to God again.

5 O if the hopes which thrill our hearts to-day
  Foreshadow aught that shall not pass away,
  And we may trust that all our days shall be
  Bound each to each by natural piety;

6 Then, as the trumpet-call, in after years
  " Lift up your hearts ! " rings pealing in our ears,
Still shall those hearts respond, with full accord,
" We lift them up, we lift them to the Lord ! "

H. M. Butler, 1833–1918.

445

LORD, I was blind, I could not see
  In Thy marred visage any grace;
  But now the beauty of Thy face
In radiant vision dawns on me.

2 Lord, I was deaf, I could not hear
  The thrilling music of Thy voice;
  But now I hear Thee and rejoice,
And mighty are Thy words, and dear.

3 Lord, I was dumb, I could not speak
  The grace and glory of Thy name;
  But now, as touched with living flame,
My lips Thine eager praises wake.

4 Lord, I was dead, I could not stir
  My lifeless soul to come to Thee;
  But now, since Thou hast quickened me,
I rise from sin's dark sepulchre.

5 For Thou hast made the blind to see,
  The deaf to hear, the dumb to speak,
  The dead to live; and lo, I break
The chains of my captivity.

W. T. Matson, 1833–99, *altd.*

446

LORD, in the fulness of my might
  I would for Thee be strong;
While runneth o'er each dear delight
  To Thee should soar my song.

2 I would not give the world my heart,
   And then profess Thy love:
I would not feel my strength depart,
   And then Thy service prove.

3 I would not with swift-wingèd zeal
   On the world's errands go:
And labour up the heavenly hill
   With weary feet and slow.

4 O not for Thee my weak desires,
   My poorer, baser part !
O not for Thee my fading fires,
   The ashes of my heart !

5 O choose me in my golden time,
   In my dear joys have part;
For Thee the glory of my prime,
   The fulness of my heart !

6 I cannot, Lord, too early take
   The covenant divine:
O ne'er the happy heart may break
   Whose earliest love was Thine.

                    T. H. Gill, 1819–1906

447

LORD of all, to whom alone
   All our hearts' desires are known,
When we stand before Thy throne,
   Jesus, hear and save !

2 Son of Man, before whose eyes
   Every secret open lies,
At Thy great and last assize,
   Jesus, hear and save !

3 Saviour, who didst not condemn
   Those who touched Thy garment's hem,
   Mercy show to us and them;
       Jesus, hear and save!

4 Lord, the way to sinners shown,
   Lord, the truth by sinners known,
   Love incarnate on the throne,
       Jesus, hear and save!   Amen.

C. A. Alington, 1872–1955.

448

LOVED with everlasting love,
    Led by grace that love to know;
Spirit, breathing from above,
    Thou hast taught me it is so.
O this full and perfect peace!
    O this transport all divine!
In a love which cannot cease
    I am His, and He is mine.

2 Heaven above is softer blue,
    Earth around is sweeter green;
Something lives in every hue,
    Christless eyes have never seen:
Birds with gladder songs o'erflow,
    Flowers with deeper beauties shine,
Since I know, as now I know,
    I am His and He is mine.

3 His for ever, only His:
    Who the Lord and me shall part?
Ah, with what a rest of bliss
    Christ can fill the loving heart!
Heaven and earth may fade and flee,
    First-born light in gloom decline;
But, while God and I shall be,
    I am His, and He is mine.

George Wade Robinson, 1838–77.

449

NOT for our sins alone
 Thy mercy, Lord, we sue;
Let fall Thy pitying glance
 On our devotions too,
What we have done for Thee,
 And what we think to do.

2 The holiest hours we spend
 In prayer upon our knees,
The times when most we deem
 Our songs of praise will please,
Thou searcher of all hearts,
 Forgiveness pour on these.

3 And all the gifts we bring,
 And all the vows we make,
And all the acts of love
 We plan for Thy dear sake,
Into Thy pardoning thought,
 O God of mercy, take.

4 Bow down Thine ear and hear,
 Open Thine eyes and see;
Our very love is shame,
 And we must come to Thee,
To make it of Thy grace
 What Thou wouldst have it be.

Henry Twells, 1823–1900

450

NOT what these hands have done
 Can save this guilty soul;
Not what this toiling flesh has borne
 Can make my spirit whole.

2 Not what I feel or do
  Can give me peace with God;
Not all my prayers, and sighs, and tears
  Can bear my heavy load.

3 Thy work alone, O Christ,
  Can ease this weight of sin;
Thy blood alone, O Lamb of God,
  Can give me peace within.

4 Thy love to me, O God,
  Not mine, O Lord, to Thee,
Can rid me of this dark unrest,
  And set my spirit free.

5 Thy grace alone, O God,
  To me can pardon speak;
Thy power alone, O Son of God,
  Can this sore bondage break.

6 I bless the Christ of God,
  I rest on life divine,
And with unfaltering lip and heart,
  I call this Saviour mine.

Horatius Bonar, 1808–89, *altd.*

451

NOW I have found the ground wherein
 Sure my soul's anchor may remain—
The wounds of Jesus, for my sin
 Before the world's foundation slain;
Whose mercy shall unshaken stay,
When heaven and earth are fled away.

2 Father, Thine everlasting grace
 Our scanty thought surpasses far,
Thy heart still melts with tenderness,
 Thy arms of love still open are
Returning sinners to receive,
That mercy they may taste and live.

3 Though waves and storms go o'er my head,
　　Though strength, and health, and friends be
　　　gone,
　Though joys be withered all and dead,
　　Though every comfort be withdrawn,
　On this my steadfast soul relies—
　Father, Thy mercy never dies !

4 Fixed on this ground will I remain,
　　Though my heart fail and flesh decay;
　This anchor shall my soul sustain,
　　When earth's foundations melt away:
　Mercy's full power I then shall prove,
　Loved with an everlasting love.

Johann Rothe, 1688–1758,
tr. John Wesley, 1703–91.

452

Now in the days of youth,
　　When life flows fresh and free,
　Thou Lord of all our hearts and lives,
　We give ourselves to Thee;
　Our joyful gift receive
　And fit us to fulfil,
　Through all our days, in all our ways,
　Our heavenly Father's will.

2 Teach us, where'er we live,
　　To act as in Thy sight,
　And do what Thou would'st have us do
　With radiant delight;
　Not choosing what is great,
　Nor spurning what is small,
　But take as from Thy hand our tasks,
　And glorify them all.

3 Teach us to love the true,
　　The beautiful and pure,
　And let us not for one short hour
　　An evil thought endure.
　But give us grace to stand
　　Decided, brave and strong,
　The lovers of all holy things,
　　The foes of all things wrong.

4 Spirit of Christ, do Thou
　　Our first bright days inspire,
　That we may live the life of love
　　And loftiest desire;
　And be by Thee prepared
　　For larger years to come,
　And for the life ineffable
　　Within the Father's home.

Walter J. Mathams, 1853-1931.

453

O MY Saviour, lifted
　　From the earth for me,
Draw me, in Thy mercy,
　　Nearer unto Thee.

2 Lift my earth-bound longings,
　　Fix them, Lord, above;
　Draw me with the magnet
　　Of Thy mighty love.

3 Lord, Thine arms are stretching
　　Ever far and wide,
　To enfold Thy children
　　To Thy loving side.

4 And I come, Lord Jesus;
　　Dare I turn away?
　No! Thy love hath conquered,
　　And I come to-day.

5 Bringing all my burdens,
   Sorrow, sin and care,
At Thy feet I lay them,
   And I leave them there.

William Walsham How, 1823–97.

454

O SAVIOUR, I have nought to plead,
   In earth beneath or heaven above,
But just my own exceeding need
   And Thy exceeding love.

2 The need will soon be past and gone,
   Exceeding great, but quickly o'er,
The love unbought is all Thine own,
   And lasts for evermore.

Jane Crewdson, 1809–63.

455

O THOU who hast redeemed of old,
And bidst me of Thy strength take hold,
   And be at peace with Thee;
Help me Thy benefits to own,
And hear me tell what Thou hast done,
   O dying Lamb, for me.

2 Vouchsafe the eye of faith to see
The Man transfixed on Calvary,
   To know Thee who Thou art,—
The one eternal God and true !
And let the sight affect, subdue,
   And break my stubborn heart.

3 Lover of souls, to rescue mine,
  Reveal the charity divine
    That suffered in my stead;
That made Thy soul a sacrifice,
And quenched in death those gracious eyes,
    And bowed that sacred head.

4 The veil of unbelief remove;
  And by Thy manifested love,
    And by Thy sprinkled blood,
Destroy the love of sin in me,
And get Thyself the victory,
    And bring me back to God. Amen.

Charles Wesley, 1707–88.

456

ONE who is all unfit to count
    As scholar in Thy school,
Thou of Thy love hast named a friend—
  O kindness wonderful !

2 Thou dwellest in unshadowed light,
    All sin and shame above—
That Thou shouldst bear our sin and shame,
    How can I tell such love ?

3 Ah, did not He the heavenly throne
    A little thing esteem,
And not unworthy for my sake
    A mortal body deem ?

4 When in His flesh they drove the nails,
    Did He not all endure ?
What name is there to fit a life
    So patient and so pure !

5 So, Love itself in human form,
    For love of me He came;
  I cannot look upon His face
    For shame, for bitter shame.

6 If there is aught of worth in me,
    It comes from Thee alone;
  Then keep me safe, for so, O Lord,
    Thou keepest but Thine own.

Narayan Vaman Tilak, 1862–1919,
tr. Nicol Macnicol, 1870–1952.

457

PSALM CXXX.

OUT of the depths I cry to Thee,
    Lord, hear me, I implore Thee;
Bend down Thy gracious ear to me,
    Regard my prayer before Thee;
If Thou rememberest each misdeed,
If each should have its rightful meed,
    Who may abide Thy presence?

2 Our pardon is Thy gift; Thy love
    And grace alone avail us;
  Our works could ne'er our guilt remove,
    The strictest life would fail us;
  That none may boast himself of aught,
  But own in fear Thy grace hath wrought
    What in him seemeth righteous.

3 And thus my hope is in the Lord
    And not in mine own merit;
  I rest upon His faithful word
    To them of contrite spirit;
  That He is merciful and just—
  Here is my comfort and my trust;
    His help I wait with patience.

4 Though great our sins and sore our woes
    His grace much more aboundeth;
His helping love no limit knows,
    Our utmost need it soundeth;
Our kind and faithful shepherd He,
Who shall at last set Israel free
    From all their sin and sorrow.

Martin Luther, 1483–1546,
tr. Catherine Winkworth, 1827–78, *altd.*

458

ROCK of ages, cleft for me,
    Let me hide myself in Thee;
Let the water and the blood,
From Thy riven side which flowed,
Be of sin the double cure;
Cleanse me from its guilt and power.

2 Not the labours of my hands
    Can fulfil Thy law's demands:
Could my zeal no respite know,
Could my tears for ever flow,
All for sin could not atone;
Thou must save, and Thou alone.

3 Nothing in my hand I bring;
    Simply to Thy cross I cling;
Naked, come to Thee for dress;
Helpless, look to Thee for grace;
Foul, I to the fountain fly,
Wash me, Saviour, or I die.

4 While I draw this fleeting breath,
    When my eyelids close in death,
When I soar to worlds unknown,
See Thee on Thy judgment-throne,
Rock of ages, cleft for me,
Let me hide myself in Thee.

A. M. Toplady, 1740–78, *altd.*

459

SAVIOUR, blessèd Saviour,
   Listen while we sing;
Hearts and voices raising
   Praises to our King:
All we have we offer,
   All we hope to be,
Body, soul, and spirit,
   All we yield to Thee.

2 Farther, ever farther,
   From Thy wounded side,
Heedlessly we wandered,
   Wandered far and wide;
Till Thou cam'st in mercy,
   Seeking young and old,
Lovingly to bear them,
   Saviour, to Thy fold.

3 Nearer, ever nearer,
   Christ, we draw to Thee,
Deep in adoration
   Bending low the knee:
Thou for our redemption
   Cam'st on earth to die;
Thou, that we might follow,
   Hast gone up on high.

4 Onward, ever onward,
   Journeying o'er the road
Worn by saints before us,
   Journeying on to God;
Leaving all behind us,
   May we hasten on,
Backward never looking,
   Till the prize is won.

5 Higher, then, and higher,
   Bear the ransomed soul,
Earthly toils forgotten,
   Saviour, to its goal;

Where, in joys unthought of,
  Saints with angels sing,
Never weary, raising
  Praises to their King.

Godfrey Thring, 1823–1903.

460

THOU hidden Love of God, whose height,
  Whose depth unfathomed, no man knows,
I see from far Thy beauteous light,
  Inly I sigh for Thy repose:
My heart is pained, nor can it be
At rest, till it finds rest in Thee.

2 'Tis mercy all, that Thou hast brought
  My mind to seek her peace in Thee:
Yet while I seek but find Thee not,
  No peace my wandering soul shall see:
O when shall all my wanderings end,
And all my steps to Thee-ward tend?

3 Is there a thing beneath the sun
  That strives with Thee my heart to share?
Ah! tear it thence, and reign alone,
  The Lord of every motion there;
Then shall my heart from earth be free,
When it has found repose in Thee.

4 Each moment draw from earth away
  My heart, that lowly waits Thy call;
Speak to my inmost soul, and say,
  I am thy love, thy God, thy all.
To feel Thy power, to hear Thy voice,
To taste Thy love, be all my choice.

Gerhard Tersteegen, 1697–1769,
tr. John Wesley, 1703–91.

(3) Obedience and Consecration

461

A CHARGE to keep I have,
A God to glorify,
A never-dying soul to save,
And fit it for the sky:

2 To serve the present age,
My calling to fulfil:
O may it all my powers engage
To do my Master's will!

3 Arm me with jealous care,
As in Thy sight to live;
And O Thy servant, Lord, prepare
A strict account to give.

4 Help me to watch and pray,
And on Thyself rely,
And let me ne'er my trust betray,
But press to realms on high.

Charles Wesley, 1707–88.

462

BE Thou my vision, O Lord of my heart,
Be all else but naught to me, save that Thou
art;
Be Thou my best thought in the day and the night,
Both waking and sleeping, Thy presence my light.

2 Be Thou my wisdom, be Thou my true word;
Be Thou ever with me, and I with Thee, Lord;
Be Thou my great Father, and I Thy true son;
Be Thou in me dwelling, and I with Thee one.

3 Be Thou my breastplate, my sword for the fight;
Be Thou my whole armour, be Thou my true might;
Be Thou my soul's shelter, be Thou my strong
tower,
O raise Thou me heavenward, great power of my
power.

4 Riches I heed not, nor man's empty praise,
Be Thou mine inheritance now and always;
Be Thou and Thou only the first in my heart;
O sovereign of heaven, my treasure Thou art.

5 High King of heaven, Thou heaven's bright sun,
O grant me its joys, after victory is won;
Great heart of my own heart, whatever befall,
Still be Thou my vision, O ruler of all.

Ancient Irish, tr. Mary Byrne, 1881–1931.
Versified by Eleanor Hull, 1861–1935, altd.

463

BLEST are the pure in heart,
For they shall see their God;
The secret of the Lord is theirs;
Their soul is Christ's abode.

2 The Lord who left the heavens,
  Our life and peace to bring,
 To dwell in lowliness with men,
  Their pattern and their king:—

3 Still to the lowly soul
  He doth Himself impart,
 And for His dwelling and His throne
  Chooseth the pure in heart.

4 Lord, we Thy presence seek:
  May ours this blessing be;
 Give us a pure and lowly heart,—
  A temple meet for Thee.

John Keble, 1792–1866.
William John Hall, 1793–1861.

464

BRIGHTLY gleams our banner,
  Pointing to the sky,
Waving on Christ's soldiers
  To their home on high:
Marching through the desert,
  Gladly thus we pray,
Still, with hearts united,
  Singing on our way.
Brightly gleams our banner,
  Pointing to the sky.
Waving on Christ's soldiers
  To their home on high!

2 Jesus, Lord and Master,
  At Thy sacred feet,
Here, with hearts rejoicing,
  See Thy children meet.
Often have we left Thee,
  Often gone astray;
Keep us, mighty Saviour,
  In the narrow way.

3 All our days direct us
   In the way we go;
   Make us still victorious
   Over every foe.
   When the march is over,
   Then come rest and peace,
   Jesus in His beauty,
   Songs that never cease.

T. J. Potter, 1827-73.
W. Walsham How, 1823-97, altd.

465

DEAR Master, in whose life I see
All that I long, but fail to be,
Let Thy clear light for ever shine,
To shame and guide this life of mine.

2 Though what I dream and what I do
In my poor days are always two,
Help me, oppressed by things undone,
O Thou, whose deeds and dreams were one.
Amen.

John Hunter, 1848-1917.

466

FAITH of our fathers, living still
In spite of dungeon, fire, and sword,
O how our hearts beat high with joy
Whene'er we hear that glorious word.
Faith of our fathers! Holy faith!
We will be true to thee till death.

2 Our fathers, chained in prisons dark,
Were still in heart and conscience free;
And blest would be their children's fate,
Though they, like them, should die for Thee.

3 Faith of our fathers ! God's great power
    Shall soon all nations win for Thee;
And through the truth that comes from God
    Mankind shall then indeed be free.

4 Faith of our fathers ! We will love
    Both friend and foe in all our strife,
And preach thee, too, as love knows how,
    By kindly words and virtuous life:
Faith of our fathers! Holy faith!
We will be true to thee till death.

F. W. Faber, 1814–63, *altd.*

467

FATHER, hear the prayer we offer:
    Not for ease that prayer shall be,
But for strength, that we may ever
    Live our lives courageously.

2 Not for ever in green pastures
    Do we ask our way to be:
But by steep and rugged pathways
    Would we strive to climb to Thee.

3 Not for ever by still waters
    Would we idly quiet stay;
But would smite the living fountains
    From the rocks along our way.

4 Be our strength in hours of weakness,
    In our wanderings be our guide;
Through endeavour, failure, danger,
    Father, be Thou at our side.

5 Let our path be bright or dreary,
    Storm or sunshine be our share;
May our souls, in hope unweary,
    Make Thy work our ceaseless prayer.

Love Maria Willis, 1824–1908.

468

FATHER, I know that all my life
   Is portioned out for me;
The changes that are sure to come
   I do not fear to see;
I ask Thee for a present mind,
   Intent on pleasing Thee.

2 I ask Thee for a thoughtful love,
   Through constant watching wise,
To meet the glad with joyful smiles,
   To wipe the weeping eyes;
A heart at leisure from itself,
   To soothe and sympathise.

3 Wherever in the world I am,
   In whatsoe'er estate,
I have a fellowship with hearts
   To keep and cultivate;
A work of lowly love to do
   For Him on whom I wait.

4 I ask Thee for the daily strength,
   To none that ask denied;
A mind to blend with outward life,
   While keeping at Thy side;
Content to fill a little space,
   If Thou be glorified.

5 In service which Thy will appoints
   There are no bonds for me;
My inmost heart is taught the truth
   That makes Thy children free;
A life of self-renouncing love
   Is one of liberty.

Anna Laetitia Waring, 1820–1910, altd.

469

FATHER, lead me day by day
Ever in Thine own good way;
Teach me to be pure and true.
Show me what I ought to do.

2 When in danger, make me brave;
Make me know that Thou canst save.
Keep me safe by Thy dear side;
Let me in Thy love abide.

3 When I'm tempted to do wrong,
Make me steadfast, wise, and strong;
And when all alone I stand,
Shield me with Thy mighty hand.

4 When my heart is full of glee,
Help me to remember Thee;
Happy most of all to know
That my Father loves me so.

5 When my work seems hard and dry,
May I press on cheerily;
Help me patiently to bear
Pain and hardship, toil and care.

6 May I see the good and bright,
When they pass before my sight;
May I hear the heavenly voice
When the pure and wise rejoice.

7 May I do the good I know,
Be Thy loving child below,
Then at last go home to Thee,
Evermore Thy child to be.

J. P. Hopps, 1834–1911.

470

FATHER of all, we come to Thee:
   We own Thy care, Thy praise we sing;
Help us our truest loyalty
   To Thee and to our land to bring.

2 Teach us to speak and do the truth,
   The false in speech and deed to shun,
So that the honour of our word
   May trusted be by everyone.

3 Help us to copy Thee, and do
   The good that lieth near at hand;
Thus, daily helping, may we learn
   How perfect is Thy law's command.

†4 O friend of all, help us to be
   The friends of all; to understand
The meaning of true brotherhood
   With every Scout, of every land.

5 Forgive us all the times that we
   Have disobedient been and wrong;
We would obey Thy holy will;
   Against temptation make us strong.

6 When troubles come and things go ill,
   Teach us to seek from Thee the grace
That turns to heaven a trustful heart,
   And to the world a smiling face.

7 Guard Thou our minds from thoughts impure,
   Our lips from all defilement stay.
We are Thy knights. O make us strong
   To follow Thee through all life's way. Amen.

E. Alec Blaxill, 1873–1953, *altd.*

† For the use of Scouts.

471

GOD be in my head,
  And in my understanding;
God be in mine eyes,
  And in my looking;
God be in my mouth,
  And in my speaking;
God be in my heart,
  And in my thinking;
God be at mine end,
  And at my departing. Amen.

Book of Hours, 1514.

472

GOD, who touchest earth with beauty,
  Make me lovely too;
With Thy Spirit re-create me,
  Make my heart anew.

2 Like Thy springs and running waters,
    Make me crystal pure;
  Like Thy rocks of towering grandeur,
    Make me strong and sure.

3 Like Thy dancing waves in sunlight,
    Make me glad and free;
  Like the straightness of the pine trees,
    Let me upright be.

4 Like the arching of the heavens,
    Lift my thoughts above;
  Turn my dreams to noble action,
    Ministries of love.

5 God, who touchest earth with beauty,
    Make me lovely too;
  Keep me ever, by Thy Spirit,
    Pure and strong and true. Amen.

Mary S. Edgar, 1889–

473

HOW shall I follow Him I serve?
　　How shall I copy Him I love,
Nor from those blessèd footsteps swerve,
　　Which lead me to His seat above?

2 Privations, sorrows, bitter scorn,
　　The life of toil, the mean abode,
The faithless kiss, the crown of thorn,—
　　Are these the consecrated road?

3 'Twas thus He suffered, though a Son,
　　Foreknowing, choosing, feeling all;
Until the perfect work was done,
　　And drunk the bitter cup of gall.

4 Lord, should my path through suffering lie,
　　Forbid it I should e'er repine;
Still let me turn to Calvary,
　　Nor heed my griefs, remembering Thine.

5 To faint, to grieve, to die for me
　　Thou camest, not Thyself to please;
And dear as earthly comforts be,
　　Shall I not love Thee more than these?

6 Yes, I would count them all but loss,
　　That I may follow after Thee:
Flesh shrinks and trembles at the cross,
　　But Thou canst give the victory.

Josiah Conder, 1789–1855.

474

HUSHED was the evening hymn,
　　The temple courts were dark;
The lamp was burning dim
　　Before the sacred ark,
When suddenly a voice divine
Rang through the silence of the shrine.

2   The old man, meek and mild,
        The priest of Israel, slept;
    His watch the temple child,
        The little Levite, kept;
    And what from Eli's sense was sealed
    The Lord to Hannah's son revealed.

3   O give me Samuel's ear,
        The open ear, O Lord,
    Alive and quick to hear
        Each whisper of Thy word—
    Like him to answer at Thy call,
    And to obey Thee first of all.

4   O give me Samuel's heart,
        A lowly heart, that waits
    Where in Thy house Thou art,
        Or watches at Thy gates
    By day and night, a heart that still
    Moves at the breathing of Thy will.

5   O give me Samuel's mind,
        A sweet, unmurmuring faith,
    Obedient and resigned
        To Thee in life and death,
    That I may read with childlike eyes
    Truths that are hidden from the wise.

                    J. D. Burns, 1823–64.

475

I NEED Thee every hour, most gracious Lord:
No tender voice like Thine can peace afford.
*I need Thee, O I need Thee; every hour I need
    Thee;
O bless me now, my Saviour! I come to Thee.*

2 I need Thee every hour; stay Thou near by;
Temptations lose their power when Thou art nigh.

3 I need Thee every hour, in joy or pain;
Come quickly and abide, or life is vain.

4 I need Thee every hour: teach me Thy will;
And Thy rich promises in me fulfil.

5 I need Thee every hour, most Holy One;
O make me Thine indeed, Thou blessèd Son.

Annie S. Hawks, 1835–1918.

476

IN sunny days, when all is bright,
When friends are near and hearts are light,
Help us, rejoicing in Thy sight,
    To do Thy will.

2 Whatever work our hands may find,
Help us, with loving, cheerful mind,
Thy laws upon our hearts to bind,
    And do Thy will.

3 Help us to serve Thee in our day,
To serve our fellows while we may,
And bravely tread the thorny way,
    When 'tis Thy will.

4 Help us to fight against all sin,
To listen to Thy voice within,
And nothing ever try to win
    Against Thy will.

5 May this great truth our glad hearts buoy,
That every good without alloy,
And every pure and lasting joy,
    Is in Thy will.

6 And when Thy heaven at last we see,
When we, O God, come home to Thee,
Still evermore our joy shall be
    To do Thy will.

Emily Waddington Haigh.

477

LOOKING upward every day,
　　Sunshine on our faces;
Pressing onward every day
　　Toward the heavenly places.

2 Growing every day in awe,
　　For Thy name is holy;
Learning every day to love
　　With a love more lowly.

3 Walking every day more close
　　To our Elder Brother;
Growing every day more true
　　Unto one another.

4 Leaving every day behind
　　Something which might hinder;
Running swifter every day,
　　Growing purer, kinder.

5 Lord, so pray we every day,
　　Hear us in Thy pity;
That we enter in at last
　　To the Holy City.

Mary Butler, 1841–1916.

478

MAKE me a captive, Lord,
　　And then I shall be free;
Force me to render up my sword,
　　And I shall conqueror be.

2 I sink in life's alarms
　　When by myself I stand;
Imprison me within Thine arms,
　　And strong shall be my hand.

3 My heart is weak and poor
  Until it master find;
It has no spring of action sure,
  It varies with the wind.

4 It cannot freely move
  Till Thou hast wrought its chain;
Enslave it with Thy matchless love,
  And deathless it shall reign.

5 My will is not my own
  Till Thou hast made it Thine;
If it would reach a monarch's throne
  It must its crown resign.

6 It only stands unbent
  Amid the clashing strife,
When on Thy bosom it has leant,
  And found in Thee its life.

George Matheson, 1842-1906

479

MASTER, speak ! Thy servant heareth,
  Waiting for Thy gracious word,
Longing for Thy voice that cheereth;
  Master, let it now be heard.
I am listening, Lord, for Thee;
  What hast Thou to say to me ?

2 Speak to me by name, O Master !
  Let me know it is to me;
Speak, that I may follow faster,
  With a step more firm and free,
Where the Shepherd leads the flock,
  In the shadow of the rock.

3 Master, speak ! though least and lowest,
    Let me not unheard depart;
 Master, speak ! for O Thou knowest
    All the yearning of my heart;
 Knowest all its truest need;
    Speak, and make me blest indeed.

4 Master, speak ! and make me ready,
    When Thy voice is truly heard,
 With obedience glad and steady
    Still to follow every word.
 I am listening, Lord, for Thee;
    Master, speak, O speak to me !

Frances Ridley Havergal, 1836–79.

480

M Y God, my Father, make me strong,
    When tasks of life seem hard and long,
 To greet them with this triumph song—
    Thy will be done.

2 Draw from my timid eyes the veil,
 To show, where earthly forces fail,
 Thy power and love must still prevail,
    Thy will be done.

3 With confident and humble mind,
 Freedom in service I would find,
 Praying through every toil assigned,
    Thy will be done.

4 Things deemed impossible I dare,
 Thine is the call and Thine the care,
 Thy wisdom shall the way prepare,
    Thy will be done.

5 All power is here and round me now,
 Faithful I stand in rule and vow,
 While 'tis not I but ever Thou;
    Thy will be done.

6 Heaven's music chimes the glad days in,
Hope soars beyond death, pain, and sin,
Faith shouts in triumph, love must win;
    Thy will be done.

Frederick Mann, 1846–1928.

481

MY spirit longs for Thee
    Within my troubled breast,
Though I unworthy be
    Of so divine a guest.

2 Of so divine a guest
    Unworthy though I be,
Yet has my heart no rest
    Unless it come from Thee.

3 Unless it come from Thee,
    In vain I look around;
In all that I can see
    No rest is to be found.

4 No rest is to be found
    But in Thy blessèd love:
O let my wish be crowned,
    And send it from above !

John Byrom, 1692–1763, altd.

482

O LORD, how happy should we be
    If we could cast our care on Thee,
If we from self could rest,
And feel at heart that One above,
In perfect wisdom, perfect love,
    Is working for the best.

2 Could we but kneel and cast our load
  E'en while we pray, upon our God;
    Then rise with lightened cheer,
  Sure that the Father, who is nigh
  To still the famished raven's cry,
    Will hear in that we fear.

3 We do not trust Him as we should;
  So chafes weak nature's restless mood
    To cast its peace away;
  But birds and flowers around us preach,
  And all the present evil teach
    Sufficient for the day.

4 Lord, make these faithless hearts of ours
  Such lessons learn from birds and flowers;
    Make them from self to cease,
  Leave all things to a Father's will,
  And taste, before Him lying still,
    E'en in affliction, peace.

Joseph Anstice, 1808-36.

483

O LORD of life, and love, and power
    How joyful life might be
If in Thy service every hour
    We lived and moved with Thee;
If eager youth in all its might
    By Thee were sanctified,
And manhood found its chief delight
    In working at Thy side !

2 'Tis ne'er too late, while life shall last,
    A new life to begin;
  'Tis ne'er too late to leave the past,
    And break with self and sin:
  And we this day, both old and young,
    Would earnestly aspire
  For hearts to nobler purpose strung,
    And purified desire.

3 Nor for ourselves alone we plead,
    But for all faithful souls
Who serve Thy cause by word or deed,
    Whose names Thy book enrols:
O speed Thy work, victorious King,
    And give Thy workers might,
That through the world Thy truth may ring,
    And all men see Thy light.

Ella Sophia Armitage, 1841–1931.

484

SAVIOUR, teach me, day by day,
Love's sweet lesson to obey;
Sweeter lesson cannot be,
Loving Him Who first loved me.

2 Teach me, I am not my own,
I am Thine, and Thine alone;
Thine to keep, to rule, to save
From all sin that would enslave.

3 With a child's glad heart of love
At Thy bidding may I move.
Prompt to serve and follow Thee,
Loving Him Who first loved me.

4 Teach me thus Thy steps to trace,
Strong to follow in Thy grace,
Learning how to love from Thee,
Loving Him Who first loved me.

Jane Leeson, 1807–82.

485

SAVIOUR, Thy dying love
    Thou gavest me,
Nor should I aught withhold,
    My Lord, from Thee;
In love my soul would bow,
My heart fulfil its vow,
Some offering bring Thee now,
    Something for Thee.

2 At the blest mercy-seat
        Pleading for me,
My feeble faith looks up,
        Jesus, to Thee :
Help me the cross to bear,
Thy wondrous love declare,
Some song to raise, or prayer —
    Something for Thee.

3 Give me a faithful heart,
        Likeness to Thee,
That each departing day
        Henceforth may see
Some work of love begun,
Some deed of kindness done,
Some wanderer sought and won—
    Something for Thee.

4 All that I am and have,
        Thy gifts so free,
In joy, in grief, through life,
        O Lord, for Thee.
And when Thy face I see,
My ransomed soul shall be,
Through all eternity,
        Something for Thee.

S. D. Phelps, 1816–95.

486

SPEAK to us, Lord, Thyself reveal,
    While here o'er earth we rove;
Speak to our hearts, and let us feel
    The kindling of Thy love.

2 With Thee conversing, we forget
    All time and toil and care;
Labour is rest, and pain is sweet,
    If Thou, my God, art here.

3 Here then, my God, vouchsafe to stay,
    And bid my heart rejoice;
My bounding heart shall own Thy sway,
    And echo to Thy voice.

4 Thou callest me to seek Thy face:
    'Tis all I wish to seek;
To attend the whispers of Thy grace,
    And hear Thee inly speak.

5 Let this my every hour employ,
    Till I Thy glory see;
Enter into my Master's joy,
    And find my heaven in Thee.

Charles Wesley, 1707–88, *altd.*

487

TEACH me, my God and King,
    In all things Thee to see,
And what I do in anything
    To do it as for Thee.

2 A man that looks on glass
    On it may stay his eye;
Or if he pleaseth, through it pass,
    And then the heaven espy.

3 All may of Thee partake:
    Nothing can be so mean,
Which with this tincture, " For Thy sake,"
    Will not grow bright and clean.

4 A servant with this clause
    Makes drudgery divine:
Who sweeps a room, as for Thy laws,
    Makes that and the action fine.

5 This is the famous stone
    That turneth all to gold:
For that which God doth touch and own
    Cannot for less be told.

                                    George Herbert, 1593–1633.

488

THE Lord is King ! I own His power,
    His right to rule each day and hour;
I own His claim on heart and will,
And His demands I would fulfil.

2 He claims my heart, to keep it clean
    From all defiling taint of sin;
He claims my will, that I may prove
How swift obedience answers love.

3 He claims my hand for active life
    In noble deeds and worthy strife;
He claims my feet, that in His ways
I may walk boldly all my days.

4 He claims my lips, that purest word
    In all my converse may be heard;
My motives, passions, thoughts, that these,
My inner life, my King may please.

5 He claims the brightness of my youth,
   My earnest strivings after truth,
   My joys, my toil, my craftsman's skill;
   All have their place, and serve His will.

6 O Lord my King, I turn to Thee;
   Thy loyal service makes me free;
   My daily task Thou shalt assign;
   For heart and will and life are Thine.

Darley Terry, 1848–1934.

489

WE bless Thee for Thy peace, O God,
   Deep as the unfathomed sea,
Which falls like sunshine on the road
   Of those who trust in Thee.

2 We ask not, Father, for repose
   Which comes from outward rest,
If we may have through all life's woes
   Thy peace within our breast,—

3 That peace which suffers and is strong,
   Trusts where it cannot see,
Deems not the trial-way too long,
   But leaves the end with Thee;

4 That peace which flows serene and deep,
   A river in the soul
Whose banks a living verdure keep—
   God's sunshine o'er the whole.

5 O Father, give our hearts this peace,
   Whate'er the outward be,
Till all life's discipline shall cease,
   And we go home to Thee.

Christian Melodies, 1858.

490

WHAT do I owe?
Nay, Lord—what do I not?
All that I am—
And all that I have got;
All that I am,
And that how small a thing,
Compared with all
Thy goodly fostering.

2   What do I owe
To this dear land of ours?
All of my best,
My time, my thoughts, my powers;
All of my best
Is yet too small to give,
That this our land
May to Thine increase live.

3   What do I owe
To all the world around?
To set Thee first,
That grace may more abound;
To set Thee first,
To hold Thee all in all,
And, come what may,
To follow Thy high call.

4   What do I owe
To those who follow on?
To build more sure
The freedom we have won;
To build more sure
The kingdoms of Thy grace,
Kingdoms secure
In truth and righteousness.

5   What do I owe
To Christ, my Lord, my King?
That all my life
Be one sweet offering;

That all my life
To noblest heights aspire,
That all I do
Be touched with holy fire.

John Oxenham, 1852–1941.

491

WHEN we walk with the Lord
In the light of His Word
What a glory He sheds on our way !
While we do His good will,
He abides with us still,
And with all who will trust and obey.

Trust and obey, for there's no other way
To be happy in Jesus,
But to trust and obey.

2   Not a burden we bear,
Not a sorrow we share,
But our toil He doth richly repay;
Not a grief nor a loss,
Not a frown nor a cross,
But is blest if we trust and obey.

3   But we never can prove
The delights of His love
Until all on the altar we lay;
For the favour He shows,
And the joy He bestows,
Are for them who will trust and obey.

4   Then in fellowship sweet
We will sit at His feet,
Or we'll walk by His side in the way;
What He says we will do,
Where He sends we will go—
Never fear, only trust and obey.

J. H. Sammis, 1846–1919.

(4) JOY AND THANKSGIVING

492

ALL my hope on God is founded;
  He doth still my trust renew.
Me through change and chance He guideth,
  Only good and only true.
    God unknown,
    He alone
Calls my heart to be His own.

2 Pride of man and earthly glory,
    Sword and crown betray his trust;
What with care and toil he buildeth,
    Tower and temple, fall to dust.
      But God's power,
      Hour by hour,
Is my temple and my tower.

3 God's great goodness aye endureth,
    Deep His wisdom, passing thought:
Splendour, light, and life attend Him,
    Beauty springeth out of nought.
      Evermore,
      From His store
New-born worlds rise and adore.

4 Daily doth the almighty giver
   Bounteous gifts on us bestow;
His desire our soul delighteth,
   Pleasure leads us where we go.
     Love doth stand
     At His hand;
   Joy doth wait on His command.

5 Still from man to God eternal
   Sacrifice of praise be done,
High above all praises praising
   For the gift of Christ His Son.
     Christ doth call
     One and all:
   Ye who follow shall not fall.

Robert Bridges, 1844–1930.
Based on Joachim Neander, 1650–80.

493

BLESSÈD assurance, Jesus is mine:
   O what a foretaste of glory divine!
Heir of salvation, purchase of God;
Born of His Spirit, washed in His blood.
This is my story, this is my song,
Praising my Saviour all the day long.

2 Perfect submission, perfect delight,
Visions of rapture burst on my sight;
Angels descending, bring from above
Echoes of mercy, whispers of love.

3 Perfect submission, all is at rest,
I in my Saviour am happy and blest;
Watching and waiting, looking above,
Filled with His goodness, lost in His love.

Frances van Alstyne, 1820–1915.

494

COME Thou fount of every blessing,
    Tune my heart to sing Thy grace;
Streams of mercy never ceasing
    Call for songs of loudest praise.
Teach me some melodious measure,
    Sung by flaming tongues above.
O the vast, the boundless treasure,
    Of my Lord's unchanging love !

2 Here I raise my Ebenezer,
    Hither by Thy help I'm come,
And I hope, by Thy good pleasure,
    Safely to arrive at home.
Jesus sought me when a stranger,
    Wandering from the fold of God;
He, to rescue me from danger,
    Interposed His precious blood.

3 O to grace how great a debtor
    Daily I'm constrained to be !
Let that grace, Lord, like a fetter
    Bind my wandering heart to Thee.
Prone to wander,—Lord, I feel it,—
    Prone to leave the God I love:
Here's my heart, O take and seal it,
    Seal it from Thy courts above.

Robert Robinson, 1735–90, *altd.*

495

COME, we that love the Lord,
    And let our joys be known;
Join in a song with sweet accord,
    And thus surround the throne.

2   The sorrows of the mind
    Be banished from the place;
Religion never was designed
    To make our pleasures less.

3   Let those refuse to sing
       That never knew our God;
  But children of the heavenly King
       May speak their joys abroad.

4   The men of grace have found
       Glory begun below;
  Celestial fruits on earthly ground
       From faith and hope may grow.

5   The hill of Zion yields
       A thousand sacred sweets,
  Before we reach the heavenly fields,
       Or walk the golden streets.

6   Then let our songs abound,
       And every tear be dry;
  We're marching through Immanuel's ground
       To fairer worlds on high.

Isaac Watts, 1674–1748, *altd.*

496

HAPPY are they, they that love God,
    Whose hearts have Christ confest,
Who by His cross have found their life,
    And neath His yoke their rest.

2 Glad is the praise, sweet are the songs,
    When they together sing;
  And strong the prayers that bow the ear
    Of heaven's eternal King.

3 Christ to their homes giveth His peace,
    And makes their loves His own:
  But ah, what tares the evil one
    Hath in His garden sown!

4 Sad were our lot, evil this earth,
    Did not its sorrows prove
The path whereby the sheep may find
    The fold of Jesus' love.

5 Then shall they know, they that love Him,
    How all their pain is good;
And death itself cannot unbind
    Their happy brotherhood.

Robert Bridges, 1844–1930.
Based on Charles Coffin, 1676–1749.

497

HOW vast the treasure we possess !
    How rich Thy bounty, King of grace !
This world is ours, and worlds to come;
Earth is our lodge, and heaven our home.

2 All things are ours;—the gifts of God,
The purchase of a Saviour's blood;
While the good Spirit shows us how
To use, and to improve them too.

3 If peace and plenty crown my days,
They help me, Lord, to speak Thy praise:
If bread of sorrows be my food,
Those sorrows work my lasting good.

4 I would not change my blest estate
For all the world calls good or great;
And while my faith can keep her hold
I envy not the sinner's gold.

5 Father, I wait Thy daily will;
   Thou shalt divide my portion still;
   Grant me on earth what seems Thee best,
   Till death and heaven reveal the rest.

Isaac Watts, 1674–1748.

498

I AM so glad that our Father in heaven
Tells of His love in the book He has given:
Wonderful things in the Bible I see;
This is the dearest, that Jesus loves me.
   I am so glad that Jesus loves me,
   Jesus loves even me.

2 Though I forget Him, and wander away,
   Still He doth love me wherever I stray;
   Back to His dear loving arms do I flee,
   When I remember that Jesus loves me.

3 O if there's only one song I can sing,
   When in His beauty I see the great King,
   This shall my song in eternity be,
   O what a wonder that Jesus loves me.

4 If one should ask of me: How can I tell?
   Glory to Jesus, I know very well;
   God's Holy Spirit with mine doth agree,
   Constantly witnessing: Jesus loves me.

Philipp Bliss, 1838–76.

499

I SOUGHT the Lord, and afterward I knew
He moved my soul to seek Him, seeking me;
It was not I that found, O Saviour true;
   No, I was found of Thee.

2 Thou didst reach forth Thy hand and mine enfold;
I walked and sank not on the storm-vexed sea;
'Twas not so much that I on Thee took hold
As Thou, dear Lord, on me.

3 I find, I walk, I love, but O the whole
Of love is but my answer, Lord, to Thee!
For Thou wert long before-hand with my soul;
Always Thou lovedst me.

Anon. 1880.

500

I THANK Thee, Lord, for life:
For Thou hast made and dowered me
With gifts of hearing, sight and speech,
With mind alert, and will that's free;
Guard all from harm, I Thee beseech.

2 I thank Thee, Lord, for health:
For day by day the joy of life
Runs through my veins with keen delight,
And I am glad amid the strife;
Keep my thoughts pure, guide me aright.

3 I thank Thee, Lord, for strength:
For as years pass, a fuller sense
Of power to dare and do is mine;
In active limb and muscle tense
I feel my strength: let it be Thine.

4 I thank Thee, Lord, for home:
Dear gift of Thine, where constant thought
Of parents' love forestalls my need;
Where care for others' weal is taught
And I am saved from self and greed.

5   I thank Thee, Lord, for hope:
What yet shall be I may not know;
  The unseen days will changes bring,
But through them all hope's star shall glow,
  And I shall have my song to sing.

J. Williams Butcher, 1857–1937.

501

Psalm xl.

I WAITED for the Lord my God,
  And patiently did bear;
At length to me He did incline,
  My voice and cry to hear.

2 He took me from a fearful pit
  And from the miry clay,
And on a rock He set my feet,
  Establishing my way.

3 He put a new song in my mouth,
  Our God to magnify:
Many shall see it, and shall fear,
  And on the Lord rely.

4 O blessèd is the man whose trust
  Upon the Lord relies,
Respecting not the proud, nor such
  As turn aside to lies.

5 O Lord my God, full many are
  The wonders Thou hast done;
Thy gracious thoughts to us-ward far
  Above all thoughts are gone.

Francis Rous, 1579–1659,
and W. Barton, 1597–1678.

502

I will sing the wondrous story
　Of the Christ who died for me,—
How He left the realms of glory
　For the cross on Calvary.
Yes, I'll sing the wondrous story
　Of the Christ who died for me,—
Sing it with His saints in glory,
　Gathered by the crystal sea.

2 I was lost: but Jesus found me,
　　Found the sheep that went astray,
Raised me up and gently led me
　　Back into the narrow way.
Days of darkness still may meet me,
　　Sorrow's paths I oft may tread;
But His presence still is with me,
　　By His guiding hand I'm led.

3 He will keep me till the river
　　Rolls its waters at my feet:
Then He'll bear me safely over,
　　Made by grace for glory meet.
Yes, I'll sing the wondrous story
　　Of the Christ who died for me,—
Sing it with His saints in glory,
　　Gathered by the crystal sea.

F. H. Rowley, 1854–1952.

503

LORD God, from whom all life
　And all true gladness springs,
Whose love and care shine everywhere
　Among earth's common things;
　Be present while we lift
　Our song to thee, and pay
Heart-gratitude for all things good
　About our path to-day.

2   We thank thee for the grace
     In friend and brother found;
For human love that points above
     To where all love is crowned:
     O may such friendship here
     Be to Thy children given,
As shall endure, deep, fair and pure,
     Till all be one in heaven.

3   But most we bless thee, Lord,
     That here Thy Spirit's breath
Blows clear and strong to baffle wrong
     And win our lives from death:
     O may each heart accept
     The entrance of Thy power,
And take Thee hence for sure defence
     And help in evil hour.

4   So, when our lives, to-day
     Within one circle brought,
Are sundered wide along the tide
     Of human work and thought,
     One song shall yet be ours,
     One life, one family,
One pathway still, by vale or hill,
     Shall lead us home to thee.

E. A. Burroughs, 1882–1935.

504

MY God, I thank Thee, Who hast made
    The earth so bright,
So full of splendour and of joy,
    Beauty and light;
So many glorious things are here,
    Noble and right.

2 I thank Thee, Lord, that Thou hast made
    Joy to abound;
So many gentle thoughts and deeds
    Circling us round,
That in the darkest spot of earth
    Some love is found.

3 I thank Thee too that all our joy
    Is touched with pain;
That shadows fall on brightest hours,
    That thorns remain:
So that earth's bliss may be our guide,
    And not our chain.

4 For Thou, Who knowest, Lord, how soon
    Our weak heart clings,
Hast given us joys, tender and true,
    Yet all with wings;
So that we see, gleaming on high,
    Diviner things.

5 I thank Thee, Lord, that Thou hast kept
    The best in store;
We have enough, yet not too much
    To long for more;
A yearning for a deeper peace
    Not known before.

6 I thank Thee, Lord, that here our souls,
    'Though amply blest,
Can never find, although they seek,
    A perfect rest,
Nor ever shall, until they lean
    On Jesus' breast.

Adelaide Anne Procter, 1825-64.

505

MY heart is resting, O my God,
   I will give thanks and sing.
My heart is at the secret source
   Of every precious thing.
I thirst for springs of heavenly life,
   And here all day they rise;
I seek the treasure of Thy love,
   And close at hand it lies.

2 I have a heritage of joy,
   That yet I must not see;
The hand that bled to make it mine
   Is keeping it for me.
And a new song is in my mouth,
   To long-loved music set:
" Glory to Thee for all the grace
   I have not tasted yet."

3 My heart is resting, O my God,
   My heart is in Thy care;
I hear the voice of joy and health
   Resounding everywhere.
" Thou art my portion," saith my soul,
   Ten thousand voices say.
The music of their glad amen
   Will never die away.

Anna Laetitia Waring, 1823–1910.

See also—
A charge to keep, 461.
All that's good, 48.
All things praise Thee, 3.
Before Jehovah's aweful
  throne, 6.
Come and rejoice with me,
  428.
For all the love, 7.
For the beauty, 8.
Lord God almighty, 62.
Lord, we thank Thee, 17.
Loved with everlasting love,
  448.
O Lord of heaven, 68.
Sing to the Lord, 29.
We thank Thee, Lord of
  heaven, 34.
When all Thy mercies, 77.

506

CHRISTIAN, dost thou see them
 On the holy ground,
How the powers of darkness
 Compass thee around ?
Christian, up and smite them,
 Counting gain but loss;
Smite them by the merit
 Of the holy cross.

2 Christian, dost thou feel them,
 How they work within,
Striving, tempting, luring,
 Goading into sin ?
Christian, never tremble,
 Never be downcast;
Gird thee for the conflict,
 Watch and pray and fast.

3 Christian, dost thou hear them,
 How they speak thee fair ?—
" Always fast and vigil ?
 Always watch and prayer ? "
Christian, answer boldly,
 " While I breathe I pray ";
Peace shall follow battle,
 Night shall end in day.

4 " Well I know thy trouble,
 O My servant true;
Thou art very weary,—
 I was weary too:
But that toil shall make thee
 Some day all Mine own,
And the end of sorrow
 Shall be near My throne."

J. M. Neale, 1818–66, altd.

507

CHRISTIAN, seek not yet repose,
   Cast thy dreams of ease away.
Thou art in the midst of foes:
   Watch and pray.

2 Principalities and powers,
   Mustering their unseen array,
Wait for thine unguarded hours:
   Watch and pray.

3 Gird thy heavenly armour on,
   Wear it ever, night and day;
Ambushed lies the evil one:
   Watch and pray.

4 Hear the victors who o'ercame;
   Still they mark each warrior's way;
All with one sweet voice exclaim,
   " Watch and pray."

5 Hear, above all, hear thy Lord,
   Him thou lovest to obey;
Hide within thy heart His word,
   " Watch and pray."

6 Watch, as if on that alone
   Hung the issue of the day;
Pray, that help may be sent down:
   Watch and pray.

Charlotte Elliott, 1789–1871.

508

SOLDIERS of Christ, arise,
   And put your armour on,
Strong in the strength which God supplies
Through His eternal Son.

2   Strong in the Lord of hosts,
      And in His mighty power;
  Who in the strength of Jesus trusts
      Is more than conqueror.

3   Stand then in His great might,
      With all His strength endued;
  And take, to arm you for the fight,
      The panoply of God.

4   To keep your armour bright
      Attend with constant care,
  Still walking in your Captain's sight,
      And watching unto prayer.

5   From strength to strength go on;
      Wrestle, and fight, and pray;
  Tread all the powers of darkness down,
      And win the well-fought day.

6   Then, having all things done,
      And every conflict passed,
  Ye may o'ercome through Christ alone,
      And stand complete at last.

Charles Wesley, 1707–88, *altd.*

509

TAKE time to be holy, speak oft with thy Lord;
Abide in Him always, and feed on His Word.
Make friends of God's children, help those who are
    weak;
Forgetting in nothing His blessing to seek.

2 Take time to be holy, the world rushes on;
Spend much time in secret with Jesus alone—
By looking to Jesus, like Him thou shalt be !
Thy friends in thy conduct His likeness shall see.

3 Take time to be holy, let Him be thy guide;
  And run not before Him, whatever betide;
  In joy or in sorrow still follow thy Lord,
  And, looking to Jesus, still trust in His Word.

4 Take time to be holy, be calm in thy soul;
  Each thought and each temper beneath His control;
  Thus led by His Spirit to fountains of love,
  Thou soon shalt be fitted for service above.

W. D. Longstaff, 1822–94.

510

" TAKE up thy cross," the Saviour said,
    " If thou wouldst My disciple be;
Take up thy cross, with willing heart,
    And humbly follow after Me."

2 Take up thy cross; let not its weight
    Fill thy weak soul with vain alarm;
His strength shall bear thy spirit up,
    And brace thy heart, and nerve thine arm.

3 Take up thy cross, nor heed the shame,
    And let thy foolish pride be still:
Thy Lord refused not e'en to die
    Upon a cross, on Calvary's hill.

4 Take up thy cross, then, in His strength,
    And calmly every danger brave;
'Twill guide thee to a better home,
    And lead to victory o'er the grave.

5 Take up thy cross, and follow Christ,
    Nor think till death to lay it down;
For only he who bears the cross
    May hope to wear the glorious crown.

C. W. Everest, 1814–77.

See also—
A charge to keep, 461.   Yield not to temptation,
Father of all, 470.   569.

511

COME, labour on !
 Who dares stand idle on the harvest-plain
While all around him waves the golden grain,
And to each servant doth the Master say,
 " Go, work to-day ! "

2   Come, labour on !
Claim the high calling angels cannot share,
To young and old the gospel-gladness bear:
Redeem the time; its hours too swiftly fly;
 The night draws nigh.

3   Come, labour on !
Away with gloomy doubt and faithless fear !
No arm so weak but may do service here;
By hands the feeblest can our God fulfil
 His righteous will.

4   Come, labour on !
No time for rest, till glows the western sky,
Till the long shadows o'er our pathway lie,
And a glad sound comes with the setting sun,
 " Servant, well done ! "

5   Come, labour on !
The toil is pleasant and the harvest sure;
Blessèd are those who to the end endure:
How full their joy, how deep their rest shall be,
 O Lord, with Thee !

Jane Borthwick, 1813–97.

512

DISMISS me not Thy service, Lord,
 But train me for Thy will;
For even I in fields so broad
 Some duties may fulfil;
And I will ask for no reward,
 Except to serve Thee still.

2 All works are good, and each is best
    As most it pleases Thee;
  Each worker pleases when the rest
    He serves in charity:
  And neither man nor work unblest
    Wilt Thou permit to be.

3 Our Master all the work has done
    He asks of us to-day;
  Sharing His service, every one
    Share too His sonship may:
  Lord, I would serve and be a son;
    Dismiss me not, I pray.

T. T. Lynch, 1818–71.

513

GO, labour on, spend, and be spent,
    Thy joy to do the Father's will;
It is the way the Master went,
    Should not the servant tread it still?

2 Go, labour on: 'tis not for nought;
    Thy earthly loss is heavenly gain;
  Men heed thee, love thee, praise thee not?
    The Master praises; what are men?

3 Go, labour on: enough while here
    If He shall praise thee, if He deign
  Thy willing heart to mark and cheer;
    No toil for Him shall be in vain.

4 Toil on, faint not, keep watch, and pray;
    Be wise the erring soul to win;
  Go forth into the world's highway,
    Compel the wanderer to come in.

5 Toil on, and in thy toil rejoice;
   For toil comes rest, for exile home;
Soon shalt thou hear the Bridegroom's voice,
   The midnight cry, " Behold, I come ! "

Horatius Bonar, 1808–89.

514

LORD, speak to me, that I may speak
   In living echoes of Thy tone;
As Thou hast sought, so let me seek
   Thy erring children, lost and lone.

2 O lead me, Lord, that I may lead
   The wandering and the wavering feet;
O feed me, Lord, that I may feed
   Thy hungering ones with manna sweet.

3 O strengthen me, that, while I stand
   Firm on the rock, and strong in Thee,
I may stretch out a loving hand
   To wrestlers with the troubled sea.

4 O teach me, Lord, that I may teach
   The precious things Thou dost impart;
And wing my words, that they may reach
   The hidden depths of many a heart.

5 O fill me with Thy fulness, Lord,
   Until my very heart o'erflow
In kindling thought and glowing word,
   Thy love to tell, Thy praise to show.

6 O use me, Lord, use even me,
   Just as Thou wilt, and when, and where,
Until Thy blessèd face I see,
   Thy rest, Thy joy, Thy glory share.

Amen.

Frances Ridley Havergal, 1836–79.

515

MY gracious Lord, I own Thy right
To every service I can pay,
And call it my supreme delight
To hear Thy dictates and obey.

2 What is my being but for Thee,
Its sure support, its noblest end;
Thy ever-smiling face to see,
And serve the cause of such a Friend?

3 I would not breathe for worldly joy,
Or to increase my worldly good;
Nor future days or powers employ
To spread a sounding name abroad.

4 'Tis to my Saviour I would live,
To Him who for my ransom died;
Nor could untainted Eden give
Such bliss as blossoms at His side.

5 His work my hoary age shall bless,
When youthful vigour is no more;
And my last hour of life confess
His love hath animating power.

Philip Doddridge, 1702-51

516

O DEAREST Lord, Thy sacred head
With thorns was pierced for me;
O pour Thy blessing on my head,
That I may think for Thee.

2 O dearest Lord, Thy sacred hands
With nails were pierced for me;
O shed Thy blessing on my hands,
That they may work for Thee.

3 O dearest Lord, Thy sacred feet
   With nails were pierced for me;
 O pour Thy blessing on my feet,
   That they may follow Thee.

4 O dearest Lord, Thy sacred heart
   With spear was pierced for me;
 O pour Thy spirit in my heart,
   That I may live for Thee.   Amen.

Father Andrew, 1869–1946

517

O GOD of truth, whose living word
   Upholds whate'er hath breath,
Look down on Thy creation, Lord,
   Enslaved by sin and death.

2 Set up Thy standard, Lord, that we,
   Who claim a heavenly birth,
May march with Thee to smite the lies
   That vex Thy groaning earth.

3 Ah ! would we join that blest array,
   And follow in the might
Of Him, the faithful and the true,
   In raiment clean and white !

4 How can we fight for truth and God,
   Poor slaves of lies and sin !
He who would fight for Thee on earth
   Must first be true within.

5 Then, God of truth, for whom we long,
   Thou who wilt hear our prayer,
Do Thine own battle in our hearts,
   And slay the falsehood there.

6 Still smite ! still burn ! till nought is left
    But God's own truth and love;
Then, Lord, as morning dew come down.
    Rest on us from above.

7 Yea, come ! then, tried as in the fire,
    From every lie set free,
Thy perfect truth shall dwell in us,
    And we shall live in Thee.

Thomas Hughes, 1822–96, altd.

518

O MASTER, let me walk with Thee
    In lowly paths of service free;
Tell me Thy secret; help me bear
The strain of toil, the fret of care.

2 Help me the slow of heart to move
By some clear winning word of love;
Teach me the wayward feet to stay,
And guide them in the homeward way.

3 Teach me Thy patience; still with Thee
In closer, dearer company,
In work that keeps faith sweet and strong,
In trust that triumphs over wrong,

4 In hope that sends a shining ray
Far down the future's broadening way;
In peace that only Thou canst give,
With Thee, O Master, let me live.   Amen.

Washington Gladden, 1836–1918, altd.

519

O THOU who camest from above
    The pure, celestial fire to impart,
Kindle a flame of sacred love
    On the mean altar of my heart.

2 There let it for Thy glory burn,
    With inextinguishable blaze;
  And, trembling, to its source return
    In humble love and fervent praise.

3 Jesus, confirm my heart's desire
    To work and speak and think for **Thee**;
  Still let me guard the holy fire,
    And still stir up Thy gift in me;

4 Ready for all Thy perfect will,
    My acts of faith and love repeat,
  Till death Thine endless mercies seal,
    And make the sacrifice complete.

Charles Wesley, 1707–88.

520

ONWARD ! Christian soldiers,
    Marching as to war,
With the cross of Jesus
    Going on before:
Christ, the royal master,
    Leads against the foe;
Forward into battle
    See His banners go !

Onward Christian soldiers!
    Marching as to war,
With the cross of Jesus
    Going on before.

2 Like a mighty army
    Moves the Church of God;
  Brothers, we are treading
    Where the saints have trod:
  We are not divided,
    All one body we,
  One in hope, in doctrine,
    One in charity.

3 Crowns and thrones may perish,
    Kingdoms rise and wane,
But the Church of Jesus
    Constant will remain:
Gates of hell can never
    'Gainst that Church prevail;
We have Christ's own promise,
    And that cannot fail.

4 Onward then, ye people!
    Join our happy throng;
Blend with ours your voices
    In the triumph-song,
" Glory, praise, and honour,
    Unto Christ the King! "
This through countless ages
    Men and angels sing.

Sabine Baring-Gould, 1834–1924, *altd.*

521

POUR down Thy Spirit from above,
    And bid all strife and discord cease,
Join heart to heart in mutual love,
    O reign among us, Prince of Peace.

2 If in the souls where love should be
    Arise the storms of fierce self-will,
Calm Thou that troubled, angry sea,
    Speak to the tempest, " Peace, be still."

3 .If rude reproach be o'er us flung,
    And slander wound as with a sword,
Rule Thou the unruly answering tongue,
    And silence every vengeful word.

4 Whene'er in this wild world we meet
    Unkindly deeds that anger move,
Teach us forgiveness,—triumph sweet,
    To conquer evil will with love.

5 In every land, in every home,
    In every heart let love increase;
Let love proclaim Thy kingdom come,
    O reign among us, Prince of peace.

William Romanis, 1824–99.

522

RESCUE the perishing, care for the dying,
    Snatch them in pity from sin and the grave;
Weep o'er the erring one, lift up the fallen,
    Tell them of Jesus, the mighty to save.
Rescue the perishing, care for the dying;
Jesus is merciful, Jesus will save.

2 Though they are slighting Him, still He is waiting,
    Waiting the penitent child to receive;
Plead with them earnestly, plead with them gently;
    He will forgive if they only believe.

3 Down in the human heart, crushed by the tempter,
    Feelings lie buried that grace can restore;
Touched by a loving hand, wakened by kindness
    Chords that were broken will vibrate once
    more.

4 Rescue the perishing,—duty demands it;
    Strength for thy labour the Lord will provide;
Back to the narrow way patiently win them;
    Tell the poor wanderer a Saviour has died.

Frances van Alstyne, 1820–1915.

523

RISE up, O men of God!
    Have done with lesser things;
Give heart and soul and mind and strength
    To serve the King of kings.

2   Rise up, O men of God !
His kingdom tarries long;
Bring in the day of brotherhood
And end the night of wrong.

3   Rise up, O men of God !
The Church for you doth wait:
His strength shall make your spirit strong,
Her service make you great.

4   Lift high the cross of Christ !
Tread where His feet have trod,
As brothers of the Son of Man
Rise up, O men of God !

*William Pierson Merrill, 1867–1954, **altd.***

524

SOLDIERS of the cross, arise !
Gird you with your armour bright;
Mighty are your enemies,
Hard the battle ye must fight.

2 O'er a faithless, fallen world
Raise your banner in the sky:
Let it float there wide unfurled;
Bear it onward; lift it high.

3 To the weary and the worn
Tell of realms where sorrows cease;
To the outcast and forlorn
Speak of mercy and of peace.

4 Guard the helpless; seek the strayed;
Comfort troubles; banish grief;
In the might of God arrayed,
Scatter sin and unbelief.

5 Be the banner still unfurled,
Still unsheathed the Spirit's sword,
Till the kingdoms of the world
Are the kingdom of the Lord.

W. Walsham How, 1823–97.

525

SOUND the battle-cry! see, the foe is nigh;
Raise the standard high for the Lord!
Gird your armour on, stand firm every one,
Rest your cause upon His holy word!

Rouse then, soldiers! rally round the banner!
Ready, steady, pass the word along;
Onward! forward! shout a loud hosanna!
Christ is captain of the mighty throng!

2 Strong to meet the foe, marching on we go,
While our cause we know must prevail;
Shield and banner bright gleaming in the light,
Battling for the right, we ne'er can fail!

3 O Thou God of all, hear us when we call;
Help us one and all, by Thy grace;
When the battle's done, and the victory won,
May we wear the crown before Thy face!

W. F. Sherwin, 1826–88.

526

SOW in the morn thy seed,
At eve hold not thy hand;
To doubt and fear give thou no heed,
Broadcast it o'er the land.

2 The good, the fruitful ground
Expect not here nor there;
O'er hill and dale, by plots 'tis found:
Go forth, then, everywhere.

3 And duly shall appear,
In verdure, beauty, strength,
The tender blade, the stalk, the ear,
And the full corn at length.

4   Thou canst not toil in vain;
     Cold, heat, and moist, and dry
Shall foster and mature the grain
     For garners in the sky.

5   Thence, when the glorious end,
     The day of God is come,
The angel reapers shall descend,
     And heaven cry, " Harvest Home ! "

James Montgomery, 1771–1854

527

TAKE my life, and let it be
     Consecrated, Lord, to Thee:
Take my moments and my days,
Let them flow in ceaseless praise.

2 Take my hands, and let them move
At the impulse of Thy love:
Take my feet, and let them be
Swift and beautiful for Thee.

3 Take my voice, and let me sing,
Always, only, for my King:
Take my lips, and let them be
Filled with messages from Thee.

4 Take my silver and my gold;
Not a mite would I withhold:
Take my intellect, and use
Every power as Thou shalt choose.

5 Take my will, and make it Thine;
It shall be no longer mine:
Take my heart—it is Thine own;
It shall be Thy royal throne.

6 Take my love; my Lord, I pour
At Thy feet its treasure-store:
Take myself, and I will be,
Ever, only, all for Thee.   Amen.

Frances Ridley Havergal, 1836–79.

528

THE wise may bring their learning,
    The rich may bring their wealth,
And some may bring their greatness,
    And some their strength and health:
We too would bring our treasures
    To offer to the King;
We have no wealth or learning,
    What gifts then shall we bring?

2 We'll bring the many duties
    We have to do each day;
We'll try our best to please Him,
    At home, at school, at play:
And better are these treasures
    To offer to our King
Than richest gifts without them;
    Yet these we all may bring.

3 We'll bring Him hearts that love Him,
    We'll bring Him thankful praise,
And souls for ever striving
    To follow in His ways:
And these shall be the treasures
    We offer to the King,
And these are gifts that ever
    Our grateful hearts may bring.

Book of Praise for Children, 1881, *altd.*

529

THOU perfect Hero-Knight,
    Help us to follow Thee,
To right the wrong, protect the weak,
    And serve Thee faithfully.

2   Thou bravest of the brave,
    We bring Thee joyful praise,
Make us unfearing, loyal, true,
    Like Thee in all our ways.

3   Thou mightiest of the strong,
      We praise Thee with our might,
   Help us to guard our purity,
      And use our strength aright.

4   Thou kingliest King of all,
      We bring Thee loyal praise,
   Help us to be true sons of Thee,
      To-day and all our days.
Alice M. Pullen, 1889-

530

WE give Thee but thine own,
    Whate'er the gift may be;
All that we have is Thine alone,
    A trust, O Lord, from Thee.

2   May we Thy bounties thus
      As stewards true receive,
   And gladly, as Thou blessest us,
      To Thee our firstfruits give.

3   For hearts are bruised and dead,
      And homes are bare and cold,
   And lambs, for whom the Shepherd bled,
      Are straying from the fold.

4   To comfort and to bless,
      To find a balm for woe,
   To tend the lone and fatherless,
      Is angels' work below.

5   The captive to release,
      To God the lost to bring,
   To teach the way of life and peace
      It is a Christ-like thing.

6   And we believe Thy word,
      Though dim our faith may be,—
   Whate'er for Thine we do, O Lord,
      We do it unto Thee.
W. Walsham How, 1823-97.

531

WE have a King who came to earth
　To win the world for God,
And we, the children of the King,
Must follow where He trod.

2 The banner that our King unfurled
　Was love to every man,
So we must try to show that love
　In all the ways we can.

3 The enemies He came to fight
　Are selfishness and sin;
Then who would be a traitor now
　And let His foemen in?

4 He bids us keep our bodies pure,
　For 'tis the pure and clean
Can see the glory of the King
　And tell what they have seen.

5 We are a little company
　But we are pledged to bring
Pure holy lives, kind joyful hearts
　To offer to the King.

Margaret Cropper, 1886-

532

WHAT purpose burns within our hearts
　　That we together here should stand,
Pledging each other mutual vows,
　And ready hand to join in hand?

2 We see in vision fair a time
　When evil shall have passed away;
And thus we dedicate our lives
　To hasten on that blessèd day;

3 To seek the truth whate'er it be,
   To follow it where'er it leads;
   To turn to facts our dreams of good,
   And coin our lives in loving deeds:

4 For this, we gather here to-day;
   To such a Church of God we bring
   Our utmost love and loyalty,
   And make our souls an offering.

Minot Judson Savage, 1841–1918.

533

WHERE cross the crowded ways of life,
  Where sound the cries of race and clan,
Above the noise of selfish strife,
We hear Thy voice, O Son of man !

2 In haunts of wretchedness and need,
   On shadowed thresholds dark with fears,
   From paths where hide the lures of greed,
   We catch the vision of Thy tears.

3 The cup of water given for Thee
   Still holds the freshness of Thy grace;
   Yet long these multitudes to see
   The sweet compassion of Thy face.

4 O Master, from the mountain-side,
   Make haste to heal those hearts of pain;
   Among these restless throngs abide;
   O tread the city's streets again;

5 Till sons of men shall learn Thy love,
   And follow where Thy feet have trod;
   Till glorious from Thy heaven above,
   Shall come the city of our God.

Frank Mason North, 1850–1935.

534

WHO is on the Lord's side?
    Who will serve the King?
Who will be His helpers
    Other lives to bring?
Who will leave the world's side?
    Who will face the foe?
Who is on the Lord's side?
    Who for Him will go?
      By Thy call of mercy,
        By Thy grace divine,
      We are on the Lord's side;
      Saviour, we are Thine.

2 Not for weight of glory,
    Not for crown and palm,
Enter we the army,
    Raise the warrior-psalm;
But for love that claimeth
    Lives for whom He died:
He whom Jesus nameth
    Must be on His side.
      By Thy love constraining,
        By Thy grace divine,
      We are on the Lord's side;
      Saviour, we are Thine.

3 Fierce may be the conflict,
    Strong may be the foe,
But the King's own army
    None can overthrow.
Round His standard ranging,
    Victory is secure,
For His truth unchanging
    Makes the triumph sure.
      Joyfully enlisting,
        By Thy grace divine,
      We are on the Lord's side;
      Saviour, we are Thine.

4 Chosen to be soldiers
   In an alien land,
Chosen, called, and faithful,
   For our captain's band,
In the service royal
   Let us not grow cold;
Let us be right loyal,
   Noble, true and bold.
      Master, Thou wilt keep us,
      By Thy grace divine,
      Always on the Lord's side,
      Saviour, always Thine.

Frances Ridley Havergal, 1836–79.

535

WORKMAN of God! O lose not heart,
   But learn what God is like;
And, in the darkest battlefield,
   Thou shalt know where to strike.

2 Ah! God is other than we think;
   His ways are far above
The heights of reason, and are reached
   Only by childlike love.

3 He hides Himself so wondrously,
   As though there were no God;
He is least seen when all the powers
   Of ill are most abroad.

4 Thrice blest is he to whom is given
   The instinct that can tell
That God is on the field when He
   Is most invisible

5 For right is right, since God is God;
    And right the day must win;
  To doubt would be disloyalty,
    To falter would be sin.

F. W. Faber, 1814–63, altd.

536

YE who are banded as comrades and **brothers,**
    Ye who confess that to Christ ye belong;
Bear, like your master, the burden of others;
    Flinch not from duty, be gentle and strong.

2 Men in the flower of young manhood are needed,
    Men who are faithful and loving and true;
Pass not the call of your Saviour unheeded;
    Forth to His service—the Lord needeth you.

3 Christ is above you and Christ is before you,
    Christ is around you and Christ is within;
His the free grace to uplift and restore you;
    His the strong arm that shall victory win.

4 All the wide world for its Saviour is yearning,
    Groaning in bondage of sin and of pain;
Comrades, go forth with hearts loyal and burning,
    All the wide world for our master to gain.

S. C. Lowry, 1855–1932.

See also—

Almighty Father, 626.
Behold us, Lord, 627.
Christ of the upward way, 538.
Eternal Ruler, 358.
Father of all, 470.
Father of men, 359.
God be in my head, 471.
In sunny days, 476.
Lead on, O King eternal, 375.

My God, my Father, 480.
Not, Lord, Thine ancient works alone, 65.
Now in the days of youth, 452.
O God of love, 663.
O Lord of life, 483.
O loving Lord, 602.
Servant of all, 632.
Stand up! 556.
The Lord is King, 488.
What do I owe, 490.

537

ALL the way my Saviour leads me;
　　What have I to ask beside ?
Can I doubt His tender mercy,
　　Who through life has been my guide ?
Heavenly peace, divinest comfort,
　　Here by faith in Him to dwell !
For I know, whate'er befall me,
　　Jesus doeth all things well.

2 All the way my Saviour leads me,
　　Cheers each winding path I tread,
Gives me grace for every trial,
　　Feeds me with the living bread.
Though my weary steps may falter,
　　And my soul athirst may be,
Gushing from the rock before me,
　　Lo, a spring of joy I see !

3 All the way my Saviour leads me;
　　O the fulness of His love !
Perfect rest to me is promised
　　In my Father's house above.
When my spirit, clothed, immortal,
　　Wings its flight to realms of day,
This my song through endless ages—
　　Jesus led me all the way !

Frances van Alstyne, 1820–1915.

538

CHRIST of the upward way,
　　My guide divine,
Where Thou hast set Thy feet
　　May I place mine:
And move and march wherever Thou hast trod,
Keeping face forward up the hill of God.

2   Give me the heart to hear
       Thy voice and will,
    That without fault or fear
       I may fulfil
Thy purpose with a glad and holy zest,
Like one who would not bring less than his best.

3   Give me the eye to see
       Each chance to serve,
    Then send me strength to rise
       With steady nerve,
And leap at once with kind and helpful deed
To the sure succour of a soul in need.

4   Give me the good stout arm
       To shield the right,
    And wield Thy sword of truth
       With all my might,
That, in the warfare I must wage for Thee,
More than a victor I may ever be.

5   Christ of the upward way,
       My guide divine,
    Where Thou hast set Thy feet,
       May I place mine;
And when Thy last call comes serene and clear,
Calm may my answer be, " Lord, I am here."
                        Amen.

W. J. Mathams, 1853–1931.

539

" FORWARD ! " be our watchword,
      Steps and voices joined;
Seek the things before us,
    Not a look behind:
Burns the fiery pillar
    At our army's head ;
Who shall dream of shrinking,
    By our captain led ?

Forward through the desert,
  Through the toil and fight:
Jordan flows before us,
  Zion beams with light.

2 Forward, flock of Jesus,
    Salt of all the earth,
  Till each yearning purpose
    Spring to glorious birth.
  Sick, they ask for healing,
    Blind, they grope for day;
  Pour upon the nations
    Wisdom's loving ray.
  Forward, out of error,
    Leave behind the night;
  Forward through the darkness,
    Forward into light.

3 Glories upon glories
    Has our God prepared,
  By the souls that love Him
    One day to be shared:
  Eye has not beheld them,
    Ear has never heard;
  Nor of these has uttered
    Thought or speech a word:
  Forward, marching forward,
    Where the heaven is bright,
  Till the veil be lifted,
    Till our faith be sight.

Henry Alford, 1810–71.

540

GRANT us Thy light, that we may know
    The wisdom Thou alone canst give;
That truth may guide where'er we go,
  And virtue bless where'er we live.

2 Grant us Thy light, that we may see
  Where error lurks in human lore,
And turn our doubting minds to Thee,
  And love Thy simple word the more.

3 Grant us Thy light, that we may learn
  How dead is life from Thee apart;
How sure is joy for all who turn
  To Thee an undivided heart.

4 Grant us Thy light, in grief and pain,
  To lift our burdened hearts above;
And count the very cross a gain,
  And bless our Father's hidden love.

5 Grant us Thy light, when, soon or late,
  All earthly scenes shall pass away,
In Thee to find the open gate
  To deathless home and endless day.

Lawrence Tuttiett, 1825–97.

541

GUIDE me, O Thou great Jehovah,
  Pilgrim through this barren land;
I am weak, but Thou art mighty;
  Hold me with Thy powerful hand:
    Bread of heaven,
  Feed me now and evermore.

2 Open now the crystal fountain,
  Whence the healing stream doth flow;
Let the fiery, cloudy pillar
  Lead me all my journey through:
    Strong deliverer,
  Be Thou still my strength and shield.

3 When I tread the verge of Jordan,
　　Bid my anxious fears subside:
Death of death, and hell's destruction,
　　Land me safe on Canaan's side:
　　　Songs of praises
　　I will ever give to Thee.

William Williams, 1717–91, *altd.*

542

HE leads us on
　　Through childhood's wondering
　　　　years,
Past all our dreamland hopes, and doubts, and
　　fears;
Draws gently back life's curtain, as we gaze
With growing marvel at His ordered ways;
　　Till childhood's days are done
　　'Tis He that leads us on.

2　　　　　He leads us on
　　By paths we do not know;
Upwards He leads us, though our steps be slow;
Though oft we faint and falter on the way,
Though storms and darkness oft obscure the day,
　　Yet, when the clouds are gone,
　　We know He leads us on.

3　　　　　He leads us on;
　　Still red the watchfires glow
Beside the paths His feet trod long ago;
He gives for guidance, through life's tangled maze,
The spacious visions seen in earlier days.
　　We know His will is done,
　　For still He leads us on.

Public Schools Hymn Book.
Based on Hiram A. Wiley.

543

JESUS, Saviour, pilot me,
Over life's tempestuous sea;
Unknown waves before me roll,
Hiding rock and treacherous shoal;
Chart and compass come from Thee:
Jesus, Saviour, pilot me!

2 As a mother stills her child,
Thou canst hush the ocean wild:
Boisterous waves obey Thy will
When Thou sayest to them " Be still ! "
Wondrous sovereign of the sea,
Jesus, Saviour, pilot me!

3 When at last I near the shore,
And the fearful breakers roar
'Twixt me and the peaceful rest—
Then, while leaning on Thy breast,
May I hear Thee say to me,
" Fear not ! I will pilot thee ! "

Edward Hopper, 1818-88.

544

JESUS, still lead on,
Till our rest be won;
And although the way be cheerless,
We will follow, calm and fearless:
Guide us by Thy hand
To our fatherland.

2   If the way be drear,
If the foe be near,
Let not faithless fears o'ertake us,
Let not faith and hope forsake us;
For, through many a foe,
To our home we go.

3   When we seek relief
      From a long-felt grief,
When oppressed by new temptations,
Lord, increase and perfect patience;
     Show us that bright shore
     Where we weep no more.

4   Jesus, still lead on
      Till our rest be won;
Heavenly leader, still direct us,
Still support, console, protect us,
     Till we safely stand
     In our fatherland.

Nikolaus von Zinzendorf, 1700–60,
tr. Jane Borthwick, 1813–97.

545

LEAD, kindly Light, amid the encircling gloom,
     Lead Thou me on;
The night is dark, and I am far from home;
     Lead Thou me on.
Keep Thou my feet; I do not ask to see
The distant scene; one step enough for me.

2 I was not ever thus, nor prayed that Thou
     Shouldst lead me on;
I loved to choose and see my path; but now
     Lead Thou me on.
I loved the garish day, and, spite of fears,
Pride ruled my will: remember not past years.

3 So long Thy power hath blest me, sure it still
     Will lead me on
O'er moor and fen, o'er crag and torrent, till
     The night is gone;
And with the morn those angel faces smile
Which I have loved long since, and lost awhile.

J. H. Newman, 1801–90.

546

LEAD us, O Father, in the paths of peace:
   Without Thy guiding hand we go astray,
And doubts appal, and sorrows still increase;
   Lead us through Christ, the true and living way.

2 Lead us, O Father, in the paths of truth:
   Unhelped by Thee, in error's maze we grope,
While passion stains and folly dims our youth,
   And age comes on uncheered by faith and hope.

3 Lead us, O Father, in the paths of right:
   Blindly we stumble when we walk alone,
Involved in shadows of a darkening night;
   Only with Thee we journey safely on.

4 Lead us, O Father, to Thy heavenly rest,
   However rough and steep the path may be,
Through joy or sorrow, as Thou deemest best,
   Until our lives are perfected in Thee.

W. H. Burleigh, 1812–71.

547

MEN true of heart and strong in faith,
   Lift up to God your voice on high;
'Tis meet and right, ye sons of men,
   The King of kings to glorify.

2 Come, Holy Spirit of the Lord,
   Thou source of life and strength divine,
Our hearts are temples made for Thee,
   Come dwell in them and make them Thine.

3 Shine in our hearts, celestial light,
   Be Thou our guide on life's rough way;
We shall not err if Thou dost lead
   And guard our steps from day to day.

4 Life holds in store great things for those
   Who walk with God and love the light:
They need no other guide but Thee
   To find the truth and do the right.

5 Help us to seek what Jesus sought,
   Things holy and of lasting worth,
The love that brings good will to men,
   The deeds that make for peace on earth.

6 Men true of heart and strong in faith,
   Praise ye the Father and the Son,
Praise ye the Spirit of the Lord,
   The triune God, the Three in One.

J. Waugh Boden, 1855–1943.

548

MY faith, it is an oaken staff,
   The traveller's well-loved aid;
My faith, it is a weapon stout,
   The soldier's trusty blade.
I'll travel on, and still be stirred
By silent thought or social word;
By all my perils undeterred
   A soldier-pilgrim staid.

2 I have a captain, and the heart
   Of every private man
Has drunk in valour from His eyes,
   Since first the war began.
He is most merciful in fight,
And of His scars a single sight
The embers of our failing might
   Into a flame can fan.

3 I have a guide, and in His steps
   When travellers have trod,
Whether beneath was flinty rock
   Or yielding grassy sod,

They cared not, but with force unspent,
Unmoved by pain, they onward went,
Unstayed by pleasures, still they bent
 Their zealous course to God.

4 My faith, it is an oaken staff,
 O let me on it lean;
My faith, it is a trusty sword,
 May falsehood find it keen.
Thy Spirit, Lord, to me impart,
O make me what Thou ever art,
Of patient and courageous heart,
 As all true saints have been.

T. T. Lynch, 1818–71.

549

MY faith looks up to Thee,
 Thou Lamb of Calvary,
  Saviour divine:
Now hear me while I pray;
Take all my guilt away;
O let me from this day
  Be wholly Thine.

2 May Thy rich grace impart
 Strength to my fainting heart,
  My zeal inspire.
As Thou hast died for me,
O may my love to Thee
Pure, warm, and changeless be,
  A living fire.

3 While life's dark maze I tread,
 And griefs around me spread,
  Be Thou my guide;
Bid darkness turn to day,
Wipe sorrow's tears away,
Nor let me ever stray
  From Thee aside.

4 When ends life's transient dream,
　When death's cold sullen stream
　　　Shall o'er me roll,
　Blest Saviour, then in love,
　Fear and distrust remove;
　O bear me safe above,
　　　A ransomed soul.

Ray Palmer, 1808–87.

550

O GOD of Bethel, by whose hand
　　Thy people still are fed;
Who through this earthly pilgrimage
　Hast all our fathers led;

2 Our vows, our prayers, we now present
　Before Thy throne of grace;
God of our fathers, be the God
　Of their succeeding race.

3 Through each perplexing path of life
　Our wandering footsteps guide.
Give us each day our daily bread,
　And raiment fit provide.

4 O spread Thy covering wings around,
　Till all our wanderings cease,
And at our Father's loved abode
　Our souls arrive in peace.

Philip Doddridge, 1702–51, *altd.*

551

O HAPPY band of pilgrims,
　　If onward ye will tread
With Jesus as your fellow
　To Jesus as your head !

2 O happy if ye labour
   As Jesus did for men;
O happy if ye hunger
   As Jesus hungered then !

3 The cross that Jesus carried
   He carried as your due;
The crown that Jesus weareth,
   He weareth it for you.

4 The trials that beset you,
   The sorrows ye endure,
The manifold temptations
   That death alone can cure,—

5 What are they but His jewels
   Of right celestial worth ?
What are they but the ladder
   Set up to heaven on earth ?

6 O happy band of pilgrims,
   Look upward to the skies,
Where such a light affliction
   Shall win you such a prize !

J. M. Neale, 1818–66, *altd.*

552

O MASTER, when Thou callest,
   No voice may say Thee nay;
For blest are they that follow
   Where Thou dost lead the way:
In freshest prime of morning,
   Or fullest glow of noon,
The note of heavenly warning
   Can never come too soon.

2 O Master, where Thou callest,
　　No foot may shrink in fear;
For they who trust Thee wholly
　　Shall find Thee ever near:
And chamber still and lonely,
　　Or busy harvest-field,
Where Thou, Lord, rulest only,
　　Shall precious produce yield.

3 O Master, when Thou callest,
　　No heart may dare refuse;
'Tis honour, highest honour,
　　When Thou dost deign to use:
Our brightest and our fairest,
　　Our dearest—all are Thine;
Thou who for each one carest,
　　We hail Thy love's design.

4 They who go forth to serve Thee,
　　We too who serve at home,
May watch and pray together
　　Until Thy kingdom come.
In Thee for aye united,
　　Our song of hope we raise,
Till that blest shore is sighted
　　Where all shall turn to praise.

Sarah G. Stock, 1838–98.

553

O WALK with God, and thou shalt find
　　How He can charm thy way,
And lead thee with a quiet mind
　　Into the perfect day:
His love shall cheer thee, like the dew
　　That bathes the drooping flower;
That love is every morning new,
　　Nor fails at evening hour.

2 O walk with God, and thou with smiles
   Shalt tread the way of tears;
His mercy every ill beguiles,
   And softens all our fears,
No fire shall harm thee, if, alas !
   Through fires He bids thee go;
Through waters when thy footsteps pass,
   They shall not overflow.

3 O walk with God, and thou shalt go
   Down death's dark vale in light,
And find thy faithful walk below
   Has reached to Zion's height.
O walk with God, if thou wouldst see
   Thy pathway thither tend;
And, lingering though thy journey be,
   'Tis heaven and home at end.

Arthur C. Coxe, 1818–96.

554

" SEEK ye first the kingdom,
      'Tis your Father's will ";
So the voice of Jesus
   Bids us follow still.
Saviour, we would hear Thee,
   Follow, find, and see;
And, in life's adventure,
   Thy disciples be.

2 As for hidden treasure,
   Or for matchless pearl,
When at last discovered,
   Men will sell their all;
So, when breaks the vision
   Of that kingdom fair,
Ours shall be its riches
   And its beauty rare.

3 As the silent leaven
  Works its secret way,
Or as grows the seed grain
  Through the night and day;
Lord, so be the increase,
  Peaceable but sure,
Of Thy word within us
  And Thy kingdom's power.

4 As the tender seedling
  Grows up tall and strong,
And the birds of heaven
  To its branches throng;
So shall all God's children
  From the east and west
Gather to His kingdom,
  In its shadow rest.

5 Humblest shall be greatest,
  Poor in spirit reign;
Home shall come the childlike
  Born through Thee again;
Eager hearts arrive there
  On the pilgrim's road.
Hail ! The kingdom glorious
  Of the living God !

Norman Elliott, 1893-.

555

SHEPHERD of eager youth,
  Guiding in love and truth
    Through devious ways,
Christ our triumphant King,
We come Thy name to sing,
And here we children bring
    Our songs of praise.

2 Thou art our Holy Lord,
  The all-subduing Word,
      Healer of strife;
  Thou didst Thyself abase,
  That from our sin's disgrace
  Thou mightest save our race
      And give us life.

3 Ever be Thou our guide,
  Our shepherd, and our pride,
      Our staff and song.
  Jesus, Thou Christ of God,
  By Thy eternal word,
  Lead us where Thou hast trod;
      Make our faith strong.

Clement of Alexandria, c. 150–215,
tr. Henry Dexter, 1821–90.

556

STAND up ! stand up for Jesus !
    Ye soldiers of the cross,
Lift high His royal banner;
    It must not suffer loss.
From victory unto victory
    His army shall He lead,
Till every foe is vanquished
    And Christ is Lord indeed.

2 Stand up ! stand up for Jesus !
    The trumpet-call obey;
  Forth to the mighty conflict
    In this His glorious day.
  Ye that are men, now serve Him
    Against unnumbered foes;
  Let courage rise with danger,
    And strength to strength oppose.

3 Stand up! stand up for Jesus!
    Stand in His strength alone;
The arm of flesh will fail you,
    Ye dare not trust your own.
Put on the gospel armour,
    Each piece put on with prayer;
Where duty calls, or danger,
    Be never wanting there.

4 Stand up! stand up for Jesus!
    The strife will not be long;
This day the noise of battle,
    The next the victor's song.
To him that overcometh
    A crown of life shall be;
He with the King of glory
    Shall reign eternally.

George Duffield, 1818–88.

557

THE days that were, the days that are,
    They all are days of God;
With psalms of cheerful trust we tread
    Where Christ's own freemen trod.

2 God of our fathers! God of Christ!
    Keep us in simple ways;
And in the calm of silent hours
    Train us for clamorous days.

3 For those who find the tempest strong,
    Make us a hiding-place,
A shadow in a weary land
    For healing and for grace.

4 When love for man is growing cold.
   And many faithless prove,
Then may the Man of sorrows come
   And teach us how to love.

5 We tarry, Lord, Thy leisure still;
   Thy best is yet to be:
Naught ever comes too late for man
   That is in time for Thee.

6 God of our fathers ! God of Christ !
   Keep us in simple ways;
And may the sharpness of the strife
   Be to Thy greater praise.

H. Elvet Lewis, 1860–1953.

558

THE Son of God goes forth to war,
   A kingly crown to gain;
His blood-red banner streams afar:
   Who follows in His train ?
Who best can drink his cup of woe,
   Triumphant over pain,
Who patient bears his cross below;
   He follows in His train.

2 The martyr first, whose eagle eye
   Could pierce beyond the grave;
Who saw his master in the sky,
   And called on Him to save:
Like Him, with pardon on his tongue,
   In midst of mortal pain,
He prayed for them that did the wrong:
   Who follows in his train ?

3 A glorious band, the chosen few
    On whom the Spirit came,
Twelve valiant saints, their hope they knew,
    And mocked the cross and flame.
They met the tyrant's brandished steel,
    The lion's gory mane;
They bowed their necks the death to feel:
    Who follows in their train?

4 A noble army, men and boys,
    The matron and the maid,
Around the Saviour's throne rejoice,
    In robes of light arrayed:
They climbed the steep ascent of heaven,
    Through peril, toil, and pain;
O God, to us may grace be given
    To follow in their train.

Reginald Heber, 1783–1826

559

THROUGH the night of doubt and sorrow
    Onward goes the pilgrim band,
Singing songs of expectation,
    Marching to the promised land.

2 Clear before us through the darkness
    Gleams and burns the guiding light;
Brother clasps the hand of brother,
    Stepping fearless through the night.

3 One the light of God's own presence
    O'er His ransomed people shed,
Chasing far the gloom and terror,
    Brightening all the path we tread;

4 One the object of our journey,
    One the faith that never tires,
One the earnest looking forward,
    One the hope our God inspires;

5 One the strain that lips of thousands
    Lift as from the heart of one;
One the conflict, one the peril,
    One the march in God begun;

6 One the gladness of rejoicing
    On the far eternal shore,
Where the one almighty Father
    Reigns in love for evermore.

B. S. Ingemann, 1789–1862,
tr. S. Baring-Gould, 1834–1924

560

WALK in the light, and thou shalt own
    Thy darkness passed away,
Because that light hath on thee shone
    In which is perfect day.

2 Walk in the light, and sin, abhorred,
    Shall ne'er defile again;
The blood of Jesus Christ thy Lord
    Shall cleanse from every stain.

3 Walk in the light, and thou shalt find
    Thy heart made truly His
Who dwells in cloudless light enshrined,
    In whom no darkness is.

4 Walk in the light, so shalt thou know
    That fellowship of love
His Spirit only can bestow
    Who reigns in light above.

5 Walk in the light, and e'en the tomb
    No fearful shade shall wear;
Glory shall chase away its gloom,
    For Christ has conquered there.

6 Walk in the light; pursue thy way
    Till faith be turned to sight,
For in the land of endless day
    God is Himself the light.

Bernard Barton, 1784–1849, altd.

561

WHO would true valour see,
    Let him come hither;
One here will constant be,
    Come wind, come weather.
There's no discouragement
Shall make him once relent
His first avowed intent
        To be a pilgrim.

2 Whoso beset him round
    With dismal stories,
Do but themselves confound;
    His strength the more is.
No lion can him fright,
He'll with a giant fight,
But he will have a right
        To be a pilgrim.

3 Hobgoblin nor foul fiend
    Can daunt his spirit:
He knows he at the end
    Shall life inherit.
Then fancies fly away,
He'll fear not what men say,
He'll labour night and day
        To be a pilgrim.

John Bunyan, 1628–88.

See also—

Brightly gleams our banner, 464.
Father, hear the prayer, 467.
I to the hills, 59.
In heavenly love abiding, 581.
Now thank we, 18.
Saviour, blessed Saviour, 459.
Sing praise to God, 28.
The God of Abraham, 30.

562

A SAFE stronghold our God is still,
    A trusty shield and weapon;
He'll help us clear from all the ill
That hath us now o'ertaken.
    The ancient prince of hell
    Hath risen with purpose fell;
    Strong mail of craft and power
    He weareth in this hour;
On earth is not his fellow.

2 With force of arms we nothing can,
    Full soon were we down-ridden;
But for us fights the proper Man
Whom God Himself hath bidden.
    Ask ye, Who is this same?
    Christ Jesus is His name,
    The Lord Sabaoth's Son;
    He, and no other one,
Shall conquer in the battle.

3 And were this world all devils o'er,
    And watching to devour us,
We lay it not to heart so sore;
    Not they can overpower us.
    And let the prince of ill
    Look grim as e'er he will,
    He harms us not a whit;
    For why? his doom is writ;
A word shall quickly slay him.

4 God's word, for all their craft and force,
    One moment shall not linger,
But, spite of hell, shall have its course:
'Tis written by His finger.

And though they take our life,
Goods, honour, children, wife,
Yet is their profit small;
These things shall vanish all,
The city of God remaineth.

Martin Luther, 1483–1546,
tr. Thomas Carlyle, 1795–1881

563

COURAGE, brother ! do not stumble,
     Though thy path be dark as night;
There's a star to guide the humble :—
     " Trust in God, and do the right."

2 Though the road be rough and dreary,
     And its end far out of sight;
Foot it bravely; strong or weary,
     Trust in God, and do the right.

3 Some will hate thee, some will love thee,
     Some will flatter, some will slight;
Cease from men, and look above thee:
     Trust in God, and do the right.

4 Simple rule and safest guiding,
     Inward peace and inward might,
Star upon our path abiding,—
     " Trust in God, and do the right."

Norman Macleod, 1812–72.

564

EPHESIANS vi. 10 ff.

GIVE me, O Christ, the strength that is in Thee,
     That I may stand in every evil hour;
Faints my poor heart except to Thee I flee,
     Resting my weakness in Thy perfect power.

2 Give me to see the foes that I must fight,
  Powers of the darkness, throned where Thou
    shouldst reign,
  Read the directings of Thy wrath aright,
  Lest, striking flesh and blood, I strike in vain.

3 Give me to wear the armour that can guard;
  Over my breast Thy blood-bought righteousness,
  Faith for my shield, when fiery darts rain hard,
  Girded with truth, and shod with zeal to bless.

4 Give me to wield the weapon that is sure,
  Taking, through prayer, Thy sword into my
    hand,
  Word of Thy wisdom, peaceable and pure,
  So, Christ my conqueror, I shall conqueror
    stand. Amen.

H. C. Carter, 1875–1954.

565

LORD Jesus, think on me,
  And purge away my sin;
From earthborn passions set me free,
  And make me pure within.

2   Lord Jesus, think on me,
      With many a care opprest;
    Let me Thy loving servant be,
      And taste Thy promised rest.

3   Lord Jesus, think on me,
      Amid the battle's strife;
    In all my pain and misery
      Be Thou my health and life.

4   Lord Jesus, think on me,
      Nor let me go astray;
    Through darkness and perplexity
      Point Thou the heavenly way.

5   Lord Jesus, think on me,
      When flows the tempest high;
   When on doth rush the enemy,
      O Saviour, be Thou nigh.

6   Lord Jesus, think on me,
      That, when the flood is past,
   I may the eternal brightness see,
      And share Thy joy at last. Amen.

Synesius of Cyrene, c. 375–430,
tr. A. W. Chatfield, 1808–96.

566

O SAFE to the Rock that is higher than I,
My soul in its conflicts and sorrows would fly,
So sinful, so weary, Thine, Thine would I be,
Thou blest Rock of ages, I'm hiding in Thee!
   Hiding in Thee ! Hiding in Thee !
   Thou blest Rock of ages, I'm hiding in Thee !

2 In the calm of the noontide, in sorrow's lone hour,
In times when temptation casts o'er me its power;
In the tempests of life, on its wide heaving sea,
Thou blest Rock of ages, I'm hiding in Thee!

3 How oft in the conflict, when pressed by the foe,
I have fled to my refuge, and breathed out my woe:
How often, when trials, like sea-billows roll,
Have I hidden in Thee, O Thou Rock of my soul

W. O. Cushing, 1823–1903.

567

R EJOICE, believer in the Lord,
   Who makes your cause His own;
The hope that's built upon His word
   Can ne'er be overthrown.

2 Though many foes beset your road,
    And feeble is your arm,
Your life is hid with Christ in God,
    Beyond the reach of harm.

3 Weak as you are, you shall not faint,
    Or fainting, shall not die;
Jesus, the strength of every saint,
    Will aid you from on high.

4 Though unperceived by mortal sense,
    Faith sees Him always near,
A guide, a glory, a defence:
    Then what have you to fear?

5 As surely as He overcame,
    And triumphed once for you,
So surely you that love His name
    Shall triumph in Him too.

John Newton, 1725–1807.

568

WILL your anchor hold in the storms of life,
    When the clouds unfold their wings of strife?
When the strong tides lift, and the cables strain,
Will your anchor drift, or firm remain?

We have an anchor that keeps the soul
Steadfast and sure while the billows roll;
Fastened to the Rock which cannot move,
Grounded firm and deep in the Saviour's love!

2 Will your anchor hold in the straits of fear,
When the breakers roar and the reef is near?
While the surges rave, and the wild winds blow,
Shall the angry waves then your bark o'erflow?

3 Will your anchor hold in the floods of death,
  When the waters cold chill your latest breath ?
  On the rising tide you can never fail,
  While your anchor holds within the veil.

4 Will your eyes behold through the morning light
  The city of gold and the harbour bright ?
  Will you anchor safe by the heavenly shore,
  When life's storms are past for evermore ?

Priscilla Owens, 1829–99.

569

YIELD not to temptation, for yielding is sin,
  Each victory will help you some other to win ;
Fight manfully onward, dark passions subdue,
Look ever to Jesus, He will carry you through.
  Ask the Saviour to help you, comfort, strengthen,
  and keep you ;
  He is willing to aid you, He will carry you
  through.

2 Shun evil companions, bad language disdain,
  God's name hold in reverence, nor take it in vain :
  Be thoughtful and earnest, kind-hearted and true
  Look ever to Jesus, He will carry you through.

3 To him that o'ercometh God giveth a crown.
  Through faith we shall conquer, though often cast
    down ;
  He who is our Saviour our strength will renew,
  Look ever to Jesus, He will carry you through.

H. R. Palmer, 1834–1907.

See also—
Fight the good fight, 289.   Lead us, heavenly Father,
Forty days and forty nights,   The Lord's my Shepherd,
  118.

570

A SOVEREIGN protector I have,
  Unseen, yet for ever at hand,
Unchangeably faithful to save,
  Almighty to rule and command.
He smiles, and my comforts abound;
  His grace as the dew shall descend,
And walls of salvation surround
  The soul He delights to defend.

2 Inspirer and hearer of prayer,
    Thou shepherd and guardian of Thine,
  My all to Thy covenant care
    I sleeping and waking resign.
  If Thou art my shield and my sun,
    The night is no darkness to me;
  And, fast as my moments roll on,
    They bring me but nearer to Thee.

A. M. Toplady. 1740–78, *altd*

571

Psalm xlii.

A S pants the hart for cooling streams,
  When heated in the chase,
So longs my soul, O God, for Thee,
  And Thy refreshing grace.

2 For Thee, my God, the living God,
    My thirsty soul doth pine:
  O when shall I behold Thy face,
    Thou majesty divine?

3 Why restless, why cast down, my soul?
    Hope still, and thou shalt sing
  The praise of Him who is thy God,
    Thy health's eternal spring.

4 To Father, Son, and Holy Ghost,
   The God whom we adore,
Be glory, as it was, is now,
   And shall be evermore.   Amen.

Nahum Tate, 1652–1715, *and*
Nicholas Brady, 1659–1726.

572

AWAKE our souls, away our fears,
      Let every trembling thought be gone;
Awake, and run the heavenly race,
   And put a cheerful courage on.

2 True, 'tis a strait and thorny road,
   And mortal spirits tire and faint;
But they forget the mighty God
   Who feeds the strength of every saint,

3 Thee, mighty God, whose matchless power
   Is ever new and ever young,
And firm endures while endless years
   Their everlasting circles run.

4 From Thee, the overflowing spring,
   Our souls shall drink a fresh supply;
While such as trust their native strength
   Shall faint away, and droop, and die.

5 Swift as an eagle cuts the air,
   We'll mount aloft to Thine abode:
On wings of love our souls shall fly,
   Nor tire amidst the heavenly road.

Isaac Watts, 1674–1748.

573

BEGONE, unbelief;
  My Saviour is near,
And for my relief
  Will surely appear.
By prayer let me wrestle,
  And He will perform;
With Christ in the vessel,
  I smile at the storm.

2 His love in time past
    Forbids me to think
  He'll leave me at last
    In trouble to sink.
  And can He have taught me
    To trust in His name,
  And thus far have brought me,
    To put me to shame?

3 Why should I complain
    Of want or distress,
  Temptation or pain?
    He told me no less:
  The heirs of salvation,
    I know from His word,
  Through much tribulation
    Must follow their Lord.

4 How bitter that cup,
    No heart can conceive,
  Which He drank quite up,
    That sinners might live.
  His way was much rougher
    And darker than mine;
  Did Jesus thus suffer,
    And shall I repine?

5 Since all that I meet
    Shall work for my good,
  The bitter is sweet,
    The medicine food.

Though painful at present,
'Twill cease before long;
And then, O how pleasant
The conqueror's song!

John Newton, 1725–1807.

574

COMMIT thou all thy griefs
And ways into His hands,
To His sure truth and tender care,
Who earth and heaven commands.

2 Who points the clouds their course,
Whom winds and seas obey,
He shall direct thy wandering feet,
He shall prepare thy way.

3 Give to the winds thy fears;
Hope, and be undismayed;
God hears thy sighs and counts thy tears;
God shall lift up thy head.

4 Through waves and clouds and storms
He gently clears thy way:
Wait thou His time; so shall this night
Soon end in joyous day.

5 Leave to His sovereign sway
To choose and to command;
So shalt thou, wondering, own His way
How wise, how strong His hand.

Paul Gerhardt, 1607–76,
tr. John Wesley, 1703–91, altd.

575

GOD is my strong salvation;
What foe have I to fear?
In darkness and temptation
My light, my help is near.

2 Though hosts encamp around me,
  Firm to the fight I stand;
What terror can confound me,
  With God at my right hand?

3 Place on the Lord reliance;
  My soul, with courage wait;
His truth be thine affiance,
  When faint and desolate.

4 His might thine heart shall strengthen,
  His love thy joy increase;
Mercy thy days shall lengthen;
  The Lord will give thee peace.

James Montgomery, 1771–1854.

576

GREAT is Thy faithfulness, O God my Father,
There is no shadow of turning with Thee;
Thou changest not, Thy compassions they fail not,
As Thou hast been Thou for ever wilt be.

Great is Thy faithfulness!
Great is Thy faithfulness!
Morning by morning new mercies I see;
All I have needed Thy hand hath provided,—
Great is Thy faithfulness, Lord, unto me!

2 Summer and winter, and spring-time and harvest,
Sun, moon and stars in their courses above,
Join with all nature in manifold witness
To Thy great faithfulness, mercy and love.

3 Pardon for sin and a peace that endureth,
Thine own dear presence to cheer and to guide;
Strength for to-day and bright hope for to-morrow,
Blessings all mine, with ten thousand beside!

T. O. Chisholm, 1866–1960.

577

HAVE faith in God, my heart,
    Trust and be unafraid;
God will fulfil in every part
    Each promise He has made.

2 Have faith in God, my mind,
    Though oft thy light burns low;
God's mercy holds a wiser plan
    Than thou canst fully know.

3 Have faith in God, my soul,
    His cross for ever stands;
And neither life nor death can pluck
    His children from His hands.

4 Lord Jesus, make me whole;
    Grant me no resting place,
Until I rest, heart, mind, and soul,
    The captive of Thy grace.

Bryn Austin Rees, 1911–

578

HOLD Thou my hand! so weak I am, and
    helpless,
I dare not take one step without Thine aid;
Hold Thou my hand! for then, O loving Saviour,
No dread of ill shall make my soul afraid.

2 Hold Thou my hand! and closer, closer draw me
To Thy dear self—my hope, my joy, my all;
Hold Thou my hand, lest haply I should wander;
    And, missing Thee, my trembling feet should
    fall.

3 Hold Thou my hand ! the way is dark before me
  Without the sunlight of Thy face divine;
But when by faith I catch its radiant glory,
  What heights of joy, what rapturous songs are
    mine !

4 Hold Thou my hand ! that when I reach the
    margin
  Of that lone river Thou didst cross for me,
A heavenly light may flash along its waters,
  And every wave like crystal bright shall be.

                    Frances van Alstyne, 1820–1915.

579

ISAIAH xliii. 1–5.

HOW firm a foundation, ye saints of the Lord,
  Is laid for your faith in His excellent word;
What more can He say than to you He hath said,
You who unto Jesus for refuge have fled ?

2 Fear not, He is with thee, O be not dismayed;
  For He is thy God, and will still give thee aid:
He'll strengthen thee, help thee, and cause thee to
    stand,
Upheld by His righteous, omnipotent hand.

3 In every condition, in sickness, in health,
  In poverty's vale, or abounding in wealth;
At home and abroad, on the land, on the sea,
As thy days may demand shall thy strength
    ever be.

4 When through the deep waters He calls thee to go,
  The rivers of grief shall not thee overflow;
For He will be with thee in trouble to bless,
And sanctify to thee thy deepest distress.

5 When through fiery trials thy pathway shall lie,
  His grace all-sufficient shall be thy supply;
The flame shall not hurt thee, His only design
Thy dross to consume and thy gold to refine.

6 The soul that on Jesus has leaned for repose
  He will not, He will not, desert to its foes;
That soul, though all hell should endeavour to
  shake,
He'll never, no never, no never forsake.

" K " in Rippon's Selection, 1787, altd.

580

IF thou but suffer God to guide thee,
  And hope in Him through all thy ways,
He'll give thee strength, whate'er betide thee,
  And bear thee through the evil days;
Who trusts in God's unchanging love
Builds on the rock that nought can move.

2 Only be still, and wait His leisure
  In cheerful hope, with heart content
To take whate'er thy Father's pleasure,
  His all-discerning love, hath sent;
Nor doubt our inmost wants are known
To Him who chose us for His own.

3 Sing, pray, and keep His ways unswerving;
  So do thine own part faithfully,
And trust His word, though undeserving,
  Thou yet shalt find it true for thee:
God never yet forsook at need
The soul that trusted Him indeed.

Georg Neumark, 1621–81,
tr. Catherine Winkworth. 1827–78.

581

IN heavenly love abiding,
    No change my heart shall fear;
And safe is such confiding,
    For nothing changes here.
The storm may roar without me,
    My heart may low be laid,
But God is round about me,
    And can I be dismayed?

2 Wherever He may guide me,
    No want shall turn me back;
My Shepherd is beside me,
    And nothing can I lack.
His wisdom ever waketh,
    His sight is never dim,
He knows the way He taketh,
    And I will walk with Him.

3 Green pastures are before me,
    Which yet I have not seen;
Bright skies will soon be o'er me,
    Where dark the clouds have been.
My hope I cannot measure,
    My path to life is free,
My Saviour has my treasure,
    And He will walk with me.

Anna Laetitia Waring, 1823–1910.

582

JESUS, I am resting, resting in the joy of what
    Thou art;
I am finding out the greatness of Thy loving heart.
Thou hast bid me gaze upon Thee, and Thy
    beauty fills my soul;
For by Thy transforming power Thou hast made
    me whole.

Jesus, I am resting, resting in the joy of what
  Thou art ;
I am finding out the greatness of Thy loving heart.

2 Simply trusting Thee, Lord Jesus, I behold Thee
   as Thou art,
 And Thy love so pure, so changeless, satisfies my
   heart:
 Satisfies its deepest longings, and supplies its every
   need,
 Compasseth me round with blessings; Thine is
   love indeed !

3 Ever lift Thy face upon me, as I work and wait
   for Thee;
 Resting neath Thy smile, Lord Jesus, earth's dark
   shadows flee.
 Brightness of my Father's glory, sunshine of my
   Father's face,
 Keep me ever trusting, resting; fill me with Thy
   grace !

                                    Jean Pigott.

583

NOT what I am, O Lord, but what Thou art,—
   That, that alone can be my soul's true rest:
Thy love, not mine, bids fear and doubt depart,
   And stills the tempest of my throbbing breast.

2 Thy name is love, I hear it from yon cross;
   Thy name is love, I hear it from yon tomb:
 All meaner love is perishable dross,
   But this shall light me through time's thickest
   gloom.

3 Girt with the love of God on every side,
   Breathing that love as heaven's own healing air,
 I work or wait, still following my guide,
   Braving each foe, escaping every snare.

4 'Tis what I know of Thee, my Lord and God,
    That fills my soul with peace, my lips with song:
Thou art my health, my joy, my staff, and rod;
    Leaning on Thee, in weakness I am strong.

5 More of Thyself, O show me hour by hour;
    More of Thy glory, O my God and Lord:
More of Thyself, in all Thy grace and power;
    More of Thy love and truth, incarnate Word!

Horatius Bonar, 1808–89.

584

PEACE, perfect peace, in this dark world of sin ?
  The blood of Jesus whispers peace within.

2 Peace, perfect peace, by thronging duties pressed ?
To do the will of Jesus, this is rest.

3 Peace, perfect peace, with sorrows surging round ?
On Jesus' bosom nought but calm is found.

4 Peace, perfect peace, with loved ones far away ?
In Jesus' keeping we are safe, and they.

5 Peace, perfect peace, our future all unknown ?
Jesus we know, and He is on the throne.

6 Peace, perfect peace, death shadowing us and
  ours ?
Jesus hath vanquished death and all its powers.

7 It is enough; earth's troubles soon shall cease,
And Jesus call us to heaven's perfect peace.

E. H. Bickersteth, 1823–1906.

585

SOMETIMES a light surprises
    The Christian while he sings;
It is the Lord who rises
    With healing in His wings.
When comforts are declining,
    He grants the soul again
A season of clear shining,
    To cheer it after rain.

2 In holy contemplation,
    We sweetly then pursue
The theme of God's salvation,
    And find it ever new.
Set free from present sorrow,
    We cheerfully can say,
" E'en let the unknown morrow
    Bring with it what it may,—

3 " It can bring with it nothing
    But He will bear us through;
Who gives the lilies clothing
    Will clothe His people too.
Beneath the spreading heavens,
    No creature but is fed;
And He who feeds the ravens
    Will give His children bread."

4 Though vine nor fig-tree neither
    Their wonted fruit should bear,
Though all the field should wither,
    Nor flocks nor herds be there,
Yet, God the same abiding,
    His praise shall tune my voice;
For, while in Him confiding,
    I cannot but rejoice.

William Cowper, 1731–1800.

586

THINE for ever ! God of love,
Hear us from Thy throne above;
Thine for ever may we be,
Here and in eternity.

2 Thine for ever ! Lord of life,
Shield us through our earthly strife;
Thou the life, the truth, the way,
Guide us to the realms of day.

3 Thine for ever ! O how blest
They who find in Thee their rest !
Saviour, guardian, heavenly friend,
O defend us to the end.

4 Thine for ever ! Thou our guide,
All our wants by Thee supplied,
All our sins by Thee forgiven,
Lead us, Lord, from earth to heaven !

Mary Fawler Maude, 1819–1913.

587

THOU hidden source of calm repose,
Thou all-sufficient love divine;
My help and refuge from my foes,
Secure I am if Thou art mine;
And lo ! from sin, and grief, and shame,
I hide me, Jesus, in Thy name.

2 Thy mighty name salvation is,
And keeps my happy soul above;
Comfort it brings, and power, and peace,
And joy, and everlasting love;
To me, with Thy dear name, are given
Pardon, and holiness, and heaven.

3 Jesus, my all-in-all Thou art—
　　My rest in toil, my ease in pain,
The medicine of my broken heart,
　　In war my peace, in loss my gain;
My smile beneath the tyrant's frown;
In shame, my glory and my crown;

4 In want, my plentiful supply;
　　In weakness, my almighty power:
In bonds, my perfect liberty;
　　My light in Satan's darkest hour;
My help and stay whene'er I call;
My life in death, my heaven, my all.

Charles Wesley, 1707–88.

588

THOUGH troubles assail and dangers affright,
　Though friends should all fail and foes all unite,
Yet one thing secures us, whatever betide,
The scripture assures us the Lord will provide.

2 The birds without barn or storehouse are fed;
From them let us learn to trust for our bread;
His saints what is fitting shall ne'er be denied,
So long as 'tis written, " The Lord will provide."

3 His call we obey, like Abram of old,
Not knowing our way, but faith makes us bold;
For, though we are strangers, we have a good
　guide,
And trust, in all dangers, the Lord will provide.

4 No strength of our own or goodness we claim;
Yet, since we have known the Saviour's great name,
In this our strong tower for safety we hide,—
The Lord is our power, the Lord will provide.

John Newton, 1725–1807.

589

THROUGH all the changing scenes of life,
    In trouble and in joy.
The praises of my God shall still
    My heart and tongue employ.

2 Of His deliverance I will boast,
    Till all that are distressed
From mine example comfort take,
    And charm their griefs to rest.

3 The hosts of God encamp around
    The dwellings of the just;
Protection He affords to all
    Who make His name their trust.

4 O magnify the Lord with me,
    With me exalt His name;
When in distress to Him I called
    He to my rescue came.

5 O make but trial of His love,
    Experience will decide
How blest are they, and only they,
    Who in His truth confide.

6 Fear Him, ye saints, and you will then
    Have nothing else to fear;
Make but His service your delight;
    Your wants shall be His care.

Nahum Tate, 1652–1715, and
Nicholas Brady, 1659–1726.

590

THROUGH the love of God our Saviour
    All will be well;
Free and changeless is His favour,
    All, all is well.
Precious is the blood that healed us,
Perfect is the grace that sealed us,
Strong the hand stretched out to shield us;
    All must be well.

2 Though we pass through tribulation,
    All will be well;
Ours is such a full salvation,
    All, all is well.
Happy, still in God confiding;
Fruitful, if in Christ abiding;
Holy, through the Spirit's guiding;
    All must be well.

3 We expect a bright to-morrow;
    All will be well;
Faith can sing through days of sorrow
    " All, all is well."
On our Father's love relying,
Jesus every need supplying,
Or in living or in dying,
    All must be well.

Mary Peters, 1813–56.

See also—

All my hope, 492.
God is love, 52.
High in the heavens, 56.
I am trusting Thee, 432.
Now I have found, 451.
O let him whose sorrow, 771.
O Lord, how happy, 482.
O love of God, 69.

The God of Abraham, 30.
The King of love, 72.
The Lord is rich, 422.
The Lord's my shepherd, 73.
Thy ceaseless, unexhausted
   love, 31.
When we walk, 491.

591

1 JOHN iv. 7.

BELOVÈD, let us love: for love is of God;
In God alone hath love its true abode.

2 Belovèd, let us love: for they who love,
They only, are His sons, born from above.

3 Belovèd, let us love: for love is rest.
And he who loveth not abides unblest.

4 Belovèd, let us love: for love is light,
And he who loveth not dwelleth in night.

5 Belovèd, let us love: for only thus
Shall we behold that God who loveth us.

Horatius Bonar, 1808–89.

592

BREATHE on me, Breath of God,
Fill me with life anew,
That I may love what Thou dost love,
And do what Thou wouldst do.

2　Breathe on me, Breath of God,
Until my heart is pure,
Until with Thee I will one will,
To do or to endure.

3　Breathe on me, Breath of God,
Till I am wholly Thine,
Until this earthly part of me
Glows with Thy fire divine.

4 Breathe on me, Breath of God,
   So shall I never die,
But live with Thee the perfect life
   Of Thine eternity.   Amen.

Edwin Hatch, 1835–89.

593

HEBREWS xiii. 20–21.

FATHER of peace, and God of love,
   We own Thy power to save,
That power by which our Shepherd rose
   Victorious o'er the grave.

2 Him from the dead Thou brought'st again,
   When, by His sacred blood,
Confirmed and sealed for evermore,
   The eternal covenant stood.

3 O may Thy spirit seal our souls,
   And mould them to Thy will,
That our weak hearts no more may stray,
   But keep Thy precepts still;

4 That to perfection's sacred height
   We nearer still may rise,
And all we think, and all we do,
   Be pleasing in Thine eyes.

Philip Doddridge, 1702–51, *altd.,*
v. 4, William Cameron, 1751–1811.

594

IT passeth knowledge, that dear love of Thine,
   My Saviour, Jesus! yet this soul of mine
Would of Thy love, in all its breadth and length,
Its height and depth, its everlasting strength,
         Know more and more.

2 It passeth telling, that dear love of Thine,
My Saviour, Jesus! yet these lips of mine
Would fain proclaim, to sinners, far and near,
A love which can remove all guilty fear,
And love beget.

3 It passeth praises, that dear love of Thine,
My Saviour Jesus! yet this heart of mine
Would sing that love, so full, so rich, so free,
Which brings a rebel sinner, such as me,
Nigh unto God.

4 But, though I cannot sing or tell or know
The fulness of Thy love, while here below,
My empty vessel I may freely bring:
O Thou who art of love the living spring,
My vessel fill.

5 O fill me, Jesus, Saviour, with Thy love;
Lead, lead me to the living fount above;
Thither may I, in simple faith, draw nigh,
And never to another fountain fly,
But unto Thee.

6 And when my Jesus face to face I see,
When at His lofty throne I bow the knee,
Then of His love, in all its breadth and length,
Its height, and depth, its everlasting strength,
My soul shall sing.

Mary Shekleton, 1827–83.

595

LOVE divine, all loves excelling,
  Joy of heaven, to earth come down,
Fix in us Thy humble dwelling,
  All Thy faithful mercies crown:
Jesus, Thou art all compassion,
  Pure, unbounded love Thou art;
Visit us with Thy salvation,
  Enter every trembling heart.

2 Breathe, O breathe Thy loving Spirit
    Into every troubled breast;
Let us all in Thee inherit,
    Let us find Thy promised rest;
Take away the love of sinning,
    Alpha and omega be;
End of faith, as its beginning,
    Set our hearts at liberty.

3 Come, almighty to deliver,
    Let us all Thy grace receive;
Suddenly return, and never,
    Never more Thy temples leave.
Thee we would be always blessing,
    Serve Thee as Thy hosts above,
Pray, and praise Thee without ceasing,
    Glory in Thy perfect love.

4 Finish, then, Thy new creation:
    Pure and spotless let us be;
Let us see Thy great salvation,
    Perfectly restored in Thee,
Changed from glory into glory,
    Till in heaven we take our place,
Till we cast our crowns before Thee,
    Lost in wonder, love, and praise.

Amen.

Charles Wesley, 1707-88

596

MAY the mind of Christ my Saviour
    Live in me from day to day,
By His love and power controlling
    All I do or say.

2 May the word of God dwell richly
    In my heart from hour to hour,
So that all may see I triumph
    Only through His power.

3 May the peace of God my Father
   Rule my life in everything,
That I may be calm to comfort
   Sick and sorrowing.

4 May the love of Jesus fill me,
   As the waters fill the sea;
Him exalting, self abasing,
   This is victory.

5 May I run the race before me,
   Strong and brave to face the foe,
Looking only unto Jesus
   As I onward go.

Kate B. Wilkinson.

597

MORE about Jesus would I know,
   More of His grace to others show;
More of His saving fulness see,
More of His love—who died for me.
   More, more about Jesus,
   More, more about Jesus;
   More of His saving fulness see,
   More of His love who died for me.

2 More about Jesus let me learn,
   More of His holy will discern;
Spirit of God, my teacher be,
Showing the things of Christ to me.

3 More about Jesus; in His Word
   Holding communion with my Lord;
Hearing His voice in every line,
Making each faithful saying mine.

4 More about Jesus; on His throne,
Riches in glory all His own;
More of His kingdom's sure increase;
More of His coming—Prince of peace.

E. E. Hewitt, 1851–1920.

598

NEARER, my God, to Thee,
    Nearer to Thee:
E'en though it be a cross
    That raiseth me,
Still all my song would be
Nearer, my God, to Thee,
    Nearer to Thee.

2 Though, like the wanderer,
    The sun gone down,
Darkness be over me,
    My rest a stone,
Yet in my dreams I'd be
Nearer, my God, to Thee,
    Nearer to Thee.

3 There let the way appear,
    Steps up to heaven;
All that Thou sendest me,
    In mercy given;
Angels to beckon me
Nearer, my God, to Thee,
    Nearer to Thee.

4 Then, with my waking thoughts
    Bright with Thy praise,
Out of my stony griefs
    Bethel I'll raise;
So by my woes to be
Nearer, my God, to Thee,
    Nearer to Thee.

5 Or, if on joyful wing
　　Cleaving the sky,
Sun, moon, and stars forgot,
　　Upwards I fly,
Still all my song shall be,
Nearer, my God, to Thee,
　　Nearer to Thee.

Sarah Fuller Adams, 1805–48.

599

O FOR a closer walk with God,
　　A calm and heavenly frame,
A light to shine upon the road
　　That leads me to the Lamb !

2 Where is the blessedness I knew
　　When first I saw the Lord ?
Where is the soul-refreshing view
　　Of Jesus and His word ?

3 What peaceful hours I once enjoyed !
　　How sweet their memory still !
But they have left an aching void
　　The world can never fill.

4 Return, O holy Dove, return,
　　Sweet messenger of rest !
I hate the sins that made Thee mourn,
　　And drove Thee from my breast.

5 The dearest idol I have known,
　　Whate'er that idol be,
Help me to tear it from Thy throne,
　　And worship only Thee.

6 So shall my walk be close with God,
　　Calm and serene my frame:
So purer light shall mark the road
　　That leads me to the Lamb.

William Cowper, 1731–1800.

600

O FOR a heart to praise my God,
　　A heart from sin set free;
A heart that's sprinkled with the blood
　　So freely shed for me;

2 A heart resigned, submissive, meek,
　　My great Redeemer's throne;
Where only Christ is heard to speak,
　　Where Jesus reigns alone.

3 A humble, lowly, contrite heart,
　　Believing, true, and clean;
Which neither life nor death can part
　　From Him that dwells within.

4 A heart in every thought renewed,
　　And full of love divine;
Perfect and right, and pure and good,
　　A copy, Lord, of Thine.

5 Thy nature, gracious Lord, impart,
　　Come quickly from above;
Write Thy new name upon my heart,
　　Thy new best name of love.

Charles Wesley, 1707–88, altd.

601

O JESUS CHRIST, grow Thou in me,
　　And all things else recede;
My heart be daily nearer Thee,
　　From sin be daily freed.

2 Each day let Thy supporting might
    My weakness still embrace;
My darkness vanish in Thy light,
    Thy life my death efface.

3 Make this poor self grow less and less,
    Be Thou my life and aim;
O make me daily through Thy grace,
    More meet to bear Thy name.

4 Daily more filled with Thee my heart,
    Daily from self more free;
Thou to whom prayer did strength impart,
    Of my prayer hearer be.

5 Fill me with gladness from above,
    Hold me by strength divine;
Lord, let the glow of Thy great love
    Through my whole being shine.

J. C. Lavater, 1741–1801,
tr. Elizabeth Lee Smith, 1817–98.

602

O LOVING Lord, who art for ever seeking
    Men of Thy mind, intent to do Thy will,
Strong in Thy strength, Thy power and grace
    bespeaking,
    Faithful to Thee, through good report and ill—

2 To Thee we come, and humbly make confession,
    Faithless so oft, in thought and word and deed,
Asking that we may have, in true possession,
    Thy free forgiveness in the hour of need.

3 In duties small be Thou our inspiration,
    In large affairs endue us with Thy might;
Through faithful service cometh full salvation;
    So may we serve, Thy will our chief delight.

4 Not disobedient to the heavenly vision,
  Faithful in all things, seeking not reward,
So, following Thee, may we fulfil our mission,
  True to ourselves, our brethren, and our Lord.

W. Vaughan Jenkins, 1868–1920.

603

O THE bitter shame and sorrow,
   That a time could ever be
When I let the Saviour's pity
Plead in vain, and proudly answered,
  " All of self, and none of Thee."

2 Yet He found me; I beheld Him
  Bleeding on the accursèd tree,
Heard Him pray, " Forgive them, Father ! "
And my wistful heart said faintly,
  " Some of self, and some of Thee."

3 Day by day His tender mercy,
  Healing, helping, full and free,
Sweet and strong, and ah ! so patient,
Brought me lower, while I whispered,
  " Less of self, and more of Thee."

4 Higher than the highest heaven,
  Deeper than the deepest sea,
Lord, Thy love at last hath conquered;
Grant me now my soul's desire,
  " None of self, and all of Thee ! "

Theodore Monod, 1836–1921.

604

O TOUCH mine eyes, that I may see
   In cloudless rapture Thy dear face,
And in that calm serenity,
  With patience run my glorious race.

2 O loose my tongue, that I may tell
    With burning words, to sinners lost,
That Thou didst come to seek and save,
    To purchase them at such a cost.

3 Unstop mine ears, that I may hear
    The softest whisper of Thy love,
To draw my heart from earthly things,
    And fix it on Thyself above.

4 Release my feet, that I may run
    The way of holiness divine;
Held by Thy hand I cannot fall,
    Filled with Thy life I'll brightly shine.

W. Spencer Walton, 1850–1906.

605

TO me to live is Christ:
    If Christ bestow His grace,
A childlike heart to me is given
That wonders after God and heaven,
    And smiles up in His face
    Whose love doth me embrace.

2 To me to live is Christ:
    If Christ with me abide,
He bringeth me victorious youth,
Rejoicing in the love of truth,
    Fearless of wrath and pride,
    Because the Lord will guide.

3 To me to live is Christ:
    If Christ my love awake,
The wisdom ripe of age is mine,
And hope, and joy, and peace divine
    At evening twilight make
    The eternal day to break.

4 So let me live to Christ,
   And death shall but disguise
The life eternal and complete,
Where age and youth and childhood meet,
   Simple and strong and wise,
   In Christ above the skies.

Walter Chalmers Smith, 1824–1908.

606

WE have not known Thee as we ought,
   Nor learned Thy wisdom, grace, and
   power:
The things of earth have filled our thought,
   And trifles of the passing hour:
Lord, give us light Thy truth to see,
And make us wise in knowing Thee.

2 We have not loved Thee as we ought,
   Nor cared that we are loved by Thee:
Thy presence we have coldly sought,
   And feebly longed Thy face to see:
Lord, give a pure and loving heart
To feel and know the love Thou art.

3 We have not served Thee as we ought;
   Alas! the duties left undone,
The work with little fervour wrought,
   The battles lost, or scarcely won !
Lord, give the zeal, and give the might,
For Thee to toil, for Thee to fight.

4 When shall we know Thee as we ought,
   When shall we love and serve aright ?
When shall we, out of trial brought,
   Be perfect in the land of light ?
Lord, may we day by day prepare
To see Thy face, and serve Thee there.

T. B. Pollock, 1836–96.

607

WE praise and bless Thee, gracious Lord,
 Our Saviour, kind and true,
For all the old things passed away,
 For all Thou hast made new.

2 New hopes, new purposes, desires,
 And joys, Thy grace has given;
Old ties are broken from the earth,
 New ties attach to heaven.

3 But yet, how much must be destroyed,
 How much renewed must be,
Ere we can fully stand complete
 In likeness, Lord, to Thee !

4 Thou, only Thou, must carry on
 The work Thou hast begun;
Of Thine own strength, Thou must impart,
 In Thine own ways to run.

5 So shall we faultless stand at last
 Before Thy Father's throne;
The blessedness for ever ours,
 The glory all Thine own !

C. J. P. Spitta, 1801–59,
tr. Jane Borthwick, 1813–97.

See also—

Come down, O Love divine, 224.

Gracious Spirit, 231.

O God, what offering, 770.

O send Thy light, 277.

Saviour, Thy dying love, 485.

Spirit of God, 240.

Thee will I love, 75.

(11) VICTORY OVER DEATH

608

AROUND the throne of God in heaven
 Thousands of children stand,
Children whose sins are all forgiven,
 A holy, happy band,
  Singing, " Glory, glory, glory ! "

2 In flowing robes of spotless white
    See every one arrayed,
Dwelling in everlasting light,
    And joys that never fade,
        Singing, " Glory, glory, glory ! "

3 What brought them to that world above,
    That heaven so bright and fair,
Where all is peace, and joy, and love ?
    How came those children there,
        Singing, " Glory, glory, glory ! "

4 On earth they sought their Saviour's grace,
    On earth they loved His name;
So now they see His blessèd face,
    And stand before the Lamb,
        Singing, " Glory, glory, glory ! "

Anne Shepherd, 1809–57.

609

FOR ever with the Lord !
    Amen, so let it be:
Life from the dead is in that word,
    'Tis immortality.
    Here in the body pent,
    Absent from Him I roam,
Yet nightly pitch my moving tent
    A day's march nearer home.

2   My Father's house on high,
        Home of my soul, how near
At times to faith's foreseeing eye
        The golden gates appear !
        Ah ! then my spirit faints
        To reach the land I love,
The bright inheritance of saints,
        Jerusalem above.

3   For ever with the Lord !
       Father, if 'tis Thy will,
  The promise of that faithful word
      E'en here to me fulfil.
      Be Thou at my right hand,
      Then can I never fail;
  Uphold Thou me, and I shall stand;
      Fight, and I must prevail.

4   So when my latest breath
      Shall rend the veil in twain,
  By death I shall escape from death,
      And life eternal gain.
      Knowing as I am known,
      How shall I love that word,
  And oft repeat before the throne,
      " For ever with the Lord ! "

James Montgomery, 1771–1854, *altd.*

610

FOR those we love within the veil
    Who once were comrades of our way,
We thank Thee, Lord; for they have won
    To cloudless day.

2 And life for them is life indeed,
    The splendid goal of earth's strait race,
And where no shadows intervene,
    They see Thy face.

3 Not as we knew them any more,
    Toil-worn and sad with burdened care,—
Erect, clear-eyed, upon their brows
    Thy name they bear

4 Free from the fret of mortal years,
    And knowing now Thy perfect will,
With quickened sense and heightened joy
    They serve Thee still.

5 O fuller, sweeter is that life,
    And larger, ampler is the air:
Eye cannot see nor heart conceive
    The glory there ;

6 Nor know to what high purpose Thou
    Dost yet employ their ripened powers,
Nor how at Thy behest they touch
    This life of ours.

7 There are no tears within their eyes,
    With love they keep perpetual tryst;
And praise and work and rest are one
    With Thee, O Christ.

W. Charter Piggott, 1872–1943.

611

GOD of the living, in whose eyes
  Unveiled Thy whole creation lies;
All souls are Thine;—we must not say
That those are dead who pass away;
From this our world of flesh set free,
We know them living unto Thee.

2 Released from earthly toil and strife
With Thee is hidden still their life;
Thine are their thoughts, their works, their powers,
All Thine, and yet most truly ours;
For well we know, where'er they be,
Our dead are living unto Thee.

3 Thy word is true, Thy will is just:
To Thee we leave them, Lord, in trust;
And bless Thee for the love which gave
Thy Son to fill a human grave,
That none might fear that world to see
Where all are living unto Thee.

4 O giver unto man of breath,
O holder of the keys of death,
O quickener of the life within,
Save us from death, the death of sin;
That body, soul, and spirit be
For ever living unto Thee !

John Ellerton, 1826–93.

612

LORD, it belongs not to my care
Whether I die or live;
To love and serve Thee is my share,
And this Thy grace must give.

2 If life be long, I will be glad
That I may long obey;
If short, yet why should I be sad
To soar to endless day ?

3 Christ leads me through no darker rooms
Than He went through before;
And he that to God's kingdom comes
Must enter by this door.

4 Come, Lord, when grace has made me meet
Thy blessèd face to see,
For if Thy work on earth be sweet,
What will Thy glory be ?

5 My knowledge of that life is small,
The eye of faith is dim;
But 'tis enough that Christ knows all,
And I shall be with Him.

Richard Baxter, 1615–91, **altd.**

613

O LORD of life, where'er they be,
Safe in Thine own eternity,
Our dead are living unto Thee:
         Hallelujah !

2 All souls are Thine, and, here or there,
They rest within Thy sheltering care;
One providence alike they share:
         Hallelujah !

3 Thy word is true, Thy ways are just;
Above the requiem " Dust to dust "
Shall rise our psalm of grateful trust:
         Hallelujah !

4 O happy they in God who rest !
No more by fear and doubt oppressed;
Living or dying, they are blest:
         Hallelujah !

F. L. Hosmer, 1840–1929

614

THERE is a land of pure delight,
   Where saints immortal reign;
Infinite day excludes the night,
   And pleasures banish pain;

2 There everlasting spring abides,
   And never-withering flowers:
Death, like a narrow sea, divides
   This heavenly land from ours.

3 Sweet fields beyond the swelling flood
   Stand dressed in living green;
So to the Jews old Canaan stood,
   While Jordan rolled between.

4 But timorous mortals start and shrink
    To cross this narrow sea,
  And linger shivering on the brink,
    And fear to launch away.

5 O could we make our doubts remove,
    Those gloomy doubts that rise,
  And see the Canaan that we love
    With unbeclouded eyes,

6 Could we but climb where Moses stood,
    And view the landscape o'er,
  Not Jordan's stream, nor death's cold flood,
    Should fright us from the shore.
                              Isaac Watts, 1674-1748.

615

THERE'S a Friend for little children
    Above the bright blue sky,
A Friend that never changes,
    Whose love will never die,
Unlike some friends by nature,
    Who change with changing years,
This Friend is always worthy
    The precious name He bears.

2 There's a home for little children
    Above the bright blue sky,
  Where Jesus reigns in glory,
    A home of peace and joy;
  No home on earth is like it,
    Nor can with it compare;
  For everyone is happy,
    Nor could be happier, there.

3 There's a song for little children
    Above the bright blue sky,
A song that will not weary,
    Though sung continually;
A song which even angels
    Can never, never sing;
They know not Christ as Saviour,
    But worship Him as King.

4 There's a crown for little children
    Above the bright blue sky;
And all who look to Jesus
    Shall wear it by-and-by,—
A crown of brightest glory,
    Which He will then bestow
On all who love the Saviour
    And walk with Him below.

Albert Midlane, 1825–1909.

616

WHEN this passing world is done,
    When has sunk yon glaring sun,
When we stand with Christ on high,
Looking o'er life's history,
Then, Lord, shall I fully know,
Not till then, how much I owe.

2 When I stand before the throne,
Dressed in beauty not my own,
When I see Thee as Thou art,
Love Thee with unsinning heart,
Then, Lord, shall I fully know,
Not till then, how much I owe.

3 When the praise of heaven I hear,
Loud as thunders to the ear,
Deep as many waters' noise,
Sweet as harp's melodious voice,
Then, Lord, shall I fully know,
Not till then, how much I owe.

4 E'en on earth, as through a glass,
  Darkly let Thy glory pass;
  Make forgiveness feel so sweet;
  Make Thy Spirit's help so meet;
  E'en on earth, Lord, make me know
  Something of how much I owe.

R. M. McCheyne, 1813–43.

See also—

Come let us join, 402.
For all the saints, 403.
Give me the wings of faith, 404.
He wants not friends, 360.
How bright these glorious spirits, 405.

I'll praise my Maker, 60.
Jerusalem the golden, 406.
O Lord of life, 650.
Ten thousand times, 407.
The sands of time, 776.
What joy to think, 408.

IX. OUR LIFE IN SOCIETY

(1) HOME AND FAMILY

617

FATHER, in Thy presence kneeling,
All our heart's desire revealing,
To Thy love, in faith, appealing—
  For our children, Lord, we pray.

2 Grant us wisdom so to train them
That no mortal evil stain them;
Young for Jesus would we gain them—
  For our children, Lord, we pray.

3 Keep them onward, upward pressing;
Courage, self-control possessing;
Bravely Christ their King confessing—
  For our children, Lord, we pray.

4 Strengthen them for high endeavour,
To Thy will unfaithful never,
God and neighbour serving ever—
  For our children, Lord, we pray.

5 Lord, on life's adventure guide them;
In Thy secret presence hide them;
To Thy love we now confide them—
  All we ask in Jesus' name. Amen.

Charles Venn Pilcher, 1879-

618

LORD of life and King of glory,
    Who didst deign a child to be,
Cradled on a mother's bosom,
    Throned upon a mother's knee:
For the children Thou hast given
    We must answer unto Thee.

2 Since the day the blessèd mother
    Thee, the world's Redeemer bore,
Thou hast crowned us with an honour
    Women never knew before;
And, that we may bear it meetly,
    We must seek Thine aid the more.

3 Grant us, then, pure hearts and patient,
    That, in all we do or say,
Little souls our deeds may copy,
    And be never led astray;
Little feet our steps may follow
    In a safe and narrow way.

4 When our growing sons and daughters
    Look on life with eager eyes,
Grant us then a deeper insight,
    And new powers of sacrifice:
Hope to trust them, faith to guide them,
    Love that nothing good denies.

5 May we keep our holy calling
    Stainless in its fair renown,
That, when all the work is over,
    And we lay the burden down,
Then the children Thou hast given
    Still may be our joy and crown.

Christian Burke, 1857–1944.

619

LORD of life, who once wast cradled
    On a human mother's knee,
Fed and clothed, and taught and guided
    Through the years of infancy:
Help and bless us, as we gather
    With our cares and needs to Thee.

2*Waking in the early morning
    To the round which each day brings;
Sitting late into the evening,
    Making garments, mending things:
Give us strength and cheerful patience
    For these common happenings.

3 Lord, we thank Thee for our children
    With their faces bright and fair,
With their laughter and their temper,
    Waking gladness, bringing care:
Teach us how to keep them upright,
    True and gallant, everywhere.

4 Show us when to hold and curb them,
    When to set them finely free,
How to keep their love and reverence
    Stainless through the years to be,
How to win their adoration
    And their loyalty to Thee.

5 And since we have often faltered,
    Missed the road and lost our way,
Known temptation, met with trouble,
    Hear us parents, as we pray:
Be Thyself their guide and master,
    Shape and fit them for their day.

W. Charter Piggott, 1872–1943.

* For Mothers

620

LORD of the home, Thine only Son
    Received a mother's tender love;
And from an earthly father won
    His vision of Thy home above.

2 Help us, O Lord, our homes to make
    Thy Holy Spirit's dwelling place;
Our hands and hearts' devotion take
    To be the servants of Thy grace.

3 Pray we that all who with us dwell,
    Thy love and joy and peace may know;
And while our lips Thy praises tell,
    May faithful lives Thy glory show.

4 Teach us to keep our homes so fair,
    That were our Lord a child once more,
He might be glad our hearth to share,
    And find a welcome at our door.

5 Lord, may Thy spirit sanctify
    Each household duty we fulfil,
May we our Master glorify
    In glad obedience to Thy will.

A. F. Bayly, 1901–

621

O HAPPY home, where Thou art loved the
    dearest,
Thou loving friend and Saviour of our
    race,
And where among the guests there never cometh
    One who can hold such high and honoured
    place !

2 O happy home, where two in heart united
   In holy faith and blessèd hope are one,
Whom death a little while alone divideth,
   And cannot end the union here begun !

3 O happy home, whose little ones are given
   Early to Thee, in humble faith and prayer,
To Thee, their friend, who from the heights of
      heaven
   Guides them, and guards with more than
      mother's care !

4 O happy home, where each one serves Thee, lowly,
   Whatever his appointed work may be,
Till every common task seems great and holy,
   When it is done, O Lord, as unto Thee !

5 O happy home, where Thou art not forgotten,
   When joy is overflowing, full and free,
O happy home, where every wounded spirit
   Is brought, physician, comforter, to Thee,—

6 Until at last, when earth's day's-work is ended,
   All meet Thee in the blessèd home above,
From whence Thou camest, where Thou hast
      ascended,
   Thy everlasting home of peace and love !

Carl Johann Philipp Spitta, 1801–59,
tr. Sarah Findlater, 1823–1907, altd.

See also—

Father all-seeing, 666.
Father who art alone, 667.
For the beauty, 8.
Friend of the home, 285.
Gracious Saviour, 286.

Holy Father, in Thy mercy, 668.
I thank Thee, Lord, 500.
Lord God, from whom, 503.
Standing forth, 342.
When mothers of Salem, 401.

622

O FATHER, all creating,
  Whose wisdom, love, and power
First bound two lives together
  In Eden's primal hour,
To-day to these Thy children
  Thine earliest gifts renew:
A home by Thee made happy,
  A love by Thee kept true.

2 O Saviour, guest most bounteous
  Of old in Galilee,
Vouc᷉ safe to-day Thy presence
  With those who call on Thee;
Their store of earthly gladness
  Transform to heavenly wine,
And teach them in the tasting
  To know the gift is Thine.

3 O Spirit of the Father,
  Breathe on them from above,
So mighty in Thy pureness,
  So tender in Thy love,
That, guarded by Thy presence,
  From sin and strife kept free,
Their lives may own Thy guidance,
  Their hearts be ruled by Thee.

4 Except Thou build it, Father,
  The house is built in vain;
Except Thou, Saviour, bless it,
  The joy will turn to pain:
But nought can break the union
  Of hearts in Thee made one;
And love Thy Spirit hallows
  Is endless love begun.

John Ellerton, 1826–93.

623

O GOD of love, to Thee we bow,
And pray for these before Thee now,
That, closely knit in holy vow,
    They may in Thee be one.

2 When days are filled with pure delight,
When paths are plain and skies are bright,
Walking by faith and not by sight,
    May they in Thee be one.

3 When stormy winds fulfil Thy will,
And all their good seems turned to ill,
Then, trusting Thee completely, still
    May they in Thee be one.

4 Whate'er in life shall be their share
Of quickening joy or burdening care,
In power to do and grace to bear,
    May they in Thee be one.

5 Eternal Love, with them abide;
In Thee for ever may they hide,
For even death cannot divide
    Those whom Thou makest one. Amen.

W. Vaughan Jenkins, 1868–1920.

624

O PERFECT Love, all human thought tran-
    scending,
Lowly we kneel in prayer before Thy throne,
That theirs may be the love which knows no
    ending
Whom Thou for evermore dost join in one.

2 O perfect Life, be Thou their full assurance
Of tender charity, and steadfast faith,
Of patient hope, and quiet brave endurance,
    With childlike trust that fears nor pain nor
    death.

3 Grant them the joy which brightens earthly
    sorrow;
  Grant them the peace which calms all earthly
    strife,
And to life's day the glorious unknown morrow
  That dawns upon eternal love and life. Amen.

Dorothy Gurney, 1858–1932.

625

TO Thee, O heavenly Father,
  Both heart and voice we raise,
For these Thy suppliant servants,
  In mingled prayer and praise:

2 Praise for the joy of loving,
  All other joys above;
Praise for the priceless blessing
  Of love's response to love;

3 Prayer that the full surrender
  Of self may perfect be,
That each be one with other,
  And both be one in Thee;

4 Prayer that Thou wilt accomplish
  The promise of to-day,
And crown the years with blessing
  That shall not pass away;

5 Praise for the hope most glorious
  That looks beyond the veil,
Where faith and hope shall vanish,
  But love shall never fail.

E. A. Welch, 1860–1932, altd.

626

ALMIGHTY Father of all things that be,
Our life, our work, we consecrate to Thee,
Whose heavens declare Thy glory from above,
Whose earth below is witness to Thy love.

2 For well we know this weary, soilèd earth
Is yet Thine own by right of its new birth,
Since that great cross upreared on Calvary
Redeemed it from its fault and shame to Thee.

3 Thine still the changeful beauty of the hills,
The purple valleys flecked with silver rills,
The ocean glistening neath the golden rays;
They all are Thine, and voiceless speak Thy praise.

4 Thou dost the strength to workman's arm impart;
From Thee the skilled musician's mystic art,
The grace of poet's pen or painter's hand,
To teach the loveliness of sea and land.

5 Then grant us, Lord, in all things Thee to own,
To dwell within the shadow of Thy throne,
To speak and work, to think, and live, and move,
Reflecting Thine own nature, which is love:

6 That so, by Christ redeemed from sin and shame,
And hallowed by Thy Spirit's cleansing flame,
Ourselves, our work, and all our powers may be
A sacrifice acceptable to Thee.

E. E. Dugmore, 1843–1925.

627

BEHOLD us, Lord, a little space
From daily tasks set free,
And met within Thy holy place
To rest awhile with Thee.

2 Around us rolls the ceaseless tide
    Of business, toil, and care;
  And scarcely can we turn aside
    For one brief hour of prayer.

3 Yet these are not the only walls
    Wherein Thou mayst be sought;
  On homeliest work Thy blessing falls,
    In truth and patience wrought.

4 Thine is the loom, the forge, the mart,
    The wealth of land and sea;
  The worlds of science and of art,
    Revealed and ruled by Thee.

5 Then let us prove our heavenly birth
    In all we do and know;
  And claim the kingdom of the earth
    For Thee, and not Thy foe.

6 Work shall be prayer, if all be wrought
    As Thou wouldst have it done;
  And prayer, by Thee inspired and taught,
    Itself with work be one.

John Ellerton, 1826–93.

628

FILL Thou my life, O Lord my God,
    In every part with praise,
  That my whole being may proclaim
    Thy being and Thy ways.

2 Not for the lips of praise alone,
    Nor e'en the praising heart
  I ask, but for a life made up
    Of praise in every part:

3 Praise in the common things of life,
    Its goings out and in;
Praise in each duty and each deed,
    However small and mean.

4 Praise in the common words I speak,
    Life's common looks and tones;
In fellowship at hearth or board
    With my beloved ones.

5 Fill every part of me with praise:
    Let my whole being speak
Of Thee and of Thy love, O Lord,
    Poor though I be and weak.

6 So shalt Thou, Lord, receive from me
    The praise and glory due;
And so shall I begin on earth
    The song for ever new.

7 So shall each duty, fret and care
    Be turned into a song;
And every winding of the way
    The echo shall prolong.

8 So shall no part of day or night
    Unblest or common be;
But all my life, in every step,
    Be fellowship with Thee.

Horatius Bonar, 1808–89, altd.

629

FORTH in Thy name, O Lord, I go,
    My daily labour to pursue,
Thee, only Thee, resolved to know
    In all I think, or speak, or do.

2 The task Thy wisdom has assigned
   O let me cheerfully fulfil;
   In all my works Thy presence find,
   And prove Thy good and perfect will.

3 Thee may I set at my right hand,
   Whose eyes my inmost secrets see;
   And labour on at Thy command,
   And offer all my works to Thee.

4 Give me to bear Thine easy yoke,
   And every moment watch and pray,
   And still to things eternal look,
   And hasten to Thy glorious day.

5 For Thee delightfully employ
   Whate'er Thy bounteous grace hath given,
   And run my course with constant joy,
   And closely walk with Thee to heaven.

Charles Wesley, 1707–88, *altd.*

630

LIFE of ages, richly poured,
Love of God, unspent and free,
Flowing in the prophet's word,
And the people's liberty !

2 Never was to chosen race
   That unstinted tide confined:
   Thine are every time and place,
   Fountain sweet of heart and mind;

3 Breathing in the thinker's creed,
   Pulsing in the hero's blood,
   Nerving noblest thought and deed,
   Freshening time with truth and good;

4 Consecrating art and song,
  Holy book and pilgrim way,
  Quelling strife and tyrant wrong,
  Widening freedom's sacred sway.

5 Life of ages, richly poured,
  Love of God, unspent and free,
  Flow still in the prophet's word,
  And the people's liberty !

Samuel Johnson, 1822–82.

631

LORD of all hopefulness, Lord of all joy,
Whose trust, ever child-like, no cares could
  destroy,
Be there at our waking, and give us, we pray,
Your bliss in our hearts, Lord, at the break of the
  day.

2 Lord of all eagerness, Lord of all faith,
  Whose strong hands were skilled at the plane and
    the lathe,
  Be there at our labours, and give us, we pray,
  Your strength in our hearts, Lord, at the noon of
    the day.

3 Lord of all kindliness, Lord of all grace,
  Your hands swift to welcome, your arms to
    embrace,
  Be there at our homing, and give us, we pray,
  Your love in our hearts, Lord, at the eve of the
    day.

4 Lord of all gentleness, Lord of all calm,
  Whose voice is contentment, whose presence is
    balm,
  Be there at our sleeping, and give us, we pray,
  Your peace in our hearts, Lord, at the end of the
    day.   Amen.

Jan Struther, 1901–53.

632

SERVANT of all, to toil for man
    Thou didst not, Lord, refuse;
Thy majesty did not disdain
    To be employed for us.

2 Son of the carpenter, receive
    This humble work of mine;
Worth to my meanest labour give,
    By joining it to Thine.

3 End of my every action Thou,
    In all things Thee I see;
Accept my hallowed labour now,
    I do it unto Thee.

4 Thy bright example I pursue,
    To Thee in all things rise;
And all I think, or speak, or do
    Is one great sacrifice.

5 Careless through outward cares I go,
    From all distraction free;
My hands are but engaged below,
    My heart is still with Thee.

Charles Wesley, 1707–88.

See also—
O God of love, 663.   Wise men seeking Jesus, 135.

(4) THE CARE OF THE SICK AND NEEDY

633

A STRANGER once did bless the earth
    Who never caused a heart to mourn,
Whose very voice gave sorrow mirth—
    And how did earth His worth return?
It spurned Him from its lowliest lot,
The meanest station owned Him not.

2 His presence was a peace to all,
    He bade the sorrowful rejoice.
Pain turned to pleasure at His call,
    Health lived and issued from His voice;
He healed the sick, and sent abroad
The dumb rejoicing in the Lord.

3 The blind met daylight in His eye,
    The joys of everlasting day;
The sick found health in His reply;
    The cripple threw his crutch away.
Yet He with troubles did remain,
And suffered poverty and pain.

4 It was for sin He suffered all
    To set the world-imprisoned free,
To cheer the weary when they call—
    And who could such a stranger be?
The God, who hears each human cry,
And came, a Saviour, from on high.

John Clare, 1793–1864, altd.

634

FATHER, whose will is life and good
    For all of mortal breath,
Bind strong the bond of brotherhood
    Of those who fight with death.

2 Empower the hands and hearts and wills
    Of friends in lands afar,
Who battle with the body's ills,
    And wage Thy holy war.

3 Where'er they heal the maimed and blind,
    Let love of Christ attend,
Proclaim the good Physician's mind,
    And prove the Saviour friend.

4 For Christ the Lord can now employ
    As agents of His will,
Restoring strength and health and joy,
    The doctor's love and skill.

5 O Father, look from heaven and bless,
    Where'er Thy servants be,
Their works of pure unselfishness,
    Made consecrate to Thee !

H. D. Rawnsley, 1851–1920, altd.

635

FROM Thee all skill and science flow,
    All pity, care, and love,
All calm and courage, faith and hope;
    O pour them from above;

2 And part them, Lord, to each and all,
    As each and all shall need,
To rise like incense, each to Thee,
    In noble thought and deed.

3 And hasten, Lord, that perfect day
    When pain and sorrow cease,
And Thy just rule shall fill the earth
    With health, and light, and peace;

4 When ever blue the sky shall gleam,
    And ever green the sod;
And man's rude work deface no more
    The paradise of God.

Charles Kingsley, 1819–75, altd.

636

LORD Christ, who on Thy heart didst bear
    The burden of our shame and sin,
And now on high dost stoop to share
    The fight without, the fear within;

2 Thy patience cannot know defeat,
    Thy pity will not be denied,
Thy loving-kindness still is great,
    Thy tender mercies still abide.

3 O brother Man, for this we pray,
    Thou brother Man and sovereign Lord,
That we Thy brethren, day by day,
    May follow Thee and keep Thy word;

4 That we may care, as Thou hast cared,
    For sick and lame, for deaf and blind,
And freely share, as Thou hast shared,
    In all the sorrows of mankind,

5 That ours may be the holy task
    To help and bless, to heal and save;
This is the happiness we ask,
    And this the service that we crave.

H. Arnold Thomas, 1848–1924, altd.

637

THINE arm, O Christ, in days of old
    Was strong to heal and save;
It triumphed o'er disease and death,
    O'er darkness and the grave.
To Thee they went, the blind, the dumb,
    The palsied and the lame,
The leper with his tainted life,
    The sick with fevered frame;

2 And lo ! Thy touch brought life and health,
    Gave speech, and strength, and sight;
And youth renewed and frenzy calmed
    Owned Thee, the Lord of light.
And now, O Lord, be near to bless,
    Almighty as of yore,
In crowded street, by restless couch,
    As by Gennesaret's shore.

3 Be Thou our great deliverer still,
 Thou Lord of life and death;
Restore and quicken, soothe and bless,
 With Thine almighty breath:
To hands that work and eyes that see
 Give wisdom's heavenly lore,
That whole and sick, and weak and strong,
 May praise Thee evermore.

E. H. Plumptre, 1821–91

638

THOU to whom the sick and dying
 Ever came, nor came in vain,
Still with healing words replying
 To the wearied cry of pain,
Hear us, Jesus, as we meet,
Suppliants at Thy mercy-seat.

2 Still the weary, sick, and dying
 Need a brother's, sister's care;
On Thy higher help relying
 May we now their burden share,
Bringing all our offerings meet,
Suppliants at Thy mercy-seat.

3 May each child of Thine be willing,
 Willing both in hand and heart,
All the law of love fulfilling,
 Ever comfort to impart,
Ever bringing offerings meet,
Suppliant to Thy mercy-seat.

4 So may sickness, sin, and sadness
 To Thy healing virtue yield,
Till the sick and sad, in gladness,
 Rescued, ransomed, cleansèd, healed,
One in Thee together meet,
Pardoned at Thy judgment-seat.

Godfrey Thring, 1823–1903.

639

ALMIGHTY Father, who for us Thy Son didst
give,
That men and nations through His precious death
    might live,
In mercy guard us, lest by sloth and selfish pride
We cause to stumble those for whom the Saviour
    died.

2 We are Thy stewards; Thine our talents, wisdom,
    skill;
Our only glory that we may Thy trust fulfil;
That we Thy pleasure in our neighbours' good
    pursue,
If Thou but workest in us both to will and do.

3 On just and unjust Thou Thy care dost freely
    shower;
Make us Thy children, free from greed and lust
    for power,
Lest human justice, yoked with man's unequal
    laws,
Oppress the needy and neglect the humble cause.

4 Let not Thy worship blind us to the claims of love;
But let Thy manna lead us to the feast above,
To seek the country which by faith we now possess,
Where Christ, our treasure, reigns in peace and
    righteousness.

George Bradford Caird, 1917–

640

GOD bless our native land,
May Thy protecting hand
    Still guard her shore;
May peace her power extend,
Foe be transformed to friend,
And Britain's rights depend
    On war no more.

2 O Lord, our monarch bless
With strength and righteousness;
    Long may she reign !
Her heart inspire and move
With wisdom from above;
And in a nation's love
    Her throne maintain.

3 May just and righteous laws
Uphold the public cause,
    And bless our isle.
Home of the brave and free,
Thou land of liberty,
We pray that still on thee
    Kind heaven may smile.

4 Nor on this land alone,
But be Thy mercies known
    From shore to shore.
Lord, make the nations see
That men should brothers be,
And form one family,
    One, the world o'er.

William Edward Hickson, 1803–70, *altd.*

641

GOD save our gracious Queen,
Long live our noble Queen,
God save the Queen!
Send her victorious,
Happy and glorious,
Long to reign over us;
God save the Queen!

2 Thy choicest gifts in store
On her be pleased to pour,
Long may she reign!
May she defend our laws,
And ever give us cause
To sing with heart and voice,
God save the Queen!

642

I VOW to thee, my country—all earthly things
above—
Entire and whole and perfect, the service of my love,
The love that asks no question: the love that
stands the test,
That lays upon the altar the dearest and the best:
The love that never falters, the love that pays the
price,
The love that makes undaunted the final sacrifice.

2 And there's another country, I've heard of long
ago—
Most dear to them that love her, most great to
them that know—
We may not count her armies: we may not see
her King—
Her fortress is a faithful heart, her pride is suffering—
And soul by soul and silently her shining bounds
increase,
And her ways are ways of gentleness and all her
paths are peace.

Cecil Spring Rice, 1859–1918.

643

JUDGE eternal, throned in splendour,
    Lord of hosts and King of kings,
With Thy living fire of judgment
    Purge this realm of bitter things:
Solace all its wide dominion
    With the healing of Thy wings.

2 Still the weary folk are pining
    For the hour that brings release:
And the city's crowded clangour
    Cries aloud for sin to cease;
And the homesteads and the woodlands
    Plead in silence for their peace.

3 Crown, O God, Thine own endeavour:
    Cleave our darkness with Thy sword:
Feed the faint and hungry heathen
    With the richness of Thy Word:
Cleanse the body of this nation
    Through the glory of the Lord.

H. Scott Holland, 1847–1918.

644

[LAND of our birth, we pledge to thee
    Our love and toil in the years to be;
When we are grown and take our place
As men and women with our race.]

2 Father in heaven, who lovest all,
    O help Thy children when they call;
That they may build from age to age
An undefilèd heritage.

3 Teach us to bear the yoke in youth
    With steadfastness and careful truth;
That in our time Thy grace may give
The truth whereby the nations live.

4 Teach us to rule ourselves alway,
   Controlled and cleanly night and day;
   That we may bring, if need arise,
   No maimed or worthless sacrifice.

5 Teach us to look in all our ends
   On Thee for judge, and not our friends;
   That we with Thee may walk, uncowed
   By fear or favour of the crowd.

6 Teach us the strength that cannot seek,
   By deed or thought, to hurt the weak;
   That, under Thee, we may possess
   Man's strength to comfort man's distress.

7 Teach us delight in simple things,
   And mirth that has no bitter springs;
   Forgiveness free of evil done
   And love to all men 'neath the sun.

[8 Land of our birth, our faith, our pride,
   For whose dear sake our fathers died,
   O Motherland, we pledge to thee
   Head, heart, and hand through the years to be.]

Rudyard Kipling, 1865-1936.

645

LOOK from Thy sphere of endless day,
   O God of mercy and of might,
In pity look on those who stray,
   Benighted in this land of light.

2 In peopled vale, in lonely glen,
   In crowded mart, by stream or sea,
How many of the sons of men
   Hear not the message sent from Thee!

3 Send forth Thy heralds, Lord, to call
   The thoughtless young, the hardened old,
A wandering flock, and bring them all
   To the good shepherd's peaceful fold.

4 Send them Thy mighty word to speak
    Till faith shall dawn, and doubt depart,
To awe the bold, to stay the weak,
    And bind and heal the broken heart.

5 So may our land, renewed again,
    Rejoice in all that's true and good,
Rich in its wealth of Christ-like men,
    Strong in a noble brotherhood.

W. C. Bryant, 1794–1878, *altd.*

646

LORD, while for all mankind we pray,
    Of every clime and coast,
O hear us for our native land,
    The land we love the most.

2 Our fathers' sepulchres are here,
    And here our kindred dwell,
Our children too; how should we love
    Another land so well?

3 O guard our shores from every foe,
    With peace our borders bless;
With prosperous times our cities crown,
    Our fields with plenteousness.

4 Unite us in the sacred love
    Of knowledge, truth, and Thee;
And let our hills and valleys shout
    The songs of liberty.

5 Lord of the nations, thus to Thee
    Our country we commend,
Be Thou her refuge and her trust,
    Her everlasting friend.

J. R. Wreford, 1800–81.

647

LORD, who in Thy perfect wisdom
  Times and seasons dost arrange,
Working out Thy changeless purpose
  In a world of ceaseless change;
Thou didst form our ancient nation,
  Guiding it through all the days,
To unfold in it Thy purpose
  To Thy glory and Thy praise.

2 To our shores remote, benighted,
   Barrier of the western waves,
Tidings in Thy love Thou sentest,
   Tidings of the cross that saves.
Saints and heroes strove and suffered
   Here Thy gospel to proclaim;
We, the heirs of their endeavour,
   Tell the honour of their name.

3 Still Thine ancient purpose standeth
   Every change and chance above;
Still Thine ancient Church remaineth,
   Witness to Thy changeless love.
Grant us vision, Lord, and courage
   To fulfil Thy work begun;
In the Church and in the nation,
   King of kings, Thy will be done.

Timothy Rees, 1874–1939, altd.

648

ECCLESIASTICUS xliv. 1–15.

NOW praise we great and famous men,
  Our fathers named in story;
And praise the Lord, who now as then,
  Reveals in man His glory.

2 Praise we the wise and brave and strong,
  Who graced their generation;
Who helped the right, and fought the wrong,
  And made our folk a nation.

3 Praise we the great of heart and mind,
  The singers sweetly gifted,
Whose music like a mighty wind
  The souls of men uplifted.

4 Praise we the peaceful men of skill,
  Who builded homes of beauty,
And, rich in art, made richer still
  The brotherhood of duty.

5 Praise we the glorious names we know,
  And they whose names have perished,
Lost in the haze of long ago,
  In silent love be cherished.

6 In peace their sacred ashes rest,
  Fulfilled their day's endeavour;
They blessed the earth, and they are blessed
  Of God and man for ever.

7 So praise we great and famous men,
  Our fathers named in story;
And praise the Lord, who now as then,
  Reveals in man His glory.

W. G. Tarrant, 1853–1928.

649

O GOD of nations, hear
    Thy people's prayer to-day,
And keep our far-off brethren near
    To Thee alway.
Though wide their skies apart,
  Bleak ice and burning sun,
Yet in their island-mother's heart
    They all are one.

2   Thine ancient promise stands,
     They shall not lack Thy care,
Though they be scattered through all lands,
     For Thou art there;
     Though far o'er land and sea
     A restless race they run,
Lord, let the love of home and Thee
     Bind all in one.

3   Lo, earth's remotest ends
     Are linked by chains of prayer;
Keep Thou, O Lord, our distant friends
     Beneath Thy care;
     And grant at last that we
     May gain that shore, where none
Shall know the sundering of the sea,
     But all be one.

F. R. Pyper, 1859–1915.

650

O LORD of life, whose power sustains
  The world unseen no less than this—
One family in Him who reigns,
    Triumphant over death, in bliss;
To Thee with thankfulness we pray,
Remembering our dead to-day.

2 As nature's healing through the years
    Reclothes the stricken battle-fields;
So mercy gives us joy for tears,
    And grief to proud remembrance yields,
And mindful hearts are glad to keep
A tryst of love with them that sleep.

3 Not names engraved in marble make
    The best memorials of the dead,
But burdens shouldered for their sake
    And tasks completed in their stead;
A braver faith and stronger prayers,
Devouter worship, nobler cares.

4 O help us in the silence, Lord,
   To hear the whispered call of love,
And day by day Thy strength afford
   Our work to do, our faith to prove.
So be Thy blessing richly shed
On our communion with our dead.

J. R. Darbyshire, 1880–1948.

651

REJOICE, O land, in God thy might;
His will obey, Him serve aright;
For thee the saints uplift their voice:
Fear not, O land, in God rejoice.

2 Glad shalt thou be, with blessing crowned,
   With joy and peace thou shalt abound;
Yea, love with thee shall make his home,
Until thou see God's Kingdom come.

3 He shall forgive thy sins untold:
   Remember thou His love of old;
Walk in His way, His word adore,
And keep His truth for evermore.

Robert Bridges, 1844–1930.

652

SON of God, eternal Saviour,
   Source of life and truth and grace,
Son of Man, whose birth amongst us
   Hallows all our human race,
Thou, our Head, who, throned in glory,
   For Thine own dost ever plead,
Fill us with Thy love and pity,
   Heal our wrongs, and help our need.

2 As Thou, Lord, hast lived for others,
    So may we for others live;
Freely have Thy gifts been granted,
    Freely may Thy servants give.
Thine the gold and Thine the silver,
    Thine the wealth of land and sea,
We but stewards of Thy bounty,
    Held in solemn trust for Thee.

3 Come, O Christ, and reign among us,
    King of love, and Prince of peace;
Hush the storm of strife and passion,
    Bid its cruel discords cease;
By Thy patient years of toiling,
    By Thy silent hours of pain,
Quench our fevered thirst of pleasure,
    Shame our selfish greed of gain.

4 Son of God, eternal Saviour,
    Source of life and truth and grace,
Son of Man, whose birth amongst us
    Hallows all our human race,
Thou who prayedst, Thou who willest
    That Thy people should be one,
Grant, O grant our hope's fruition:
    Here on earth Thy will be done.   Amen.

S. C. Lowry, 1855–1932.

653

TO Thee, our God, we fly
    For mercy and for grace;
O hear our lowly cry,
    And hide not Thou Thy face.
O Lord, stretch forth Thy mighty hand,
And guard and bless our fatherland.

2   Arise, O Lord of hosts !
        Be jealous for Thy name,
    And drive from out our coasts
        The sins that put to shame:

3 The powers ordained by Thee
    With heavenly wisdom bless;
May they Thy servants be,
    And rule in righteousness:

4 The Church of Thy dear Son
    Inflame with love's pure fire;
Bind her once more in one,
    And life and truth inspire:

5 Give peace, Lord, in our time,
    O let no foe draw nigh,
Nor lawless deed of crime
    Insult Thy majesty:

6 Though all unworthy, still
    Thy people, Lord, are we;
And for our God we will
    None other have but Thee.

W. Walsham How, 1823–97.

654

WHEN wilt Thou save the people,
    O God of mercy, when?
Not kings alone but nations;
    Not thrones and crowns, but men!
Flowers of Thy heart, O God, are they;
Let them not pass, like weeds, away,
Their heritage a sunless day:
    God save the people!

2 Shall crime bring crime for ever,
    Strength aiding still the strong?
Is it Thy will, O Father,
    That man shall toil for wrong?
" No," say Thy mountains; " No," Thy skies;
Man's clouded sun shall brightly rise,
And songs ascend instead of sighs:
    God save the people!

3 When wilt Thou save the people,
     O God of mercy, when ?
   The people, Lord, the people !
     Not thrones and crowns, but men !
   God save the people; Thine they are,
   Thy children, as Thine angels fair;
   From vice, oppression, and despair,
       God save the people !

Ebenezer Elliott, 1781–1849, *altd.*

655

WHERE restless crowds are thronging
     Along the city ways,
Where pride and greed and turmoil
   Consume the fevered days,
Where vain ambitions banish
   All thoughts of praise and prayer,
The people's spirits waver:
   But Thou, O Christ, art there.

2 In scenes of want and sorrow
     And haunts of flagrant wrong,
   In homes where kindness falters,
     And strife and fear are strong,
   In busy street of barter,
     In lonely thoroughfare,
   The people's spirits languish:
     But Thou, O Christ, art there.

3 O Christ, behold Thy people—
     They press on every hand !
   Bring light to all the cities
     Of our beloved land.
   May all our bitter striving
     Give way to visions fair
   Of righteousness and justice:
     For Thou, O Christ, art there.

Thomas Curtis Clark, 1877–1953.

656

WHOM oceans part, O Lord, unite
To love Thy name and seek Thy light;
Though from each other far we be,
Let none, O Christ, be far from Thee.

2 On many a distant island shore
Still let men see heaven's opened door;
Mid silent hills, beneath fresh skies,
Let Bethel's shining ladder rise.

3 Bring thoughts of home and Christian ways
To those who miss sweet Sabbath days;
The long-forgotten prayer recall
To those who sin, and mourn their fall.

4 Our sons and daughters guide in truth;
Take for Thyself the flower of youth;
Afar from home, through gain or loss
Keep them true-hearted to Thy cross.

5 Whom oceans part, O Lord, unite—
One commonwealth for God and right.
A ransomed people, strong and free,
To bring the whole wide world to Thee !

H. Elvet Lewis, 1860-1953.

See also—

Lord, Thy kingdom bring triumphant, 382.
O day of God, 187.
These things shall be, 196.

Thy kingdom come ! on bended knee, 398.
What do I owe, 490.
Where cross the crowded ways, 533.

(6) INTERNATIONAL RELATIONS

657

ALMIGHTY Father, who dost give
The gift of life to all who live,
Look down on all earth's sin and strife,
And lift us to a nobler life.

2 Lift up our hearts, O King of kings,
 To brighter hopes and kindlier things,
 To visions of a larger good,
 And holier dreams of brotherhood.

3 Thy world is weary of its pain,
 Of selfish greed and fruitless gain,
 Of tarnished honour, falsely strong,
 And all its ancient deeds of wrong.

4 Hear Thou the prayer Thy servants pray,
 Uprising from all lands to-day,
 And o'er the vanquished powers of sin
 O bring Thy great salvation in.

J. H. B. Masterman, 1867–1933.

658

ISAIAH ii. 2–5.

BEHOLD the mountain of the Lord
 In latter days shall rise
On mountain tops, above the hills,
 And draw the wondering eyes.

2 To this the joyful nations round,
 All tribes and tongues, shall flow;
Up to the hill of God, they'll say,
 And to His house we'll go.

3 The beam that shines from Zion's hill
 Shall lighten every land;
The King who reigns in Salem's towers
 Shall all the world command.

4 No strife shall vex, nor hostile feuds
 Disturb those peaceful years;
To ploughshares men shall beat their swords,
 To pruning-hooks their spears.

5 No longer hosts encountering hosts
   Their millions slain deplore;
They hang the trumpet in the hall,
   And study war no more.

6 Come, then, O come, from every land,
   To worship at His shrine;
And, walking in the light of God,
   With holy beauties shine.

Scottish Paraphrases, **1781**.

659

CHRIST is the world's true light,
   Its captain of salvation,
The daystar clear and bright
   Of every man and nation;
New life, new hope awakes,
   Where'er men own His sway:
Freedom her bondage breaks,
   And night is turned to day.

2 In Christ all races meet,
   Their ancient feuds forgetting,
The whole round world complete,
   From sunrise to its setting:
When Christ is throned as Lord,
   Men shall forsake their fear,
To ploughshare beat the sword,
   To pruning-hook the spear.

3 One Lord, in one great name
   Unite us all who own Thee;
Cast out our pride and shame
   That hinder to enthrone Thee;
The world has waited long,
   Has travailed long in pain;
To heal its ancient wrong,
   Come, Prince of peace, and reign.

G. W. Briggs, 1875–1959.

660

GRANT us Thy peace; for Thou alone canst
    bend
Our faltering purpose to a nobler end;
Thy love alone can teach our hearts to see
The fellowship that binds all lives in Thee.

2 Grant us Thy peace; for men have filled the years
With greed and envy and with foolish fears,
With squandered treasures and ignoble gain,
And fruitless harvests that we reap in vain.

3 Grant us Thy peace; till all our strife shall seem
The hateful memory of some evil dream;
Till that new song ring out that shall not cease,
" In heaven Thy glory and on earth Thy peace ! "
                            Amen.

J. H. B. Masterman, 1867–1933.

661

IN Christ there is no East or West,
    In Him no South or North,
But one great fellowship of love
    Throughout the whole wide earth.

2 In Him shall true hearts everywhere
    Their high communion find:
His service is the golden cord
    Close-binding all mankind.

3 Join hands then, brothers of the faith,
    Whate'er your race may be !
Who serves my Father as a son
    Is surely kin to me.

4 In Christ now meet both East and West,
    In Him meet South and North,
All Christly souls are one in Him,
    Throughout the whole wide earth.

John Oxenham, 1852–1941.

662

O BROTHER man, fold to thy heart thy
brother:
Where pity dwells, the peace of God is there;
To worship rightly is to love each other,
Each smile a hymn, each kindly deed a prayer.

2 Follow with reverent steps the great example
Of Him whose holy work was doing good:
So shall the wide earth be our Father's temple,
Each loving life a psalm of gratitude.

3 Then shall all shackles fall: the stormy clangour
Of wild war music o'er the earth shall cease;
Love shall tread out the baleful fire of anger,
And in its ashes plant the tree of peace.

J. G. Whittier, 1807–92.

663

O GOD of love, O King of peace,
Make wars throughout the world to cease;
The wrath of sinful men restrain;
Give peace, O God, give peace again.

2 Remember, Lord, Thy works of old,
The wonders that our fathers told;
Remember not our sin's dark stain;
Give peace, O God, give peace again.

3 Whom shall we trust but Thee, O Lord?
Where rest but on Thy faithful word?
None ever called on Thee in vain;
Give peace, O God, give peace again.

4 Where saints and angels dwell above,
All hearts are knit in holy love;
O bind us in that heavenly chain;
Give peace, O God, give peace again.   Amen.

H. W. Baker, 1821–77.

664

THE Saviour's precious blood
 Hath made all nations one.
United let us praise this deed
 The Father's love hath done.

2 In this vast world of men,
 A world so full of sin,
No other theme can be our prayer
 Than this—Thy Kingdom come.

3 In this sad world of war
 Can peace be ever found ?
Unless the love of Christ prevail,
 True peace will not abound.

4 The Master's new command
 Was " Love each other well."
O brothers, let us all unite
 To do His holy will.

tr. William Scott and Yung Oon Kim, 1950.

See also—

O day of God, 187.
O God of love, 66.
Rejoice, O people, 389.
Sing we the King, 191.

These things shall be, 196.
Thy kingdom come, O God, 397.
Thy kingdom come ! on bended
 knee, 398.

(7) TRAVELLERS AND ABSENT FRIENDS

665

ETERNAL Father, strong to save,
 Whose arm hath bound the restless wave,
Who bidd'st the mighty ocean deep
Its own appointed limits keep,
 O hear us when we cry to Thee
 For those in peril on the sea.

2 O Christ, whose voice the waters heard,
And hushed their raging at Thy word,
Who walkedst on the foaming deep,
And calm amid the storm didst sleep,
 O hear us when we cry to Thee
 For those in peril on the sea.

3 O Holy Spirit, who didst brood
Upon the chaos dark and rude,
And bid its angry tumult cease,
And give, for wild confusion, peace,
 O hear us when we cry to Thee
 For those in peril on the sea.

4 O Trinity of love and power
Our brethren shield in danger's hour.
From rock and tempest, fire and foe,
Protect them wheresoe'er they go;
 Thus evermore shall rise to Thee
 Glad hymns of praise from land and sea.

William Whiting, 1825–78, altd.

666

FATHER all-seeing, friend of all creation,
 Life of Thy children, still Thy love revealing,
For all our loved ones, now far absent from us,
 We are appealing.

2 Working or playing, Lord, be Thou their leader;
 And if alarm or sickness should oppress them,
Teach them to trust Thee, knowing that in all
  things
 Thy love will bless them.

3 In all temptation be their strength and comfort;
 Guide them in weakness, sanctifying, shielding;
Through Him who, tempted every day as we are,
 Lived without yielding.

4 When they are lonely, be Thou their companion,
Hold them in safety, strengthen their en-
deavour;
Grant them to follow where Thy voice shall call
them,
Now and for ever.   Amen.

Maud Bell, 1868–

667

FATHER, who art alone
    Our helper and our stay,
O hear us, as we plead
    For loved ones far away,
And shield with Thine almighty hand
Our wanderers by sea and land.

2   For Thou, our Father God,
        Art present everywhere,
    And bendest low Thine ear
        To catch the faintest prayer,
    Waiting rich blessings to bestow
    On all Thy children here below.

3   O compass with Thy love
        The daily path they tread;
    And may Thy light and truth
        Upon their hearts be shed,
    That, one in all things with Thy will,
    Heaven's peace and joy their souls may fill.

4   Guard them from every harm
        When dangers shall assail,
    And teach them that Thy power
        Can never, never fail;
    We cannot with our loved ones be,
    But trust them, Father, unto Thee.

5 We all are travellers here
   Along life's various road,
   Meeting and parting oft
    Till we shall mount to God—
At home at last, with those we love,
Within the fatherland above.

Edith Jones, 1849–1929.

668

HOLY Father, in Thy mercy,
   Hear Thy children's prayer;
Keep our loved ones, in their absence,
   Neath Thy care.

2 Jesus, Saviour, let Thy presence
   Be their light and guide;
Keep, O keep them, in their weakness,
   At Thy side.

3 When in sorrow, when in danger,
   When in loneliness,
In Thy love look down and comfort
   Their distress.

4 May the joy of Thy salvation
   Be their strength and stay;
May they love and may they praise Thee
   Day by day.

5 Holy Spirit, let Thy teaching
   Sanctify their life;
Send Thy grace that they may conquer
   In the strife.

6 Father, Son, and Holy Spirit,
   God the One in Three,
Bless them, guide them, save them, keep them
   Near to Thee. Amen.

Isabel Stevenson, 1843–90.

669

O LORD, be with us when we sail
  Upon the lonely deep,
Our guard when on the silent deck
  The midnight watch we keep.

2 We need not fear, though all around
    Mid rising winds we hear
The multitude of waters surge,
    For Thou, O God, art near.

3 The calm, the breeze, the gale, the storm,
    That pass from land to land,
All, all are Thine, are held within
    The hollow of Thy hand.

4 As when on blue Gennesaret
    Rose high the angry wave,
And Thy disciples quailed in dread,
    One word of Thine could save,

5 So when the fiercer storms arise
    From man's unbridled will,
Be Thou, Lord, present in our hearts
    To whisper, " Peace, be still ! "

6 Across this troubled tide of life
    Thyself our pilot be,
Until we reach that better land,
    The land that knows no sea.

E. A. Dayman, 1807–90.

670

THOU who dost rule on high,
  Our Father and our friend,
All those who ride the sky
  We now to Thee commend.
For though among the stars they move,
They cannot rise beyond Thy love.

2 Alone in boundless space,
  May they be still with Thee;
 The glory of Thy face
  Among the heavens see;
For Thou, by land and sea and air,
Art with Thy children everywhere.

3 When tempests loose their power
  And dangers gather round;
 In Thee, in that dread hour,
  May their defence be found;
O may that peace possess their mind
Which all Thy trusting children find.

4 And soon from pole to pole
  Thy kingdom, Lord, arise;
 And peace alone control
  The commerce of the skies;
Till all the gifts Thou givest men,
We to Thy glory give again.

R. W. Littlewood, 1908–

See also—
Forget them not, 368. Whom oceans part, 656.
God be with you, 761.

X. TIMES AND SEASONS

For the Christian Year, see Section II, Hymns 38–47; Section IV, Hymns 78–221; and Section V, Hymns 222–240.
For Church Anniversaries, etc., see Section VII (2), Hymns 266–283.

(1) MORNING

671

AT Thy feet, O Christ, we lay
Thine own gift of this new day;
Doubt of what it holds in store
Makes us crave Thine aid the more;
Lest it prove a time of loss,
Mark it, Saviour, with Thy cross.

2 If it flow on calm and bright,
Be Thyself our chief delight;
If it bring unknown distress,
Good is all that Thou canst bless;
Only, while its hours begin,
Pray we, keep them clear of sin.

3 Fain would we Thy word embrace,
Live each moment in Thy grace,
All our selves to Thee consign,
Fold up all our wills in Thine,
Think, and speak, and do, and be,
Simply that which pleases Thee.

4 Hear us, Lord, and that right soon;
Hear, and grant the choicest boon
That Thy love can e'er impart,
Loyal singleness of heart;
So shall this and all our days,
Christ our God, show forth Thy praise.

William Bright, 1824–1901.

672

AWAKE, my soul, and with the sun
Thy daily stage of duty run:
Shake off dull sloth, and joyful rise
To pay thy morning sacrifice.

2 Wake, and lift up thyself, my heart,
And with the angels bear thy part,
Who all night long unwearied sing
High praise to the eternal King.

3 May I like them in God delight,
Have all day long my God in sight,
Perform like them my Maker's will,
And celebrate His glories still.

4 Lord, I my vows to Thee renew;
Scatter my sins as morning dew;
Guard my first springs of thought and will,
And with Thyself my spirit fill.

5 Direct, control, suggest, this day,
All I design, or do, or say,
That all my powers, with all their might,
In Thy sole glory may unite.

6 Glory to Thee, who safe hast kept,
And hast refreshed me while I slept;
Grant, Lord, when I from death shall wake,
I may of endless life partake.

7 Praise God, from whom all blessings flow,
Praise Him, all creatures here below,
Praise Him above, ye heavenly host,
Praise Father, Son, and Holy Ghost.

Amen.

Thomas Ken, 1637–1711.

673

CHRIST, whose glory fills the skies,
   Christ the true, the only light,
Sun of righteousness, arise,
   Triumph o'er the shades of night:
Day-spring from on high, be near;
Day-star, in my heart appear.

2 Dark and cheerless is the morn,
   Unaccompanied by Thee;
Joyless is the day's return,
   Till Thy mercy's beams I see;
Till they inward light impart,
Glad my eyes, and warm my heart.

3 Visit then this soul of mine;
   Pierce the gloom of sin and grief;
Fill me, radiancy divine;
   Scatter all my unbelief;
More and more Thyself display,
Shining to the perfect day.

Charles Wesley, 1707–88.

674

COME, my soul, thou must be waking;
   Now is breaking
O'er the earth another day.
Come to Him who made this splendour;
   See thou render
All thy feeble strength can pay.

2 Gladly hail the light returning;
   Ready burning
Be the incense of thy powers.
For the night is safely ended;
   God hath tended
With His care thy helpless hours.

3 Pray that He may prosper ever
    Each endeavour
When thine aim is good and true;
But that He may ever thwart thee,
    And convert thee,
From the ill thou wouldst pursue.

4 May'st thou then on life's last morrow,
    Free from sorrow,
Pass away in slumber sweet;
And, released from death's dark sadness,
    Rise in gladness,
That far brighter sun to greet.

Friedrich von Canitz, 1654–99,
tr. H. J. Buckoll, 1803–71, altd.

675

FATHER, we praise Thee, now the night is over;
    Active and watchful, stand we all before
        Thee;
Singing we offer prayer and meditation:
    Thus we adore Thee.

2 Monarch of all things, fit us for Thy mansions;
    Banish our weakness, health and wholeness
        sending;
Bring us to heaven, where Thy saints united
    Joy without ending.

3 All-holy Father, Son, and equal Spirit,
    Trinity blessèd, send us Thy salvation;
Thine is the glory, gleaming and resounding
    Through all creation.

Attributed to Gregory the Great, 540–604,
tr. Percy Dearmer, 1867–1936.

676

PSALMS xix. 4, 8; lxxiii. 24.

GOD of the morning, at whose voice
   The cheerful sun makes haste to rise,
And like a giant doth rejoice
   To run his journey through the skies !

2 O like the sun, may I fulfil
   The appointed duties of the day,
With ready mind and active will
   March on, and keep my heavenly way !

3 But I shall rove and lose the race
   If God, my sun, should disappear,
And leave me in this world's wide maze
   To follow every wandering star.

4 Lord ! Thy commands are clean and pure,
   Enlightening our beclouded eyes;
Thy threatenings just, Thy promise sure;
   Thy gospel makes the simple wise.

5 Give me Thy counsel for my guide;
   And then receive me to Thy bliss:
All my desires and hopes beside
   Are faint and cold compared with this.

Isaac Watts, 1674–1748.

677

LORD God of morning and of night,
   We thank Thee for Thy gift of light;
As in the dawn the shadows fly,
We seem to find Thee now more nigh.

2 Fresh hopes have wakened in the heart,
   Fresh force to do our daily part;
The kindly hours of sleep restore
Our drooping strength to serve Thee more.

3 Yet, whilst Thy will we would pursue,
Oft what we would we cannot do;
The sun may stand in noonday skies,
But on the soul thick midnight lies.

4 O Lord of light, 'tis Thou alone
Canst make our darkened hearts Thine own:
O then be with us, Lord, that we,
In Thy great day may wake to Thee.

5 Praise God, our maker and our friend;
Praise Him through time, till time shall end;
Till psalm and song His name adore
Through heaven's great day of evermore.

F. T. Palgrave, 1824–97.

678

NEW every morning is the love
Our wakening and uprising prove;
Through sleep and darkness safely brought,
Restored to life, and power, and thought.

2 New mercies, each returning day,
Hover around us while we pray;
New perils past, new sins forgiven,
New thoughts of God, new hopes of heaven.

3 If on our daily course our mind
Be set to hallow all we find,
New treasures still, of countless price,
God will provide for sacrifice.

4 Old friends, old scenes, will lovelier be,
As more of heaven in each we see;
Some softening gleam of love and prayer
Will dawn on every cross and care.

5 The trivial round, the common task,
   Will furnish all we ought to ask;
   Room to deny ourselves; a road
   To bring us daily nearer God.

6 Only, O Lord, in Thy dear love
   Fit us for perfect rest above;
   And help us, this and every day,
   To live more nearly as we pray.

John Keble, 1792 1866, altd.

679

NOW that the sun is gleaming bright,
   Implore we, bending low,
That He, the uncreated light,
   May guide us as we go.

2 No sinful word, nor deed of wrong,
   Nor thoughts that idly rove,
But simple truth be on our tongue,
   And in our hearts be love.

3 And while the hours in order flow,
   O Christ, securely fence
Our gates, beleaguered by the foe,
   The gate of every sense.

4 And grant that to Thine honour, Lord,
   Our daily toil may tend;
That we begin it at Thy word,
   And in Thy favour end.

Latin, 8th cent.
tr. John Henry Newman, 1801–90, altd.

680

O JESUS, Lord of heavenly grace,
Thou brightness of Thy Father's face,
Thou fountain of eternal light
Whose beams disperse the shades of night;

2 Come, holy sun of heavenly love,
Send down Thy radiance from above,
And to our inmost hearts convey
Thy Holy Spirit's cloudless ray.

3 And we the Father's help will claim,
And sing the Father's glorious name;
His powerful succour we implore,
That we may stand, to fall no more.

4 May He our actions deign to bless,
And loose the bonds of wickedness;
From sudden falls our feet defend,
And guide us safely to the end.

5 O hallowed be the approaching day;
Let meekness be our morning ray,
And faithful love our noonday light,
And hope our sunset, calm and bright.

6 O Christ, with each returning morn
Thine image to our hearts is borne;
O may we ever clearly see
Our Saviour and our God in Thee.

Ambrose, 340-97,
tr. John Chandler, 1806-76.

681

O LORD of life, Thy quickening voice
Awakes my morning song;
In gladsome words I would rejoice
That I to Thee belong.

2 I see Thy light, I feel Thy wind;
   Earth is Thy uttered word;
Whatever wakes my heart and mind,
   Thy presence is, my Lord.

3 Therefore I choose my highest part,
   And turn my face to Thee;
Therefore I stir my inmost heart
   To worship fervently.

4 Lord, let me live and act this day,
   Still rising from the dead.
Lord, make my spirit good and gay—
   Give me my daily bread.

5 Within my heart speak, Lord, speak on,
   My heart alive to keep
Till comes the night, and, labour done,
   In Thee I fall asleep.

George Macdonald, 1824–1905.

682

R ISE, my soul, adore thy Maker!
   Angels praise;
     Join thy lays,
With them be partaker.
Father, Lord of every spirit,
   In Thy light
   Lead me right,
Through my Saviour's merit.

2 O my Jesus, God almighty,
   Pray for me,
    Till I see
Thee in Salem's city.
Holy Ghost, by Jesus given,
   Be my guide,
   Lest my pride
Shut me out of heaven.

3 Thou this night wast my protector:
    With me stay
    All the day,
Ever my director.
Holy, holy, holy giver
    Of all good,
    Life and food,
Reign, adored for ever !

John Cennick, 1708-55, altd.

683

STILL, still with Thee, when purple morning breaketh,
When the bird waketh, and the shadows flee:
Fairer than morning, lovelier than the daylight,
Dawns the sweet consciousness, I am with Thee.

2 Alone with Thee, amid the mystic shadows,
    The solemn hush of nature newly born;
Alone with Thee, in breathless adoration,
    In the calm dew and freshness of the morn.

3 Still, still with Thee; as to each newborn morning
    A fresh and solemn splendour still is given,
So does this blessèd consciousness awaking,
    Breathe each day nearness unto Thee and heaven.

4 When sinks the soul, subdued by toil to slumber,
    Its closing eye looks up to Thee in prayer;
Sweet the repose beneath Thy wings' o'ershading,
    But sweeter still to wake and find Thee there.

5 So shall it be at last, in that bright morning
    When the soul waketh, and life's shadows flee;
O in that hour, fairer than daylight dawning,
    Shall rise the glorious thought, I am with Thee :

Harriet Beecher Stowe 1812-96.

684

SWEETLY the holy hymn
Breaks on the morning air;
Before the world with smoke is dim
We meet to offer prayer.

2 While flowers are wet with dew,
Dew of our souls, descend;
Ere yet the sun the day renew,
O Lord, Thy Spirit send.

3 Upon the battlefield,
Before the fight begins,
We seek, O Lord, Thy sheltering shield,
To guard us from our sins.

4 Ere yet our vessel sails
Upon the stream of day,
We plead, O Lord, for heavenly gales
To speed us on our way.

5 On the lone mountain side,
Before the morning's light,
The Man of sorrows wept and cried,
And rose refreshed with might.

6 O hear us, then, for we
Are very weak and frail;
We make the Saviour's name our plea,
And surely must prevail.

Charles Haddon Spurgeon, 1834–92.

685

WHEN morning gilds the skies,
My heart awaking cries,
" May Jesus Christ be praised ! "
Alike at work and prayer
To Jesus I repair;
" May Jesus Christ be praised ! "

2 When sleep her balm denies,
   My silent spirit sighs,
        "May Jesus Christ be praised!"
   The night becomes as day,
   When from the heart we say,
        "May Jesus Christ be praised!"

3 When evil thoughts molest,
   With this I shield my breast,
        "May Jesus Christ be praised!"
   The powers of darkness fear,
   When this sweet chant they hear,
        "May Jesus Christ be praised!"

4 Does sadness fill my mind?
   A solace here I find,
        "May Jesus Christ be praised!"
   Or fades my earthly bliss?
   My comfort still is this,
        "May Jesus Christ be praised!"

5 To God the Word on high,
   The hosts of angels cry,
        "May Jesus Christ be praised!"
   Let mortals, too, upraise
   Their voice in hymns of praise,
        "May Jesus Christ be praised!"

6 Let earth's wide circle round
   In joyful notes resound,
        "May Jesus Christ be praised!"
   Let air, and sea, and sky,
   From depth to height reply,
        "May Jesus Christ be praised!"

tr. from the German by
E. Caswall, 1814–78.

686

ABIDE with me: fast falls the eventide;
The darkness deepens: Lord, with me abide;
When other helpers fail, and comforts flee,
Help of the helpless, O abide with me.

2 Swift to its close ebbs out life's little day;
Earth's joys grow dim, its glories pass away;
Change and decay in all around I see:
O Thou who changest not, abide with me.

3 I need Thy presence every passing hour;
What but Thy grace can foil the tempter's power?
Who like Thyself my guide and stay can be?
Through cloud and sunshine, O abide with me.

4 I fear no foe, with Thee at hand to bless;
Ills have no weight, and tears no bitterness;
Where, death, thy sting? where, grave, thy victory?
I triumph still if Thou abide with me.

5 Hold Thou Thy cross before my closing eyes,
Shine through the gloom, and point me to the
    skies:
Heaven's morning breaks, and earth's vain
    shadows flee;
In life, in death, O Lord, abide with me.

H. F. Lyte, 1793–1847.

687

AS darker, darker fall around
    The shadows of the night,
We gather here, with hymn and prayer,
    To seek the eternal light.

2 Father in heaven, to Thee are known
   Our many hopes and fears,
   Our heavy weight of mortal toil,
   Our bitterness of tears.

3 We pray Thee for all absent friends,
   Who have been with us here;
   And in our secret heart we name
   The distant and the dear.

4 For weary eyes, and aching hearts,
   And feet that from Thee rove,
   The sick, the poor, the tried, the fallen,
   We pray Thee, God of love.

5 We bring to Thee our hopes and fears,
   And at Thy footstool lay;
   And, Father, Thou who lovest all
   Wilt hear us when we pray.

Hymn of Calabrian Shepherds

688

AT even, when the sun was set,
   The sick, O Lord, around Thee lay;
O in what divers pains they met !
   O with what joy they went away !

2 Once more 'tis eventide, and we,
   Oppressed with various ills, draw near;
What if Thy form we cannot see ?
   We know and feel that Thou art here.

3 O Saviour Christ, our woes dispel:
   For some are sick, and some are sad,
And some have never loved Thee well,
   And some have lost the love they had;

4 And none, O Lord, have perfect rest,
    For none are wholly free from sin;
  And they who fain would serve Thee best
    Are conscious most of wrong within.

5 O Saviour Christ, Thou too art man;
    Thou hast been troubled, tempted, tried;
  Thy kind but searching glance can scan
    The very wounds that shame would hide.

6 Thy touch has still its ancient power,
    No word from Thee can fruitless fall;
  Hear in this solemn evening hour,
    And in Thy mercy heal us all.

Henry Twells, 1823–1900.

689

DAY is dying in the west,
  Heaven is touching earth with rest;
Wait and worship while the night
Sets her evening lamps alight
    Through all the sky.

Holy, holy, holy, Lord God of hosts:
Heaven and earth are full of Thee,
Heaven and earth are praising Thee,
    O Lord most high.

2 Lord of life, beneath the dome
  Of the universe Thy home,
  Gather us, who seek Thy face,
  To the fold of Thy embrace;
    For Thou art nigh.

3 While the deepening shadows fall
  Heart of love enfolding all,
  Through the glory and the grace
  Of the stars that veil Thy face,
    Our hearts ascend.

4 When for ever from our sight
Pass the stars, the day, the night,
Lord of angels, on our eyes
Let eternal morn arise,
    And shadows end.

Mary Lathbury, 1841–1913.

690

ERE I sleep, for every favour
    This day showed
      By my God,
I will bless my Saviour.

2 O my Lord, what shall I render
    To Thy name,
      Still the same,
Gracious, good, and tender ?

3 Thou hast ordered all my goings
    In Thy way,
      Heard me pray,
Sanctified my doings.

4 Visit me with Thy salvation,
    Let Thy care
      Now be near
Round my habitation.

5 Thou my rock, my guard, my tower,
    Safely keep,
      While I sleep,
Me, with all Thy power.

6 So, whene'er in death I slumber,
    Let me rise
      With the wise,
Counted in their number.

John Cennick, 1718–55.

691

FAR in the west the sunset's golden splendour
    Floods with its glory all the sky above,
Calling Thy children prayer and praise to render
    To Thee, our Father, God of perfect love !

2 Thine is a love that bore the cross to save us,
    Thine is a love that broke the bonds of death;
E'en in the midst of mortal pain forgave us,
    Pleading our pardon with Thy dying breath.

3 No human heart can match Thy love so tender,
    No human mind can tell its farthest bound,
Nor height, nor depth, nor all creation's splendour
    Knoweth the limits where Thy love is found !

4 Thine is the kingdom, Thine the power and glory,
    On Thee the countless angel-hosts attend !
Yet still Thy love is earth's most wondrous story,
    Yet still my soul may own Thee Saviour, Friend.

Leslie H. Moore, 1909–

692

FATHER, in high heaven dwelling,
    May our evening song be telling
    Of Thy mercy large and free:
Through the day Thy love hath fed us,
Through the day Thy care hath led us,
    With divinest charity.

2 This day's sins, O pardon, Saviour,
    Evil thoughts, perverse behaviour,
        Envy, pride, and vanity;
From the world, the flesh, deliver,
Save us now, and save us ever,
    O Thou Lamb of Calvary !

3 Whilst the night-dews are distilling,
  Holy Ghost, each heart be filling
    With Thine own serenity:
  Softly let our eyes be closing,
  Loving souls on Thee reposing,
    Ever blessèd Trinity.

George Rawson, 1807–89.

693

FATHER of love and power,
  Guard Thou our evening hour,
    Shield with Thy might:
  For all Thy care this day
  Our grateful thanks we pay,
  And to our Father pray,
    Bless us to-night.

2 Jesus, Immanuel,
  Come in Thy love to dwell
    In hearts contrite:
  For many sins we grieve,
  But we Thy grace receive,
  And in Thy word believe:
    Bless us to-night.

3 Spirit of truth and love,
  Life-giving, holy Dove,
    Shed forth Thy light:
  Heal every inward smart,
  Still every throbbing heart,
  And Thine own peace impart;
    Bless us to-night.   Amen.

George Rawson, 1807–89.

694

GLORY to Thee, my God, this night
  For all the blessings of the light:
Keep me, O keep me, King of kings,
Beneath Thine own almighty wings.

2 Forgive me, Lord, for Thy dear Son,
The ill that I this day have done;
That with the world, myself, and Thee,
I, ere I sleep, at peace may be.

3 Teach me to live, that I may dread
The grave as little as my bed;
Teach me to die, that so I may
Rise glorious at the judgment day.

4 O may my soul on Thee repose,
And may sweet sleep mine eyelids close,
Sleep, that shall me more vigorous make
To serve my God when I awake.

5 If in the night I sleepless lie,
My soul with heavenly thoughts supply;
Let no ill dreams disturb my rest,
No powers of darkness me molest.

6 Praise God from whom all blessings flow;
Praise Him, all creatures here below;
Praise Him above, ye heavenly host;
Praise Father, Son, and Holy Ghost.   Amen.

Thomas Ken, 1637–1711, *altd.*

695

HAIL, gladdening Light of His pure glory
    poured
Who is the immortal Father, heavenly, blest,
Holiest of holies, Jesus Christ, our Lord !
  Now we are come to the sun's hour of rest,
  The lights of evening round us shine,
We hymn the Father, Son, and Holy Spirit divine.
  Worthiest art Thou at all times to be sung
  With undefilèd tongue,
Son of our God, giver of life, alone:
Therefore in all the world Thy glories, Lord, they
    own.

Greek, 3rd cent.,
tr. John Keble, 1792–1866.

696

HOW calmly the evening once more is descend-
 ing,
 As kind as a promise, as still as a prayer;
O wing of the Lord, in Thy shelter befriending,
 May we and our households continue to share !

2 The sky, like the kingdom of heaven, is open;
 O enter, my soul, at the glorious gates;
The silence and smile of His love are the token,
 Who now for all comers invitingly waits.

3 We come to be soothed with His merciful healing,
 The dews of the night cure the wounds of the
  day;
We come, our life's worth and its brevity feeling,
 With thanks for the past, for the future we pray.

4 Lord, save us from folly; be with us in sorrow;
 Sustain us in work till the time of our rest;
When earth's day is over, may heaven's to-morrow
 Dawn on us, of homes long expected possessed.

Thomas Toke Lynch, 1818–71.

697

NOW God be with us, for the night is closing,
 The light and darkness are of His disposing,
And neath His shadow here to rest we yield us,
 For He will shield us.

2 As Thy belovèd, soothe the sick and weeping;
 And bid the sufferer lose his griefs in sleeping;
Widows and orphans, we to Thee commend them,
 Do Thou befriend them.

3 We have no refuge, none on earth to aid us,
 Save Thee, O Father, who Thine own hast made
  us;
 But Thy dear presence will not leave us lonely
  Who seek Thee only.

4 Let our last thoughts be Thine when sleep o'ertakes
  us;
 Our earliest thoughts be Thine when morning
  wakes us;
 All day serve Thee, in all that we are doing,
  Thy praise pursuing.

Petrus Herbert, ?–1571,
tr. Catherine Winkworth, 1827–78.

698

NOW the day is over,
 Night is drawing nigh,
Shadows of the evening
 Steal across the sky.

2 Now the darkness gathers,
 Stars begin to peep,
Birds, and beasts, and flowers
 Soon will be asleep.

3 Jesus, give the weary
 Calm and sweet repose;
With Thy tenderest blessing
 May our eyelids close.

4 Comfort every sufferer
 Watching late in pain;
Those who plan some evil
 From their sin restrain.

5 When the morning wakens,
    Then may I arise
  Pure, and fresh, and sinless
    In Thy holy eyes.

6 Glory to the Father,
    Glory to the Son,
  And to Thee, blest Spirit,
    Whilst all ages run.

S. Baring-Gould, 1834–1924.

699

O GLADSOME light, O grace
  Of God the Father's face,
The eternal splendour wearing;
  Celestial, holy, blest,
  Our Saviour Jesus Christ,
Joyful in Thine appearing.

2   Now, ere day fadeth quite,
    We see the evening light,
  Our wonted hymn outpouring;
    Father of might unknown,
    Thee, His incarnate Son,
  And Holy Spirit adoring.

3   To Thee of right belongs
    All praise of holy songs,
  O Son of God, lifegiver;
    Thee, therefore, O Most High,
    The world doth glorify,
  And shall exalt for ever.

3rd cent.,
tr. Robert Bridges, 1844–1930.

700

O SAVIOUR, bless us ere we go;
   Thy word into our minds instil;
And make our lukewarm hearts to glow
   With lowly love and fervent will.
Through life's long day and death's dark night,
O holy Jesus, be our light.

2 Grant us, dear Lord, from evil ways
   True absolution and release;
And bless us, more than in past days,
   With purity and inward peace.

3 Do more than pardon; give us joy,
   Sweet fear, and sober liberty,
And loving hearts without alloy,
   That only long to be like Thee.

4 For all we love, the poor, the sad,
   The sinful, unto Thee we call;
O let Thy mercy make us glad;
   Thou art our Jesus and our all.
Through life's long day and death's dark night,
O holy Jesus, be our light.

Amen.

F. W. Faber, 1814–63.

701

O UR day of praise is ended,
   Its peaceful hours all flown,
We come to close its worship,
   O Lord, before Thy throne;
We bless Thee for this earnest
   Of better rest above,
This token of Thy kindness,
   This pledge of boundless love.

2 We would prolong its moments,
   And linger yet awhile
Amid its closing shadows,
   Illumined by Thy smile.
Our souls shall know no darkness
   While we may look to Thee;
Our eyes shall ne'er grow weary
   While we Thy face can see.

3 O Jesus, our dear Saviour,
   To Thee our songs we raise;
Our hearts, by care untroubled,
   Uplift themselves in praise;
For to God's truce with labour
   More glory Thou hast given,
And sabbaths now are sweeter
   Since Christ the Lord has risen.

4 O Lord, again we bless Thee
   For such a day as this,
So rich in ancient glories,
   So bright with hopes of bliss:
O may we reach Thy perfect,
   Thine endless, day of rest:
Then lay our earth-worn spirits
   Upon our Father's breast.

T. V. Tymms, 1842–1921.

702

SAVIOUR, again to Thy dear name we raise
With one accord our parting hymn of praise;
We stand to bless Thee ere our worship cease,
Then, lowly kneeling, wait Thy word of peace.

2 Grant us Thy peace upon our homeward way;
With Thee began, with Thee shall end the day;
Guard Thou the lips from sin, the hearts from
   shame,
That in this house have called upon Thy name.

3 Grant us Thy peace, Lord, through the coming
   night,
Turn Thou for us its darkness into light;
From harm and danger keep Thy children free,
For dark and light are both alike to Thee.

4 Grant us Thy peace throughout our earthly life,
Our balm in sorrow, and our stay in strife;
Then, when Thy voice shall bid our conflict cease,
Call us, O Lord, to Thine eternal peace.

John Ellerton, 1826–93.

703

SUN of my soul, Thou Saviour dear,
It is not night if Thou be near;
O may no earth-born cloud arise
To hide Thee from Thy servant's eyes.

2 When the soft dews of kindly sleep
My wearied eyelids gently steep,
Be my last thought, how sweet to rest
For ever on my Saviour's breast.

3 Abide with me from morn till eve,
For without Thee I cannot live;
Abide with me when night is nigh,
For without Thee I dare not die.

4 If some poor wandering child of Thine
Have spurned to-day the voice divine,
Now, Lord, the gracious work begin;
Let him no more lie down in sin.

5 Watch by the sick; enrich the poor
With blessings from Thy boundless store;
Be every mourner's sleep to-night,
Like infant's slumbers, pure and light.

6 Come near and bless us when we wake.
Ere through the world our way we take;
Till in the ocean of Thy love
We lose ourselves in heaven above.   Amen.

John Keble, 1792–1866, altd.

704

THE day departs;
Our souls and hearts
Long for that better morrow,
When Christ shall set His people free
From every care and sorrow.

2   The sunshine bright
Is lost in night;
O Lord, Thyself unveiling,
Shine on our souls with beams of love,
All darkness there dispelling.

3   The land above,
Of peace and love,
No earthly beams need brighten;
For all its borders Christ Himself
Doth with His glory lighten.

4   May we be there,
That joy to share,
Glad hallelujahs singing;
With all the ransomed evermore
Our joyful praises bringing.

5   Lord Jesus, Thou
Our refuge now,
Forsake Thy servants never;
Uphold and guide that we may stand
Before Thy throne for ever.

Johann Freylinghausen, 1670–1739,
tr. Jane Borthwick, 1813–97, altd.

705

THE day is past and over:
    All thanks, O Lord, to Thee;
We pray Thee now that sinless
    The hours of dark may be.
O Jesus, keep us in Thy sight,
And guard us through the coming night.

2 The joys of day are over:
    We lift our hearts to Thee;
And ask Thee that offenceless
    The hours of dark may be.
O Jesus, keep us in Thy sight,
And guard us through the coming night.

3 The toils of day are over:
    We raise the hymn to Thee,
And ask that free from peril
    The hours of dark may be.
O Jesus, keep us in Thy sight,
And guard us through the coming night.

4 Be Thou our souls' preserver,
    O God, for Thou dost know
How many are the perils
    Through which we have to go.
Lover of men, O hear our call,
And guard and save us from them all.
                              Amen.

Greek, c. 6th cent.,
tr. J. M. Neale, 1818–66.

706

THE day Thou gavest, Lord, is ended,
    The darkness falls at Thy behest;
To Thee our morning hymns ascended,
    Thy praise shall hallow now our rest.

2 We thank Thee that Thy Church unsleeping,
    While earth rolls onward into light,
  Through all the world her watch is keeping
    And rests not now by day or night.

3 As o'er each continent and island
    The dawn leads on another day,
  The voice of prayer is never silent,
    Nor dies the strain of praise away.

4 The sun, that bids us rest, is waking
    Our brethren neath the western sky.
  And hour by hour fresh lips are making
    Thy wondrous doings heard on high.

5 So be it, Lord; Thy throne shall never,
    Like earth's proud empires, pass away;
  But stand, and rule, and grow for ever,
    Till all Thy creatures own Thy sway.

John Ellerton, 1826–93.

707

THE duteous day now closeth,
  Each flower and tree reposeth,
    Shade creeps o'er wild and wood:
Let us, as night is falling,
On God our maker calling,
    Give thanks to Him, the giver good.

2 Now all the heavenly splendour
    Breaks forth in starlight tender
      From myriad worlds unknown;
  And man, the marvel seeing,
  Forgets his selfish being,
      For joy of beauty not his own.

3 His care he drowneth yonder,
  Lost in the abyss of wonder;
    To heaven his soul doth steal:
  This life he disesteemeth,
  The day it is that dreameth,
    That doth from truth his vision seal.

4 Awhile his mortal blindness
  May miss God's loving-kindness,
    And grope in faithless strife:
  But when life's day is over
  Shall death's fair night discover
    The fields of everlasting life.

Robert Bridges, 1844–1930.
Based on Paulus Gerhardt, 1607–76.

708

THE radiant morn hath passed away,
    And spent too soon her golden store;
The shadows of departing day
    Creep on once more.

2 Our life is but an autumn day,
    Its glorious noon how quickly past !
Lead us, O Christ, Thou living way,
    Safe home at last.

3 O by Thy soul-inspiring grace
    Uplift our hearts to realms on high;
Help us to look to that bright place,
    Beyond the sky,

4 Where light, and life, and joy, and peace
    In undivided empire reign,
And thronging angels never cease
    Their deathless strain;

5 Where saints are clothed in spotless white,
    And evening shadows never fall;
Where Thou, eternal light of light,
    Art Lord of all.

Godfrey Thring, 1823–1903.

709

THE sun is sinking fast,
　The daylight dies;
Let love awake, and pay
　Her evening sacrifice.

2 As Christ upon the cross
　In death reclined,
Into His Father's hands
　His parting soul resigned,

3 So now herself my soul
　Would wholly give
Into His sacred charge
　In whom all spirits live;

4 So now beneath His eye
　Would calmly rest,
Without a wish or thought
　Abiding in the breast,

5 Save that His will be done
　Whate'er betide;
Dead to herself, and dead
　In Him to all beside.

6 Thus would I live; yet now
　Not I, but He
In all His power and love
　Henceforth alive in me,

7 One sacred Trinity,
　One Lord divine;
Myself for ever His,
　And He for ever mine !

Latin, 18th cent.,
tr. Edward Caswall, 1814–78.

(3) OLD AND NEW YEAR

710

ACROSS the sky the shades of night
This winter's eve are fleeting.
We come to Thee, the life and light,
In solemn worship meeting,
And as the year's last hours go by
We lift to Thee our earnest cry,
Once more Thy love entreating.

2 Before the cross subdued we bow,
To Thee our prayers addressing;
Recounting all Thy mercies now,
And all our sins confessing;
Beseeching Thee, this coming year,
To hold us in Thy faith and fear,
And crown us with Thy blessing.

3 We gather up in this brief hour
The memory of Thy mercies;
Thy wondrous goodness, love, and power
Our grateful song rehearses;
For Thou hast been our strength and stay
In many a dark and dreary day
Of sorrow and reverses.

4 Then, O great God, in years to come,
Whatever fate betide us,
Right onward through our journey home
Be Thou at hand to guide us;
Nor leave us till, at close of life,
Safe from all peril, toil, and strife,
Heaven shall receive and hide us.

James Hamilton, 1819–96.

711

AT Thy feet, our God and Father,
Who hast blessed us all our days,
We with grateful hearts would gather,
To begin the year with praise,—

2 Praise for light so brightly shining
On our steps from heaven above,
Praise for mercies daily twining
Round us golden cords of love.

3 Jesus, for Thy love most tender,
On the cross for sinners shown,
We would praise Thee, and surrender
All our hearts to be Thine own.

4 With so blest a friend provided,
We upon our way would go,
Sure of being safely guided,
Guarded well from every foe.

5 Every day will be the brighter
When Thy gracious face we see;
Every burden will be lighter
When we bear it, Lord, with Thee.

6 Spread Thy love's broad banner o'er us;
Give us strength to serve and wait,
Till the glory breaks before us,
Through the City's open gate.

James Drummond Burns, 1823-64.

712

COME, let us anew
Our journey pursue,
Roll round with the year,
And never stand still till the Master appear.

2   His adorable will
          Let us gladly fulfil,
And our talents improve
By the patience of hope, and the labour of love.

3   Our life is a dream;
          Our time as a stream
Glides swiftly away,
And the fugitive moment refuses to stay.

4   The arrow is flown,
          The moment is gone;
The millennial year
Rushes on to our view, and eternity's here.

5   O that each in the day
          Of His coming may say,
" I have fought my way through,
I have finished the work Thou didst give me to do."

6   O that each from his Lord
          May receive the glad word,
" Well and faithfully done !
Enter into My joy, and sit down on My throne."

Charles Wesley, 1707–88.

713

FATHER, let me dedicate
    All this year to Thee,
In whatever worldly state
    Thou wouldst have me be:
Not from sorrow, pain, or care
    Freedom dare I claim;
This alone shall be my prayer,
    " Glorify Thy name."

2 Can a child presume to choose
    Where or how to live?
Can a father's love refuse
    All the best to give?
More Thou givest every day
    Than the best can claim;
Nor withholdest aught that may
    Glorify Thy name.

3 If Thou callest to the cross,
    And its shadow come,
Turning all my gain to loss,
    Shrouding heart and home:
Let me think how Thy dear Son
    To His glory came,
And in deepest woe pray on,
    " Glorify Thy name."

4 If in mercy Thou wilt spare
    Joys that yet are mine,
If on life, serene and fair,
    Brighter rays may shine,
Let my glad heart, while it sings,
    Thee in all proclaim;
And whate'er the future brings,
    Glorify Thy name.

L. Tuttiett, 1825–97.

714

FOR Thy mercy and Thy grace,
    Faithful through another year,
Hear our song of thankfulness,
    Father and Redeemer, hear.

2 Lo, our sins on Thee we cast,
    Lo, to Thee we now arise
And, forgetting all the past,
    Press towards our glorious prize.

3 Dark the future: let Thy light
   Guide us, bright and morning star;
Fierce our foes, and hard the fight:
   Arm us, Saviour, for the war.

4 In our weakness and distress,
   Rock of strength, be Thou our stay;
In the pathless wilderness
   Be our true and living way.

5 Keep us faithful, keep us pure,
   Keep us evermore Thine own.
Help, O help us to endure;
   Fit us for the promised crown.

H. Downton, 1818–85.

715

GREAT God, we sing that guiding hand
By which supported still we stand;
The opening year Thy mercy shows;
That mercy crowns it till its close.

2 By day, by night, at home, abroad,
Still are we guarded by our God;
By His incessant bounty fed,
By His unerring counsel led.

3 With grateful hearts the past we own;
The future, all to us unknown,
We to Thy guardian care commit,
And peaceful leave before Thy feet.

4 In scenes exalted or depressed,
Thou art our joy and Thou our rest;
Thy goodness all our hopes shall raise,
Adored through all our changing days.

5 When death shall interrupt these songs,
   And seal in silence mortal tongues,
   Our helper God, in whom we trust,
   Shall keep our souls and guard our dust.

Philip Doddridge, 1702–51

716

MARCH on, my soul, with strength,
   March forward, void of fear;
He who hath led will lead,
   While year succeedeth year;
And as thou goest on thy way,
His hand shall hold thee day by day.

2 March on, my soul, with strength,
   In ease thou darest not dwell;
High duty calls thee forth;
   Then up, and quit thee well!
Take up thy cross, take up thy sword,
And fight the battles of thy Lord!

3 March on, my soul, with strength,
   With strength, but not thine own;
The conquest thou shalt gain,
   Through Christ thy Lord alone;
His grace shall nerve thy feeble arm,
His love preserve thee safe from harm.

4 March on, my soul, with strength,
   From strength to strength march on;
Warfare shall end at length,
   All foes be overthrown.
Then, O my soul, if faithful now,
The crown of life awaits thy brow.

William Wright, 1859–1924.

717

O THOU whose love has brought us here,
   Our Lord and King,
Within these walls, so dear to us,
   Thy praise shall ring.
To-day, with joy and peace and hope,
   Thy people sing.

2 With joy we meet the friends we love,
   Before Thy throne,
Our voices raised with one accord
   Thy name to own;
Whilst those we miss are still Thy care,
   Nor are alone.

3 The peace which lifts us near to Thee
   Is ours to-day;
The sacred calm of trustful faith
   Drives care away;
That Thou wilt free from every fear,
   Thy servants pray.

4 With hope we face the paths untrod
   Which none can see;
For Thou wilt guide our stumbling feet
   And near us be;
May each year's service find us still
   Nearer to Thee.

H. Wheeler Robinson, 1872–1945.

718

THE old year's long campaign is o'er;
   Behold a new begun;
Not yet is closed the holy war,
   Not yet the triumph won.
Out of its still and deep repose
   We hear the old year say,
" Go forth again to meet your foes,
   Ye children of the day.

2 " Go forth, firm faith in every heart,
   Bright hope on every helm,
Through that shall pierce no fiery dart,
   And this no fear o'erwhelm:
Go in the spirit and the might
   Of Him who led the way;
Close with the legions of the night,
   Ye children of the day."

3 So forth we go to meet the strife,
   We will not fear nor fly;
We love the holy warrior's life,
   His death we hope to die:
We slumber not, that charge in view,
   " Toil on, while toil ye may,
Then night shall be no night to you,
   Ye children of the day."

4 Lord God, our glory, Three in One,
   Thine own sustain, defend;
And give, though dim this earthly sun,
   Thy true light to the end,
Till morning tread the darkness down,
   And night be swept away,
And never-ending triumph crown
   The children of the day.

S. J. Stone, 1839–1900.

See also—
Now thank we all our God, 18.

(4) THE SEASONS

719

HARK, my soul, how everything
  Strives to serve our bounteous King;
Each a double tribute pays,
Sings its part, and then obeys.

2 Nature's chief and sweetest choir
   Him with cheerful notes admire;
   Chanting every day their lauds,
   While the grove their song applauds.

3 Though their voices lower be,
   Streams have too their melody;
   Night and day they warbling run,
   Never pause, but still sing on.

4 All the flowers that gild the spring
   Hither their still music bring;
   If heaven bless them, thankful, they
   Smell more sweet, and look more gay.

5 Wake! for shame, my sluggish heart,
   Wake! and gladly sing thy part;
   Learn of birds, and springs, and flowers,
   How to use thy nobler powers.

6 Call whole nature to thy aid,
   Since 'twas He whole nature made;
   Join in one eternal song,
   Who to one God all belong.

J. Austin, 1613–69.

720

THE glory of the spring how sweet!
   The new-born life how glad!
What joy the happy earth to greet,
   In new, bright raiment clad!

2 Divine renewer, Thee I bless;
   I greet Thy going forth;
I love Thee in the loveliness
   Of Thy renewèd earth.

3 But O these wonders of Thy grace,
　　These nobler works of Thine,
　These marvels sweeter far to trace,
　　These new births more divine,

4 This new-born glow of faith so strong,
　　This bloom of love so fair,
　This new-born ecstasy of song
　　And fragrancy of prayer !

5 Creator Spirit, work in me
　　These wonders sweet of Thine;
　Divine renewer, graciously
　　Renew this heart of mine.

6 Still let new life and strength upspring,
　　Still let new joy be given;
　And grant the glad new song to ring
　　Through the new earth and heaven.

T. H. Gill, 1819–1906, altd.

721

HERE, Lord, we offer Thee all that is fairest,
　　Bloom from the garden, and flowers from
　the field,
Gifts for the stricken ones, knowing Thou carest
　More for the love than the wealth that we yield.

2 Send, Lord, by these to the sick and the dying,
　　Speak to their hearts with a message of peace;
　Comfort the sad, who in weakness are lying,
　　Grant the departing a gentle release.

3 Raise, Lord, to health again those who have
　　sickened;
　Fair be their lives as the roses in bloom;
　Give, of Thy grace, to the souls Thou hast
　　quickened
　Gladness for sorrow, and brightness for gloom.

A. G. W. Blunt, 1827–1902.

722

SUMMER suns are glowing
  Over land and sea,
Happy light is flowing,
  Bountiful and free.
Everything rejoices
  In the mellow rays;
All earth's thousand voices
  Swell the psalm of praise.

2 God's free mercy streameth
  Over all the world,
And His banner gleameth,
  Everywhere unfurled.
Broad and deep and glorious
  As the heaven above,
Shines in might victorious
  His eternal love.

3 Lord, upon our blindness
  Thy pure radiance pour;
For Thy loving-kindness
  Make us love Thee more.
And when clouds are drifting
  Dark across our sky,
Then, the veil uplifting,
  Father, be Thou nigh.

4 We will never doubt Thee,
  Though Thou veil Thy light;
Life is dark without Thee;
  Death with Thee is bright.
Light of light, shine o'er us
  On our pilgrim way;
Go Thou still before us
  To the endless day.

W. Walsham How, 1823–97.

723

'TIS winter now; the fallen snow
    Has left the heavens all coldly clear;
Through leafless boughs the sharp winds blow,
    And all the earth lies dead and drear.

2 And yet God's love is not withdrawn;
    His life within the keen air breathes;
His beauty paints the crimson dawn,
    And clothes the boughs with glittering wreaths.

3 And though abroad the sharp winds blow,
    And skies are chill, and frosts are keen,
Home closer draws her circle now,
    And warmer glows her light within.

4 O God, who giv'st the winter's cold,
    As well as summer's joyous rays,
Us warmly in Thy love enfold,
    And keep us through life's wintry days.

Samuel Longfellow, 1819–92.

(5) HARVEST

724

COME, ye thankful people, come,
    Raise the song of harvest home!
All is safely gathered in
Ere the winter storms begin;
God, our Maker, doth provide
For our needs to be supplied:
Come to God's own temple, come,
Raise the song of harvest-home.

2 All the world is God's own field,
Fruit unto His praise to yield;
Wheat and tares together sown,
Unto joy or sorrow grown;

First the blade, and then the ear,
Then the full corn shall appear:
Lord of harvest, grant that we
Wholesome grain and pure may be.

3 For the Lord our God shall come,
And shall take His harvest home,
From His field shall in that day
All offences purge away,
Give His angels charge at last
In the fire the tares to cast,
But the fruitful ears to store
In His garner evermore.

4 Even so, Lord, quickly come,
Bring Thy final harvest home;
Gather Thou Thy people in,
Free from sorrow, free from sin;
There, for ever purified,
In Thy garner to abide:
Come, with all Thine angels, come,
Raise the glorious harvest-home.

Henry Alford, 1810–71.

725

FAIR waved the golden corn
In Canaan's pleasant land,
When, full of joy, some shining morn,
Went forth the reaper-band.

2 To God, so good and great,
Their cheerful thanks they pour,
Then carry to His temple-gate
The choicest of their store.

3 Like Israel, Lord, we give
Our earliest fruits to Thee,
And pray that, long as we shall live,
We may Thy children be.

4   Thine is our youthful prime,
      And life and all its powers;
  Be with us in our morning time,
      And bless our evening hours.

5   In wisdom let us grow,
      As years and strength are given,
  That we may serve Thy Church below
      And join Thy saints in heaven.

J. H. Gurney, 1802–62.

726

GOD, whose farm is all creation,
    Take the gratitude we give;
Take the finest of our harvest,
    Crops we grow that men may live.

2 Take our ploughing, seeding, reaping,
    Hopes and fears of sun and rain,
All our thinking, planning, waiting,
    Ripened in this fruit and grain.

3 All our labour, all our watching,
    All our calendar of care,
In these crops of your creation,
    Take, O God: they are our prayer.

John Arlott, 1914–

727

NOW sing we a song for the harvest:
    Thanksgiving and honour and praise
For all that the bountiful giver
    Hath given to gladden our days,

2 For grasses of upland and lowland,
    For fruits of the garden and field,
  For gold which the mine and the furrow
    To delver and husbandman yield;

3 And thanks for the harvest of beauty,
    For that which the hands cannot hold,
  The harvest eyes only can gather,
    And only our hearts can enfold.

4 We reap it on mountain and moorland;
    We glean it from meadow and lea;
  We garner it in from the cloudland;
    We bind it in sheaves from the sea.

5 But the song goes yet deeper and higher;
    There are harvests that eye cannot see,
  They ripen on mountains of duty,
    Are reaped by the brave and the free.

6 O Thou who art Lord of the harvest,
    The giver who gladdens our days,
  Our hearts are for ever repeating
    Thanksgiving and honour and praise.

J. W. Chadwick, 1840–1904.

728

PRAISE, O praise, the Lord of harvest,—
    Providence and love !
Praise Him in His earthly temples,
    And above !

2 Praise Him, every living creature,
    By His goodness fed,
  Whose rich mercy daily giveth
    Daily bread.

3 Sing Him thanks for all the bounties
        Of His gracious hand;
    Smiling peace and welcome plenty
        O'er our land.

4 Speed, O speed, that glorious harvest
        Of the souls of men,
    When Christ's members, here long-scattered,
        Meet again.

5 Glory to the Lord of harvest,
        Holy Three in One!
    To the Father, Son, and Spirit,
        Praise be done!   Amen.

James Hamilton, 1819–96

729

PRAISE we now the God of heaven,
    Laud and magnify His worth;
By His hand alone is given
    Boon of harvest for our dearth;
        Hallelujah!
    God hath visited the earth!

2 Praise to God, who calls us ever
    In His harvesting to share;
May He own our poor endeavour,
    Find us faithful everywhere;
        Hallelujah!
    For our handiwork is prayer.

3 Praise to God, who makes us brothers,
    From our striving bids us cease,
Teaches us to share with others
    All the good of earth's increase;
        Hallelujah!
    In His harvest field is peace.

4 Praise to God ! His word abideth
  While the changing seasons roll,
Praise to Him ! His love provideth
  Hidden manna for the soul;
    Hallelujah !
  Evermore His name extol !

H. R. Moxley, 1881–

730

Psalm lxv.

S ING to the Lord of harvest,
    Sing songs of love and praise;
With joyful hearts and voices
  Your hallelujahs raise.
By Him the rolling seasons
  In fruitful order move;
Sing to the Lord of harvest
  A song of happy love.

2 By Him the clouds drop fatness,
    The deserts bloom and spring,
The hills leap up in gladness,
    The valleys laugh and sing.
He filleth with His fullness
    All things with large increase,
He crowns the year with goodness,
    With plenty and with peace.

3 Bring now in glad thanksgiving
    The gifts His goodness gave,
The golden sheaves of harvest,
    The souls He died to save.
Your hearts lay down before Him
    When at His feet ye fall,
And with your lives adore Him,
    Who gave His life for all.

J. S. B. Monsell, 1811–75.

731

TO Thee, O Lord, our hearts we raise
    In hymns of adoration,
To Thee bring sacrifice of praise
    With shouts of exultation;
Bright robes of gold the fields adorn,
    The hills with joy are ringing,
The valleys stand so thick with corn
    That even they are singing.

2 And now, on this our festal day,
    Thy bounteous hand confessing,
Before Thee thankfully we lay
    The first fruits of Thy blessing:
By Thee the souls of men are fed
    With gifts of grace supernal,
Thou who dost give us earthly bread
    Give us the bread eternal.

3 We bear the burden of the day,
    And often toil seems dreary,
But labour ends with sunset ray,
    And rest comes for the weary;
May we, the angel-reaping o'er,
    Stand at the last accepted,
Christ's golden sheaves for evermore
    To garners bright elected.

4 O blessèd is that land of God,
    Where saints abide for ever,
Where golden fields spread far and broad,
    Where flows the crystal river;
The strains of all its holy throng
    With ours to-day are blending;
Thrice blessèd is that harvest-song
    Which never hath an ending.

W. C. Dix, 1837–98.

732

WE plough the fields and scatter
 The good seed on the land,
But it is fed and watered
 By God's almighty hand;
He sends the snow in winter,
 The warmth to swell the grain,
The breezes and the sunshine
 And soft refreshing rain.

All good gifts around us
 Are sent from heaven above,
Then thank the Lord, O thank the Lord,
 For all His love.

2 He only is the Maker
 Of all things near and far;
He paints the wayside flower,
 He lights the evening star;
The wind and waves obey Him,
 By Him the birds are fed;
Much more to us, His children,
 He gives our daily bread.

3 We thank Thee then, O Father,
 For all things bright and good,
The seed-time and the harvest,
 Our life, our health, our food.
Accept the gifts we offer
 For all Thy love imparts,
And what Thou most desirest,
 Our humble, thankful hearts.

Matthias Claudius, 1740–1815,
tr. Jane Montgomery Campbell, 1817–78.

See also—
 O Lord of heaven, 68. **When the corn, 757.**

XI. FOR YOUNGER CHILDREN
See also Index of Hymns Suitable for Young People.

733

All things bright and beautiful,
  All creatures great and small,
All things wise and wonderful,
  The Lord God made them all.

2 Each little flower that opens,
    Each little bird that sings,
  He made their glowing colours,
    He made their tiny wings.

3 The purple-headed mountain,
    The river running by,
  The sunset, and the morning
    That brightens up the sky;

4 The cold wind in the winter,
    The pleasant summer sun,
  The ripe fruits in the garden,
    He made them every one.

5 He gave us eyes to see them,
    And lips that we might tell
  How great is God almighty,
    Who has made all things well.
                  Cecil Frances Alexander, 1818–95.

734

AWAY in a manger, no crib for a bed,
The little Lord Jesus laid down His sweet head.
The stars in the bright sky looked down where He
  lay,
The little Lord Jesus asleep on the hay.

2 The cattle are lowing, the baby awakes,
But little Lord Jesus no crying He makes.
I love Thee, Lord Jesus ! look down from the sky,
And stay by my side until morning is nigh.

3 Be near me, Lord Jesus; I ask Thee to stay
Close by me for ever, and love me, I pray.
Bless all the dear children in Thy tender care,
And fit us for heaven to live with Thee there.

Anon.

735

CHILDREN of Jerusalem
Sang the praise of Jesus' name:
Children, too, of modern days,
Join to sing the Saviour's praise.
*Hark ! While children's voices sing
Loud hosannas to our King.*

2 We are taught to love the Lord,
We are taught to read His word,
We are taught the way to heaven:
Praise for all to God be given.

3 Parents, teachers, old and young,
All unite to swell the song;
Higher and yet higher rise,
Till hosannas reach the skies.

John Henley, 1800-42.

736

Morning

FATHER, we thank Thee for the night,
And for the pleasant morning light;
For rest and food and loving care,
And all that makes the day so fair.

2 Help us to do the things we should,
  To be to others kind and good;
  In all we do at work or play
  To grow more loving every day.

Rebecca J. Weston.

737

FOR air and sunshine pure and sweet,
  We thank our heavenly Father;
For grass that grows beneath our feet,
  We thank our heavenly Father;
For lovely flowers and blossoms gay,
For trees and woods in bright array,
For birds that sing in joyful lay,
  We thank our heavenly Father.

2 For leafy trees with fruit and shade,
  We thank our heavenly Father;
For things of beauty He has made,
  We thank our heavenly Father;
For daily blessings, full and free,
For leading where we cannot see,
For all His care o'er you and me,
  We thank our heavenly Father.

3 For Jesus, born a little child,
  We thank our heavenly Father;
For Jesus, loving, kind, and mild,
  We thank our heavenly Father;
For Jesus Christ, the children's Friend,
Who to us all His love doth send;
For Him who helps us to the end,
  We thank our heavenly Father.

Child Songs.

738

FOR sun and moon and stars
　　We thank Thee, Lord of light,
For happy play by day,
　　And quiet sleep at night.
Children yellow, black, and brown
Watch the same red sun go down;
And the moon which lights our sky
Guards their sleep with loving eye.

2　　For friends and grass and trees
　　　　We thank Thee, Lord of love;
　　For smiling flowers and earth
　　　　And sunny skies above.
Children living far away
Love the flowers bright and gay,
Love the trees so straight and tall,
And the blue sky over all.

3　　We know Thy tender love,
　　　　We thank Thee for Thy care,
　　For light and fields and flowers,
　　　　And all things everywhere.
Children live across the sea
Who have never heard of Thee:
We who know Thy love can pray,
" Bless the children far away."

Anon., 1929.

739

GENTLE Jesus, meek and mild,
　　Look upon a little child;
Pity my simplicity,
Suffer me to come to Thee.

2 Fain I would be as Thou art;
　Give me Thy obedient heart;
　Thou art pitiful and kind,
　Let me have Thy loving mind.

3 Let me, above all, fulfil
   God my heavenly Father's will,
   Never His good Spirit grieve,
   Only to His glory live.

4 Thou didst live to God alone,
   Thou didst never seek Thine own,
   Thou Thyself didst never please,
   God was all Thy happiness.

5 Loving Jesus, gentle Lamb,
   In Thy gracious hands I am;
   Make me, Saviour, what Thou art,
   Live Thyself within my heart.

6 I shall then show forth Thy praise,
   Serve Thee all my happy days;
   Then the world shall always see
   Christ, the holy child, in me.

Charles Wesley, 1707–88.

740

GOD has given us a book full of stories,
   Which was made for His people of old,
It begins with the tale of a garden,
   And ends with the city of gold.

2 But the best is the story of Jesus,
   Of the babe with the ox in the stall,
Of the song that was sung by the angels,
   The most beautiful story of all.

3 There are stories for parents and children,
   For the old who are ready to rest,
But for all who can read them or listen,
   The story of Jesus is best.

4 For it tells how He came from the Father,
   His far-away children to call,
To bring the lost sheep to their Shepherd—
The most beautiful story of all.
                    Maria Penstone, 1859–1910.

741

GOD make my life a shining light,
    Within the world to glow;
A little flame that burneth bright
Wherever I may go.

2 God make my life a lovely flower,
    That giveth joy to all;
Content to bloom in native bower,
    Although the place be small.

3 God make my life a happy song,
    That comforteth the sad;
That helpeth others to be strong,
    And makes the singer glad.

4 God make my life a sturdy staff,
    Whereon the weak may rest;
That so what health and strength I have
    May serve my neighbours best.

5 God make my life a tuneful hymn
    Of tenderness and praise,
Of faith that never waxeth dim,
    In all His wondrous ways.
            Matilda Betham-Edwards, 1836–1919, altd.

742

GOD my Father, loving me,
  Gave His Son my friend to be;
Gave His Son my form to take,
And to suffer for my sake.

2 Jesus still remains the same
    As in days of old He came;
    As my brother by my side
    Still He seeks my steps to guide.

3 How can I repay Thy love,
    Lord of all the hosts above?
    What have I, a child, to bring
    Unto Thee, Thou heavenly King?

4 I have but myself to give,
    Let me for Thy service live;
    Let me follow, day by day,
    Where Thou showest me the way.

G. W. Briggs, 1875–1959.

743

GOD who hath made the daisies,
    And every lovely thing,
He will accept our praises,
    And hearken while we sing:
He says, though we are simple,
    Though ignorant we be,
" *Suffer the little children,*
And let them come to Me."

2 Though we are young and simple,
    In praise we may be bold;
The children in the temple
    He heard in days of old;
And if our hearts are humble
    He says to you and me,

3 He sees the bird that wingeth
    Its way o'er earth and sky;
He hears the lark that singeth
    Up in the heaven so high;
But sees the heart's low breathings
    And says, well pleased to see,

4 Therefore we will come near Him,
  And joyfully we'll sing;
No cause to shrink or fear Him,
  We'll make our voices ring;
For in our temple speaking,
  He says to you and me,
" *Suffer the little children,*
And let them come to Me."

Edwin Paxton Hood, 1820–85.

744

GOD who made the earth,
  The air, the sky, the sea,
Who gave the light its birth,
  Careth for me.

2 God who made the grass,
  The flower, the fruit, the tree,
The day and night to pass,
  Careth for me.

3 God who made the sun,
  The moon, the stars, is He
Who, when life's clouds come on,
  Careth for me.

4 God who sent His Son
  To die on Calvary,
He, if I lean on Him,
  Will care for me.

Sarah Betts Rhodes, 1824–1904.

745

IT is the joyful Easter time,
  Let all sing hallelujah !
The merry bells ring out their chime,
  ' But now is Christ arisen.'

2 The church is bright with flowers gay,
  And all Christ's people praise and pray,
For Jesus rose on Easter day;
  Sing joyful hallelujah !

A. M. Milner-Barry, 1875–1940.

746

JESUS bids us shine
    With a pure, clear light,
Like a little candle
    Burning in the night.
In this world is darkness;
    So let us shine,
You in your small corner,
    And I in mine.

2 Jesus bids us shine,
    First of all for Him;
Well He sees and knows it,
    If our light grows dim.
He looks down from heaven
    To see us shine,
You in your small corner,
    And I in mine.

3 Jesus bids us shine,
    Then, for all around;
Many kinds of darkness
    In the world are found—
Sin, and want, and sorrow;
    So we must shine,
You in your small corner,
    And I in mine.

Susan Warner, 1819–85.

747

JESUS, friend of little children,
    Be a friend to me;
Take my hand, and ever keep me
    Close to Thee.

2 Show me what my love should cherish,
    What, too, it should shun;
Lest my feet on harmful errands
    Swift should run.

3 Teach me how to grow in goodness,
    Daily as I grow:
Thou hast been a child, and surely
    Thou dost know.

4 Step by step, O lead me onward,
    Upward into youth;
Wiser, stronger, still becoming
    In Thy truth.

5 Never leave me, nor forsake me,
    Ever be my friend:
For I need Thee from life's dawning
    To its end.

W. J. Mathams, 1853–1931, altd.

748

JESUS, high in glory,
    Lend a listening ear;
When we bow before Thee,
    Children's praises hear.

2 Though Thou art so holy,
    Heaven's almighty King,
Thou will stoop to listen
    When Thy praise we sing.

3 Save us, Lord, from sinning;
   Watch us day by day;
Help us now to love Thee;
   Take our sins away.

4 Strengthen us for duty,
   While on earth we live;
May we to Thy service
   Our best talents give.

5 Then, when Thou shalt call us
   To our heavenly home,
We will gladly answer,
   Saviour, Lord, we come !
Harriet M'Keever, 1807–86.

749

JESUS loves me ! this I know,
   For the Bible tells me so;
Little ones to Him belong;
They are weak, but He is strong.
     Yes! Jesus loves me!
     The Bible tells me so.

2 Jesus loves me ! He who died
Heaven's gate to open wide;
He will wash away my sin,
Let His little child come in.

3 Jesus loves me ! He will stay
Close beside me all the way;
Then His little child will take
Up to heaven, for His dear sake.
Anna Warner, 1820–1915.

750

JESUS, tender shepherd, hear me,
Bless Thy little lamb to-night;
Through the darkness be Thou near me,
Keep me safe till morning light.

2 Through this day Thine hand has led me,
And I thank Thee for Thy care;
Thou hast clothed me, warmed and fed me,
Listen to my evening prayer.

3 Let my sins be all forgiven;
Bless the friends I love so well;
Take me, when I die, to heaven,
Happy there with Thee to dwell. Amen.

Mary Lundie Duncan, 1814–40.

751

LONG ago when Jesus
Walked in Galilee,
Children found a welcome
At the Saviour's knee.

2 Now He gives the children
Born in every land,
Dark and fair, a blessing
From His loving hand.

3 Redskin, white and yellow,
Black and brown draw near.
Then, since He receives them,
We too hold them dear.

A. F. Bayly, 1901–

752

O what can little hands do
　　To please the King of Heaven ?
The little hands their share may take
And other people happy make:
　　Such grace to mine be given !

2 O what can little lips do
　　To please the King of Heaven ?
The little lips can praise and pray,
And gentle words of kindness say:
　　Such grace to mine be given !

3 O what can little eyes do
　　To please the King of Heaven ?
The little eyes can upward look,
And learn to read God's holy book:
　　Such grace to mine be given !

4 O what can little hearts do
　　To please the King of Heaven ?
Our hearts, if God His Spirit send,
Can love and trust their Saviour-Friend:
　　Such grace to mine be given !

5 Though small is all that we can do
　　To please the King of Heaven,
When hearts and hands and lips unite
To serve the Saviour with delight,
　　Then perfect grace is given.

Anon.

753

PRAISE Him, praise Him, all ye little children,
　　He is love, He is love.

2 Thank Him, thank Him, all ye little children,
   He is love, He is love.

3 Love Him, love Him, all ye little children,
   He is love, He is love.

4 Crown Him, crown Him, all ye little children
   He is love, He is love.

5 Serve Him, serve Him, all ye little children,
   He is love, He is love.

Anon., c. 1890.

754

THANK you for the world so sweet;
   Thank you for the food we eat;
Thank you for the birds that sing:
   Thank you, God, for everything !

Edith Leatham, **1870–1939.**

755

THE little flowers came through the ground
   At Easter-time, at Easter-time,
They raised their heads and looked around,
   At happy Easter-time :
And every little flower did say,
" Good people, bless this holy day,
For Christ is risen, the angels say,
   At happy Easter-time."

2 The pure white lily raised its cup,
   The crocus to the sky looked up,
   " We'll hear the song of love," they say,
   " Its glory shines on us to-day,
   O may it shine on us alway,
      At happy Easter-time."

3 'Twas long and long and long ago,
But still the pure white lilies blow,
And still the little flower doth say,
" Good people, bless this holy day,
For Christ is risen, the angels say,
At happy Easter-time."

Laura E. Richards, 1850–1943.

756

THOU who once on mother's knee
Wast a little one like me,
When I wake, or go to bed,
Lay Thy hands upon my head;
Let me feel Thee very near,
Jesus Christ, our Saviour dear.

2 Be beside me in the light,
Be close by me through the night;
Make me gentle, kind, and true,
Do what I am bid to do;
Help and cheer me when I fret,
And forgive when I forget. Amen.

F. T. Palgrave, 1824–97.

757

Harvest

WHEN the corn is planted
In the deep dark bed,
Mothers know their children
Will have daily bread.

2 God sends sun and showers,
Birds sing overhead,
While the corn is growing
For our daily bread.

3 When the corn is gathered,
   Stored in barn and shed,
Then we all are thankful
   For our daily bread.

4 Father high in heaven,
   All by Thee are fed;
Hear Thy children praise Thee
   For our daily bread.

Anon.

XII. THE CLOSE OF WORSHIP:
DOXOLOGIES AND FAREWELL HYMNS

758

COME, dearest Lord, descend and dwell
By faith and love in every breast;
Then shall we know, and taste, and feel
The joys that cannot be expressed.

2 Come, fill our hearts with inward strength;
Make our enlargèd souls possess
And learn the height and breadth and length
Of Thine unmeasurable grace.

3 Now to the God whose power can do
More than our thoughts or wishes know,
Be everlasting honours done
By all the Church, through Christ His Son.
                                        Amen.

Isaac Watts, 1674–1748.

759

FAREWELL, my friends beloved,
    Time passes fleetly;
When moments are improved,
    Time passes sweetly:
In Jesus we are one;
When our few years are gone
Before the shining throne
    We'll meet in glory.

2 The woes of life we feel,
  And its temptations;
But let us nobly fill
  Our proper stations:
Soldiers of Christ, hold fast,
The war will soon be past;
When victory comes at last,
  We'll meet in glory.

3 And O what joys shall crown
  That happy meeting!
We'll bow before the throne,
  Each other greeting;
Refreshed again we start,
Though for awhile we part,
Yet, always joined in heart,
  We'll meet in glory.

Joseph Harbottle, 1798-1864.

760

PSALM cxvii.

FROM all that dwell below the skies,
  Let the Creator's praise arise;
Let the Redeemer's name be sung
Through every land, by every tongue.

2 Eternal are Thy mercies, Lord;
Eternal truth attends Thy word.
Thy praise shall sound from shore to shore,
Till suns shall rise and set no more.

Isaac Watts, 1674-1748.

761

GOD be with you till we meet again,
  By His counsels guide, uphold you,
With His sheep securely fold you:
God be with you till we meet again.

2 God be with you till we meet again,
    Neath His wings protecting hide you,
    Daily manna still provide you:
God be with you till we meet again.

3 God be with you till we meet again,
    When life's perils thick confound you,
    Put His arms unfailing round you:
God be with you till we meet again.

4 God be with you till we meet again,
    Keep love's banner floating o'er you,
    Smite death's threatening wave before you:
God be with you till we meet again.

Jeremiah Rankin, 1828-1904.

762

LORD, dismiss us with Thy blessing,
    Fill our hearts with joy and peace;
Let us each, Thy love possessing,
    Triumph in redeeming grace:
        O refresh us,
    Travelling through this wilderness.

2 Thanks we give and adoration,
    For Thy gospel's joyful sound;
May the fruits of Thy salvation
    In our hearts and lives abound:
        May Thy presence
    With us evermore be found.

3 So, whene'er the signal's given
    Us from earth to call away,
Borne on angels' wings to heaven,
    Glad the summons to obey,
        May we ever
    Reign with Christ in endless day.

John Fawcett, 1740-1817.

763

MAY the grace of Christ our Saviour,
And the Father's boundless love,
With the Holy Spirit's favour,
Rest upon us from above.

2 Thus may we abide in union
With each other and the Lord;
And possess in sweet communion
Joys which earth cannot afford. Amen.

John Newton, 1725-1807.

764

HEBREWS xiii. 20-21.

NOW may He, who from the dead
Brought the shepherd of the sheep,
Jesus Christ, our king and head,
All our souls in safety keep.

2 May He teach us to fulfil
What is pleasing in His sight;
Perfect us in all His will,
And preserve us day and night.

3 To that dear Redeemer's praise,
Who the covenant sealed with blood,
Let our hearts and voices raise
Loud thanksgivings to our God.   Amen.

John Newton, 1725-1807.

765

O God our Father, who dost make us one,
Heart bound to heart, in love of Thy dear Son,
Now as we part and go our several ways,
Touch every lip, may every voice be praise―

2 Praise for the fellowship that here we find,
The fellowship of heart and soul and mind,
Praise for the bonds of love and brotherhood,
Bonds wrought by Thee, who makest all things
good.

3 Lord, make us strong, for Thou alone dost know
How oft we turn our faces from the foe;
How oft, when claimed by dark temptation's hour,
We lose our hold on Thee, and of Thy power.

4 Go with us, Lord, from here; we only ask
That Thou be sharer in our daily task;
So, side by side with Thee, shall each one know
The blessedness of heaven begun below.

W. Vaughan Jenkins, 1868–1920.

766

PRAISE God, from whom all blessings flow,
Praise Him, all creatures here below,
Praise Him above, ye heavenly host,
Praise Father, Son, and Holy Ghost.   Amen.

Thomas Ken, 1637–1711.

See also—
O Saviour, bless us ere we go, 700.
Saviour, again to Thy dear name, 702.

767

COME, O Thou Traveller unknown,
Whom still I hold, but cannot see !
My company before is gone,
   And I am left alone with Thee ;
With Thee all night I mean to stay,
And wrestle till the break of day.

2 I need not tell Thee who I am,
My misery and sin declare ;
Thyself hast called me by my name ;
   Look on Thy hands, and read it there ;
But who I ask Thee, who art Thou ?
Tell me Thy name, and tell me now.

3 Wilt Thou not yet to me reveal
Thy new, unutterable name ?
Tell me, I still beseech Thee, tell ;
   To know it now resolved I am ;
Wrestling, I will not let Thee go,
Till I Thy name, Thy nature know.

4 Yield to me now ; for I am weak,
   But confident in self-despair ;
Speak to my heart, in blessings speak,
   Be conquered by my instant prayer ;
Speak, or Thou never hence shalt move,
And tell me if Thy name is Love.

5 'Tis Love ! 'tis Love ! Thou diedst for me !
   I hear Thy whisper in my heart ;
The morning breaks, the shadows flee,
   Pure, universal Love Thou art ;
To me, to all, Thy mercies move :
Thy nature and Thy name is Love.

6 I know Thee, Saviour, who Thou art,
   Jesus, the feeble sinner's friend;
Nor wilt Thou with the night depart,
   But stay and love me to the end;
Thy mercies never shall remove;
Thy nature and Thy name is Love.

7 The Sun of Righteousness on me
   Hath risen with healing in His wings;
Withered my nature's strength, from Thee
   My soul its life and succour brings;
My help is all laid up above:
Thy nature and Thy name is Love.

8 Contented now upon my thigh
   I halt, till life's short journey end;
All helplessness, all weakness, I
   On Thee alone for strength depend;
Through all eternity to prove
Thy nature and Thy name is Love.

Charles Wesley, 1707–88.

768

JESU, priceless treasure,
   Source of purest pleasure,
Truest friend to me;
How my heart hath panted
Till it well nigh fainted,
   Thirsting, Lord, for Thee.
Thine I am, O spotless Lamb,
I will suffer nought to hide Thee,
   Nought I ask beside Thee.

2 In Thine arm I rest me;
Foes who would molest me
   Cannot reach me here;
Though the earth be shaking,

Every heart be quaking,
  Jesus calms my fear;
Sin and hell in conflict fell
With their bitter storms assail me:
  Jesus will not fail me.

3 Hence all fears and sadness !
  For the Lord of gladness,
    Jesus, enters in;
  Those who love the Father,
  Though the storms may gather,
    Still have peace within;
  Yea, whate'er I here must bear,
  Still in Thee lies purest pleasure,
    Jesu, priceless treasure !

Johann Franck, 1618–77,
tr. Catherine Winkworth, 1827–78.

769

NONE other Lamb, none other name,
  None other hope in heaven or earth or sea,
None other hiding-place from guilt and shame,
  None beside Thee !

2 My faith burns low, my hope burns low;
  Only my heart's desire cries out in me
By the deep thunder of its want and woe,
  Cries out to Thee.

3 Lord, Thou art life, though I be dead;
  Love's fire Thou art, however cold I be:
Nor heaven have I, nor place to lay my head,
  Nor home, but Thee.

Christina Georgina Rossetti, 1830–94.

770

O GOD, what offering shall I give
To Thee, the Lord of earth and skies?
My spirit, soul, and flesh receive,
A holy, living sacrifice:
Small as it is, 'tis all my store;
More shouldst Thou have, if I had more.

2 Now, O my God, Thou hast my soul,
No longer mine, but Thine I am;
Guard Thou Thine own, possess it whole,
Cheer it with hope, with love inflame;
Thou hast my spirit, there display
Thy glory to the perfect day.

3 Take Thou my flesh, Thy hallowed shrine,
Devote it solely to Thy will;
Here let Thy light for ever shine,
This house still let Thy presence fill:
O source of life; live, dwell, and move
In me, till all my life be love!

4 Send down Thy likeness from above,
And let this my adorning be;
Clothe me with wisdom, patience, love,
With lowliness and purity,
Than gold and pearls more precious far,
And brighter than the morning star.

5 Lord, arm me with Thy Spirit's might,
Since I am called by Thy great name;
In Thee let all my thoughts unite,
Of all my works be Thou the aim:
Thy love attend me all my days,
And my sole business be Thy praise.

Joachim Lange, 1670–1744,
tr. John Wesley, 1703–91, *altd.*

771

O LET him whose sorrow
   No relief can find,
Trust in God, and borrow
   Ease for heart and mind.

2 Where the mourner, weeping,
   Sheds the secret tear,
God His watch is keeping,
   Though none else be near.

3 God will never leave thee;
   All thy wants He knows,
Feels the pains that grieve thee,
   Sees thy cares and woes.

4 If in grief thou languish,
   He will dry the tear,
Who His children's anguish
   Soothes with succour near.

5 All thy woe and sadness,
   In this world below,
Balance not the gladness
   Thou in heaven shalt know,

6 When thy gracious Saviour,
   In the realms above,
Crowns thee with His favour,
   Fills thee with His love.

Heinrich Oswald, 1751–1834,
tr. Frances Cox, 1812–97.

772

O LOVE divine, how sweet thou art !
  When shall I find my willing heart
   All taken up by thee ?
I thirst, I faint, I die to prove
The greatness of redeeming love,
   The love of Christ to me.

2 Stronger His love than death and hell;
    Its riches are unsearchable:
        The first-born sons of light
    Desire in vain its depth to see;
    They cannot reach the mystery,
        The length, and breadth, and height.

3 God only knows the love of God:
    O that it now were shed abroad
        In this poor stony heart!
    For love I sigh, for love I pine;
    This only portion, Lord, be mine,
        Be mine this better part.

4 O that I could for ever sit
    With Mary at the Master's feet;
        Be this my happy choice.
    My only care, delight, and bliss,
    My joy, my heaven on earth be this,
        To hear the Bridegroom's voice.

                    Charles Wesley, 1707–88, altd.

773

SHOW me myself, O holy Lord;
    Help me to look within;
I will not turn me from the sight
    Of all my sin.

2 Just as it is in Thy pure eyes
    Would I behold my heart,—
Bring every hidden spot to light,
    Nor shrink the smart.

3 Not mine, the purity of heart
    That shall at last see God;
Not mine, the following in the steps
    The Saviour trod:

4 Not mine, the life I thought to live
   When first I took His name;—
Mine but the right to weep and grieve
   Over my shame.

5 Yet, Lord, I thank Thee for the sight
   Thou hast vouchsafed to me;
And humbled to the dust, I shrink
   Closer to Thee;

6 And if Thy love will not disown
   So frail a heart as mine,
Chasten and cleanse it as Thou wilt,
   But keep it Thine !   Amen.

Plymouth Hymnal, 1893

774

STILL with Thee, O my God,
   I would desire to be;
By day, by night, at home, abroad,
   I would be still with Thee.

2   With Thee, when dawn comes in
        And calls me back to care;
Each day returning to begin
        With Thee, my God, in prayer.

3   With Thee, amid the crowd
        That throngs the busy mart;
To hear Thy voice, 'mid clamour loud,
        Speak softly to my heart.

4   With Thee, when day is done,
        And evening calms the mind;
The setting, as the rising sun,
        With Thee my heart would find.

5   With Thee, when darkness brings
       The signal of repose;
    Calm in the shadow of Thy wings,
       Mine eyelids I would close.

6   With Thee, in Thee, by faith
       Abiding I would be.
    By day, by night, in life, in death,
       I would be still with Thee.

James Drummond Burns, 1823–64.

775

Abide in Me, and I in you.

THAT mystic word of Thine, O sovereign Lord,
    Is all too pure, too high, too deep for me;
Weary of striving, and with longing faint,
    I breathe it back again in prayer to Thee.

2 Abide in me, I pray, and I in Thee;
    From this good hour, O leave me never more.
Then shall the discord cease, the wound be healed,
    The lifelong bleeding of the soul be o'er.

3 Abide in me; o'ershadow by Thy love
    Each half-formed purpose, and dark thought of
       sin;
Quench, ere it rise, each selfish, low desire,
    And keep my soul as Thine, calm and divine.

4 Abide in me; there have been moments blest
    When I have heard Thy voice and felt Thy
       power;
Then evil lost its grasp, and passion, hushed,
    Owned the divine enchantment of the hour.

5 These were but seasons, beautiful and rare;
   Abide in me, and they shall ever be;
Fulfil at once Thy precept and my prayer—
   Come and abide in me, and I in Thee.

Harriet Beecher Stowe, 1812–96.

776

THE sands of time are sinking,
   The dawn of heaven breaks;
The summer morn I've sighed for,
   The fair, sweet morn, awakes.
Dark, dark hath been the midnight,
   But dayspring is at hand,
And glory, glory dwelleth
   In Immanuel's land.

2 The King there, in His beauty,
   Without a veil is seen;
It were a well-spent journey,
   Though seven deaths lay between:
The Lamb, with His fair army,
   Doth on Mount Zion stand,
And glory, glory dwelleth
   In Immanuel's land.

3 O Christ, He is the fountain,
   The deep, sweet well of love;
The streams on earth I've tasted,
   More deep I'll drink above:
There, to an ocean fulness,
   His mercy doth expand,
And glory, glory dwelleth
   In Immanuel's land.

4 With mercy and with judgment,
   My web of time He wove;
And aye the dews of sorrow
   Were lustred with His love;

I'll bless the hand that guided,
  I'll bless the heart that planned,
When throned where glory dwelleth
  In Immanuel's land.

5 The bride eyes not her garment,
    But her dear bridegroom's face;
  I will not gaze at glory,
    But on my King of grace,
  Not at the crown He giveth,
    But on His piercèd hand:
  The Lamb is all the glory
    Of Immanuel's land.

6 I've wrestled on towards heaven,
    'Gainst storm and wind and tide;
  Now, like a weary traveller
    That leaneth on his guide,
  Amid the shades of evening,
    While sinks life's lingering sand,
  I hail the glory dawning
    From Immanuel's land.

Anne Cousin, 1824–1906.

777

WHEN on my day of life the night is falling
And, in the winds from unsunned spaces
    blown,
I hear far voices out of darkness calling
  My feet to paths unknown.

2 Thou who hast made my home of life so pleasant,
    Leave not its tenant when its walls decay;
  O love divine, O helper ever present,
    Be Thou my strength and stay.

3 Be near me when all else is from me drifting,—
    Earth, sky, home's pictures, days of shade and
        shine,
  And kindly faces to my own uplifting
    The love which answers mine.

4 I have but Thee, my Father; let Thy Spirit
    Be with me then to comfort and uphold;
  No gate of pearl, no branch of palm I merit,
    Nor street of shining gold.

5 Suffice it if—my good and ill unreckoned,
    And both forgiven through Thine abounding
        grace—
  I find myself by hands familiar beckoned
    Unto my fitting place.

6 Some humble door among Thy many mansions,
    Some sheltering shade where sin and striving
        cease,
  And flows for ever through heaven's green
        expansions
    The river of Thy peace.

7 There from the music round about me stealing
    I fain would learn the new and holy song,
  And find at last, beneath Thy trees of healing,
    The life for which I long.

J. G. Whittier, 1802–92.

XIV.

DIRECTIONS FOR CHANTING

IT cannot be too strongly stressed that the chants should be sung in speech-rhythm. This means that the natural flow and accentuation of the words must be preserved, and every word be sung with the deliberation of a good actor declaiming dignified prose, and not subordinated to a melody with a fixed rhythm. The notes of the chant, in fact, have no definite time values; the chant is simply a series of notes on which the verse is recited.

The "*recitation*" (*i.e.* the words preceding the first bar-line) should be unhurried, and pass without any pause into the following part of the chant. There must be no counting of beats in either part.

The *bar-lines* in the words correspond to the bar-lines in the chant. The *dot* shows the point where the chord changes inside a bar. In a four-syllable bar, two syllables are to be sung to each chord unless the dot indicates otherwise. An *asterisk* (*) indicates a place for a breath to be taken. A *slur* under the words at the end of a verse or half-verse (*e.g.* Te Deum, verse 4) indicates that the singing should continue at that point without a break. *Commas etc.* are to be treated as in ordinary speech—many call for no break whatever. A final "*-ed*" is to be pronounced as a separate syllable only when it is customary to do so in normal speech (*e.g.* " bless-ed ").

A. CANTICLES

For the following Canticles see the Psalm in its proper sequence:

Deus misereatur	Psalm 67	813
Venite	Psalm 95	821
Cantate Domino	Psalm 98	823
Jubilate	Psalm 100	824

778

TE DEUM LAUDAMUS

1 We praise | Thee O | God:
  We acknowledge | Thee to | be the | Lord.

2 All the earth doth | worship | Thee:
  The | Father | ever|lasting.

3 To Thee all angels | cry a|loud:
  The heavens and | all the | powers·there|in.

4 To Thee | cherubim·and | seraphim: ◡
  Con|tin·ual|ly do | cry

5 Holy | holy | holy:
  Lord | God of | Saba|oth,

6 Heaven and | earth are | full: ◡
  Of the | majes·ty | of Thy | glory.

7 The glorious company of the a|postles | praise
  Thee:
  The goodly fellowship | of the | prophets |
  praise Thee;

8 The noble army of | martyrs | praise Thee:
  The holy church throughout all the | world·
  doth ac|knowledge | Thee,

9 The Father of an | infin · ite | majesty:
  Thine honourable true and only Son, * also
  the | Holy | Ghost the | Comforter.

10 Thou art the King of | glory · O | Christ:
   Thou art the ever|lasting | Son · of the | Father.

11 When Thou tookest upon Thee to de|liver | man:
   Thou didst not ab|hor the | Virgin's | womb.

12 When Thou hadst overcome the | sharpness · of |
     death:
   Thou didst open the kingdom of | heaven · to |
     all be|lievers.

13 Thou sittest at the | right hand · of | God:
   In the | glory | of the | Father.

14 We be|lieve that | Thou: ⌣
   Shalt | come to | be our | Judge.

15 We therefore pray Thee | help Thy | servants:
   Whom Thou hast re|deemed · with Thy |
     precious | blood.

2nd half

16 Make them to be numbered | with Thy | saints:
   In | glory | ever|lasting.

17 O Lord save Thy people and | bless Thine |
     heritage:
   Govern them and | lift them | up for | ever.

18 Day by day we | magni · fy | Thee:
   And we worship Thy | name · ever | world
     with · out | end.

19 Vouchsafe O Lord to keep us this | day with·out |
    sin :
    O Lord have mercy up|on us·have | mercy·
    up|on us;

20 O Lord let Thy mercy lighten upon us * as our |
    trust·is in | Thee :
    O Lord in Thee have I trusted, * let me | never |
    be con|founded.

779

MAGNIFICAT

LUKE i. 46–55.

1 My soul doth | magnify·the | Lord :
    And my spirit hath re|joiced in | God my |
    Saviour.

2 For | He hath·re|garded : ◡
    The | lowli·ness | of His | handmaiden.

3 For be|hold from | henceforth :
    All gener|ations·shall | call me | blessed,

4 For He that is | mighty·hath | magnified me :
    And | holy | is His | name,

5 And His mercy is on | them that | fear him :
    Through|out all | gener|ations.

6 He hath shewed | strength·with His | arm :
    He hath scattered the proud in the imagin-|
    ation | of their | hearts.

7 He hath put down the | mighty from their | seat :
    And hath ex|alted·the | humble·and | meek.

8 He hath filled the | hungry with good | things:
And the rich He | hath sent | empty·a|way.

9 He re|membering·His | mercy:
Hath | holpen·His | servant | Israel,

10 As He | promised to our | forefathers:
Abraham | and his | seed for | ever.

Glory | be·to the | Father:
And to the Son | and·to the | Holy | Ghost;
As it was in the be|ginning·is | now:
And ever shall be, | world·without | end. A|men

780

BENEDICTUS
LUKE i. 68–79.

1 Blessed be the Lord | God of | Israel:
For He hath visited | and re|deemed His | people,

2 And hath raised up a mighty sal|vation | for us:
In the | house·of His | servant | David,

3 As He spake by the mouth of His | holy | prophets:
Which have been | since the | world be|gan,

4 That we should be | saved·from our | enemies:
And from the | hands of | all that | hate us;

5 To perform the mercy promised to our fore-
fathers, * and to remember His | holy | covenant:
To perform the oath which He sware to our
forefather | Abraham·that | He would | give
us,

6 That we being delivered out of the hand of our
   enemies * might | serve Him without | fear:
   In holiness and righteousness before Him | all
   the | days·of our | life.

7 And thou child shalt be called the | prophet of
   the | highest:
   For thou shalt go before the face of the | Lord·
   to pre|pare His | ways,

8 To give knowledge of salvation | unto·His |
   people:
   For the re|mission | of their | sins,

9 Through the tender | mercy of our | God:
   Whereby the dayspring from on | high hath |
   visit·ed | us,

10 To give light to them that sit in darkness and in
   the | shadow·of | death:
   And to guide our feet | into·the | way of |
   peace.
                                         GLORIA.

781

NUNC DIMITTIS

LUKE ii. 29–32.

1 Lord now lettest Thou Thy servant de|part in |
   peace:
   Ac|cording | to Thy | word.

2 For mine eyes have | seen·Thy sal|vation:
   Which Thou hast pre|pared before the | face
   of·all | people,

3 To be a light to | lighten·the | Gentiles:
   And to be the | glory of Thy | people | Israel.
                                         GLORIA.

782

GLORIA IN EXCELSIS

1 Glory be to | God on | high:
   And in earth | peace, good|will·towards | men.

2 We praise Thee, we | bless·Thee, we | worship
   Thee:
   We glorify Thee, we give thanks to | Thee for |
   Thy great | glory,

3 O Lord God, heavenly King, God the | Father·
   Al|mighty:
   O Lord, the only begotten | Son | Jesus | Christ.

4 O Lord God, Lamb of God, | Son·of the | Father:
   That takest away the sins of the | world have |
   mercy·up|on us.

5 Thou that takest away the sins of the world have |
   mercy·up|on us:
   Thou that takest away the sins of the | world
   re|ceive our | prayer.

6 Thou that sittest at the right hand of God the
   Father * have | mercy·up|on us:
   For Thou only art holy, | Thou·only | art the |
   Lord.

7 Thou only, O Christ, with the Holy | Ghost·art
   most | high:
   In the | glory·of | God the | Father.

783

SALVATOR MUNDI

1 O Saviour of the world the | Son Lord | Jesus:
   Stir up Thy strength and | help us·we | humbly·
   be|seech Thee.

2 By Thy Cross and precious blood Thou | hast re|deemed us:
   Save us and | help us·we | humbly·be|seech Thee.

3 Thou didst save Thy disciples when | ready·to | perish:
   Hear us and | save us·we | humbly·be|seech Thee.

4 Let the pitifulness of | Thy great | mercy : ‿
   Loose us from our | sins we | humbly·be|seech Thee.

5 Make it appear that Thou art our Saviour and | mighty·De|liverer:
   O save us that we may | praise Thee·we | humbly·be|seech Thee.

6 Draw near according to Thy promise from the | throne of·Thy | glory:
   Look down and hear our | crying·we | humbly· be|seech Thee.

7 Come again and dwell with us, O | Lord Christ | Jesus:
   Abide with us for | ever·we | humbly·be|seech Thee.

8 And when Thou shalt appear with | power and great | glory:
   May we be made like unto | Thee·in Thy | glorious | kingdom.

9 Thanks be to | Thee, O | Lord:
   Halle|lujah. | A|men.

784

BENEDICITE

(Canticle of the Three Children)

1 O all ye works of the Lord | bless·ye the | Lord:
 Praise Him and | magni·fy | Him for | ever.

2 O ye angels of the Lord | bless·ye the | Lord:
 Praise Him and | magni·fy | Him for | ever.

3 O ye heavens | bless·ye the | Lord:
 Praise Him and | magni·fy | Him for | ever.

4 O ye sun, moon and stars | bless·ye the | Lord:
 Praise Him and | magni·fy | Him for | ever.

5 O ye winter and summer | bless·ye the | Lord:
 Praise Him and | magni·fy | Him for | ever.

6 O ye nights and days | bless·ye the | Lord:
 Praise Him and | magni·fy | Him for | ever.

7 O let the earth | bless the | Lord:
 Yea let it praise Him and | magni·fy | Him
 for | ever.

8 O ye seas and floods | bless·ye the | Lord:
 Praise Him and | magni·fy | Him for | ever.

9 O all ye that move in the waters | bless·ye the |
 Lord:
 Praise Him and | magni·fy | Him for | ever.

10 O ye fowls of the air | bless·ye the | Lord:
 Praise Him and | magni·fy | Him for | ever.

11 O ye beasts and cattle | bless·ye the | Lord:
 Praise Him and | magni·fy | Him for | ever.

12 O ye children of men | bless·ye the | Lord:
 Praise Him and | magni·fy | Him for | ever.

13 O ye servants of the Lord | bless·ye the | Lord:
   Praise Him and | magni·fy | Him for | ever.

14 O ye souls of the righteous | bless·ye the | Lord:
   Praise Him and | magni·fy | Him for | ever.

2nd half

15 O ye holy and humble men of heart | bless·ye
   the | Lord:
   Praise Him and | magni·fy | Him for | ever.

GLORIA.

785

THE EASTER CANTICLE

1 Christ our Passover is | sácri·ficed | for us:
   Therefore | let us | keep the | feast,

2 Not with the old leaven, * nor with the leaven of |
   malice·and | wickedness:
   But with the unleavened | bread·of sin|cerity·
   and | truth.

3 Christ being risen from the dead | dieth·no | more:
   Death hath | no more·dom|inion | over Him.

4 For in that He died, * He died | once·unto | sin:
   But in that He liveth, * He | liveth | unto | God.

5 Likewise reckon ye also yourselves to be dead in-|
   deed·unto | sin:
   But alive unto God through | Jesus | Christ
   our | Lord.

6 Christ is | risen from the | dead:
   And become the | firstfruits·of | them that |
   slept.

7 For since by | man came | death:
   By man came also the resur|rection | of the |dead.

8 For as in | Adam·all | die:
  Even so in Christ shall | all be | made a|live.

9 Thanks be to God which | giveth us the | victory:
  Through our | Lord | Jesus | Christ.

786

LET US NOW PRAISE FAMOUS MEN

ECCLESIASTICUS xliv.

1 Let us now praise | famous | men:
  And our | fathers | that be|gat us.

2 The Lord hath wrought great | glory·by | them:
  Through His great | power | from·the be-|
  ginning.

3 Such as did bear rule in their kingdoms, * men
  re|nowned·for their | power:
  Giving counsel by their under|standing and
  de|claring | prophecies;

4 Leaders of the people | by their | counsels:
  And by their knowledge of | learning | meet·
  for the | people,

5 Wise and eloquent | in·their in|structions:
  Such as found out musical tunes and re|cited |
  verses·in | writing;

6 Rich men | furnished with a|bility:
  Living peaceably | in their | habi|tations;

7 All these were honoured in their | gener|ations;
  And were the | glory | of their | times.

8 There be of them that have left a | name be|hind
  them:
  That their | praises | might·be re|ported.

9 And some there be which have | no me|morial:
    Who are perished as | though·they had | never |
    been,

10 And are become as though they had | never·
    been | born :
    And their | children | after | them.

11 But these were | merci·ful | men :
    Whose righteousness | hath not | been for-|
    gotten ;

12 With their seed shall continually remain a | good
    in|heritance :
    And their | children are with|in the | covenant.

13 Their seed | standeth | fast :
    And their | children | for their | sakes.

14 Their seed shall re|main for|ever :
    And their | glory·shall | not be blotted | out.

15 Their bodies are | buried·in | peace :
    But their name | liveth·for | ever|more.

16 The people will | tell of·their | wisdom :
    And the congre|gation·will | shew·forth their |
    praise.

                                   GLORIA.

B. PSALMS

The text for the Psalms is that of the Authorised Version, though a Revised Version or other reading has occasionally been used.

787

PSALM 1

The Two Ways

1 Blessed is the man that walketh not in the counsel |
    of the · un|godly:
  Nor standeth in the way of sinners, * nor | sitteth
  in the | seat · of the | scornful.

2 But his delight is in the | law · of the | Lord:
  And in His law doth he | medi · tate | day and |
    night.

3 And he shall be like a tree planted by the | rivers ·
    of | water:
  That bringeth | forth his | fruit · in his | season.

4 His leaf also | shall not | wither:
  And whatso|ever · he | doeth · shall | prosper.

5 The ungodly | are not | so:
  But are like the chaff which the | wind | driveth ·
  a|way.

6 Therefore the ungodly shall not | stand · in the |
    judgment:
  Nor sinners in the congre|gation | of the |
  righteous.

7 For the Lord knoweth the | way · of the | righteous:
  But the | way · of the un|godly · shall | perish.

GLORIA.

788

PSALM 5 (Selection)

A Morning Prayer

1 Give ear to my | words O | Lord:
Con|sider·my | medi|tation.

2 Hearken unto the voice of my cry, my | King·and
my | God:
For unto | Thee·will I | make my | prayer.

3 My voice shalt Thou hear in the | morning·O |
Lord:
In the morning will I direct my prayer unto |
Thee and | will look | up.

4 As for me, I will come into Thy house in the
multitude | of Thy | mercy:
And in Thy fear will I worship | toward·Thy |
holy | temple.

5 Lead me O Lord in Thy righteousness be|cause of·
mine | enemies:
Make Thy way | straight be|fore my | face.

6 Let all those that put their trust in | Thee re|joice:
Let them | ever | shout for | joy.

7 Because Thou de|fendest | them:
Let them also that love Thy | name be | joyful·
in | Thee.

8 For Thou Lord wilt | bless the | righteous:
With favour wilt Thou | compass·him | as·with
a | shield.

GLORIA.

789

PSALM 8

GOD'S HIGH CALLING OF MAN

1 O Lord our Lord, how excellent is Thy name in |
    all the | earth:
  Who hast set Thy | glory·a|bove the | heavens.

2 Out of the mouths of babes and sucklings hast
    Thou ordained strength be|cause of·Thine |
    enemies:
  That Thou mightest still the | ene·my | and·the
    a|venger.

3 When I consider Thy heavens, the | work of·Thy |
    fingers:
  The moon and the | stars which | Thou·hast
    or|dained,

4 What is man that Thou art | mindful·of | him:
  And the son of man | that Thou | visit·est |
    him?

5 For Thou hast made him a little | lower than the |
    angels:
  And hast | crowned him·with | glory·and |
    honour.

6 Thou madest him to have dominion over the |
    works of·Thy | hands:
  Thou hast put | all things | under·his | feet,

7 All | sheep and | oxen:
  Yea and the | beasts | of the | field,

8 The fowl of the air and the | fish·of the | sea:
  And whatsoever | passeth through the | paths·
    of the | sea.

9 O | Lord our | Lord:
  How excellent is Thy | name in | all the | earth.
                                    GLORIA.

790

PSALM 15

THE TRUE WORSHIPPER

1 Lord who shall a|bide·in Thy | tabernacle:
Who shall | dwell·in Thy | holy | hill ?

2 He that walketh uprightly and | worketh |
righteousness:
And | speaketh·the | truth·from his | heart;

3 He that backbiteth not | with his | tongue:
Nor doeth evil to his neighbour, nor taketh up
a re|proach a|gainst his | neighbour; .

4 In whose eyes a vile person | is con|temned:
But he honoureth | them that | fear the | Lord;

5 He that sweareth to his own hurt and | changeth |
not:
He that putteth not out his money to usury, *
nor taketh re|ward a|gainst the | innocent.

6 He that | doeth·these | things:
Shall | ne|ver be | moved.

GLORIA.

791

PSALM 16 (Selection)

LIFE IN GOD NOW AND FOR EVER

1 Preserve | me O | God:
For in | Thee·do I | put my | trust.

2 I have said unto the Lord, | Thou art·my | Lord:
I | have no | good be·yond | Thee.

3 As for the saints that are | in the | earth:
   They are the excellent in | whom is | all·my
     de|light.

4 The Lord is the portion of mine inheritance and |
     of my | cup:
   Thou | shalt main|tain my | lot.

5 The lines are fallen unto me in | pleasant |
     places:
   Yea I | have a | goodly | heritage.

6 I will bless the Lord who hath | given·me|
   counsel:
   My heart also in|structeth·me | in the | night
   seasons.

7 I have set the Lord | always·be|fore me:
   Because He is at my right hand | I shall | not
   be | moved.

8 Therefore my heart is glad and my | soul re-|
   joiceth:
   My flesh | also·shall | rest in | hope.

9 For Thou wilt not leave my | soul·in the | grave:
   Neither wilt Thou suffer Thine | holy·one to |
   see cor|ruption.

10 Thou wilt shew me the | path of | life:
   In Thy presence is fulness of joy; * at Thy
   right hand there are | pleasures·for | ever-|
   more.

                            GLORIA.

792

PSALM 19

GOD'S GLORY IN THE HEAVENS AND IN HIS WORD

1 The heavens declare the | glory·of | God:
   And the | firma·ment | sheweth·His | handy-
   work.

2 Day unto day | utter·eth | speech:
  And | night·unto | night·sheweth | knowledge.

3 There is no | speech nor | language:
  Where their | voice | is not | heard.

4 Their sound is gone out through | all the | earth:
  And their | words·to the | end·of the | world.

5 In them hath He set a tabernacle | for the | sun:
  Which is as a bridegroom coming out of his
  chamber, * and rejoiceth as a | strong·man
  to | run a | race.

6 His going forth is from the end of the heaven, *
  and his | circuit·unto the | ends of it:
  And there is nothing | hid·from the | heat
  there|of.

7 The law of the Lord is perfect, con|verting·the |
  soul:
  The testimony of the Lord is | sure·making |
  wise the | simple.

8 The statutes of the Lord are right, re|joicing·
  the | heart:
  The commandment of the Lord is | pure,
  en|lightening·the | eyes.

9 The fear of the Lord is clean, en|during·for|ever:
  The judgments of the Lord are true and |
  righteous | alto|gether.

10 More to be desired are they than gold, * yea
   than | much fine | gold:
   Sweeter also than | honey | and the | honey-
   comb.

11 Moreover by them is Thy | servant | warned:
   And in keeping of them | there is | great
   re|ward.

12 Who can under|stand his | errors ? :
   Cleanse Thou | me from | secret | faults.

13 Keep back Thy servant also from pre|sumptuous |
   sins :
   Let them not | have do|minion | over me.

14 Then shall | I be | upright :
   And I shall be innocent | from the | great
   trans|gression.

2nd half

15 Let the words of my mouth and the meditation
   of my heart * be acceptable | in Thy | sight :
   O Lord my | strength and | my re|deemer.

                                    GLORIA.

793

PSALM 22 (Selection)

OUR FATHERS' GOD AND OURS

1 Thou art holy O Thou that inhabitest the |
   praises·of | Israel :
   Our fathers trusted in Thee, * they | trusted·
   and | Thou·didst de|liver them.

2 They cried unto Thee and | were de|livered :
   They trusted in Thee | and were | not con-|
   founded.

3 Be not far from me for | trouble·is | near :
   For | there is | none to | help.

4 Be not Thou far from | me O | Lord :
   O my | strength | haste·Thee to | help me.

5 I will declare Thy name | unto·my | brethren :
   In the midst of the congre|gation | will I |
   praise Thee.

6 O praise the Lord | ye that | fear Him:
  All ye the seed of Jacob glorify Him, * and
  fear Him | all·ye the | seed of | Israel.

7 For He hath not despised nor abhorred the
  affliction | of·the af|flicted:
  Neither hath He hid His face from him, * but
  when he | cried·unto | Him He | heard.

8 My praise shall be of Thee in the |great·congre-|
  gation:
  I will pay my | vows·before | them that | fear
  Him.

9 The meek shall | eat·and be | satisfied:
  They shall | praise the | Lord that | seek Him.

10 Your heart shall | live for | ever:
   All the ends of the world shall re|member·
   and | turn·to the | Lord.

11 And all the | kindreds of the | nations:
   Shall | wor|ship be|fore Thee.

12 For the kingdom | is the | Lord's:
   And He is the | governor·a|mong the | nations

GLORIA.

794

PSALM 23

THE GOOD SHEPHERD

1 The Lord | is my | shepherd:
  I | shall | not | want.

2 He maketh me to lie down in | green | pastures:
  He leadeth me be|side the | still | waters.

3 He res|toreth·my | soul:
   He leadeth me in the paths of | righteous·ness |
   for His | name's sake.

4 Yea though I walk through the valley of the
   shadow of death, * I will | fear no | evil:
   For Thou art with me, Thy | rod·and Thy |
   staff they | comfort me.

5 Thou preparest a table before me in the | presence
   of mine | enemies:
   Thou anointest my head with | oil, my | cup·
   runneth | over.

6 Surely goodness and mercy shall follow me all
   the | days·of my | life:
   And I will dwell in the | house·of the | Lord
   for | ever.

GLORIA.

795

PSALM 24

THE KING OF GLORY

1 The earth is the Lord's and the | fulness·there|of:
   The world and | they that | dwell there|in.

2 For He hath founded it up|on the | seas:
   And es|tablished it up|on the | floods.

3 Who shall ascend into the | hill·of the | Lord:
   Or who shall | stand·in His | holy | place?

4 He that hath clean hands and a | pure | heart:
   Who hath not lifted up his soul unto | vanity·
   nor | sworn de|ceitfully.

5 He shall receive the | blessing of the | Lord:
   And righteousness from the | God of | his
   sal|vation.

6 This is the generation of | them that | seek Him:
That seek Thy | face O | God of | Jacob.

7 Lift up your heads O ye gates, * and be ye lift up
ye ever|lasting | doors:
And the King of | glory | shall come | in.

8 Who is this | King of | glory?:
The Lord strong and mighty, the | Lord |
mighty·in | battle.

9 Lift up your heads O ye gates, * even lift them up
ye ever|lasting | doors:
And the King of | glory | shall come | in.

10 Who is this | King of | glory?:
The Lord of hosts, | He·is the | King of | glory.

GLORIA.

796

PSALM 25 (Selection)

TRUST IN GOD'S MERCY

1 Unto Thee O Lord do I lift up my soul, * O my
God I | trust in | Thee:
Let me not be ashamed, * let not mine |
ene·mies | triumph | over me.

2 Yea let none that wait on | Thee·be a|shamed:
Let them be ashamed which trans|gress with-|
out | cause.

3 Shew me Thy ways O Lord and | teach me·Thy |
paths:
Lead me | in Thy | truth and | teach me.

4 For Thou art the God of | my sal|vation:
On | Thee·do I | wait·all the | day.

5 Remember O Lord Thy tender mercies and Thy |
    loving|kindnesses :
    For | they have · been | ever · of | old.

6 Remember not the sins of my youth | nor · my
    trans|gressions :
    According to Thy mercy remember Thou me
    for Thy | goodness' | sake O | Lord.

7 Good and upright | is the | Lord :
    Therefore will He teach | sinners | in the | way.

8 The meek will He | guide in | judgment :
    And the | meek · will He | teach His | way.

9 All the paths of the Lord are | mercy · and | truth :
    Unto such as keep His | cove · nant | and His |
    testimonies.

10 For Thy | name's · sake O | Lord :
    Pardon mine in|iquity · for | it is | great.

11 What man is he that | feareth · the | Lord ? :
    Him shall He teach in the | way that | He shall |
    choose.

12 The secret of the Lord is with | them that | fear
    Him :
    And | He will | shew them · His | covenant.

                                 GLORIA.

797

PSALM 27 (Selection)

The Lord is My Light

1 The Lord is my light and my salvation. | Whom ·
    shall I | fear ? :
    The Lord is the strength of my life. * Of |
    whom · shall I | be a|fraid ?

2 Though an host should encamp against me, my |
heart·shall not | fear:
Though war should rise against me, * in | this
will | I be | confident.

3 One thing have I desired of the Lord, | that·will
I | seek after:
That I may dwell in the house of the | Lord·
all the | days of·my | life,

4 To behold the | beauty of the | Lord:
And to en|quire | in His | temple.

5 For in the | time of | trouble:
He shall | hide me | in·His pa|vilion.

6 In the secret of His tabernacle | shall He | hide me:
He shall | set me·up|on a | rock.

7 Hear O Lord when I | cry·with my | voice:
Have mercy | also·up|on me·and | answer me.

8 When Thou saidst, | Seek ye·My | face:
My heart said unto Thee, Thy | face Lord |
will I | seek.

9 Thou hast | been my | help:
Leave me not, neither forsake me O | God
of | my sal|vation.

10 Teach me Thy | way O | Lord:
And | lead me | in a·plain | path.

11 I had fainted unless I had believed to see the |
goodness of the | Lord:
In the | land | of the | living.

12 Wait on the Lord, | be of·good | courage:
And He shall strengthen thine heart; * | wait
I | say·on the | Lord.

                                    GLORIA.

798

REJOICING IN DELIVERANCE

1 I will extol Thee O Lord for Thou hast | lifted ·
me | up :
And hast not made my | foes · to re|joice · over |
me.

2 O Lord my God I | cried · unto | Thee :
And | Thou hast | heal-ed | me.

3 Sing unto the Lord O ye | saints of | His :
And give thanks at the re|membrance | of His |
holiness.

4 For His anger endureth but a moment; * in His |
favour · is | life :
Weeping may endure for a night, * but | joy ·
cometh | in the | morning.

5 And in my prosperity I said, I shall | never · be |
moved :
Lord by Thy favour Thou hast made my |
mountain · to | stand | strong.

6 Thou didst hide Thy face and | I was | troubled :
I cried to Thee O Lord, * and unto the | Lord I |
made · suppli|cation.

7 Hear O Lord and have | mercy · up|on me :
O | Lord be | Thou my | helper.

8 Thou hast turned for me my | mourning into |
dancing :
Thou hast put off my sackcloth and | girded |
me with | gladness.

9 To the end that my soul may sing praise to Thee
and | not be | silent:
O Lord my God, I will give | thanks·unto |
Thee for | ever.

GLORIA.

799

PSALM 31 (Selection)

THE TRUSTWORTHINESS OF GOD

1 In Thee O Lord do I | put my | trust:
Let me never be ashamed, * de|liver·me | in
Thy | righteousness.

2 Bow down thine ear to me, de|liver·me | speedily:
Be Thou my strong rock for an | house·of
de|fence to | save me.

3 For Thou art my | rock·and my | fortress:
Therefore for Thy | name's sake | lead me·
and | guide me.

4 Into Thine hand I com|mit my | spirit:
Thou hast re|deemed me·O | Lord·God of |
truth.

5 I will be glad and re|joice·in Thy | mercy:
For Thou hast considered my trouble, * Thou
hast | known my | soul·in ad|versities,

6 And hast not shut me up into the | hand·of the |
enemy:
Thou hast set my | feet·in a | large | room.

7 O how great is Thy goodness which Thou hast
laid up for | them that | fear Thee:
Which Thou hast wrought for them that trust
in Thee be|fore the | sons of | men.

8 Thou shalt hide them in the secret of Thy
presence from the | pride of | man:
Thou shalt keep them secretly in a pa|vilion
from the | strife of | tongues.

9 Blessed | be the | Lord:
For He hath showed me His marvellous |
kindness | in a·strong | city.

10 For I said in my haste, I am cut off from
be|fore Thine | eyes:
Nevertheless Thou heardest the voice of my
suppli|cations when I | cried·unto | Thee.

11 O love the Lord all | ye His | saints:
For the Lord preserveth the faithful, * and
plentifully re|wardeth·the | proud | doer.

12 Be of good courage and He shall | strengthen·
your | heart:
All | ye that | hope·in the | Lord.

GLORIA.

800

PSALM 32 (Selection)

THE JOY OF FORGIVENESS

1 Blessed is he whose transgression is forgiven, *
whose | sin is | covered:
Blessed is the man unto whom the Lord
imputeth not iniquity, * and in whose |
spirit·there | is no | guile.

2 I acknowledged my | sin·unto | Thee:
And mine in|iqui·ty | have I·not | hid.

3 I said, I will confess my transgressions | unto·the |
Lord:
And Thou forgavest the in|iqui · ty | of my | sin.

4 For this shall everyone that is godly | pray·unto |
  Thee:
  In a | time·when Thou | mayest·be | found.

5 Surely in the | floods of·great | waters:
  Thy shall | not come | nigh·unto | him.

6 Thou art my hiding-place, * Thou shalt pre|serve
  me·from | trouble:
  Thou shalt compass me a|bout with | songs·of
  de|liverance.

7 I will instruct thee and teach thee in the way
  which | thou shalt | go:
  I will | guide thee | with mine | eye.

8 Be ye not as the horse or as the mule which
  have | no·under|standing:
  Whose mouth must be held in with bit and
  bridle, * else they will | not come | near·
  unto | thee.

9 Many sorrows shall | be·to the | wicked:
  But he that trusteth in the Lord | mercy·
  shall | compass him a|bout.

10 Be glad in the Lord and re|joice ye | righteous:
   And shout for joy all | ye·that are | upright·
   in | heart.

GLORIA.

801

PSALM 33 (Selection)

THE STRENGTH OF A NATION

1 Blessed is the nation whose | God·is the | Lord:
  And the people whom He hath | chosen for
  His | own in|heritance.

2 The Lord | looketh·from | heaven:
   He beholdeth | all the | sons of | men.

3 From the place of His | habi|tation:
   He looketh upon all the in|habi·tants | of the | earth.

4 He fashioneth their | hearts a|like:
   He con|sider·eth | all their | works.

5 There is no king saved by the multitude | of an | host:
   A mighty man is not de|livered | by much | strength.

6 Behold the eye of the Lord is upon | them that | fear Him:
   Upon | them that | hope·in His | mercy.

7 To deliver their | soul from | death:
   And to | keep·them a|live in | famine.

8 Our soul | waited for the | Lord:
   He is our | help | and our | shield.

9 For our heart shall re|joice in | Him:
   Because we have trusted | in His | holy | name.

10 Let Thy mercy O | Lord·be up|on us:
   According | as we | hope in | Thee.

GLORIA.

802

PSALM 34 (Selection)

THE SECRET OF LIFE

1 I will bless the | Lord at | all times:
   His praise shall con|tinual·ly | be·in my | mouth.

2 My soul shall make her | boast · in the | Lord :
  The humble shall | hear there|of · and be | glad.

3 O magnify the | Lord with | me :
  And let us ex|alt His | name to|gether.

4 I sought the Lord | and He | heard me :
  And de|livered me from | all my | fears.

5 They looked unto Him | and were | lightened :
  And their | faces · were | not a|shamed.

6 This poor man cried and the Lord heard him, *
  and saved him out of | all his | troubles :
  The angel of the Lord encampeth round them
  that | fear Him | and de|livereth them.

7 O taste and see that the | Lord is | good :
  Blessed is the | man that | trusteth · in | Him.

8 O fear the Lord | ye His | saints :
  For there is no | want to | them that | fear Him.

9 The young lions do lack and | suffer | hunger :
  But they that seek the Lord shall | not want |
  any · good | thing.

10 Come ye children | hearken unto | me :
  I will | teach you · the | fear · of the | Lord.

11 What man is he that de|sireth | life :
  And loveth many | days that | he may · see |
  good ?

12 Keep thy tongue from evil, and thy lips from |
  speaking | guile :
  Depart from evil and do good, | seek peace |
  and pur|sue it.

13 The eyes of the Lord are up|on the | righteous :
  And His ears are | open | unto · their | cry.

14 The face of the Lord is against | them that·do |
    evil:
    To cut off the re|membrance·of | them·from
    the | earth.

15 The righteous cry and the | Lord | heareth:
    And delivereth them | out of | all their |
    troubles.

16 The Lord is nigh unto them that are of a |
    broken | heart:
    And saveth such as | be·of a | contrite | spirit.

17 Many are the af|flictions of the | righteous:
    But the Lord de|livereth·him | out of·them |
    all.

18 The Lord redeemeth the | soul of·His | servants:
    And none of them that | trust in | Him·shall
    be | desolate.
                     GLORIA.

803

PSALM 36 (Selection)

THE FOUNTAIN OF LIFE

1 Thy mercy O Lord is | in the | heavens:
    And Thy faithfulness | reacheth | unto·the |
    clouds.

2 Thy righteousness is like the great mountains, *
    Thy judgments | are a·great | deep:
    O Lord Thou pre|servest | man and | beast.

3 How excellent is Thy loving|kindness·O | God:
    Therefore the children of men put their trust
    under the | shadow | of Thy | wings.

4 They shall be abundantly satisfied with the | fatness
        of Thy | house :
    And Thou shalt make them drink of the | river |
        of Thy | pleasures,

5 For with Thee is the | fountain · of | life :
    In Thy | light shall | we see | light.

6 O continue Thy loving-kindness unto | them that |
        know Thee :
    And Thy righteousness | to the | upright · in |
        heart.

                                        GLORIA.

804

PSALM 37 (Selection)

A CALL TO PATIENCE

1 Fret not thyself because of | evil|doers :
    Neither be thou envious against the | workers |
        of in|iquity,

2 For they shall soon be cut down | like the | grass :
    And | wither | as the · green | herb.

3 Trust in the | Lord and · do | good :
    So shalt thou dwell in the land, and | veri · ly |
        thou shalt · be | fed.

4 Delight thyself also | in the | Lord :
    And He shall | give thee the de|sires of · thine |
        heart.

5 Commit thy way | unto · the | Lord :
    Trust also in Him and | He shall | bring it · to |
        pass.

6 And He shall bring forth thy righteousness | as
the | light:
And thy | judgment | as the | noon-day.

7 O | rest·in the | Lord:
And wait | patient|ly for | Him.

8 Fret not thyself because of him who prospereth |
in his | way:
Because of the man who bringeth | wicked·
de|vices·to | pass.

9 Cease from anger and for|sake | wrath:
Fret not thy|self in any|wise to·do | evil.

10 For evil-doers shall | be cut | off:
But those that wait upon the Lord | they·shall
in|herit·the | earth.

11 For yet a little while and the wicked | shall not |
be:
Yea thou shalt diligently consider his | place·
and it | shall not | be.

12 But the meek shall in|herit·the | earth:
And shall delight themselves | in·the a|bund-
ance·of | peace.

GLORIA.

805

PSALM 40 (Selection)

WHAT SHALL I RENDER?

1 I waited patiently | for the | Lord:
And He inclined unto | me and | heard my |
cry.

2 He brought me out of an horrible pit, * out of
the | miry | clay:
And set my feet upon a | rock·and es|tab-
lished·my | goings.

3 And He hath put a new song in my mouth, even |
praise·to our | God:
Many shall see it and | fear and | trust·in the |
Lord.

4 Blessed is the man that maketh the | Lord His |
trust:
And respecteth not the proud, nor such as |
turn a|side to | lies.

5 Many O Lord my God are Thy wonderful works
which | Thou hast | done:
And Thy thoughts which are towards us, * they
cannot be reckoned up in | order | unto |
Thee.

6 If I would declare and | speak of | them:
They are | more than | can be | numbered.

7 Sacrifice and offering Thou didst | not de|sire:
Mine ears hast Thou opened, * burnt offering
and sin offering | hast Thou | not re|quired.

8 Then said I, lo I come; * in the volume of the
book it is | written·of | me:
I delight to do Thy will O my God, * yea Thy |
law·is with|in my | heart.

9 Withhold not Thou Thy tender mercies from |
me O | Lord:
Let Thy loving-kindness and Thy | truth
con|tinually·pre|serve me.

10 Let all those that seek Thee rejoice and be | glad
in | Thee:
Let such as love Thy salvation say con|tinually·
the | Lord be | magnified.

11 But I am | poor and | needy:
    Yet the | Lord | thinketh·up|on me.

12 Thou art my | help and my de|liverer:
    Make no | tarry·ing | O my | God.

GLORIA.

806

PSALMS 42 and 43 (Selection)

HOPE THOU IN GOD

1 As the hart panteth | after·the | waterbrooks:
    So panteth my | soul·after | Thee O | God.

2 My soul thirsteth for God, for the | living | God·
    When shall I | come·and ap|pear be·fore |
    God?

3 My tears have been my meat | day and | night:
    While they continually say unto me, | Where
    is | now thy | God?

4 When I re|member·these | things:
    I pour | out my | soul in | me.

5 For I had | gone·with the | multitude:
    I went with | them·to the | house of | God

6 With the voice of | joy and | praise:
    With a | multi·tude | that kept | holy-day.

7 Why art thou cast down | O my | soul:
    And why art | thou dis|quieted·with|in me?

8 Hope | thou in | God:
    For I shall yet praise Him who is the health
    of my | counten·ance | and my | God.

9 The Lord will command His loving|kindness in
    the | daytime:
    And in the night His song shall be with me, *
    and my | prayer·to the | God of·my | life.

10 I will say unto | God my | rock:
    Why hast | Thou for|gotten | me?

11 Why | go I | mourning:
    Because of the op|pression | of the | enemy?

12 As with a sword in my bones my | enemies·
    re|proach me:
    While they say daily unto me, | Where is | now
    thy | God?

13 Why art thou cast down | O my | soul:
    And why art | thou dis|quieted·with|in me?

14 Hope | thou in | God :
    For I shall yet praise Him who is the health of
    my | counten·ance | and my | God.

15 O send out Thy light and Thy truth, | let them |
    lead me:
    Let them bring me unto Thy holy | hill and | to
    Thy | tabernacles.

16 Then will I go unto the altar of God, unto God
    my ex|ceeding | joy:
    Yea upon the harp will I | praise Thee·O | God
    my | God.

17 Why art thou cast down | O my | soul:
    And why art | thou dis|quieted·with|in me?

18 Hope | thou in | God:
    For I shall yet praise Him who is the health
    of my | counten·ance | and my | God.

GLORIA.

807

PSALM 46

GOD OUR REFUGE

1 God is our | refuge · and | strength :
   A very | present | help in | trouble.

2 Therefore will not we fear though the | earth · be re|moved :
   And though the mountains be carried | into · the | midst · of the | sea.

3 Though the waters thereof | roar · and be | troubled :
   Though the mountains | shake · with the | swelling · there|of.

4 The Lord of | hosts is | with us :
   The God of | Jacob | is our | refuge.

5 There is a river the streams whereof shall make glad the | city · of | God :
   The holy place of the tabernacles | of the | Most | High.

6 God is in the midst of her, she shall | not be | moved :
   God shall | help her · and | that right | early.

7 The nations raged, the | kingdoms · were | moved :
   He uttered His | voice, the | earth | melted.

8 The Lord of | hosts is | with us :
   The God of | Jacob | is our | refuge.

9 Come behold the | works · of the | Lord :
   What desolations | He hath | made · in the | earth.

10 He maketh wars to cease unto the | end · of the |
    earth :
    He breaketh the bow and cutteth the spear in
    sunder, * He burneth the | chariot | in the |
    fire.

11 Be still and know that | I am | God :
    I will be exalted among the nations, * I will be
    ex|alted | in the | earth.

12 The Lord of | hosts is | with us :
    The God of | Jacob | is our | refuge.

GLORIA.

808

PSALM 47 (Selection)

REJOICE, THE LORD IS KING

1 O clap your hands | all ye | people :
    Shout unto | God · with the | voice of | triumph.

2 For the Lord most | high is | terrible :
    He is a great | King · over | all the | earth.

3 He shall choose our in|heri · tance | for us :
    The excellency of | Jacob | whom He | loved.

4 God is gone | up · with a | shout :
    The | Lord · with the | sound · of a | trumpet.

5 Sing praises to | God, sing | praises :
    Sing praises | unto · our | King, sing | praises.

6 For God is the King of | all the | earth :
    Sing ye | praises · with | under|standing.

7 God reigneth | over · the | nations :
    God sitteth up|on the | throne of · His | holiness.

8 The princes of the people are | gathered·to|gether :
   Even the | people of the | God of | Abraham.

9 For the shields of the earth be|long·unto | God :
   And | He is | greatly·ex|alted.

GLORIA

809

PSALM 51 (Selection)

A Prayer for Pardon and Cleansing

1 Have mercy upon me O God according to Thy |
   loving|kindness :
   According unto the multitude of Thy tender
   mercies | blot out | my trans|gressions.

2 Wash me throughly from | mine in|iquity :
   And | cleanse me | from my | sin.

3 For I ac|knowledge my trans|gressions :
   And my | sin is | ever·be|fore me.

4 Against Thee, Thee only have I sinned * and done
   this | evil in Thy | sight :
   That Thou mightest be justified when Thou |
   speakest and be | clear·when Thou | judgest.

5 Hide Thy | face·from my | sins :
   And | blot out | all·mine in|iquities.

6 Create in me a clean | heart O | God :
   And re|new a·right | spirit·with|in me.

7 Cast me not a|way·from Thy | presence :
   And take not Thy | holy | spirit | from me.

8 Restore unto me the | joy of Thy sal|vation :
   And up|hold me·with | Thy free | spirit.

9 Then will I teach trans|gressors·Thy | ways:
  And sinners shall be con|verted | unto | Thee

10 O Lord open | Thou my | lips:
  And my | mouth·shall shew | forth Thy | praise.

11 For Thou desirest not sacrifice, | else·would I |
  give it:
  Thou de|lightest | not in·burnt | offering.

12 The sacrifices of God are a | broken | spirit:
  A broken and a contrite heart O | God·Thou
  wilt | not des|pise.

GLORIA.

810

PSALM 63 (Selection)

THE SOUL'S THIRST FOR GOD

1 O God | Thou art·my | God:
  Early will I seek Thee, my | soul | thirsteth·
  for | Thee.

2 My flesh | longeth·for | Thee:
  In a dry and thirsty land | where no | water | is.

3 To see Thy | power and Thy | glory:
  As I have | seen Thee | in the | sanctuary.

4 Because Thy loving-kindness is | better·than | life:
  My | lips shall | praise | Thee.

5 Thus will I bless Thee | while I | live:
  I will | lift up·my | hands in·Thy | name.

6 My soul shall be satisfied as with | marrow·and |
  fatness:
  And my mouth shall | praise Thee·with |
  joyful | lips.

7 When I remember Thee up|on my | bed :
   And | meditate · on | Thee · in the | night watches

8 Because Thou hast | been my | help :
   Therefore in the shadow of Thy | wings will | I
   re|joice.

GLORIA.

811

PSALM 65

A HARVEST THANKSGIVING

1 Praise waiteth for Thee O | God in | Zion :
   And unto | Thee · shall the | vow · be per|formed.

2 O Thou that | hearest | prayer :
   Unto | Thee shall | all flesh | come.

3 Iniquities pre|vail a|gainst me :
   As for our transgressions | Thou shalt | purge ·
   them a|way.

4 Blessed is the man | whom Thou | choosest :
   And causest to approach unto Thee that | he
   may | dwell · in Thy | courts.

5 We shall be satisfied with the goodness | of Thy |
   house :
   Even | of Thy | holy | temple.

6 By terrible things in righteousness wilt Thou |
   answer | us :
   O | God of | our sal|vation.

7 Who art the confidence of all the | ends · of the |
   earth :
   And of them that are a|far off · up|on the | sea.

8 Which **by His** strength setteth | fast the |
   mountains:
   Being | girded·a|bout with | power,

9 Which stilleth the | noise·of the | seas:
   The noise of their waves and the | tumult | of
   the | people.

10 They also that dwell in the uttermost parts are
   a|fraid·at Thy | tokens:
   Thou makest the outgoings of the | morning·
   and | evening to re|joice.

11 Thou visitest the | earth and | waterest it:
   Thou greatly enrichest it with the river of |
   God·which is | full of | water.

12 Thou pre|parest·them | corn:
   When Thou hast | so pro|vided | for it.

13 Thou waterest the ridges there|of a|bundantly:
   Thou | settlest·the | furrows·there|of.

14 Thou makest it soft with showers, * Thou
   blessest the | springing·there|of:
   Thou crownest the year with Thy | goodness
   and Thy | paths drop | fatness.

15 They drop upon the | pastures of the | wilderness:
   And the little hills re|joice on | every | side.

16 The pastures are | clothed with | flocks:
   The valleys also are covered over with corn, *
   they shout for | joy, they | also | sing.

GLORIA.

812

PSALM 66 (Selection)

GOD HAS HEARD ME

1 Make a joyful noise unto God | all ye | lands:
   Sing forth the | honour | of His | Name.

2 Make His | praise | glorious:
   Say unto God, How | terrible·art | Thou·in
   Thy | works.

3 Through the | greatness of Thy | power:
   Shall Thine enemies sub|mit them|selves·unto |
   Thee.

4 All the earth shall | worship | Thee:
   And shall sing unto Thee, | they shall | sing·to
   Thy | name.

5 Come and hear all | ye that·fear | God:
   And I will declare what | He hath | done·for
   my | soul.

6 I cried unto | Him·with my | mouth:
   And | He·was ex|tolled·with my | tongue.

7 If I regard iniquity in my heart the | Lord·will
   not | hear me:
   But | veri·ly | God hath | heard me.

8 He hath attended to the | voice·of my | prayer:
   Blessed be God which hath not turned away
   my | prayer·nor His | mercy | from me.

                                          GLORIA.

813

PSALM 67

THE HOPE OF THE WORLD

1 God be merciful unto | us and | bless us:
   And cause His | face to | shine up|on us.

2 That Thy way may be | known up·on | earth:
   Thy saving | health a|mong all | nations.

3 Let the people | praise · Thee O | God:
　　Yea let | all the | people | praise Thee.

4 O let the nations be glad and | sing for | joy:
　　For Thou shalt judge the people righteously, *
　　and | govern · the | nations · on | earth.

5 Let the people | praise · Thee O | God:
　　Yea let | all the | people | praise Thee.

6 Then shall the earth | yield her | increase:
　　And God, even our own | God shall | give us ·
　　His | blessing.

2nd half

7 God | shall | bless us:
　　And all the | ends · of the | earth shall | fear Him.

GLORIA.

814

PSALM 72 (Selection)

THE BLESSINGS OF MESSIAH'S REIGN

1 Give the king Thy judgments O God * and Thy
　　righteousness | unto the · king's | son:
　　He shall judge Thy people with righteousness |
　　and Thy | poor with | judgment.

2 The mountains | shall bring | peace:
　　And the little hills | righteous · ness | unto · the |
　　people.

3 He shall judge the | poor · of the | people:
　　He shall save the children of the needy, * and
　　shall | break in | pieces the op|pressor.

4 They shall fear Thee as long as the sun and |
　　moon en|dure:
　　Through|out all | gener|ations.

5 He shall come down like rain upon the | mown |
    grass :
  As | showers · that | water · the | earth.

6 In his days shall the | righteous | flourish :
  And abundance of peace so | long · as the |
    moon en|dureth.

7 He shall have dominion also from | sea to | sea :
  And from the river | unto · the | ends · of the |
    earth.

8 Yea all kings shall | fall down · be|fore him :
  All | nations · shall | do him | service.

9 For he shall deliver the needy | when he | crieth :
  The poor also and | him that | hath no | helper.

10 He shall spare the | poor and | needy :
  And shall | save the | souls · of the | needy.

11 He shall redeem their soul from de|ceit and |
    violence :
  And precious shall their | blood be | in his | sight.

12 And he shall live, and to him shall be given of the |
    gold of | Sheba :
  Prayer also shall be made for him continually, *
  and | daily · shall | he be | praised.

13 His name shall en|dure for | ever :
  His name shall be con|tinued · as | long · as the |
    sun,

14 And men shall be | blessed in | him :
  All | nations · shall | call him | blessed.

15 Blessed be the Lord God the | God of | Israel :
  Who only | doeth | wondrous | things,

16 And blessed be His glorious | name for | ever :
  And let the whole | earth be | filled · with His |
    glory.

                                  GLORIA.

815

PSALM 84

THE HOUSE OF GOD

1 How lovely are Thy dwellings O | Lord of |
    hosts :
  My soul longeth, yea even | fainteth for the |
    courts · of the | Lord.

2 My heart | and my | flesh : ⌣
  Crieth | out · for the | living | God.

3 Yea the sparrow hath | found · her an | house :
  And the swallow a nest for herself where | she
    may | lay her | young,

4 Even Thine altars O | Lord of | hosts :
  My | King | and my | God.

5 Blessed are they that | dwell in · Thy | house :
  They will be | alway | praising | Thee.

6 Blessed is the man whose | strength · is in | Thee :
  In whose | heart · are the | highways · to | Zion.

7 Passing through the valley of weeping they make
    it a | place of | springs :
  Yea the early rain | cover · eth | it with |
    blessings.

8 They go from | strength to | strength :
  Every one of them ap|peareth be · fore | God
    in | Zion.

9 O Lord God of hosts | hear my | prayer :
  Give | ear O | God of | Jacob.

10 Behold O | God our | shield :
  And look upon the | face of | Thine an|ointed.

11 For a day | in Thy | courts: ‿
    Is | better | than a | thousand.

12 I had rather be a doorkeeper in the | house of·
    my | God:
    Than to | dwell·in the | tents of | wickedness.

13 For the Lord God is a | sun and | shield:
    The Lord will give grace and glory, * no good
    thing will He withhold from | them that |
    walk up|rightly.

14 O | Lord of | hosts:
    Blessed is the | man that | trusteth·in | Thee.

                            GLORIA.

816

PSALM 85 (Selection)

CONFIDENCE IN GOD'S MERCY

1 Lord Thou hast been favourable | unto·Thy |
    land:
    Thou hast brought | back the·cap|tivity·of |
    Jacob.

2 Thou hast forgiven the iniquity | of Thy | people:
    Thou hast | covered | all their | sin.

3 Wilt Thou be angry with | us for | ever:
    Wilt Thou draw out Thine | anger·to | all·
    gener|ations?

4 Wilt Thou not revive us again that Thy people
    may re|joice in | Thee?:
    Shew us Thy mercy O | Lord and | grant us
    Thy sal|vation.

5 I will hear what God the | Lord will | speak:
　　For He will speak peace unto His people and
　　　to His saints, * but | let them·not | turn
　　　again to | folly.

6 Surely His salvation is nigh | them that | fear
　　　Him:
　　That | glory·may | dwell in·our | land.

7 Mercy and truth are | met to|gether:
　　Righteousness and | peace have | kissed each |
　　　other.

8 Truth shall spring | out·of the | earth:
　　And | righteousness·shall | look·down from |
　　　heaven.

9 Yea the Lord shall give | that·which is | good:
　　And our | land shall | yield her | increase.

10 Righteousness shall | go be|fore Him:
　　And shall | set us in the | way·of His | steps.

GLORIA.

817

PSALM 86 (Selection)

IN THE DAY OF TROUBLE

1 Be merciful unto | me O | Lord:
　　For I | daily | cry·unto | Thee.

2 Rejoice the | soul of·Thy | servant:
　　For unto Thee O | Lord·do I | lift·up my | soul.

3 For Thou Lord art good and | ready to for|give:
　　And plenteous in mercy unto | all·them that |
　　call up·on | Thee.

4 Give ear O Lord | unto·my | prayer:
And attend to the | voice of·my | suppli-|
cations.

5 In the day of my trouble I will | call up·on | Thee:
For | Thou wilt | answer | me.

6 Among the gods there is none like unto | Thee
O | Lord:
Neither are there any | works like | unto | Thy
works.

7 All nations whom Thou hast made shall come
and worship before | Thee O | Lord:
And shall | glori|fy Thy | name,

8 For | Thou art | great:
And doest wondrous things, | Thou art | God
a|lone.

9 Teach me Thy way O Lord, I will | walk in·
Thy | truth:
Unite my | heart to | fear Thy | name.

10 I will praise Thee O Lord my God with | all my |
heart:
And I will glorify Thy | name for | ever|more.

11 For Thou O Lord art a God full of com|passion·
and | gracious:
Longsuffering and | plenteous·in | mercy·and |
truth.

12 O turn unto me and have | mercy·up|on me:
Give Thy strength unto Thy servant and | save
the | son of·Thine | handmaid.

GLORIA.

818

A FAITHFUL CREATOR

1 I will sing of the mercies of the | Lord for | ever:
   With my mouth will I make known Thy |
   faithfulness·to | all·gener|ations.

2 For I have said, Mercy shall be | built·up for |
   ever:
   Thy faithfulness shalt Thou es|tablish | in the |
   heavens.

3 And the heavens shall praise Thy | wonders·O |
   Lord:
   Thy faithfulness also in the congre|gation | of
   the | saints.

4 For who in the heaven can be compared | unto·
   the | Lord:
   Who among the sons of the mighty can be |
   likened | unto·the | Lord?

5 God is greatly to be feared in the as|sembly of
   the | saints:
   And to be had in reverence of | all·them that |
   are a|bout Him.

6 O Lord God of hosts, who is a strong Lord |
   like·unto | Thee:
   Or to Thy | faithful·ness | round a|bout Thee?

7 Thou rulest the | raging of the | sea:
   When the waves thereof a|rise Thou | stillest |
   them.

8 The heavens are Thine, the earth | also·is |
   Thine:
   As for the world and the fulness thereof | Thou
   hast | founded | them.

9 Thou hast a | mighty | arm:
   Strong is Thy hand and | high is | Thy right |
   hand.

10 Justice and judgment are the habitation | of Thy |
   throne:
   Mercy and truth shall | go be|fore Thy | face.

11 Blessed is the people that know the | joyful |
   sound:
   They shall walk O | Lord·in the | light of·Thy |
   countenance.

12 In Thy name shall they re|joice·all the | day:
   And in Thy righteousness | shall they | be
   ex|alted.

13 For Thou art the | glory of their | strength:
   And in Thy favour our | horn shall | be
   ex|alted.

14 For the Lord is | our de|fence:
   And the Holy One of | Is·rael | is our | King.

GLORIA.

819

PSALM 90 (Selection)

OUR ETERNAL HOME

1 Lord Thou hast been our dwelling-place in | all·
   gener|ations:
   Before the | mountains | were brought | forth

2 Or ever Thou hadst formed the | earth·and the |
   world:
   Even from everlasting to ever|lasting | Thou
   art | God.

3 Thou turnest | man·to des|truction:
   And sayest, Re|turn ye | children·of | men.

4 For a thousand years in Thy sight are but as
　　yesterday | when·it is | past:
　　And | as a | watch·in the | night.

5 Thou carriest them away as with a flood, | they
　　are as a | sleep:
　　In the morning they are like | grass which |
　　groweth | up;

6 In the morning it flourisheth and | groweth | up:
　　In the evening | it is·cut | down and | withereth.

7 The days of our years are threescore | years and |
　　ten:
　　And if by reason of strength | they be | four-
　　score | years,

8 Yet is their strength | labour·and | sorrow:
　　For it is soon cut | off·and we | fly a|way.

9 So teach us to | number·our | days:
　　That we may ap|ply our | hearts·unto |
　　wisdom.

10 O satisfy us | early with Thy | mercy:
　　That we may re|joice·and be | glad·all our |
　　days.

11 Make us glad according to the days wherein |
　　Thou·hast af|flicted us:
　　And the | years·wherein | we have·seen | evil.

12 Let Thy work appear | unto·Thy | servants:
　　And Thy | glory | unto·their | children.

2nd half

13 And let the beauty of the Lord our | God·be
　　up|on us:
　　And establish Thou the work of our hands
　　upon us, * yea the work of our | hands
　　es|tablish·Thou | it.
　　　　　　　　　　　　　　　　GLORIA.

820

PSALM 92 (Selection)

A Thanksgiving

1 It is a good thing to give thanks | unto·the |
    Lord:
    And to sing praises | unto·Thy | name·O most |
    High,

2 To shew forth Thy loving-kindness | in the |
    morning:
    And Thy | faithful·ness | every | night

3 Upon an instrument of ten strings and up|on the |
    psaltery:
    Upon the | harp·with a | solemn | sound.

4 For Thou Lord hast made me | glad·through
    Thy | work:
    I will | triumph in the | works of·Thy | hands.

5 O Lord how | great·are Thy | works:
    And Thy | thoughts are | very | deep.

6 A brutish man | knoweth | not:
    And a | fool·doth not | under|stand this.

7 The righteous shall flourish like the palm tree, *
    he shall grow like a | cedar·in | Lebanon:
    Those that be planted in the house of the Lord
    shall | flourish in the | courts·of our | God.

8 To shew that the | Lord is | upright:
    He is my rock and there is | no un|righteous·
    ness | in Him.

GLORIA.

821

PSALM 95 (Selection)

A CALL TO WORSHIP

1 O come let us | sing unto the | Lord:
  Let us heartily rejoice in the | strength of | our
  sal|vation.

2 Let us come before His | presence·with | thanks-
  giving:
  And shew ourselves | glad in | Him with | psalms.

3 For the Lord is a | great | God:
  And a great | King a|bove all | gods.

4 In His hand are all the | corners of the | earth:
  And the | strength·of the | hills is·His | also.

5 The sea is | His·and He | made it:
  And His | hands pre|pared the·dry | land.

6 O come let us | worship and bow | down:
  Let us kneel be|fore the | Lord our | Maker.

7 For He is the | Lord our | God:
  And we are the people of His | pasture and the |
  sheep of·His | hand.

GLORIA.

822

PSALM 96

THE JUDGE OF ALL THE EARTH

1 O sing unto the | Lord a·new | song:
  Sing unto the | Lord | all the | earth.

2 Sing unto the Lord, | bless His | name:
  Shew forth His sal|vation·from | day to | day.

3 Declare His glory a|mong the | nations:
His | wonders · a|mong all | people.

4 For the Lord is great and | greatly to be | praised:
He is to be | feared a|bove all | gods.

5 For all the gods of the | nations · are | idols:
But it is the | Lord that | made the | heavens.

6 Honour and majesty | are be|fore Him:
Strength and | beauty · are | in His | sanctuary.

7 Give unto the Lord O ye | kindreds of the |
people:
Give unto the | Lord | glory · and | strength.

8 Give unto the Lord the glory due | unto · His ɪ
name:
Bring an offering and | come in|to His | courts.

9 O worship the Lord in the | beauty · of | holiness:
Fear be|fore Him | all the | earth.

10 Say among the nations that the Lord reigneth. *
The world also shall be established that it |
shall · not be | moved:
He shall | judge the | people | righteously.

11 Let the heavens rejoice and let the | earth be |
glad:
Let the sea | roar · and the | fulness · there|of.

12 Let the field be joyful and all that | is there|in:
Then shall all the trees of the wood re|joice
be|fore the | Lord.

13 For | He | cometh:
For He | cometh · to | judge the | earth.

14 He shall judge the | world with | righteousness:
And the | people | with His | truth.

GLORIA.

823

PSALM 98

The Salvation of Our God

1 O sing unto the | Lord a·new | song:
For | He hath·done | marvel·lous | things.

2 His right hand and His | holy | arm: ⌣
Hath | gotten | Him the | victory.

3 The Lord hath made known | His sal|vation:
His righteousness hath He openly | shewed·in
the | sight·of the | nations.

4 He hath remembered His mercy and His truth
toward the | house of | Israel:
All the ends of the earth have | seen the·
sal|vation of our | God.

5 Make a joyful noise unto the | Lord·all the |
earth:
Make a loud | noise·and re|joice and·sing |
praise.

6 Sing unto the | Lord·with the | harp:
With the | harp·and the | voice·of a | psalm,

7 With trumpets and | sound of | cornet:
Make a joyful noise be|fore the | Lord the |
King.

8 Let the sea roar and the | fulness·there|of:
The world and | they that | dwell there|in.

9 Let the floods | clap their | hands:
Let the hills be joyful to|gether·be|fore the |
Lord.

10 For He cometh to | judge the | earth:
With righteousness shall He judge the | world·
and the | people·with | equity.

GLORIA.

824

PSALM 100

THE JOY OF WORSHIP

1 Make a joyful noise unto the Lord | all ye | lands:
 Serve the Lord with gladness, | come before
 His | presence·with | singing.

2 Know ye that the | Lord·He is | God:
 It is He that hath made us and not we
 ourselves, * we are His | people and the |
 sheep of·His | pasture.

3 Enter into His gates with thanksgiving * and into
 His | courts with | praise:
 Be thankful unto | Him and | bless His | name.

4 For the Lord is good, His mercy is | ever|lasting:
 And His truth en|dureth·to | all·gener|ations.

GLORIA.

825

PSALM 103

GOD'S EVERLASTING KINDNESS

1 Bless the Lord | O my | soul:
 And all that is within me | bless His | holy |
 name.

2 Bless the Lord | O my | soul:
 And for|get not | all His | benefits;

3 Who forgiveth | all·thine in|iquities:
 Who | healeth | all·thy dis|eases;

4 Who redeemeth thy | life·from des|truction:
 Who crowneth thee with loving|kindness·and |
 tender | mercies;

5 Who satisfieth thy | mouth with · good | things :
   So that thy | youth · is re|newed · like the | eagle's.

6 The Lord executeth | righteousness and | judg-
   ment :
   For | all that | are op|pressed.

7 He made known His | ways · unto | Moses :
   His acts | unto · the | children · of | Israel.

8 The Lord is | merciful and | gracious :
   Slow to | anger · and | plenteous · in | mercy.

9 He will not | always | chide :
   Neither will He | keep His | anger · for | ever.

10 He hath not dealt with us | after · our | sins :
   Nor rewarded us ac|cording · to | our in|iquities.

11 For as the heaven is high a|bove the | earth :
   So great is His | mercy · toward | them that | fear Him.

12 As far as the | east is from the | west :
   So far hath He re|moved · our trans|gressions | from us.

13 Like as a father | pitieth · His | children :
   So the Lord | piti · eth | them that | fear Him.

14 For He | knoweth · our | frame :
   He re|membereth · that | we are | dust.

15 As for man, his | days · are as | grass :
   As a | flower of the | field · so he | flourisheth ;

16 For the wind passeth over it | and · it is | gone :
   And the | place thereof · shall | know it · no | more.

17 But the mercy of the Lord is from everlasting to
  everlasting upon | them that | fear Him :
  And His righteousness | unto | children's |
  children,

18 To such as | keep His | covenant :
  And to those that re|member His com-|
  mandments·to | do them.

19 The Lord hath prepared His | throne·in the |
  heavens :
  And His kingdom | ruleth | over | all.

20 Bless the Lord ye His angels that ex|cel in |
  strength :
  That do His commandments hearkening |
  unto·the | voice of·His | word.

21 Bless ye the Lord all | ye His | hosts :
  Ye ministers of | His that | do His | pleasure.

22 Bless the Lord all His works in all places of |
  His do|minion :
  Bless the | Lord | O my | soul.

GLORIA.

826

PSALM 104 (Selection)

THE WONDERS OF CREATION

1 Bless the Lord | O my | soul :
  O Lord my God Thou art very great, * Thou
  art | clothed with | honour·and | majesty ;

2 Who coverest Thyself with light | as·with a |
  garment :
  Who stretchest out the | heavens | like a |
  curtain ;

3 Who layeth the beams of His | chambers in the |
    waters:
    Who maketh the clouds His chariot, * Who
    walketh up|on the | wings·of the | wind;

4 Who maketh His | angels | spirits:
    His | ministers·a | flaming | fire;

5 Who laid the found|ations of the | earth:
    That it should | not·be re|moved for|ever.

6 Thou coveredst it with the deep | as·with a |
    garment:
    The waters | stood a|bove the | mountains.

7 At Thy re|buke they | fled:
    At the voice of Thy | thunder·they | hasted·
    a|way.

8 They go up by the mountains, they go | down·by
    the | valleys:
    Unto the place which | Thou hast | founded |
    for them.

9 Thou hast set a bound that they may | not pass |
    over:
    That they turn not a|gain to | cover·the | earth.

10 He sendeth the springs | into·the | valleys:
    Which | run a|mong the | hills.

11 They give drink to every | beast·of the | field:
    The wild | asses | quench their | thirst.

12 By them shall the fowls of the heaven have their |
    habi|tation:
    Which | sing a|mong the | branches.

13 He watereth the | hills·from His | chambers:
    The earth is satisfied | with the | fruit of·Thy |
    works.

14 He causeth the grass to | grow·for the | cattle:
And | herb·for the | service·of | man,

15 That he may bring forth food | out·of the |
earth:
And wine that maketh | glad the | heart of |
man,

16 And oil to make his | face to | shine:
And | bread which | strengtheneth·man's |
heart.

17 The trees of the Lord are | full of | sap:
The cedars of | Lebanon·which | He hath |
planted,

18 Where the birds | make their | nests:
As for the stork the | fir trees | are her | house.

19 The high hills are a refuge for the | wild | goats:
And the | stony | rocks·for the | conies.

20 He appointed the | moon for | seasons:
The sun | knoweth·his | going | down.

21 Thou makest darkness | and·it is | night:
Wherein **all the** | beasts·of the | forest·creep |
forth.

22 The young lions roar | after·their | prey:
And | seek their | meat from | God.

23 The sun ariseth, they gather them|selves to-|
gether:
And | lay them | down·in their | dens.

24 Man goeth forth | unto·his | work:
And to his | labour·un|til the | evening.

2nd half

25 O Lord how manifold | are Thy | works:
In wisdom hast Thou made them all, * the |
earth is | full of·Thy | riches.

GLORIA.

827

PSALM 111

WORTHY TO BE PRAISED

1 I will praise the Lord with my whole heart in the
    as|sembly of the | upright:
  And | in the | congre|gation.

2 The works of the | Lord are | great:
  Sought out of all | them·that have | pleasure·
    there|in.

3 His work is | honourable·and | glorious:
  And His | righteousness en|dureth·for | ever.

4 He made His wonderful | works to be re|mem-
    bered:
  The Lord is | gracious·and | full·of com-|
    passion.

5 He hath given meat unto | them that | fear Him:
  He will ever be | mindful | of His | covenant.

6 He hath shewed His people the | power·of His |
    works:
  That He may give them the | herit·age | of
    the | nations.

7 The works of His hands are | verity·and |
    judgment:
  And | all·His com|mandments·are | sure.

8 They stand fast for | ever·and | ever:
  And are | done in | truth and | uprightness.

9 He sent redemption | unto·His | people:
  He hath commanded His covenant for ever, *
    Holy and | rever·end | is His | name.

10 The fear of the Lord is the be|ginning·of | wisdom :
    A good understanding have all they that do His commandments, * His | praise en-| dureth·for | ever.

GLORIA.

828

PSALM 115 (Selection)

A Very Present Help

1 Not unto us O Lord, not unto us, * but unto Thy | name give | glory :
    For Thy | mercy·and | for Thy | truth's sake.

2 Wherefore should the heathen say, Where is | now their | God ? :
    Our God is in the heavens, * He hath | done· whatso|ever He hath | pleased.

3 O Israel | trust·in the | Lord :
    He is our | help | and our | shield.

4 O house of Aaron | trust·in the | Lord :
    He is our | help | and our | shield.

5 Ye that fear the Lord | trust·in the | Lord :
    He is our | help | and our | shield.

6 The Lord hath been mindful of us, | He will | bless us :
    He will bless them that fear the | Lord, both | small and | great.

7 The Lord shall increase you more and more, | you· and your | children :
    Ye are blessed of the | Lord·which made | heaven·and | earth.

8 The heaven, even the | heavens · are the | Lord's :
But the earth hath He | given · to the|children ·
of | men.

2nd half

9 We will | bless the | Lord :
From this time forth and for | ever · more. | Praise
the | Lord.

GLORIA.

829

PSALM 116 (Selection)

A HYMN OF GRATITUDE

1 I | love the | Lord :
Because He hath heard my | voice · and my |
suppli|cations.

2 Because He hath inclined His | ear · unto | me :
Therefore will I call upon | Him as | long as ·
I | live.

3 The sorrows of death | compassed | me :
I | found | trouble · and | sorrow.

4 Then called I upon the | name · of the | Lord :
O Lord I be|seech Thee · de|liver · my | soul.

5 Gracious is the | Lord and | righteous :
Yea our | God is | merci|ful.

6 The Lord pre|serveth · the | simple :
I was in | miser · y | and He | helped me.

7 Return unto thy | rest · O my | soul :
For the Lord hath dealt | bounti|fully with |
thee.

8 For thou hast delivered my | soul from | death :
   Mine eyes from | tears·and my | feet from |
     falling.

9 I will walk be|fore the | Lord :
   In the | land | of the | living.

10 What shall I render | unto·the | Lord :
   For | all His | benefits·to|wards me ?

11 I will take the | cup of·sal|vation :
   And | call upon the | name·of the | Lord.

12 I will pay my vows now | unto·the | Lord :
   In the | presence·of | all His | people.

13 Precious in the | sight·of the | Lord : ⌣
   Is the | death | of His | saints.

14 I will offer to Thee the | sacrifice·of | thanks-
     giving :
   And will | call upon the | name·of the | Lord.

15 I will pay my vows now | unto·the | Lord :
   In the | presence·of | all His | people.

16 In the courts of the | Lord's | house :
   In the | midst of·thee | O Je|rusalem.

GLORIA.

830

PSALM 118 (Selection)

THANKSGIVING FOR DELIVERANCE

1 O give thanks unto the Lord for | He is | good :
   For His | mercy·en|dureth·for | ever.

2 The Lord is my | strength and | song :
   And | is be|come·my sal|vation.

3 The voice of rejoicing and salvation is in the |
    dwellings of the | righteous :
    The right hand of the | Lord | doeth | valiantly.

4 The right hand of the | Lord · is ex|alted :
    The right hand of the | Lord | doeth | valiantly.

5 I shall not | die but | live :
    And de|clare the | works · of the | Lord.

6 The Lord hath | chastened · me | sore :
    But He hath not given me | over | unto | death.

7 Open to me the | gates of | righteousness :
    I will go into them * and | I will | praise the | Lord.

8 This is the | gate · of the | Lord :
    Into | which the | righteous · shall | enter.

9 I will praise Thee for | Thou hast | heard me :
    And | art be|come · my sal|vation.

10 The stone which the | builders · re|fused :
    Is become the | headstone | of the | corner.

11 This is the | Lord's | doing :
    It is | marvel · lous | in our | eyes.

12 This is the day which the | Lord hath | made :
    We will re|joice · and be | glad in | it.

13 Save now I be|seech Thee · O | Lord :
    O Lord I be|seech Thee | send now · pros|perity.

14 Blessed be he that cometh in the | name · of the |
    Lord :
    We have blessed you | out of · the | house · of
    the | Lord.

15 Thou art my God and | I will | praise Thee :
    Thou art my | God and | I will · ex|alt Thee.

16 O give thanks unto the Lord for | He is | good:
For His | mercy·en|dureth·for | ever.

GLORIA.

831

PSALM 119 (Selection)

A MEDITATION ON GOD'S LAW

Part I

1 Blessed are the unde|filed·in the | way:
Who | walk·in the | law·of the | Lord.

2 Blessed are they that | keep His | testimonies:
And that | seek Him | with the·whole | heart.

3 They also | do·no in|iquity:
They | walk |·in His | ways.

4 Thou hast commanded us to keep Thy | precepts |
diligently:
O that my ways were di|rected·to | keep Thy |
statutes.

5 Then shall I | not·be a|shamed:
When I have re|spect·unto | all·Thy com-|
mandments.

6 I will praise Thee with uprightness of heart * when
I shall have learned Thy | righteous | judg-
ments:
I will keep Thy statutes. | O for|sake me·not |
utterly.

GLORIA.

832

PSALM 119

Part II

1 Wherewithal shall a young man | cleanse his | way ? :
  By taking heed thereto ac|cording | to Thy | word.

2 With my whole heart | have I | sought Thee :
  O let me not | wander | from · Thy com|mand-ments.

3 Thy word have I | hid · in my | heart :
  That I | might not | sin a|gainst Thee.

4 Blessed art | Thou O | Lord :
  O | teach me | Thy | statutes.

5 With my lips have | I de|clared : ⌣
  All the | judgments | of Thy | mouth.

6 I have rejoiced in the | way of · Thy | testimonies :
  As | much as | in all | riches.

7 I will meditate | in Thy | precepts :
  And have res|pect un|to Thy | ways.

8 I will delight myself | in Thy | statutes :
  I will | not for|get Thy | word.

GLORIA.

833

PSALM 119

Part III

1 Open Thou mine eyes that I may behold wondrous things | out of · Thy | law :
  I will run the way of Thy commandments when | Thou · shalt en|large my | heart.

2 Teach me O Lord the | way of·Thy | statutes:
  And I shall | keep it | unto·the | end.

3 Thy statutes have been my songs in the | house
    of·my | pilgrimage:
  O how I love Thy law; * it is my medi|tation |
    all the | day.

4 How sweet are Thy words | unto·my | taste:
  Yea sweeter than | honey | to my | mouth.

5 Through Thy precepts I get | under|standing:
  Therefore I | hate·every | false | way.

6 Thy word is a lamp | unto·my | feet:
  And a | light | unto·my | path.

7 Accept I beseech Thee the freewill offerings of
    my | mouth O | Lord:
  And | teach | me Thy | judgments.

8 The entrance of Thy words | giveth | light:
  It giveth under|standing | unto·the | simple.

9 Order my steps | in Thy | word:
  And let not any iniquity | have do|minion |
    over me.

10 Thy word is very pure, therefore Thy | servant |
    loveth it:
  Thy word is true from the beginning, * and
    every one of Thy righteous | judgments·
    en|dureth·for | ever.

                              GLORIA.

834

PSALM 121

THE SLEEPLESS GUARDIAN

1 I will lift up mine eyes | unto·the | hills:
  From | whence | cometh·my | help?

2 My help | cometh from the | Lord:
  Which | made | heaven and | earth.

3 He will not suffer thy | foot·to be | moved:
  He that | keepeth·thee | will not | slumber.

4 Behold He that | keepeth | Israel:
  Shall | neither | slumber·nor | sleep.

5 The Lord | is thy | keeper:
  The Lord is thy | shade up|on thy·right | hand.

6 The sun shall not | smite thee·by | day:
  Nei|ther the | moon by | night.

7 The Lord shall preserve thee from | all | evil:
  He | shall pre|serve thy | soul.

8 The Lord shall preserve thy going out and thy |
    coming | in:
  From this time forth and | even·for | ever|more.

GLORIA.

835

PSALM 122

THE JOY OF PUBLIC WORSHIP

1 I was glad when they said unto me, * Let us go
    into the | house·of the | Lord:
  Our feet shall stand with|in thy | gates·O
    Je|rusalem.

2 Jerusalem is | builded as a | city:
  That | is com|pact to|gether.

3 Whither the tribes go up, the | tribes·of the |
    Lord:
  Unto the testimony of Israel * to give | thanks·
    to the | name·of the | Lord.

4 For there are set | thrones of | judgment:
  The | thrones · of the | house of | David.

5 Pray for the | peace · of Je|rusalem:
  They shall | prosper · that | love | thee.

6 Peace be with|in thy | walls:
  And pros|perity · with|in thy | palaces.

7 For my brethren and com|panions' | sakes:
  I will now say, | Peace | be with|in thee.

8 Because of the house of the | Lord our | God:
  I will | seek to | do thee | good.

GLORIA.

836

PSALM 124

DELIVERANCE COMES FROM GOD

1 If it had not been the Lord who was on our side, *
  now may | Israel | say:
  If it had not been the Lord who was on our
  side * when | men rose | up a|gainst us,

2 Then they had swallowed us | up a|live:
  When their | wrath was | kindled · a|gainst us.

3 Then the waters had overwhelmed us, * the stream
  had gone | over · our | soul:
  Then the proud | waters had gone | over · our |
  soul.

4 Blessed | be the | Lord:
  Who hath not | given us · as a | prey · to their |
  teeth.

5 Our soul is escaped as a bird out of the | snare · of
   the | fowlers :
   The snare is | broken · and | we are · es|caped.

6 Our help is in the | name · of the | Lord :
   Who | made | heaven · and | earth.

GLORIA.

837

PSALM 126

PRAISE FOR THE PAST AND TRUST FOR THE FUTURE

1 When the Lord turned again the cap|tivity · of |
   Zion :
   We were | like · unto | them that | dream.

2 Then was our mouth | filled with | laughter :
   And our | tongue with | songs of | joy.

3 Then said they among the heathen, * The Lord
   hath done great | things for | them :
   The Lord hath done great things for us |
   whereof | we are | glad.

4 Turn again our captivity O Lord as the | streams ·
   in the | south :
   They that sow in | tears shall | reap in | joy.

5 He that goeth forth and weepeth, bearing |
   precious | seed :
   Shall doubtless come again with rejoicing, |
   bringing · his | sheaves | with him.

GLORIA.

838

PSALM 130

A Cry for Succour

1 Out of the depths have I cried unto | Thee O |
   Lord :
   O | Lord | hear my | voice.

2 Let Thine | ears·be at|tentive : ⌣
   To the | voice·of my | suppli|cations.

3 If Thou Lord shouldst | mark in|iquities :
   O | Lord | who shall | stand ?

4 But there is for|giveness·with | Thee :
   That | Thou | mayest·be | feared.

5 I wait for the Lord, my | soul doth | wait :
   And | in His | word·do I | hope.

6 My soul waiteth for the Lord more than they
   that | watch·for the | morning :
   I say, more than | they that | watch·for the |
   morning.

7 Let Israel | hope·in the | Lord :
   For | with the | Lord·there is | mercy,

8 And with Him is | plenteous·re|demption :
   And He shall redeem | Israel·from | all·his
   in|iquities.

                                        GLORIA.

839

PSALM 138 (Selection)

God's Aid in Trouble

1 I will praise Thee with my | whole | heart :
   I will sing | praises | unto | Thee.

2 I will | praise Thy | name :
For Thy | loving|kindness·and | truth.

3 In the day when I cried, | Thou didst | answer me :
And | strengthen me with | strength·in my | soul.

4 All the kings of the earth shall | praise Thee·O |
Lord :
When they | hear the | words of·Thy | mouth.

5 Yea they shall sing in the | ways·of the | Lord :
For great is the | glory | of the | Lord.

6 Though the Lord be high, * yet hath He respect |
unto·the | lowly :
But the | proud He | knoweth·a|far off.

7 Though I walk in the midst of trouble, | Thou·
wilt re|vive me :
And | Thy right | hand shall | save me.

8 The Lord will perfect | that·which con|cerneth me :
Thy mercy O Lord endureth for ever; * forsake
not the | works of | thine own | hands.

GLORIA.

840

PSALM 139 (Selection)

THE SEARCHING PRESENCE

1 O Lord Thou hast | searched me·and | known
me :
Thou knowest my downsitting and mine up-
rising, * Thou under|standest·my | thoughts
a|far off.

2 Thou compassest my path and my | lying | down :
And art ac|quainted·with | all my | ways.

3 For there is not a | word in·my | tongue:
  But lo, O Lord, Thou | knowest·it | alto|gether.

4 Thou hast beset me be|hind·and be|fore:
  And | laid Thine | hand up|on me.

5 Such knowledge is too | wonderful·for | me:
  It is high, I | cannot·at|tain | unto it.

6 Whither shall I | go·from Thy | spirit:
  Or whither | shall I | flee·from Thy | presence?

7 If I ascend up into heaven | Thou art | there:
  If I make my bed in the | grave be|hold·Thou
  art | there.

8 If I take the wings of the morning and dwell in
  the uttermost | parts·of the | sea:
  Even there shall Thy hand lead me, * and |
  Thy right | hand shall | hold me.

9 If I say, Surely the | darkness·shall | cover me:
  Even the | night·shall be | light a|bout me.

10 Yea the darkness hideth not from Thee, * but
  the night | shineth as the | day:
  The darkness and the light are | both a|like to |
  Thee.

11 How precious also are Thy thoughts unto | me
  O | God:
  How | great·is the | sum of | them.

12 If I should count them they are more in number |
  than the | sand:
  When I awake | I am | still with | Thee.

13 Search me O God and | know my | heart:
  Try | me and | know my | thoughts,

14 And see if there be any | wicked·way | in me:
  And | lead me in the | way·ever|lasting.

GLORIA.

841

PSALM 143 (Selection)

A Prayer for Guidance

1 Hear my prayer O Lord, * give ear to my |
suppli|cations :
    In Thy faithfulness and | in Thy | righteous·
    ness | answer me.

2 And enter not into judgment | with Thy | servant :
    For in Thy sight shall | no man | living·be |
    justified.

3 I remember the days of old, * I meditate on | all
    Thy | works :
    I muse on the works of Thy hands, * I | stretch·
    forth my | hands·unto | Thee.

4 My soul thirsteth after Thee as a | thirsty | land :
    Hear me speedily O Lord for my spirit faileth ; * |
    hide·not Thy | face from | me.

5 Cause me to hear Thy loving|kindness in the |
    morning :
    For in | Thee·do I | put my | trust.

6 Cause me to know the way wherein | I should |
    walk :
    For I | lift up·my | soul·unto | Thee.

7 Teach me to do Thy will for | Thou art·my | God :
    Thy spirit is good ; * lead me | into·the | land
    of | uprightness.

8 Quicken me O Lord for | Thy name's | sake :
    For Thy righteousness' sake | bring my | soul·
    out of | trouble.

GLORIA.

842

GOD'S GOODNESS TO ALL

1 I will extol Thee my | God O | king:
And I will bless Thy | name for|ever·and | ever.

2 Every | day·will I | bless Thee:
And I will praise Thy | name for | ever·and |
ever.

3 Great is the Lord and | greatly to be | praised:
And His | greatness | is un|searchable.

4 One generation shall praise Thy | works·to
an|other:
And shall de|clare Thy | mighty | acts.

5 I will speak of the glorious | honour of Thy |
majesty:
And | of Thy | wondrous | works.

6 And men shall speak of the might of Thy |
terri·ble | acts:
And | I·will de|clare Thy | greatness.

7 They shall abundantly utter the memory of |
Thy great | goodness:
And | men shall | sing·of Thy | righteousness.

8 The Lord is gracious and | full of·com|passion:
Slow to | anger and of | great | mercy.

9 The Lord is | good to | all:
And His tender mercies are | over | all His |
works.

10 All Thy works shall | praise Thee·O | Lord:
And Thy | saints shall | bless | Thee.

11 They shall speak of the | glory of Thy | kingdom:
   And | talk | of Thy | power.

12 To make known to the sons of men His | mighty |
       acts:
   And the glorious | majes·ty | of His | kingdom.

13 Thy kingdom is an ever|lasting | kingdom:
   And Thy dominion endureth through|out all |
       gener|ations.

14 The Lord upholdeth | all that | fall:
   And raiseth up all | those that | be bowed |
       down.

15 The eyes of all | wait up·on | Thee:
   And Thou givest | them their | meat in·due |
       season.

16 Thou | openest·Thy | hand:
   And satisfieth the desire of | every | living |
       thing.

17 The Lord is righteous in | all His | works:
   And | holy·in | all His | ways.

18 The Lord is nigh unto all them that | call up·on |
       Him:
   To all that | call up·on | Him in | truth.

19 He will fulfil the desire of | them that | fear Him:
   He also will | hear their | cry·and will | save
       them.

20 My mouth shall speak the | praise·of the | Lord:
   And let all flesh bless His holy | name for |
       ever·and | ever.

                                        GLORIA.

843

THE UNFAILING DELIVERER

1 Praise ye the Lord. * Praise the Lord | O my |
    soul:
    While I | live·will I | praise the | Lord.

2 I will sing praises | unto·my | God:
    While | I have | any | being.

3 Put not your trust in princes, * nor in the | son
    of | man:
    In | whom there | is no | help.

4 Happy is he who hath the God of | Jacob for
    his | help:
    Whose | hope is in the | Lord his | God,

5 Which made heaven and earth, * the sea and all
    that | therein | is:
    Which | keepeth | truth for | ever;

6 Which executeth judgment | for·the op|pressed:
    Which | giveth | food·to the | hungry.

7 The Lord | looseth·the | prisoners:
    The Lord | openeth·the | eyes·of the | blind.

8 The Lord raiseth | them that are bowed | down:
    The | Lord | loveth·the | righteous.

9 The Lord preserveth the strangers, * He relieveth
    the | fatherless·and | widow:
    But the way of the wicked He | turneth |
    upside | down.

10 The Lord shall | reign for|ever:
    Even thy God O Zion unto all gener|ations. |
    Praise·ye the | Lord.

                                    GLORIA.

844

THE DIVINE PROVIDENCE

1 Praise ye the Lord, * for it is good to sing
   praises | unto·our | God:
   For it is | pleasant·and | praise is | comely.

2 He healeth the | broken·in | heart:
   And | bindeth | up their | wounds.

3 He telleth the | number of the | stars:
   He | calleth·them | all·by their | names.

4 Great is our God | and of·great | power:
   His | under|standing·is | infinite.

5 Sing unto the | Lord with·thanks|giving:
   Sing praise up|on the | harp·to our | God,

6 Who covereth the heaven with clouds, * who
   prepareth | rain·for the | earth:
   Who maketh grass to | grow up|on the |
   mountains.

7 He giveth to the | beast his | food:
   And to the | young | ravens·which | cry.

8 Praise the Lord | O Je|rusalem:
   Yea | praise thy | God O | Zion.

9 For He hath strengthened the | bars of·thy |
   gates:
   He hath | blessed thy | children·with|in thee.

10 He maketh | peace·in thy | borders:
   And filleth thee with the | finest | of the | wheat.

11 He sendeth forth His com|mandment·on | earth:
   His word | runneth | very | swiftly.

12 He giveth | snow like | wool:
And | scattereth·the | hoar frost·like | ashes.

13 He casteth forth His | ice like | morsels:
Who can | stand be|fore His | cold ?

14 He sendeth out His word and | melteth | them:
He causeth His wind to | blow·and the | waters | flow.

15 He sheweth His | word·unto | Jacob:
His statutes and His | judgments | unto | Israel.

16 He hath not dealt so with | any | nation:
And as for His judgments, they have not | known them. | Praise·ye the | Lord.

GLORIA.

845

PSALM 148 (Selection)

NATURE'S HYMN OF PRAISE

1 Praise ye the | Lord·from the | heavens:
O | praise Him | in the | heights.

2 Praise ye Him | all His | angels:
O | praise Him | all His | hosts.

3 Praise ye Him | sun and | moon:
Praise Him | all ye | stars of | light.

4 Praise Him ye | heavens·of | heavens:
And ye waters that | are a|bove the | heavens.

5 Let them praise the | name·of the | Lord:
For He commanded | and they | were cre|ated.

6 He hath also stablished them for | ever · and |
    ever :
   He hath made a de|cree which | shall not | pass.

7 Praise the Lord from the earth * ye | dragons
    and all | deeps :
   Fire and hail, snow and vapours, * stormy |
    wind ful|filling · His | word,

8 Mountains and all hills, fruitful | trees and · all |
    cedars :
   Beasts and all cattle, | creeping things and |
    flying | fowl,

9 Kings of the | earth and · all | people :
   Princes and all | judges | of the | earth,

10 Young men and maidens, | old · men and |
    children :
   Let them | praise the | name · of the | Lord.

2nd half

11 For His name a|lone is | excellent :
   His glory is a|bove the | earth and | heaven.

                         GLORIA.

846

PSALM 150

A JUBILANT DOXOLOGY

1 Praise ye the Lord. * Praise | God · in His |
    sanctuary :
   Praise Him in the | firma · ment | of His | power.

2 Praise Him for His | mighty | acts :
   Praise Him ac|cording to His | excel · lent |
    greatness.

3 Praise Him with the | sound · of the | trumpet :
    ·Praise Him up|on the | lute and | harp.

4 Praise Him with the | timbrel · and | dance :
    Praise Him up|on the | strings and | organs.

5 Praise Him upon the | loud | cymbals :
    Praise Him upon the | high | sounding | cymbals

6 Let everything | that hath | breath : ⌣
    Praise the | Lord. | Praise · ye the | Lord.

                                GLORIA.

C. OTHER PASSAGES OF SCRIPTURE

These are intended for alternate reading, the congregation reading the verses in italics.

In many of these passages the text is that of the Revised Standard Version. Where this is not indicated by the letters R.S.V. the text is that of the Authorised Version, though occasionally a preferred rendering from the Revised Version has been used.

The quotations from the Revised Standard Version of the Bible, copyrighted 1946 and 1952, are here made by courtesy of Thomas Nelson and Sons, Ltd., Edinburgh.

847

1 CHRONICLES xxix. 10–13.

BLESSED be Thou, Lord God of Israel our Father, for ever and ever.

Thine, O Lord, is the greatness, and the power, and the glory, and the victory, and the majesty : for all that is in the heaven and in the earth is Thine ; Thine is the kingdom, O Lord, and Thou art exalted as head above all.

Both riches and honour come of Thee, and Thou reignest over all ; and in Thine hand is power and might ; and in Thine hand it is to make great, and to give strength unto all.

Now therefore, our God, we thank Thee, and praise Thy glorious name.

848

2 CHRONICLES vi. 14, 18–21, 41.

O LORD God of Israel, there is no God like Thee in the heaven, nor in the earth ; which keepest covenant, and shewest mercy unto Thy servants, that walk before Thee with all their hearts :

But will God in very deed dwell with men on the earth? behold, heaven and the heaven of heavens cannot contain Thee; how much less this house which I have built!

Have respect therefore to the prayer of Thy servant, and to his supplication, O Lord my God, to hearken unto the cry and the prayer which Thy servant prayeth before Thee:

That Thine eyes may be open upon this house day and night, upon the place whereof Thou hast said that Thou wouldest put Thy name there; to hearken unto the prayer which Thy servant prayeth toward this place.

Hearken therefore unto the supplications of Thy servant, and of Thy people Israel, which they shall make towards this place: hear Thou from Thy dwelling place, even from heaven; and when Thou hearest, forgive.

Now therefore arise, O Lord God, into Thy resting place, Thou, and the ark of Thy strength; let Thy priests, O Lord God, be clothed with salvation, and let Thy saints rejoice in goodness.

849

JOB xxviii. 12–15, 18–21, 23–28.

WHERE shall wisdom be found? and where is the place of understanding?

Man knoweth not the price thereof; neither is it found in the land of the living.

The depth saith, It is not in me: and the sea saith, It is not with me.

It cannot be gotten for gold, neither shall silver be weighed for the price thereof.

No mention shall be made of coral, or of pearls: for the price of wisdom is above rubies.

The topaz of Ethiopia shall not equal it, neither shall it be valued with pure gold.

Whence then cometh wisdom? and where is the place of understanding?

Seeing it is hid from the eyes of all living, and kept close from the fowls of the air.

God understandeth the way thereof, and He knoweth the place thereof.

For He looketh to the ends of the earth, and seeth under the whole heaven;

To make the weight for the winds; and He weigheth the waters by measure.

When He made a decree for the rain, and a way for the lightning of the thunder:

Then did He see it, and declare it; He prepared it, yea, and searched it out.

And unto man He said, Behold, the fear of the Lord, that is wisdom; and to depart from evil is under-standing.

850

PROVERBS iii. 5, 6, 11–13, 17–22a, 23, 26.

TRUST in the Lord with all thine heart; and lean not unto thine own understanding.

In all thy ways acknowledge Him, and He shall direct thy paths.

My son, despise not the chastening of the Lord; neither be weary of His correction:

For whom the Lord loveth He correcteth; even as a father the son in whom he delighteth.

Happy is the man that findeth wisdom, and the man that getteth understanding.

Her ways are ways of pleasantness, and all her paths are peace.

She is a tree of life to them that lay hold upon her: and happy is every one that retaineth her.

The Lord by wisdom hath founded the earth; by understanding hath He established the heavens.

By His knowledge the depths are broken up, and the clouds drop down the dew.

My son, let not them depart from thine eyes : keep sound wisdom and discretion :
So shall they be life unto thy soul.
Then shalt thou walk in thy way safely, and thy foot shall not stumble.
For the Lord shall be thy confidence, and shall keep thy foot from being taken.

851

ISAIAH xii. R.S.V.

I WILL give thanks to Thee, O Lord, for though Thou wast angry with me, Thy anger turned away, and Thou didst comfort me.
Behold God is my salvation, I will trust, and will not be afraid ; for the Lord God is my strength and my song, and He has become my salvation.
With joy you will draw water from the wells of salvation.
And you will say in that day, " Give thanks to the Lord, call upon His name ; make known His deeds among the nations, proclaim that His name is exalted.
Sing praises to the Lord for He has done gloriously; let this be known in all the earth.
Shout, and sing for joy, O inhabitant of Zion, for great in your midst is the Holy One of Israel."

852

ISAIAH xxv. 1, 4a, 8, 9 ; xxvi. 3, 4. R.S.V.

O LORD, Thou art my God; I will exalt Thee, I will praise Thy name; for Thou hast done wonderful things, plans formed of old, faithful and sure.
For Thou hast been a stronghold to the poor, a stronghold to the needy in his distress, a shelter from the storm and a shade from the heat.

The Lord will swallow up death for ever, and the Lord God will wipe away tears from all faces, and the reproach of His people He will take away from all the earth; for the Lord has spoken.

It will be said on that day, " Lo, this is our God ; we have waited for Him that He might save us. This is the Lord ; we have waited for Him ; let us be glad and rejoice in His salvation."

Thou dost keep him in perfect peace, whose mind is stayed on Thee, because he trusts in Thee.

Trust in the Lord for ever, for the Lord God is an everlasting rock.

853

ISAIAH XXXV. 1–8a, 9–10.

THE wilderness and the solitary place shall be glad for them; and the desert shall rejoice, and blossom as the rose.

It shall blossom abundantly, and rejoice even with joy and singing : the glory of Lebanon shall be given unto it, the excellency of Carmel and Sharon, they shall see the glory of the Lord, and the excellency of our God.

Strengthen ye the weak hands, and confirm the feeble knees.

Say to them that are of a fearful heart, Be strong, fear not : behold, your God will come with vengeance, even God with a recompence : He will come and save you.

Then the eyes of the blind shall be opened, and the ears of the deaf shall be unstopped.

Then shall the lame man leap as an hart, and the tongue of the dumb sing : for in the wilderness shall waters break out, and streams in the desert.

And the parched ground shall become a pool, and the thirsty land springs of water: in the habitation of dragons, where each lay, shall be grass with reeds and rushes.

*And an highway shall be there, and a way, and it
shall be called the way of holiness ;*

No lion shall be there, not any ravenous beast
shall go up thereon, it shall not be found there ;
but the redeemed shall walk there :

*And the ransomed of the Lord shall return, and
come to Zion with songs and everlasting joy upon
their heads : they shall obtain joy and gladness, and
sorrow and sighing shall flee away.*

854

ISAIAH xl. 1–11, 25–31.

COMFORT ye, comfort ye my people, saith your
God.

*Speak ye comfortably to Jerusalem, and cry unto
her, that her warfare is accomplished, that her
iniquity is pardoned : that she hath received of the
Lord's hand double for all her sins.*

The voice of him that crieth, Prepare ye in the
wilderness the way of the Lord, make straight in the
desert a highway for our God.

*Every valley shall be exalted, and every mountain
and hill shall be made low; and the crooked shall be
made straight, and the rough places plain :*

And the glory of the Lord shall be revealed, and
all flesh shall see it together: for the mouth of the
Lord hath spoken it.

*The voice said, Cry. And he said, What shall I
cry ? All flesh is grass, and all the goodliness thereof
is as the flower of the field :*

The grass withereth, the flower fadeth: because
the spirit of the Lord bloweth upon it: surely the
people is grass.

*The grass withereth, the flower fadeth : but the
word of our God shall stand for ever.*

O thou that bringest good tidings to Zion, get
thee up into the high mountain; O thou, that
bringest good tidings to Jerusalem, lift up thy voice

with strength; lift it up, be not afraid; say unto the cities of Judah, Behold your God!

Behold, the Lord God will come with strong hand, and His arm shall rule for Him: behold His reward is with Him, and His work before Him.

He shall feed His flock like a shepherd: He shall gather the lambs with His arm, and carry them in His bosom, and shall gently lead those that are with young.

To whom then will ye liken Me, or shall I be equal? saith the Holy One.

Lift up your eyes on high, and behold who hath created these, that bringeth out their host by number: He calleth them all by name; by the greatness of His might, for that He is strong in power, not one faileth.

Why sayest thou, O Jacob, and speakest, O Israel, My way is hid from the Lord, and my judgment is passed over from my God?

Hast thou not known? hast thou not heard, that the everlasting God, the Lord, the Creator of the ends of the earth, fainteth not, neither is weary? there is no searching of His understanding.

He giveth power to the faint; and to them that have no might He increaseth strength.

Even the youths shall faint and be weary, and the young men shall utterly fall:

But they that wait upon the Lord shall renew their strength; they shall mount up with wings as eagles; they shall run, and not be weary; and they shall walk, and not faint.

855

Isaiah lii. 7–10.

HOW beautiful upon the mountains are the feet of him that bringeth good tidings, that publisheth peace; that bringeth good tidings of good, that publisheth salvation; that saith unto Zion, Thy God reigneth!

Thy watchmen shall lift up the voice; with the voice together shall they sing: for they shall see eye to eye, when the Lord shall bring again Zion.

Break forth into joy, sing together, ye waste places of Jerusalem: for the Lord hath comforted His people, He hath redeemed Jerusalem.

The Lord hath made bare His holy arm in the eyes of all the nations; and all the ends of the earth shall see the salvation of our God.

856

ISAIAH lii. 13–liii. R.S.V.

BEHOLD, my servant shall prosper, he shall be exalted and lifted up, and shall be very high.

As many were astonished at him—his appearance was so marred, beyond human semblance, and his form beyond that of the sons of men—

so shall he startle many nations; kings shall shut their mouths because of him; for that which has not been told them they shall see, and that which they have not heard they shall understand.

Who has believed what we have heard? And to whom has the arm of the Lord been revealed?

For he grew up before him like a young plant, and like a root out of dry ground; he had no form or comeliness that we should look at him, and no beauty that we should desire him.

He was despised and rejected by men; a man of sorrows and acquainted with grief; and as one from whom men hide their faces he was despised and we esteemed him not.

Surely he has borne our griefs and carried our sorrows; yet we esteemed him stricken, smitten by God, and afflicted.

But he was wounded for our transgressions, he was bruised for our iniquities; upon him was the chastisement that made us whole, and with his stripes we are healed.

All we like sheep have gone astray; we have

turned every one to his own way; and the Lord has laid on him the iniquity of us all.

He was oppressed, and he was afflicted, yet he opened not his mouth; like a lamb that is led to the slaughter, and like a sheep that before its shearers is dumb, so he opened not his mouth.

By oppression and judgment he was taken away; and as for his generation, who considered that he was cut off out of the land of the living, stricken for the transgression of my people?

And they made his grave with the wicked and with a rich man in his death, although he had done no violence, and there was no deceit in his mouth.

Yet it was the will of the Lord to bruise him; He has put him to grief; when he makes himself an offering for sin, he shall see his offspring, he shall prolong his days; the will of the Lord shall prosper in his hand;

he shall see the fruit of the travail of his soul and be satisfied; by his knowledge shall the righteous one, my servant, make many to be accounted righteous; and he shall bear their iniquities.

Therefore I will divide him a portion with the great, and he shall divide the spoil with the strong; because he poured out his soul to death, and was numbered with the transgressors; yet he bore the sin of many, and made intercession for the transgressors.

857

Isaiah lv. 1–3, 6–13.

HO every one that thirsteth, come ye to the waters, and he that hath no money; come ye, buy and eat; yea, come, buy wine and milk without money and without price.

Wherefore do ye spend money for that which is not bread? and your labour for that which satisfieth not? Hearken diligently unto me, and eat ye that which is good, and let your soul delight itself in fatness.

Incline your ear, and come unto me; hear, and your soul shall live; and I will make an everlasting covenant with you, even the sure mercies of David.

Seek ye the Lord while He may be found, call ye upon Him while He is near :

Let the wicked forsake his way, and the unrighteous man his thoughts: and let him return unto the Lord, and He will have mercy upon him; and to our God, for He will abundantly pardon.

For my thoughts are not your thoughts, neither are your ways my ways, saith the Lord.

For as the heavens are higher than the earth, so are my ways higher than your ways, and my thoughts than your thoughts.

For as the rain cometh down, and the snow from heaven, and returneth not thither, but watereth the earth, and maketh it bring forth and bud, that it may give seed to the sower, and bread to the eater :

So shall my word be that goeth forth out of my mouth: it shall not return unto me void, but it shall accomplish that which I please, and it shall prosper in the thing whereto I sent it.

For ye shall go out with joy, and be led forth with peace : the mountains and the hills shall break forth before you into singing, and all the trees of the field shall clap their hands.

Instead of the thorn shall come up the fir tree, and instead of the brier shall come up the myrtle tree: and it shall be to the Lord for a name, for an everlasting sign that shall not be cut off.

858

Isaiah lx. 1–3, 11, 18–20.

ARISE, shine; for thy light is come, and the glory of the Lord is risen upon thee.

For, behold, the darkness shall cover the earth, and gross darkness the people : but the Lord shall arise upon thee, and His glory shall be seen upon thee.

And the Gentiles shall come to thy light, and kings to the brightness of thy rising.

Therefore thy gates shall be open continually ; they shall not be shut day nor night ; that men may bring unto thee the forces of the Gentiles, and that their kings may be brought.

Violence shall no more be heard in thy land, wasting nor destruction within thy borders; but thou shalt call thy walls Salvation, and thy gates Praise.

The sun shall be no more thy light by day ; neither for brightness shall the moon give light unto thee : but the Lord shall be unto thee an everlasting light, and thy God thy glory.

Thy sun shall no more go down; neither shall thy moon withdraw itself: for the Lord shall be thine everlasting light, and the days of thy mourning shall be ended.

859

MICAH iv. 1–4. R.S.V.

IT shall come to pass in the latter days that the mountain of the house of the Lord shall be established as the highest of the mountains, and shall be raised up above the hills ; and peoples shall flow to it,

and many nations shall come and say : " Come, let us go up to the mountain of the Lord, to the house of the God of Jacob ; that He may teach us His ways and we may walk in His paths."

For out of Zion shall go forth the law, and the word of the Lord from Jerusalem.

He shall judge between many peoples, and shall decide for strong nations afar off; and they shall beat their swords into plowshares, and their spears into pruning hooks ;

nation shall not lift up sword against nation, neither shall they learn war any more ;

*but they shall sit every man under his vine and under
his fig tree, and none shall make them afraid;*
for the mouth of the Lord of hosts has spoken.

860

DEUT. xxx. 11 ff ; ROMANS x. 4–9. R.S.V.

THIS commandment which I command you this
day is not too hard for you, neither is it far off.

*It is not in heaven, that you should say " Who will
go up for us to heaven, and bring it to us, that we may
hear it and do it? "*

Neither is it beyond the sea, that you should say,
" Who will go over the sea for us, and bring it to us,
that we may hear it and do it? "

*But the word is very near you ; it is in your mouth
and in your heart, so that you can do it.*

See, I have set before you this day life and good,
death and evil.

*If you obey the commandments of the Lord your
God which I command you this day, by loving the
Lord your God, by walking in His ways, and by
keeping His commandments and His statutes and His
ordinances, then you shall live and multiply, and the
Lord your God will bless you in the land which you are
entering to take possession of it.*

But if your heart turns away, and you will not hear,
but are drawn away to worship other gods and serve
them,

*I declare to you this day, that you shall perish ; you
shall not live long in the land which you are going over
the Jordan to enter and possess.*

I call heaven and earth to witness against you this
day, that I have set before you life and death,
blessing and curse; therefore choose life, that you
and your descendants may live.

*Loving the Lord your God, obeying His voice, and
cleaving to Him ; for that means life to you and
length of days, that you may dwell in the land which*

the Lord swore to your fathers, to Abraham, to Isaac, and to Jacob, to give them.

For Christ is the end of the law, that every one who has faith may be justified.

Moses writes that the man who practises the righteousness which is based on the law shall live by it.

But the righteousness based on faith says, Do not say in your heart, " Who will ascend into heaven ? " (that is, to bring Christ down)

or " Who will descend into the abyss ? " (that is, to bring Christ up from the dead).

But what does it say ? The word is near you, on your lips and in your heart (that is, the word of faith which we preach);

because, if you confess with your lips that Jesus is Lord and believe in your heart that God raised Him from the dead, you will be saved.

861

MATTHEW v. 3-10.

BLESSED are the poor in spirit :
for theirs is the kingdom of heaven.
Blessed are they that mourn :
for they shall be comforted.
Blessed are the meek :
for they shall inherit the earth.
Blessed are they which do hunger and thirst after righteousness :
for they shall be filled.
Blessed are the merciful :
for they shall obtain mercy.
Blessed are the pure in heart :
for they shall see God.
Blessed are the peace makers :
for they shall be called the children of God.
Blessed are they which are persecuted for righteousness' sake :
for theirs is the kingdom of heaven.

862

JOHN i. 1–5, 9–14, 16–18. R.S.V.

IN the beginning was the Word, and the Word was with God, and the Word was God.

He was in the beginning with God;

all things were made through Him, and without Him was not anything made that was made.

In Him was life, and the life was the light of men.

The light shines in the darkness, and the darkness has not overcome it.

The true light that enlightens every man was coming into the world.

He was in the world, and the world was made through Him, yet the world knew Him not.

He came to His own home, and His own people received Him not.

But to all who received Him, who believed in His name, He gave power to become children of God,

who were born, not of blood nor of the will of the flesh nor of the will of man, but of God.

And the Word became flesh and dwelt among us, full of grace and truth; we have beheld His glory, glory as of the only Son from the Father.

And from His fullness have we all received, grace upon grace.

For the law was given through Moses; grace and truth came through Jesus Christ.

No one has ever seen God; the only Son, Who is in the bosom of the Father. He has made Him known.

863

1 CORINTHIANS xiii. R.S.V.

IF I speak in the tongues of men and of angels, but have not love, I am a noisy gong or a clanging cymbal.

And if I have prophetic powers, and understand all mysteries and all knowledge, and if I have all faith,

*so as to remove mountains, but have not love, I am
nothing.*

If I give away all I have, and if I deliver my body
to be burned, but have not love, I gain nothing.

*Love is patient and kind; love is not jealous or
boastful;*

it is not arrogant or rude. Love does not insist
on its own way; it is not irritable or resentful;

*it does not rejoice at wrong, but rejoices in the
right.*

Love bears all things, believes all things, hopes all
things, endures all things.

*Love never ends; as for prophecy, it will pass
away; as for tongues, they will cease; as for
knowledge, it will pass away.*

For our knowledge is imperfect and our prophecy
is imperfect;

*but when the perfect comes, the imperfect will pass
away.*

When I was a child, I spoke like a child, I thought
like a child, I reasoned like a child; when I became
a man, I gave up childish ways.

*For now we see in a mirror dimly, but then face to
face. Now I know in part; then I shall understand
fully, even as I have been fully understood.*

So faith, hope, love abide, these three; but the
greatest of these is love.

864

EPHESIANS iii. 14–21.

FOR this reason I bow my knees before the
Father, from whom every family in heaven and
on earth is named,

*that according to the riches of His glory He may
grant you to be strengthened with might through His
Spirit in the inner man,*

and that Christ may dwell in your hearts through faith; that you, being rooted and grounded in love,
may have power to comprehend with all the saints what is the breadth and length and height and depth,
and to know the love of Christ which surpasses knowledge, that you may be filled with all the fulness of God.
Now to Him who by the power at work within us is able to do far more abundantly than all that we ask or think,
to Him be glory in the church and in Christ Jesus to all generations, for ever and ever.   Amen.

865

EPHESIANS iv. 1–7, 11–13. R.S.V.

I THEREFORE, a prisoner for the Lord, beg you to lead a life worthy of the calling to which you have been called,
with all lowliness and meekness, with patience, forbearing one another in love,
eager to maintain the unity of the Spirit in the bond of peace.
There is one body and one Spirit, just as you were called to the one hope that belongs to your call,
one Lord, one faith, one baptism,
one God and Father of us all, who is above all and through all and in all.
But grace was given to each of us according to the measure of Christ's gift.
And His gifts were that some should be apostles, some prophets, some evangelists, some pastors and teachers,
for the equipment of the saints, for the work of ministry, for building up the body of Christ,
until we all attain to the unity of the faith and of the knowledge of the Son of God, to mature manhood, to the measure of the stature of the fullness of Christ.

866

EPHESIANS vi. 10–18.

FINALLY, my brethren, be strong in the Lord, and in the power of His might.

Put on the whole armour of God, that ye may be able to stand against the wiles of the devil.

For we wrestle not against flesh and blood, but against principalities, against powers, against the rulers of the darkness of this world, against spiritual wickedness in high places.

Wherefore take unto you the whole armour of God, that ye may be able to withstand in the evil day, and having done all, to stand.

Stand therefore, having your loins girt about with truth, and having on the breastplate of righteousness;

And your feet shod with the preparation of the gospel of peace ;

Above all, taking the shield of faith, wherewith ye shall be able to quench all the fiery darts of the wicked.

And take the helmet of salvation, and the sword of the Spirit, which is the word of God :

Praying always with all prayer and supplication in the Spirit, and watching thereunto with all perseverance and supplication for all saints.

867

PHILIPPIANS ii. 1–11. R.S.V.

SO if there is any encouragement in Christ, any incentive of love, any participation in the Spirit, any affection and sympathy,

complete my joy by being of the same mind, having the same love, being in full accord and of one mind.

Do nothing from selfishness or conceit, but in humility count others better than yourselves.

Let each of you look not only to his own interests, but also to the interests of others.

Have this mind among yourselves, which you have in Christ Jesus,

who, though He was in the form of God, did not count equality with God a thing to be grasped,

but emptied Himself, taking the form of a servant, being born in the likeness of men.

And being found in human form He humbled Himself and became obedient unto death, even death on a cross.

Therefore God has highly exalted Him and bestowed on Him the name which is above every name,

that at the name of Jesus every knee should bow, in heaven and on earth and under the earth,

and every tongue confess that Jesus Christ is Lord, to the glory of God the Father.

868

PHILIPPIANS iv. 4–9. R.S.V.

REJOICE in the Lord always; again I will say, Rejoice.

Let all men know your forbearance. The Lord is at hand.

Have no anxiety about anything, but in everything by prayer and supplication with thanksgiving let your requests be made known to God.

And the peace of God, which passes all understanding, will keep your hearts and your minds in Christ Jesus.

Finally, brethren, whatever is true, whatever is honourable, whatever is just, whatever is pure, whatever is lovely, whatever is gracious, if there is any excellence, if there is anything worthy of praise, think about these things.

What you have learned and received and heard and seen in me, do ; and the God of peace will be with you.

869

Colossians i. 12–23. R.S.V.

WE give thanks to the Father who has qualified us to share in the inheritance of the saints in light.

He has delivered us from the dominion of darkness and transferred us to the kingdom of his beloved Son,

in whom we have redemption, the forgiveness of sins.

He is the image of the invisible God, the first-born of all creation ;

for in Him all things were created, in heaven and on earth, visible and invisible, whether thrones or dominions or principalities or authorities—all things were created through Him and for Him.

He is before all things, and in Him all things hold together.

He is the head of the body, the church; He is the beginning, the first-born from the dead, that in everything He might be pre-eminent.

For in Him all the fullness of God was pleased to dwell,

and through Him to reconcile to Himself all things, whether on earth or in heaven, making peace by the blood of His cross.

And you, who once were estranged and hostile in mind, doing evil deeds,

He has now reconciled in His body of flesh by His death, in order to present you holy and blameless and irreproachable before Him,

provided that you continue in the faith, stable and steadfast, not shifting from the hope of the gospel.

870

Hebrews xi. 1, 6–10, 24–27, 32–40 ; xii. 1–2. R.S.V.

NOW faith is the assurance of things hoped for, the conviction of things not seen,

And without faith it is impossible to please God.

For whoever would draw near to God must believe that He exists and that He rewards those who seek Him.

By faith Noah, being warned by God concerning events as yet unseen, took heed and constructed an ark for the saving of his household; by this he condemned the world and became an heir of the righteousness which comes by faith.

By faith Abraham obeyed when he was called to go out to a place which he was to receive as an inheritance; and he went out, not knowing where he was to go.

By faith he sojourned in the land of promise, as in a foreign land, living in tents with Isaac and Jacob, heirs with him of the same promise.

For he looked forward to the city which has foundations, whose builder and maker is God.

By faith Moses, when he was grown up, refused to be called the son of Pharaoh's daughter,

choosing rather to share ill-treatment with the people of God than to enjoy the fleeting pleasures of sin.

He considered abuse suffered for the Christ greater wealth than the treasures of Egypt, for he looked to the reward.

By faith he left Egypt, not being afraid of the anger of the king; for he endured as seeing Him who is invisible.

And what more shall I say? For time would fail me to tell of Gideon, Barak, Samson, Jephthah, of David and Samuel and the prophets—who through faith conquered kingdoms, enforced justice, received promises, stopped the mouths of lions,

quenched raging fire, escaped the edge of the sword, won strength out of weakness, became mighty in war, put foreign armies to flight.

Women received their dead by resurrection. Some were tortured, refusing to accept release that they might rise again to a better life.

Others suffered mocking and scourging, and even chains and imprisonment.

They were stoned, they were sawn in two, they were killed with the sword; they went about in skins of sheep and goats, destitute, afflicted, ill-treated—

of whom the world was not worthy—wandering over deserts and mountains, and in dens and caves of the earth.

And all these, though well-attested by their faith, did not receive what was promised,

since God had foreseen something better for us, that apart from us they should not be made perfect.

Therefore, since we are surrounded by so great a cloud of witnesses, let us also lay aside every weight, and sin which clings so closely, and let us run with perseverance the race that is set before us,

looking to Jesus the pioneer and perfecter of our faith, who for the joy that was set before Him endured the cross, despising the shame, and is seated at the right hand of the throne of God.

871

REVELATION vii. 9–17. R.S.V.

AFTER this I looked, and behold, a great multitude which no man could number, from every nation, from all tribes and peoples and tongues, standing before the throne and before the Lamb, clothed in white robes, with palm branches in their hands,

and crying out with a loud voice, " Salvation belongs to our God who sits upon the throne, and to the Lamb ! "

And all the angels stood round the throne and round the elders and the four living creatures, and they fell on their faces before the throne and worshipped God, saying,

" Amen ! Blessing and glory and wisdom and thanksgiving and honour and power and might be to our God for ever and ever ! Amen."

Then one of the elders addressed me, saying,

" Who are these, clothed in white robes, and whence have they come ? "

I said to him, " Sir, you know." And he said to me, " These are they who have come out of the great tribulation ; they have washed their robes and made them white in the blood of the Lamb.

Therefore are they before the throne of God, and serve Him day and night within His temple; and He who sits upon the throne will shelter them with His presence.

They shall hunger no more, neither thirst any more ; the sun shall not strike them, nor any scorching heat.

For the Lamb in the midst of the throne will be their shepherd, and He will guide them to springs of living water; and God will wipe away every tear from their eyes."

872

REVELATION xxi. 2–7, 22–27 ; xxii. 1–5. R.S.V.

AND I saw the holy city, new Jerusalem, coming down out of heaven from God, prepared as a bride adorned for her husband;

and I heard a great voice from the throne saying, " Behold, the dwelling of God is with men. He will dwell with them, and they shall be His people, and God Himself will be with them ;

He will wipe away every tear from their eyes, and death shall be no more, neither shall there be mourning nor crying nor pain any more, for the former things have passed away."

And He who sat upon the throne said, " Behold, I make all things new." Also He said, " Write this, for these words are trustworthy and true."

And He said to me, " It is done ! I am the Alpha and the Omega, the beginning and the end. To the thirsty I will give waters without price from the fountain of the water of life.

He who conquers shall have this heritage, and I will be his God and he shall be my son."

And I saw no temple in the city, for its temple is the Lord God the Almighty and the Lamb.

And the city has no need of sun or moon to shine upon it, for the glory of God is its light, and its lamp is the Lamb.

By its light shall the nations walk; and the kings of the earth shall bring their glory into it,

and its gates shall never be shut by day—and there shall be no night there ;

they shall bring into it the glory and the honour of the nations.

But nothing unclean shall enter it, nor any one who practices abomination or falsehood, but only those who are written in the Lamb's book of life.

Then He showed me the river of the water of life, bright as crystal, flowing from the throne of God and of the Lamb through the middle of the street of the city ;

also, on either side of the river, the tree of life with its twelve kinds of fruit, yielding its fruit each month ; and the leaves of the tree were for the healing of the nations.

There shall no more be anything accursed, but the throne of God and of the Lamb shall be in it, and His servants shall worship Him;

they shall see His face, and His name shall be on their foreheads.

And night shall be no more; they need no light of lamp or sun, for the Lord God will be their light, and they shall reign for ever and ever.

873

THE COMMANDMENTS
WITH NEW TESTAMENT COMMENTS

THOU shalt have no other gods before me: but thou shalt love the Lord thy God with all thy heart, and with all thy soul, and with all thy strength, and with all thy mind.

Lord, have mercy upon us, and incline our hearts to keep this law.

Thou shalt not make unto thyself any graven image: for God is a Spirit, and they that worship Him must worship Him in spirit and in truth.

Lord, have mercy upon us, and incline our hearts to keep this law.

Thou shalt not take the name of the Lord thy God in vain: but shalt serve Him acceptably with reverence and godly fear.

Lord, have mercy upon us, and incline our hearts to keep this law.

Remember the Sabbath day to keep it holy: and forsake not the assembling of yourselves together; for the Sabbath was made for man.

Lord, have mercy upon us, and incline our hearts to keep this law.

Honour thy father and thy mother: and be kindly affectioned one to another, that ye may be the children of your Father who is in heaven.

Lord, have mercy upon us, and incline our hearts to keep this law.

Thou shalt not kill: and be not angry with thy brother without a cause; but overcome evil with good.

Lord, have mercy upon us, and incline our hearts to keep this law.

Thou shalt not commit adultery: but glorify God in your body and in your spirit, which are God's.

Lord, have mercy upon us, and incline our hearts to keep this law.

Thou shalt not steal: but provide things honest in the sight of all men, and render to every man his due.

Lord, have mercy upon us, and incline our hearts to keep this law.

Thou shalt not bear false witness against thy neighbour: for love thinketh no evil, and rejoiceth not in iniquity, but rejoiceth in the truth.

Lord, have mercy upon us, and incline our hearts to keep this law.

Thou shalt not covet anything that is thy neighbour's: but do unto others as ye would that others should do unto you; and love thy neighbour as thyself; for love is the fulfilling of the law.

Lord, have mercy upon us, and write all these laws in our hearts, we beseech Thee.

874

BAPTISM

MATT. iii. 13–17 ; ROM. vi. 3–6, 11 ; GALATS. iii. 27 ; MATT. xxviii. 19–20. R.S.V.

THEN Jesus came from Galilee to the Jordan to John, to be baptised by him.

John would have prevented Him, saying, " I need to be baptised by you, and do you come to me ? "

But Jesus answered him, " Let it be so now; for thus it is fitting for us to fulfil all righteousness." Then he consented.

And when Jesus was baptised, He went up immediately from the water, and behold, the heavens were opened and He saw the Spirit of God descending like a dove, and alighting on Him,

and lo, a voice from heaven, saying, " This is my beloved Son, with whom I am well pleased."

Do you not know that all of us who have been baptised into Christ Jesus were baptised into His death ?

We were buried therefore with Him by baptism into death, so that as Christ was raised from the dead by the glory of the Father, we too might walk in newness of life.

For if we have been united with Him in a death like His, we shall certainly be united with Him in a resurrection like His.

We know that our old self was crucified with Him so that the sinful body might be destroyed, and we might no longer be enslaved to sin.

So you also must consider yourselves dead to sin and alive to God in Christ Jesus.

For as many of you as were baptised into Christ have put on Christ.

Go therefore and make disciples of all nations, baptising them in the name of the Father and of the Son and of the Holy Spirit,

teaching them to observe all that I have commanded you; and lo, I am with you always, to the close of the age.

875

THE LORD'S SUPPER

1 JOHN iv. 9–10; 1 TIM. i. 15; JOHN vi. 35; MATT. v. 6; 1 COR. xi. 23–26; PSALM cxvi. 12–14, 17.

IN this was manifested the love of God toward us, because that God sent His only begotten Son into the world, that we might live through Him.

Herein is love, not that we loved God, but that He loved us, and sent His Son to be the propitiation for our sins.

This is a faithful saying, and worthy of all acceptation, that Christ Jesus came into the world to save sinners.

And Jesus said unto them, I am the bread of life : he that cometh to me shall never hunger ; and he that believeth on me shall never thirst.

Blessed are they which do hunger and thirst after righteousness:

For they shall be filled.

The Lord Jesus the same night in which he was betrayed took bread, and when he had given thanks, He brake it, and said:

Take, eat ; this is my body, which is broken for you: this do ye in remembrance of me.

After the same manner also He took the cup, when He had supped, saying:

This cup is the new testament in my blood : this do ye, as oft as ye drink it, in remembrance of me.

For as often as ye eat this bread, and drink this cup, ye do shew the Lord's death till He come.

What shall I render unto the Lord for all His benefits toward me?

I will take the cup of salvation, and call upon the name of the Lord.

I will pay my vows unto the Lord now in the presence of all His people.

I will offer to thee the sacrifice of thanksgiving and will call upon the name of the Lord.

876

INTERNATIONAL PEACE

PSALM xxxiii. 12; PROVERBS xiv. 34; ISAIAH xxxii. 17;
ISAIAH ii. 2–5 R.S.V.; EPHESIANS ii. 14–18 R.S.V.;
ACTS x. 34–35 R.S.V.; COLOSSIANS iii. 11; LUKE ii. 14.

B LESSED is the nation whose God is the Lord.
Righteousness exalteth a nation: but sin is a reproach to any people.

And the work of righteousness shall be peace; and the effect of righteousness quietness and assurance for ever.

It shall come to pass in the latter days that the mountain of the house of the Lord shall be established as the highest of the mountains, and shall be raised above the hills; and all nations shall flow to it,

and many nations shall come and say: " Come, let us go up to the mountain of the Lord, to the house of the God of Jacob; that He may teach us His ways and that we may walk in His paths."

For out of Zion shall go forth the law, and the word of the Lord from Jerusalem.

He shall judge between the nations, and shall decide for many peoples; and they shall beat their swords into plowshares, and their spears into pruning hooks;

nation shall not lift up sword against nation, neither shall they learn war any more.

Come ye, and let us walk in the light of the Lord.

*For He is our peace, who has made us both one,
and has broken down the dividing wall of hostility,
that He might create in Himself one new man in
place of the two, so making peace,*

and might reconcile us both to God in one body
through the cross, thereby bringing the hostility to
an end.

*And He came and preached peace to you who were
far off and peace to those who were near ;*

for through Him we both have access in one
Spirit to the Father.

*God shows no partiality, but in every nation any
one who fears Him and does what is right is acceptable
to Him.*

There is neither Greek nor Jew, circumcision nor
uncircumcision, barbarian, Scythian, bond nor free:
but Christ is all and in all.

*Glory to God in the highest, and on earth peace,
goodwill toward men.*

877

THE MISSIONARY CALL

ACTS xvii. 26–28 R.S.V.; ROMANS x. 12–15 R.S.V.; ACTS
xiii. 2–4 R.S.V.; EPHESIANS iii. 8, 11 R.S.V.; 2 CORIN-
THIANS v. 19 R.S.V.; 1 JOHN ii. 2; JOHN iii. 16; ACTS i.
8 R.S.V.

GOD made from one every nation of men to
live on all the face of the earth, having deter-
mined allotted periods and the boundaries of their
habitation,

*that they should seek God, in the hope that they
might feel after Him and find Him.*

Yet He is not far from each one of us, for in Him
we live and move and have our being.

*For there is no distinction between Jew and Greek ;
the same Lord is Lord of all and bestows His riches
upon all who call upon Him.*

For every one who calls upon the name of the Lord will be saved.

But how are men to call upon Him in whom they have not believed? and how are they to believe in Him of whom they have never heard? And how are they to hear without a preacher?

And how can men preach unless they are sent?

The Holy Spirit said, " Set apart for me Barnabas and Saul for the work to which I have called them."

Then after fasting and praying they laid their hands on them and sent them off.

So, being sent out by the Holy Spirit, they went down to Seleucia; and from there they sailed to Cyprus.

To me, though I am the very least of all the saints, this grace was given, to preach to the Gentiles the unsearchable riches of Christ,

according to the eternal purpose which He has realised in Christ Jesus our Lord.

God was in Christ reconciling the world to Himself, not counting their trespasses against them, and entrusting to us the message of reconciliation.

And He is the propitiation for our sins; and not for ours only, but also for the whole world.

For God so loved the world that He gave His only-begotten Son, that whosoever believeth in Him should not perish but have everlasting life.

Jesus said: " You shall receive power when the Holy Spirit has come upon you; and you shall be my witnesses in Jerusalem and in all Judea and Samaria and to the end of the earth."

878

THE CHRISTIAN HOME

DEUT. vi. 4–7; EPHES. v. 33 R.S.V.; EPHES. vi. 1–2 R.S.V.;
COL. iii. 12–14, 17 R.S.V.

HEAR, O Israel: the Lord our God is one Lord. And thou shalt love the Lord thy God with all thine heart, and with all thy soul, and with all thy might. And these words which I command thee this day shall be in thine heart.

And thou shalt teach them diligently unto thy children, and shalt talk of them when thou sittest in thine house.

Husbands, let each of you love his wife as himself, and let the wife see that she respects her husband.

Children, obey your parents in the Lord, for this is right. Honour your father and mother. Fathers, do not provoke your children to anger, but bring them up in the discipline and instruction of the Lord.

Put on then, as God's chosen ones, holy and beloved, compassion, kindness, lowliness, meekness and patience,

forbearing one another and, if one has a complaint against another, forgiving each other ; as the Lord has forgiven you, so you also must forgive.

And above all these put on love, which binds everything together in perfect harmony.

And whatever you do, in word or deed, do everything in the name of the Lord Jesus, giving thanks to God the Father through Him.

879

THE HEAVENLY WORSHIP

REVELATION iv. 8, 11; xv. 3–4; xix. 6–7; v. 12–13; vii. 12
R.S.V.

HOLY, holy, holy, is the Lord God almighty, *who was and is and is to come* !

Worthy art Thou, our Lord and God, to receive glory and honour and power,

for Thou didst create all things, and by Thy will they existed and were created.

Great and wonderful are Thy deeds, O Lord God the almighty !

Just and true are Thy ways, O King of the ages !

Who shall not fear and glorify Thy name, O Lord ?

For Thou alone art holy.
All nations shall come and worship Thee,
for Thy judgments have been revealed.
Hallelujah ! For the Lord God, the almighty
reigns.
Let us rejoice and exult and give Him the glory.
Worthy is the Lamb who was slain,
to receive power and wealth and wisdom and might and honour and glory and blessing !
To Him who sits upon the throne and to the Lamb
be blessing and honour and glory and might for ever
and ever ! Amen.
Blessing and glory and wisdom and thanksgiving and honour and power and might be to our God for ever and ever ! Amen.

880

OLD TESTAMENT BEATITUDES

Psalm lxxxiv. 5; xxxii. 1; i. 2; cxix. 2; xl. 4; lxviii. 19;
lxxii. 18 f; cxiii. 3.

BLESSED is the man whose strength is in the
Lord, and in whose heart are the highways to
Zion.
Grant us this blessing, O Lord.
Blessed is the man whose transgression is forgiven
and whose sin is covered.
Grant us this blessing, O Lord.
Blessed is the man whose delight is in the law of the
Lord and who doth meditate therein day and night.
Grant us this blessing, O Lord.
Blessed are they who keep the testimonies of the
Lord and that seek Him with the whole heart.
Grant us this blessing, O Lord.
Blessed is the man that maketh the Lord his trust.
Grant us this blessing, O Lord.
Blessed be God who daily beareth our burden,
even the God who is our salvation.
Blessed be His holy name.

Blessed be the Lord God who only doeth wondrous things and blessed be His glorious name for ever, and let the whole earth be filled with His glory.

Blessed be His holy name.

From the rising of the sun unto the going down of the same, the Lord's name is to be praised.

881

THE FRUIT OF THE SPIRIT

GAL. v. 22–26; ROM. viii. 5, 6, 12–16, R.S.V.

THE fruit of the Spirit is love, joy, peace, patience, kindness, goodness, faithfulness, gentleness, self-control;

against such there is no law.

And those who belong to Christ Jesus have crucified the flesh with its passions and desires.

If we live by the Spirit, let us also walk by the Spirit.

Let us have no self-conceit, no provoking of one another, no envy of one another.

Those who live according to the Spirit set their minds on the things of the Spirit.

To set the mind on the flesh is death, but to set the mind on the Spirit is life and peace.

So then, brethren, we are debtors, not to the flesh, to live according to the flesh—

for if you live according to the flesh you will die,

but if by the Spirit you put to death the deeds of the body you will live.

For all who are led by the Spirit of God are sons of God.

For you did not receive the spirit of slavery to fall back into fear, but you have received the spirit of sonship.

When we cry " Abba ! Father ! " it is the Spirit Himself bearing witness with our spirit that we are children of God.

882

A SCRIPTURAL DECLARATION OF FAITH

JOHN iv. 24; 1 JOHN i. 5, 7; iv. 16, 7, 10; 2 COR. v. 19; JOHN iii. 16; GAL. i. 1; 2 COR. iv. 14; 1 JOHN iii, 2; iv. 13; i. 9; v. 11; 2 COR. ix. 15.

GOD is Spirit, and they that worship Him must worship Him in spirit and in truth.
Glory be to God on high.
God is Light. If we walk in the light as He is in the light, we have fellowship one with another.
Glory be to God on high.
God is Love. Everyone that loveth is born of God and knoweth God. Herein is love, not that we loved God, but that He loved us, and sent His Son to be the propitiation for our sins.
Glory be to God on high.
God was in Christ, reconciling the world unto Himself, not imputing their trespasses unto them.
Glory be to God on high.
God so loved the world that He gave His only begotten Son, that whosoever believeth in Him should not perish but have everlasting life.
Glory be to God on high.
God the Father raised Him from the dead, and He which raised up the Lord Jesus shall raise up us also by Jesus.
Glory be to God on high.
Now are we the children of God. Hereby know we that we dwell in Him and He in us, because He hath given us of His Spirit.
Thanks be to God.
If we confess our sins He is faithful and just to forgive us our sins and to cleanse us from all unrighteousness.
Thanks be to God.
God hath given unto us eternal life, and this life is in His Son.
Thanks be unto God for His unspeakable gift.

883

CHRISTIAN CITIZENSHIP

PSALM xxxiii. 12; lxxxv. 8–13; PROVERBS xiv. 34; AMOS v. 15; MICAH vi. 8; 1 PETER ii. 13–17 R.S.V.; ROM. xiii. 5, 7–10 R.S.V.; MATT. xxii. 21.

BLESSED is the nation whose God is the Lord; *and the people whom He hath chosen for His own inheritance.*

I will hear what God the Lord will speak; *for He will speak peace unto His people, and to His saints :*
but let them not turn again to folly.
Surely His salvation is nigh them that fear Him ; that glory may dwell in our land.

Mercy and truth are met together; righteousness and peace have kissed each other.
Truth shall spring out of the earth; and righteousness shall look down from heaven.

Yea, the Lord shall give that which is good; and our land shall yield her increase.
Righteousness shall go before Him ; and shall set us in the way of His steps.

Righteousness exalteth a nation; but sin is a reproach to any people.
Hate the evil and love the good, and establish justice in the gate.

What doth the Lord require of thee but to do justly and to love mercy and to walk humbly with thy God.

Be subject for the Lord's sake to every human institution, whether it be to the emperor as supreme, or to governors as sent by Him to punish those who do wrong and to praise those who do right.

For it is God's will that by doing right you should put to silence the ignorance of foolish men.

Live as free men, yet without using your freedom ⸱ a pretext for evil ; but live as servants of God.

Honour all men. Love the brotherhood. Fear God. Honour the emperor.

Therefore one must be subject, not only to avoid God's wrath, but also for the sake of conscience.

Pay all of them their dues, taxes to whom taxes are due, revenue to whom revenue is due, respect to whom respect is due, honour to whom honour is due.

Owe no one anything, except to love one another; for he who loves his neighbour has fulfilled the law.

The commandments, " You shall not commit adultery, You shall not kill, You shall not steal, You shall not covet ", and any other commandment, are summed up in this sentence,

" You shall love your neighbour as yourself."

Love does no wrong to a neighbour; therefore love is the fulfilling of the law.

Render therefore unto Caesar the things which are Caesar's; and unto God the things that are God's.

884

CHRISTIAN GIVING

EXODUS xxv. 1–2; xxxv. 4–5, 21; xxxvi. 4–5; 2 COR. ix. 7; viii. 12; PHIL. iv. 19; 2 COR. viii. 9; ix. 15.

THE Lord spake unto Moses, saying, Speak unto the children of Israel, that they bring me an offering; of every man that giveth it willingly with his heart ye shall take my offering.

And Moses spake unto all the congregation of the children of Israel, saying, This is the thing which the Lord commanded, saying,

Take ye from among you an offering unto the Lord: whoever is of a willing heart, let him bring it, an offering of the Lord, gold and silver and brass.

And they came, every one whose heart stirred him up, and every one whom his spirit made willing, and they brought the Lord's offering to the work of the tabernacle of the congregation and for all his service.

And all the wise men that wrought all the work of the sanctuary came and spake unto Moses, saying,

The people bring much more than enough for the service of the work which the Lord commanded to make.

Every man according as he purposeth in his heart, so let him give;

not grudgingly or of necessity : for God loveth a cheerful giver.

For if there be first a willing mind, it is accepted according to that a man hath and not according to that he hath not.

And my God shall supply every need of yours according to his riches in glory in Christ Jesus.

For ye know the grace of our Lord Jesus Christ that though He was rich yet for your sakes He became poor, that ye through His poverty might become rich.

Thanks be to God for His unspeakable gift.

HYMNS SUITABLE FOR YOUNG PEOPLE

I. GOD OUR FATHER

1. *Praise and Thanksgiving*

All creatures of our God and King	1
All people that on earth	2
All that's good and great	48
For all the love	7
For the beauty of the earth	8
God is good	10
I thank Thee, Lord, for life	500
Immortal, invisible	61
Let all the world	13
Let the whole creation	14
Let us with a gladsome mind	15
Lord God almighty	62
Lord God, from whom all life	503
Lord, we thank Thee	17
Now thank we all our God	18
O Lord of heaven	68
O love of God	69
O worship the King	22
Our God, our help	71
Praise my soul	23
Praise the Lord	24
Praise we God	45
Sing to the Lord	29

2. *His Works in Creation*

All things bright and beautiful	733
All things praise Thee	3
All things which live	49
Angels holy	5
For the beauty of the earth	8
God who made the earth	744
God who touchest earth	472
How dearly God must love us	57
I sing the almighty power	58
The spacious firmament	74
There is a book	76
We thank You, Lord of heaven	34

II. OUR LORD JESUS CHRIST

1. *His Advent and Birth*

2. *His Life and Ministry*

3. *His Suffering and Death*

V. THE CHURCH

1. *Its Nature and Purpose*

2. *Its Worship*

3. *Its World-wide Mission*

VI. THE CHRISTIAN LIFE

1. *Decision*

2. *Consecration*

3. *Forgiveness*

4. *Character*

INDEX OF SCRIPTURE
PASSAGES

INDEX OF HYMNS AND CANTICLES

SURSUM CORDA

Minister : Lift up your hearts.
People : We lift them up unto the Lord.
Minister : Let us give thanks unto our Lord God.
People : It is meet and right so to do.
Minister : It is very meet, right, and our bounden duty, that we should at all times and in all places, give thanks unto Thee, O Lord, Holy Father, Almighty, Everlasting God.

Minister and People : Therefore with angels and archangels, and with all the company of heaven, we laud and magnify Thy glorious name; evermore praising Thee and saying: Holy, holy, holy, Lord God of hosts, heaven and earth are full of Thy glory: Glory be to Thee, O Lord most high. Amen.

BENEDICTIONS

THE Lord bless you and keep you. The Lord make His face to shine upon you and be gracious unto you. The Lord lift up His countenance upon you, and give you peace. Amen.

THE peace of God which passeth all understanding, keep your hearts and minds in the knowledge and love of God, and of His Son, Jesus Christ, our Lord; and the blessing of God almighty, the Father, the Son, and the Holy Spirit, be upon you and remain with you always. Amen.

THE grace of our Lord Jesus Christ, and the love of God, and the communion of the Holy Spirit, be with you all. Amen.

NOW the God of peace, that brought again from the dead our Lord Jesus, that great shepherd of the sheep, through the blood of the everlasting covenant, make you perfect in every good work to do His will, working in you that which is well-pleasing in His sight, through Jesus Christ, to whom be glory for ever and ever. Amen.